Gunner Green's War (1938–1946)

Gunner Green's War (1938–1946)

L. J. GREEN

The Pentland Press
Edinburgh – Cambridge – Durham – USA

First published in 1999 by
The Pentland Press Ltd
1 Hutton Close
South Church
Bishop Auckland
Durham

ISBN 1-85821-694-x

Typeset in Bell 12/15
by Carnegie Publishing, Carnegie House, Chatsworth Road, Lancaster LA1 4SL
Printed and bound by Bookcraft Ltd. Bath

To my wife Angela, without whom this book would have been written — probably — but certainly never published.

Contents

Illustrations

Chapter One

In Which I Become
a Trainee Warrior

There was no doubt about it, in 1938 when I was seventeen war clouds were on the horizon and no matter what I said or did one thing was certain: I would become involved. I had been a member of the Wesleyan church in Putney, was still a member of the Band of Hope based there and had heard all about the horrors of the Great War and so should have been a person with strong pacific leanings. On the other hand I had spent much time listening to political speakers in Hyde Park and on the Putney towpath and their message was clear – war was on the way whether I liked it or not. So it gradually dawned on me I had a choice: wait to be called up or get myself a bit of pre-war training.

I had been urged for some time by an old school acquaintance named Croker to follow him to the Putney drill hall of an artillery outfit based in Lytton Grove, off Putney Hill. I never did understand why I was influenced so much by him. He was not a particular buddy of mine. Like me he was well built but was much coarser with more fat and didn't seem capable of using his brain overmuch. He had been one of the gang led by the school dunce Lee, with whom I teamed up for a while and was thus involved in all sorts of adventures in and around Putney until I discovered that our hero and leader, Lee, was a first class thief. I had never been keen on that ball game and so had withdrawn and had seen no more of the gang including Croker until I happened to bump into him one day and he eventually persuaded me to join the Territorial Army at Lytton Grove.

Before I was allowed into the fighting force known as the

'Saturday Night Soldiers' I had to have a medical. This meant paying a visit to a very well-built Irish doctor with a surgery in one of the roads off the High Street. He had a ruddy complexion, a big booming voice and an air of always living out of doors, and seemed to be under instructions to pass as medically fit anything capable of moving. He didn't bother overmuch with the medical checks, merely commenting on the size of my powerful looking thighs and surmising correctly that I was a keen cyclist.

So, there I was in, varicose leg and bespectacled eyes and all. Hitler could take care, the British were beginning to stir.

I had no idea that I would receive any money. I imagined a volunteer was a volunteer and was more likely to pay for the privilege than be paid. But I discovered I was to be paid five pounds for joining, receive five pounds bounty a year for twelve appearances at the drill hall and a fiver if I attended the annual fortnightly camp. Bear in mind my wages were well under five pounds a week so the money wasn't a bad rake-off.

Drill nights were not what I had expected. There never seemed to be much training going on except at the bar where most of the gunners and others seemed to reside, training hard for future boozing careers. There was a large hall where, from time to time, some sort of desultory training went on, marching up and down, knees bend and saluting. Saluting seemed to be one of the things which obsessed the Territorial Army. It seemed to be just as important as firing a gun. We had some lectures and now and again, weather permitting, we would march out to the concreted area at the back of the drill hall for a bit of gun drill. I might add that gun drill was another obsession and at times could be both a day- and a nightmare.

We had a couple of Great War left-overs in the form of two three-inch AckAck guns and now and again we practised on them with wooden shells, shells, both dummy and live, being known not as shells but as rounds. Shells are of course the outer coverings of peanuts and the like.

No one knew quite who was who. There were usually a couple

of officers around, some sergeants and bombardiers but everyone seemed to be matey with everybody else and there was never any question of 'pulling rank'. We were in fact civilians mucking about in two-piece brown overalls which gradually became impregnated with that peculiar smell given off by oils used in gunnery. We were indeed Saturday night soldiers.

Bit by bit we were issued with khaki uniforms and I must say that these items were always received with laughter, derision and at times amazement. When we were all togged up we were clearly in uniforms abandoned after the First World War. We were issued with hard peaked caps with chin straps to hold the caps on because we were officially horse artillery. We had khaki jackets which buttoned up to the neck and — wait for it — wait for it — riding breeches! These had to be blancoed on those parts which came into, or used to come into, contact with a horse. We were issued with ammo boots and puttees. Ammunition boots were heavily studded, iron toed or steel-capped affairs, we thought, designed to stop anyone wearing them from running away. In fact they were designed for a special purpose, which we were to discover for ourselves later on, in action. The puttees were a confounded nuisance, made long enough to be wound from ankles to just below the knees, probably made for Great War Flanders mud and to keep lice well positioned on human legs. As someone pointed out, 'By the time we've got these perishing things on Jerry will have bombed us into Kingdom come!' We of course assumed that the powers that were would insist upon us being properly dressed for going into battle. Every gunner wore a lanyard round his left shoulder. Without it he wasn't properly dressed and this bit of string with the loop at the end had to be constantly blancoed white.

Although we never wore the uniform without the lanyard we never used one and I cannot even remember getting the reason for their one time use. It was probably something to do with a firing mechanism. I suppose, like the artillery badge with its motto, *'Ubique Quo Fas Et Gloria Ducunt'*, it was an emblem of pride. I found as the years went by that no matter how cynical one might become, how anti-army – and most were – we had the feeling of being better than anyone else in khaki including generals – except possibly the Gurkhas. Maybe it was something handed down from generation to generation from the time when the rest of the army was under the command of the Horse Guards and the artillery was the responsibility of the Master of the Ordnance. At any rate no one was properly dressed unless he was wearing his blancoed lanyard, his cap and badge and his ammo boots.

The annual camp of 1938 was to be held at Weybourne on the coast of Norfolk and much to my father's disgust I said I intended to attend it. He didn't approve because in those days a week was the general rule for an annual holiday and as far as he was concerned two weeks holiday was unheard of especially if he was expected to make my wages up. Then again I had joined him in his jobbing building business a couple of years before, the work had grown and I suppose, though he would never have admitted it, he would miss me helping him out.

My mother naturally didn't approve but then she was so often in a non-approving mood so what the hell!

In the meantime I had tried to get my old school mate and boon companion Will Simmonds to join me in the outfit, but his father wouldn't let him, saying that he, Will's father, had been in the artillery during the war and he wasn't going to let his son have anything to do with it.

On Saturday 30th July I spent a great deal of time with spit and polish trying to make the somewhat old-hat uniform and equipment a bit soldier-like. I was not over successful then and neither was I any better in the whole of my military career. Smartness and I were never good bed-fellows.

The army supplied shirts but not vests nor pants nor socks. One could be minutely inspected on the outside but no one bothered about the state of the underclothes on the inside.

In due course we were issued with a housewife which turned out to be a sewing kit and not a female human being, plus cleaning kit including brushes and a brass button cleaner which, when pushed in round a button, prevented the brass polish from staining the cloth. Polish was never issued, we had to buy that.

On the Sunday morning I took myself off to Liverpool Street Station, having said farewell to them there civilians and carefully avoiding places *en route* where I might have met friends or neighbours. Like so many of my fellow volunteers I was feeling a right Charlie in all that get-up, plus haversack, pack, water bottle and kitbag. By the time I reached the station I was a ball of sweat. Sweat was and still is a handicap and it was a problem on active service.

Upon arrival at the station I copped my first fatigue of the campaign – I found myself on the baggage party. Not only was I to sweat under my own clobber but was to do a bit of extra perspiring handling other people's. What the devil, I wondered, had I done to deserve a start like this?

At ten past five we arrived at Weybourne station and after detraining, the main body marched in style to the camp, headed by a band; we slaves of the baggage party sweated under a warm sky manhandling all that damned baggage.

We spent a couple of hours drawing bedding, blankets (there were never any sheets) and palliasses to be filled with straw. This business, we soon discovered, was a tricky one. If a palliasse was stuffed with too much straw, until it began to powder after use, one was liable to roll off the damned thing. If one was a bit skimpy with the straw a hard bed was inevitable. The art was to get it just right.

Our first meal was first rate, roast beef, greens, potatoes, apricots and custard. If an army marches on its stomach we were in for a lot of it and I must say we never had cause for complaint about the food at Weybourne. After an MO's inspection we toddled off to our country-smelling beds in the well-worn tents – the camp was in use all summer.

Here I might take the opportunity to point to another army obsession – the FFI – full frontal inspection. From camp to camp, from station to station along the roads of war, we had the demand for trousers down for a 'Short Arm Inspection'. I remember on one occasion one medical bod lifting up the rows of testicles with a pencil and I wondered how the pencil felt!

On Monday I got my first cookhouse fatigue and after peeling spuds and washing greasy dixies in cold water and dirty sand all day I was too tired to do anything but flop out on my bed or, as it became known, my flea pit.

On the Tuesday afternoon I happened to be floating about as a spare bod with nothing in particular to do, so a certain Sergeant Haines borrowed me and thus I found myself as a number eight ammunition number on a three-inch gun, wearing a gasmask which made the job of loading well nigh impossible. I came to the immediate conclusion that the next war had better be fought without the need for gasmasks otherwise I would be forced to resign.

My job was to fuse a round with a fuse key and in my turn ram a round into the breech of the gun; the breech would be slammed shut and the gun fired. One can imagine that most of us had heard only fireworks going bang, so when we first heard the crack of a three-inch gun it frightened the life out of us, at any rate it did me. The danger to any gun loader in peacetime, let alone war, was immediately apparent. The gun had what was known as an over door breech block. After the round had been rammed home by the gloved hand of a loader, the breech operator slammed the breech block shut and locked it with a downward thrust of the breech block operating handle and then the gun was fired. The point being if the loader was a bit slow and the number five breech operator a bit quick the loader could lose his hand as had happened in the past.

Another problem was the concern of the number three who operated the elevating wheel. The nasty crack of the three-inch could cause the operator to jump and loosen his hold on the elevating wheel and it could spin out of his grasp and the wheel handle could break an arm. It happened to an operator at the camp.

In ideal conditions, and at the camp ideal conditions prevailed, the loaders could happily punch up rounds without difficulty.

We used to wonder what would happen in real warfare. Would Jerry be so obliging as to adopt our gunnery theories which included constant speed, constant height and constant direction? Would he fly at a decent height at the edge of the horizon so that the gun loaders wouldn't have a difficult time of it? Or would the fool fly directly over our gunsites with unsportsman-like intentions? Well, in that case, as he approached the gunsite the firing angle would become more acute until with him over-head, the loaders would have to lie on their backs to punch rounds home, a thing we found impossible. In any case there would be the danger of a round falling back onto a prone gunner's stomach giving rise to the possibility of a stomach ache. Later on we found the answer. When Jerry flew above our heads we would cease firing until he had shot past.

I have mentioned the awful crack of the three-inch gun and still can remember the first time I heard it. There had been no firing at all for the first three days of the camp; there were too many small white clouds floating about in the sky. Then I found myself on a lorry taking ammunition from point A to point B and at one moment we were right under the barrel of a gun when some fool cried, 'Fire!' and off it went. I think all of us jumped higher than the gun barrel, thinking ourselves on the way to eternity.

We had a sergeant in our section, 'Daddy' Stream, who was a pain in our collective neck as he described how he was going to turn us into true fighting men ready to dash the enemy to pieces in Flanders Fields – everyone assumed the battle would commence there. Arriving at the camp our somewhat pasty-faced sergeant was in charge of a gun. The first time his gun fired his face turned paler than usual, he paused for a second or two and then took off we thought for those same Flanders Fields he was always talking about. At any rate he took off and the last we saw of him was his backside as he went through the main gate at a considerable gallop.

So, there we were, part-time amateur soldiers having, on the whole, a whale of a time, firing guns when there were no clouds in the sky to impede vision and not firing when clouds appeared. We fired at sleeves towed by aircraft or at the pilotless plane, the Queen Bee which was in no circumstances to be brought down, though it was doubtful if that was ever possible. All three of the 54th's batteries were at camp, 160, 161 and 162 and it was decided to use all three batteries in one big night shoot. As someone remarked, 'Gawd, if we don't do too well in daylight what'll it be like in the dark? Jerry should worry.'

We never found out. The clouds rolled up, the shoot was cancelled and we went back to camp from the gunpark to a midnight supper of sausages, greens, potatoes, bread and cocoa.

At Weybourne I discovered I had made one mistake which was already bearing unwelcome consequences.

At the time I signed on I had become disenchanted with religion. At the Sunday school I had been something of a star when it came to religious knowledge and at one time had been second in an all England exam. But politics had made inroads on all that so that when I was asked what denomination I was I advised the clerk to please himself what he put me down as. As a consequence I was registered as C of E which I hadn't been since the day I had been christened. At the camp I discovered that church parades were compulsory. Roman Catholics, Jews, Free Church people would be fallen out to make their own way to wherever they wanted to go, even if it was in the general direction of the pub. Meanwhile we poor C of E suckers were marched off to adorn a nearby state church. For me it was the beginning of a long series of debates with clergymen which culminated in an agreement to allow anyone to walk to church or not, as they wished. But that solution lay a long way ahead.

In camp the jolly fortnight was wound up with a sports meeting in which our battery took the honours, while I took myself off to have a long look at Norwich cathedral. Toward the end of our stint at Weybourne we were introduced to the new wonder gun, the 3.7, which was to play such a major role in the AckAck world in the war that was coming. I think each battery was allowed to fire two rounds of which four were registered as direct hits.

We turned in about half an hour after midnight on our last night only to be roused up at two o'clock in the morning, which was most upsetting after our mighty efforts of the past fortnight. Staggering out of our tent we discovered that most of the battery personnel were togged up in either army shirts or in some cissy cases civvy pyjamas, wearing tin hats and fists at the ready, having been alerted to the possibility of an attack upon us by the other two batteries. It was said that some folk were tired of pretending and wanted a real battle. Nothing happened. It was a false alarm and so we all went back to bed. We retired at 3.15 a.m., were roused up an hour later for no apparent reason, and then went to breakfast at 6 a.m. Then, while togged up in full marching order, we retired to the Naafi until we were marched off to the station, to home and to the world of the civilian population.

That was the world of unease, speculation, trouble, unrest and the growing fear of war. Though in my case, having listened to the arguments of the self-styled communist Burns on Putney towpath, I agreed with him that war was not about to break out – yet. The powers that were were not ready. Burns had advised his audiences that it would in all probability start in the September of 1939!

Mark you, in that period of excursions and alarums we did get some humorous pieces of information, as when news went round that in Germany when a private car bumped into a tank the car damaged the tank! Hitler, it was said, was furious. When the war did get going there were a lot of people, particularly infantrymen and tank men, who wished the tiger tank had been made of cardboard as the car-bashed tank was said to have been.

The Sudeten Germans in Czechoslovakia were making nuisances of themselves throughout August. They were a large minority in a country made up of minorities and were demanding reunion with ye old Fatherland Germany and that was causing an uproar. Hitler kept threatening, the democracies kept fumbling or was it stalling? Meanwhile the Russians, who seemed to want to do something about it all, were ignored. Then the French suggested that, as Hitler said he wouldn't dream of attacking France, except in self-defence, it might be a good idea if someone slipped over to Berlin and gave the Chancellor, that is Hitler, a good talking to. It was known that Hitler did not want to attack Britain not even in self defence, so perhaps the British prime minister, Neville Chamberlain, who, after all, came from a decent family, could pop over and sort out that upstart cove Adolf. So Chamberlain nipped on to a plane and popped over to have a chat with the nastiest character since Genghis Khan.

All kinds of rumours were flying about, truth and fiction well mixed up. While dear old Neville kept popping over to see the modern Genghis it was said that Henlein, the leader of the Sudeten Germans, had taken a powder and was being hunted by the Czech police, that he had a price on his head and the Czechs if forced to it would give Hitler and his mob a bloody nose. After all, didn't they have a pretty big arms industry? Then we began to hear that France and Britain had agreed that the Sudeten lands should be handed back to Germany. After all, that seemed eminently reasonable since those lands were German anyway.

This really did set the cat amongst the pigeons. The Czechs said, 'We'll fight.' The Germans said, 'What's ours is ours.' The Poles then said, if the Germans get what they shouldn't have, we want our cut of Czechoslovakia, that bit we should have.

Meanwhile the Russians were putting their oar in in trying to get anyone interested in opposing Hitler to do something about it. But no one took any notice of that sort of thing; the Russians were beyond the pale. What a mess!

In the end the Czechs agreed angrily to have their country stripped of the Sudeten lands, thus starting riots in Prague and facing the fact that they no longer had any defences worth bothering about. Hitler said once that he had no more territorial ambitions in Europe. As a mate of mine said, 'Blimey, if you believe that you'll believe anything.'

The cauldron was on the boil. The French started mobilising their troops, others followed suit and Britain did the decent thing and mobilised the navy. Now as soon as they started in on the navy it was pretty clear the defence of the country was next on the agenda and that certainly meant us – the AckAck.

On 26th August I went to bed with a heavy cold as company while expecting to hear at any moment the knock on the door from a telegraph boy. I couldn't sleep. Radios were blaring all over the place and all attention was focused on one thing – Hitler's speech. It seemed that he wanted his own way and that he meant to get it and be damned what anyone else might think of things. Then I got up – by order. The telegram boy had delivered his missile.

I was to report to Lytton Grove immediately in full war harness and with one day's rations. So I pulled my war togs out from under my bed and got dressed. Having got dressed I found my brother was delighted. I never discovered whether he was genuinely interested in the welfare of his military elder brother or whether he was glad to be shot of me. My mother wept of course, my father was noncommittal as usual and one or two of the neighbours seemed, even at that early stage, anxious for me to 'Thrash those Germans.'

My brother Victor came up with me but soon sheered off. Inside the hall all was chaos. Khaki-clad figures were rushing about all over the place, lorries were coming and going, guns were being towed away to unknown destinations (if they were three-inch probably to the local junk heap) and sections of gunners were being marched off to some defensible frontier or other.

With a companion I settled down on the floor of the hall in a quiet corner, feeling I needed to protect my cold from all possible draughts. We covered ourselves with newspapers, taking care to include our faces. We had decided upon, at least for the time being, a quiet life. I had already learned a very good military rule – keep a low profile. I had become an old soldier at the ripe old age of seventeen.

Chapter Two

Battle Stations for a Warrior

C Section, or that part of it which could be rounded up, was paraded while my mate and I rested quietly in our corner. The section was to be trained on Lewis guns, those noisy things of which we had one or maybe two though we had no ammunition. Night had been replaced by day and now that too was fading away. By now news of the goings on in the regimental battle stations was filtering through. Later still we heard something of the Lewis gunners. One crew was detailed off as the AckAck defence of Dartford. The two characters concerned found themselves situated on the top of a huge gas container with one Lewis gun, no tripod and no ammunition. They discussed their situation carefully and decided that if Jerry turned up, one of them would hold the Lewis at the hip, waggle it at the hostile and so frighten the enemy off. Finally odd bods were rounded up and sent off to various compass points while the last six of us were detailed off as headquarters staff, thus ensuring that they had selected a body of men devoted to their own welfare and so probably good material for looking after others.

Our first task was to go by lorry to Hyde Park and draw ammunition for that part of the outfit stationed at the front. Upon arrival we discovered that there was no ammo where they said it ought to be so we returned to headquarters empty-handed. Then, noting that most people did not seem to know what was going on, we took advantage of the situation and three of us nipped home for a bath and some civvy victuals. I assured my parents that the way the war was going on I would be home on such visits from time to time to help bolster civilian morale. But that night we were shipped off to our battle headquarters at Eltham in South London. Our slow progress across the metropolis was cheered on by children while we were inundated with jokes from lorry and bus drivers who seemed to think we were some sort of Fred Karno's outfit.

London parks were undergoing a kind of land-based sea change with trenches being dug and spoil being flung into long barrow-like heaps while public buildings were disappearing at least on their lower floors behind piles of sandbags. We understood fortunes were in the making by the sandbag manufacturers. But that was to be expected, was it not? Meanwhile children were being prepared for evacuation into the country. Our headquarters turned out to be the home of an engineering unit, South End Hall, Foots Cray Road, Eltham. Not a bad billet. Only one drawback: no straw palliasses, only three blankets and a place on a floor. But as compared with our front line troops we were in the middle of luxury.

Meanwhile Chamberlain and his French counterpart went over and had a very successful talk with a very understanding Hitler with the result that Czechoslovakia was to be partitioned off and Hitler was to get what he really and truly wanted, the Sudeten lands. This meant 'Peace in Our Time', or at least that was what was announced when the prime minister waved his piece of paper on his return from a visit to Genghis. But of course our role in things had to go on until someone told us to stand down. So we were kept busy on such jobs as cleaning lavatories, making tea, sweeping up, smoking too many cigarettes and doing an occasional errand or two.

One day I had to take a message to one of the gunsites. The last news we had had of guns was when one, being towed, swung sharply round a corner in a busy high street so that the barrel gave a lamp post a mighty swipe and bent the top over – our first casualty.

Now here were some guns stuck in the middle of what at one time had been a sports field, a field which at the time of my arrival there had been turned into a sea of mud. The gun crews and instrument operators were housed in the sports club building at one side of the field. To man the guns, the crews had to hobble through a sea of Flanders type mud thus making themselves and the guns somewhat messy. Here I should explain that during the whole of this warlike period the rain had deluged all over the place as if the god of weather had been making an effort to get the place as Flanderish as possible.

Everyone wondered at the prospect before us in those early days. If it was like this in England, what the devil would it be like in France? Everyone of course assumed that the war would be a continuation of the impasse brought about during the Great War.

The sentry at the gate looked at the letter in my hand and nodded toward the pavilion.

'Down there, cock, that's where you've gotta go.'

I looked at the sentry, looked at the pavilion, looked at the mud, compared the state of my boots with his and said, 'Me, I'm headquarters staff, my brief stops here at your garden gate, so you take it.' I placed the letter into his somewhat grimy hand and shoved off. If there was a reply someone else could fetch it along to headquarters.

With the ending of the crisis we had to start packing up. For me and my friends it was plain sailing but for the mudlarkers their troubles were far from over. A couple of guns got stuck in mud in the middle of a field and would not budge. A towing matador failed to tow them out and only got itself bogged down. The only thing to do was to wait in the rain and cold wind until the arrival of a scammell, the vehicle which would pull anything out of anywhere in any condition. As for our light defences on the top of the Dartford gasholder, we knew all was well there, since if there had been any trouble the explosion would have been heard and felt throughout southern England.

So toward the end of our two weeks on active service the strategical withdrawal from Hackney marshes and other places was well under way. This was our first experience of such an operation but certainly not the last. We also came to understand through experience that we, in the British army, never retreated, it was always to be a 'strategical withdrawal', often drawing the enemy on so that we could knock his block off. It didn't always work out that way though.

Rumours went round we would be on active service until the middle of October, then the middle of November and then Christmas. In the event the expense of it all must have been too great because we were stood down before any of the dates bandied about.

By Tuesday 4th October stores were still being ferried back to Lytton Grove and the guns had already been put to bed.

I had been a hospital orderly for a few days at Eltham so on the fifth of the month I helped to load up one of the commandeered commercial vans with hospital stores and then, with the sergeant in charge driving as if fleeing from Jerry (in a strategical manner of course) and a bombardier and me hanging on for dear life, we dashed back to Putney.

Once there, we of the overworked headquarters staff, following in the footsteps of others, asked for leave. But as we were preparing to step back into the civilian world again, the battle-weary troops discovered that all leave had been cancelled, guards were placed on all exits and entrances and no one, not even a mouse, was allowed to leave. Such is the way of the military.

For my part I didn't mind a bit. I had in my pack fifty cigarettes, two pounds of bacon, several packets of biscuits and an outsize tin of pineapple given to me by an understanding ward sister. I could hang on for a bit longer if need be.

Then leave was on again and I collected a twenty-four hour pass and went home, I daresay like a conquering hero. At any rate I went home much to the relief of my family.

I returned on the Friday morning expecting to have a rest after the fatigue of leave but instead found myself assisting in the job of rolling up fourteen hundred army blankets into bundles of ten. Then, given leave from 6.30 p.m. to midnight, I went to the pictures.

The following morning, feeling bored, I joined a working party for Dartford. I must have been sickening for something, volunteering like that!

Arriving in the area we found ourselves in a right old desolate place beside the Thames where we filled in muddy trenches of the Flanders Fields type and piled muddy old sleepers on to a couple of lorries. As soon as we had finished we had our bully beef and biscuits and then headed for home via Woolwich ferry. Arriving at the drill hall we found that everyone had gone home so we downed tools at once and did likewise.

I have done all kinds of things in my life. I have built with my own home-made bricks, laid my own drains, roofed roofs, laid a ring main, written verse, largely doggerel, and unperformed plays — so I thought I'd have a go at a book.

I dedicate it to all who served in the war, and remember those who didn't have such a humorous war — such as the prisoners of the Japanese; tank crews; young airmen and naval men, in particular those merchant seamen who went to war with no weapon in their hand but courage.

We remember

We were there
Years and years ago,
On desert dust, Norwegian snow,
In jungle sweat
And icy seas
Where smoke trails met . . .
And women serving teas.

Yes, we were there
In manhood's bloom
Nurses to care —
Facing, facing doom.
Most came home,
Many stayed away
And wherever we may roam
We remember those who had to stay.
Yes, we remember,
They too were there.

Chapter Three

In the Eye of the Storm

I went back to the building trade, my father and our business. Back to the civilian way of life so different from the one I had so recently adopted. My father was a hard-working character who believed in charging his customers only the exact number of hours worked and in those hours worked we really did get stuck into things. The result of this honesty was that often we would get paid for half a day or a few hours. In consequence of this my father always had plenty of work though not all that amount of money. He would never be a rich retired builder.

We repaired roofs, did plumbing, bricklaying, decorating, painting and all kinds of odd jobs. You name it, we did it. In retrospect I can see how good my dad was at decorating but how indifferent when it was a matter of plumbing. I soon learned after the war that it was better to employ a craftsman for a specific job than do a botched job oneself.

The contrast between then and now is stark. Every area of London had its quota of jobbing builders with their hand trucks and therefore limited area of operation. Overheads in consequence were low and bills could be reasonable. Today those jobbing builders have vanished from the scene and are replaced by mostly young men rushing around in vans of all shapes and sizes doing work all over the place. In fact it is quite usual to see builders' vans parked in London belonging to builders domiciled way outside London. And the small job is not very apparent either. Usually one sees roofs being reslated in entirety and rarely can we see a few slates or tiles being put into place on an old roof. The result of course is high prices and the growth of high prices has produced the 'Cowboy builder'.

Our longest journey with truck was from Danemere Street

just short of Putney Common to a turning just off Tooting Broadway. Many times have I pushed our truck over there and we have spent a day hard at it and then at the end of the day, we have loaded the truck and pushed it back to the yard in Danemere Street. There wasn't too much energy left for making a nuisance of oneself in the evenings. It was a fair old push home, from the Broadway, along Garret Lane Wandsworth, along Wandsworth High Street, down Putney Bridge Road and then along the Lower Road to the yard.

Incidentally, this was an improvement upon my grandfather's situation when he was a young man. He had walked to work and back every day from Fulham Broadway to Tooting.

But mostly we worked in Putney and Fulham from eight in the morning until half past five in the evening, adding on time for returning to the yard. Many a time and oft in winter we have worked on by candlelight to get a job completed to enable us to keep the prices down. As a great deal of our interior work was what was known as landlord's work, this is a quick job at low cost, there was no hanging about. A further interesting feature of that kind of work was the vast amount of cream, green and brown used in painting. Pastel shades were only for those who could afford their luxury. The other thing to be noted is that most houses in those days had bugs browsing or dozing in the walls. This was made easy for the bugs because of the habit of hanging pictures on walls with nails, thus creating a mass of holes behind wallpapers, many of which had been on the walls for many years. It was not unusual to strip from walls fourteen layers of paper. The old man would never paper over old wallpaper.

So it was pretty well all work and not too much time for play. Indeed, if we had been called upon to do as much work in the Saturday night army we would have probably started a mutiny.

In those years immediately before the outbreak of war in 1939, nearly everyone was a cinema goer, apart perhaps, from my grandfather who only seemed to be concerned with his demolition business, the sale of second hand timber and dealing in scrap metal in his Felsham Road yard. My brother and I, along with a cousin Bertie, spent a great deal of our time playing in that yard which not only had stacks of second hand timber but also a huge manure pile from the horses of 'Chummy Hudson', the greengrocer who used to stable his horses in the stables at the side of the two cottages on the site.

That manure pile had been the cause of some irritation on the part of us younger fry. There was always a pot of tea on the go in my grandmother's kitchen but we young'uns could only have any after the adults had finished so that our tea was always lukewarm or downright cold. In summer the blowflies from the manure heap − which was larger than a house − would find pleasure in flopping into the tea, forcing us to flick 'em out. Indeed, how times have changed! The Middle East taught me to hate all flies and the war also brought a change of hygiene. Before the war we never had lavatory paper, only squares of newspaper, and washing hands was not a general habit.

The yard had several unusual denizens. One was Billy the goat who seemed to relish anything at all edible. He once saw a woollen jumper hanging on a washing line, the property of my mother. Billy decided that the jumper looked a very juicy green grassy morsel so helped himself to one arm of the jumper! Armless in the yard amid goats! We kids were fascinated by the way Billy ate anything. We used to feed him soap to watch the bubbles come out of his mouth. Then one day that goat discovered a half hundredweight tin of plum jam. He ate it but it wasn't plum jam, it was red lead.

Then there was the goose. My grandmother had always had a hard time with my grandfather and when the latter was away on one of his frequent journeys to far flung fields of demolition she would give herself solace in the public bar of the Half Moon pub at the bottom of Bigg's Row. Everyone knew she was solacing because the goose would waddle down after her and sit outside the door until she emerged to shoo him away, though he never would oblige. We wondered if he was a spy in the pay of our grandfather.

An observation on the pre-war cinema, the Hippodrome in

particular. This was an old vaudeville theatre turned cinema where at one stage we used to get taken by my parents to the gallery – entrance fee fourpence (old style). But I was always peeved because like many gallery goers my father would always buy a bag of peanuts from a red nosed old bloke who sold them at the gallery door. Thus we would find ourselves trying to listen to the not over clear talkies while the rest of the audience went about the business of shelling peanuts!

Later on when in our teens we despised the gallery we would attend either the circle or the stalls. All cinemas in those days had their long queues with people waiting patiently to get in. Often those waiting outside would be quite content to miss the B picture in their desire to see the main picture. At the Hippodrome there were times when one could get in in standing-room only, which meant standing at the back of the stalls until a seat became available. The Hippodrome was so designed that the floor of the circle came down so low that it neatly cut off the heads of the film actors on the screen so that when in 'standing room only' one was liable to only see the moving bodies of the screen actors and thus one didn't know who the devil was who. However cinema audiences were not deterred by little things like that.

Then there was the football. Putney Common on Saturday afternoon was the scene of play between a number of amateur clubs. The footballers there always gave me the impression that while they were not out to kill each other they never minded if an arm or leg got broken; it could mean a temporary lay off work. The big footballing attraction was of course Fulham football club, to which place I was taken when I could only see what was going on by being held firmly on a crash barrier. They were the days of the five and a half day working week so that men would stream into the football grounds straight from work, often enough in their working clothes since the supply of overalls did not seem to be general. I was always intrigued by one particular thing – the busmen's hat. On a certain day in spring on would go the white cloth covers of the busmen's hats and there they would remain until a day in autumn when they would be removed and there was always a good sprinkling of busmen in those pre-war football crowds.

I never came across any violence in those matches. Was it because most folk were too tired to muck about or were they a different breed to so many of the modern football fraternity? Certainly if a woman happened to be in the vicinity in the crowd and someone, forgetting himself, started swearing, he soon got told to knock it off. The last time I ventured into a football ground in the eighties I was appalled not only at the male swearing but the women's too!

Then there was the wireless, not the radio but the wireless. It was the time of the wet battery when they had to be taken to a shop to be recharged. Our first wireless had entered our home sometime in the early thirties so that it was something relatively new to us but even in those short years it had come to dominate our lives along with the cinema.

It brought the world into the homes of ordinary people. There were good things about it of course but there were bad things too. I suppose one of the good was the introduction into those homes of light entertainment and music, though whenever a chamber concert was announced I would be the first to rush to the switch and turn that stuff off. It was only during the war that I discovered how much of an idiot I had been.

The wireless bombarded all and sundry with bad news: Hitler, Mussolini, Franco, Spain, the Japanese attack on China. Though China was a long way away and in any case it had always been fashionable for someone to attack China.

We were told of the death of George V, we knew all about the new King Edward VIII and his abdication and the accession of Brother George. We were told about re-armament, while being assured that there would be no war; after all, hadn't Mr Chamberlain seen to that?

But of course he hadn't seen to that. The prophets I had listened to on the Putney towing path and in Hyde Park were proved right, the powers that be, were not ready for war yet.

Chamberlain was attacked right from the time he waved his

bit of paper about, announcing 'Peace in Our Time'. He wasn't helped by the news that Franco Spanish warships had attacked and sunk Spanish government ships and of all places in the North Sea! Everyone up till then had been under the impression that the North Sea was *our* sea and what the devil were foreigners doing fighting in *our* sea?

The air raid wardens who had been stood down were not happy. They had been urged to volunteer and had spent a great deal of their time handing out gas masks to the general public. They had had no pay and were a bit short of cash after the crisis. But they had been volunteers and that was that. If they hadn't volunteered they would have been unpatriotic but would have been in work and drawn their pay.

Then another bit of patriotism was brought to light. Sandbags, timber and corrugated iron had been ordered for slit trenches and air raid shelters. Immediately the patriotic businessmen of Britain had raised the price of sandbags from 2½ *d.* to 10½ *d.* and 11½ *d;* sand from 7*s.* 6*d.* to £1 a yard and no one seemed to know what the new price of timber was except that it was a good deal dearer than it had been. There was talk of a government enquiry, councils refusing to pay and suppliers of unwanted material refusing to take the goods back.

All the time looming in the background was the menace of the dictators and in particular that Charlie Chaplinesque figure – Hitler.

In Britain Sir Oswald Mosley and his fascists were stirring up trouble and in particular attacking Jews in the East End of London with the result that anti-fascist groups, usually led by communists, fought running battles with the Mosleyites while, it seemed to many people, the police looked on and even seemed to be protecting the fascists.

But it was the German Jew who suffered the most along with others such as socialists, communists, trade unionists and anyone else the Nazis didn't like. News came through of purges of Jews, of concentration camps and tremendous suffering and masses of people fleeing from the ever growing Nazi terror.

In the middle of it all came the festive season.

Merry Christmas all!

But the Christmas spirit was not all that brilliant. It was dawning on more and more people that war was inevitable. As time went by Hitler's demands increased. Eventually he not only took over the whole of the weakened Czech state including the mighty Skoda works but the free port of Memel as well. Mussolini, not to be outdone, took over the tiny state of Albania to swell his growing empire while the Japanese continued to wreak disaster in China.

In March the Spanish Republican fleet gave up the struggle and surrendered itself to the French in Tunisia. Franco Spain came into existence and that meant the territory of the Axis powers was greatly extended, an alarming prospect in the face of the coming war. Meanwhile the Russians kept urging a pact between them and the Western allies against the Axis powers but the Allies weren't keen. In the end the Russians became browned off with the tardiness of the West and did a deal with the Nazis, whereby when Germany seized one half of Poland the Russians would take the other half. The Russians then, realising the need to strengthen their fortifications around Leningrad, offered to do a deal with the Finns, a deal which would have been fairly advantageous to the Finns but at the prompting of anti-communist forces the Finns refused and under Marshal Mannerheim they went to war with the Russians. As that war developed we heard of the usual atrocities, this time perpetrated by the Russians, and how, for example, a file of Finnish heroes had defeated ten thousand Red Army men in the snow.

In time the war was brought to an end, the Russians got what they wanted and as far as I recall the Finns didn't do badly out of the final settlement either. In Britain air raid shelters were offered for sale.

Early in 1939 experiments were carried out with cone shaped air raid shelters and it was decided they could be issued free to people with a weekly income of five pounds or less but that the richer folk would have to pay for them. Later on shelters were offered free to families with an income of £250 or less per annum. There was a great deal of argument about those shelters. One of the contentions was that a half-submerged shelter would spoil the garden!

In the first world war conscription had to be introduced once it started to sink in that there was no honour and glory in being blown to bits in Flanders mud. In 1939 the government didn't hang about. Three hundred and ten thousand young men between the ages of twenty and twenty-one were called to serve for six months then to be put into the Territorials or the army reserve for four years less the six months.

Cambridge won the boat race by four lengths and Blue Peter won the Derby. Derby day, always on a Wednesday, presumably to keep it exclusive, saw the turn-out of the upper crust in vintage cars, Rolls-Royces, grey suits and toppers with the ladies in all their finery. Many of them passed through Putney on the way to the Derby on Derby day, something much more important than what Hitler could do.

In the boxing world Two-Ton Tony Galento, down from a weight of twenty-two stone to seventeen, had been training hard on beer, cigars and steaks and was said to have remarked, in reference to the world champion Joe Louis, 'I'll moider that bum Louis.' In the event Galento hammered Louis for the first two rounds and even went so far as to floor the champion. But in the fourth round, Louis, no doubt sure that he was not a bum, sailed into the challenger and knocked him all round the ring with such effect that the referee stopped the fight and Two-Ton had to have twenty-two stitches in what no doubt he himself would have called 'My Mooee'.

And what a memory: England beat the West Indies in the first test match *easily*! But in the world at large the gloom was deepening. On 14th July the first of the conscripts went into camps to begin their training.

During the year there were three submarine disasters, one American, one French and one British, the last being the *Thetis* which was raised and used during the war. Blackouts were being prepared, traffic lights were being blacked out, leaving a mere cross for the light to be identified by. This was no doubt a very good ploy to deceive the enemy, either enemy planes or invading tanks, though it might have been better to black the lights out altogether, thus denying enemy tanks the knowledge as to when to stop and go on.

Sticky paper was being offered for window panes, sandbags were being filled and trenches dug.

Hitler was getting impatient and was clearly not going to stand for any Polish nonsense, while Britain and France were not going to stand for Hitler's nonsense. The uneasy peace was coming to an end along with the League of Nations. We were on the threshold of a war in which one or two nations were to fling their armed might into a great many parts of the world, irrespective of whether or not other nations wanted to stay neutral. We were to hear of millions of dead, twenty million in the Soviet Union alone, before the ghastly thing came to a close with the introduction of the atom bomb and its use, not by the evil forces of fascism but by the democratic leaders of the Allies.

Chapter Four

Limbering up for the Duffy

The year 1939 was one of political turmoil and of expanding war. War in China, war in Spain, Ethiopia conquered by the unwarlike Italians under the leadership of the somewhat comical dictator Mussolini, and later on the Finns and the Russians would be disputing territory around Leningrad. It was all about juggling for position in readiness for what was so clearly inevitable – a massive war in which powerful nations would ride roughshod over small ones. One did not have to be a prophet to foretell what was coming.

In Britain, although there was a great deal of official talk about 'Peace in Our Time' and 'No more War', there was feverish activity behind the scenes: evacuation plans, conscription plans, rationing, military and naval bustle and we in the AckAck were to have a month's service and not two weeks, half the time at a war site, the other at a firing camp at Watchet.

There had been changes within the 54th regiment. It had been expanded and a fourth battery had been added, the 312 of which, I found, I was a member. We very soon discovered that it carried a special section known as X. This was made up of well washed, well heeled, well spoken, well nigh useless (from a gunnery point of view) upper crust lawyers, solicitors and bank bods who were there to get some army flavouring before becoming officers. In their case, money no object. An interesting thing about those characters was that while we, the lumpen lot, drank beer or scrumpy in the public bar, they took their shorts in the saloon.

My brother helped me up to the drill hall with my gear, including tin hat, gas mask, kit bag, haversack, water bottle and attaché case, though I wore my own ammo boots and riding breeches and carried my own overcoat, the ever lovable and constant companion until it fell to pieces, 'bum freezer'.

Victor pushed off home. He was sixteen and would have to wait for his call-up papers which he would receive in due course. After this he would be embarked as an infantryman onto a sea of battle nastiness which would affect him for ever after. Me, I had a different war but then not only was I in the RA but I was one of them there 'Fred Karno's lot', wasn't I?

Meanwhile my daddy would have to soldier on on his tod until I got back from this war limbering-up business. His builder's board might carry the sign J. GREEN & SON but Sonny was off somewhere else playing at being a soldier. As for my particular bit of the army, how much more advanced were we now that we were that much nearer a duffy with Jerry? During the crisis I had opened a cupboard, a broom cupboard, and discovered the total small arms collection of our outfit: four Lee Enfield rifles used for guard purposes.

Would there be more now?

Some of us climbed into a Green Line coach as the first move in our advance to our war station and having got ourselves as comfortable as possible were turfed out again and herded into an old banger of a coach, thus allowing us to assume the Green Line was commandeered for the Sam Browne Belters and their allies in X section.

At our war site in Essex near Billericay we were under canvas and I might as well say right away that as usual the weather man was not on our side. In fact it was on that site that we discovered that automatically offered after three days rain there was an issue of rum.

Reveille was at 6 a.m. and then the rest of the day would find us constantly at it, mostly gun drilling. This was one of the tyrannies of the RA. It was with us night and day, that damned gun drill. Fall in, number off, take post, elevate, depress, traverse. It was a positive nightmare.

But in fact it was for the good of our souls. It was irksome, tiresome, a damned nuisance but when it came to action against a determined and ruthless enemy the instinct to operate in hellish conditions saved lives.

The new 3.7 guns were on the site, far superior monsters to the old three-inch oven door things. To start with, the breech on a 3.7 was far better. Gone was the dangerous slamming shut and instead we had the pleasure of knowing that when a round was thrust into the 'spout' the breech would slide across and indeed would knock a hand out of the way and into safety. As time went by things improved even more until the time came when a fused round was bunged into a tray, the tray was swung in line with the breech, a toggle rammed the round home, the breech closed and bang, off it went. Safety first! Good idea.

There were two types of gun, the static and the mobile. The former was a straightforward fixed affair, bolted firmly into a concrete base. All a crew had to do was to dance around the thing a few thousand times, elevating and depressing, turning it through its full 360 degree arc and pretending to fire it until all actions could be done in one's sleep.

The mobile was very different. It was basically the same gun but it entailed more work and fast work at that, which no one involved could duck out of because the slower the operators moved in bringing a gun into action, the more chance an enemy had of stopping you altogether. So everyone had to move and move fast. The whole operation to take minutes, the ideal being to take no time at all in coming into action.

The towing lorry would stop, the crew leap out of the matador, unhook the gun, then away matador. Out would come sledge hammers, down would come the four legs, into the spike holes would go the spikes, they would be hammered home thus se-curing the gun, the ammunition would be laid out in a circle, breech block opened, traversing and elevating commence accord-ing to the dictates of the instruments, the first round fused and in the breech, the number five would bang down his firing lever and bang! Away went the round. There were two types of ammunition, shrapnel and high explosive, but in peace time our experience of such things was, to say the least, minimal.

Pretty straightforward in the light of day. Less so in the pitch dark.

So the training proceeded with all that taking post and elevating and depressing and ramming home until the novelty had completely worn off and we were browned off. The weather man didn't help. He seemed intent upon giving us plenty of training too. In his case he seemed to want to harden us all off for a future endurance test in Flanders mud. At times it was so wet we seemed to live permanently in our weatherproof capes which after a time failed to be weatherproof. I often wondered what mums would think if they knew how their dear sons were suffering.

Then of course as usual there were the fatigue duties, the necessary but irksome things that all military men of lower rank have to endure.

The unpopular one was cookhouse fatigue which meant a day in and around the cookhouse cleaning greasy dixies in cold water and dirty sand, or peeling spuds. We found that cooks were naturally mean and one had to be extremely astute to get anything out of them. They always seemed to be in cahoots with the War Office in an endeavour to save money at the expense of military stomachs. What I mean is, not that we were badly fed on the war site or in camp but that it was hard to scrounge anything extra.

One of the main chores in the cookhouse fatigue was peeling potatoes or, in military parlance, spud bashing. The title was apt when it is considered how many ways in which a potato can be peeled. The peelers could be graded into the careful, the finicky, the conscientious, the careless, the savage and those who just didn't care and were so slow that they were a burden to others. Finally there was the spud basher who would prove to his fellow sufferers how useless he was by putting more potato into the swill bin than into the bucket of spuds. I often wondered whether the lack of control over the potato operation could lose us the war and I was sure the German counterpart would be more thorough than any of us. But whatever category a man fell into he was always part of a 'mothers' meeting'. A group would sit round the spud bucket and swill bin plus potato sacks and while murdering potatoes would natter about everything under the sun unless there was among them one of those characters who had the knack of telling smutty jokes all day long without repeating himself.

One of the easiest things to get on to was what was known as jankers, that is punishment for minor misdemeanours. Such punishments could include days on spud bashing or latrine cleaning or other such uncongenial tasks. Guard duties were another series of pains in the proverbial neck. Here there was always apparent an official mania for spit and polish. Buttons were to shine, lanyards to be blancoed white, whiter than white, and when ankle puttees replaced the leg type and riding breeches they were to be greener than green. Rifle barrels had to have rifle bores shining brighter than any bright moon and woe betide the poor blighter who had neglected to spend hours with a pull-through on his bore.

Guard duties were usually night affairs, guard mountings were always based on bull shine and then came the sentry bit, butt salute for those Captain and under and the full works for Majors and above. From that point of view the first two shifts were the worst, after which time most folks were either in bed or out of camp and far away.

Those duties under which most of us suffered became fairly fixed as time went by and altered little throughout the war years. It seemed to be that despite the fact that the army was crawling with labour there was always a chronic shortage of people to carry out the mundane work of any unit. When I was young I was never very mechanically minded and really did have clumsy hands, but from an early date I found myself a limber gunner, an important rank without authority and without such things as stripes on arms. The limber gunner was in fact a nursemaid to a gun. He was the one who kept it clean and in working order, doing minor repairs when necessary and passing on the major ones to an artificer. Funnily enough, I never came across anyone who was a limber gunner who wasn't conscientious in his work and in fact in Palestine we all used to work far longer hours than anyone else without thinking twice about it. I suppose it was inbred in all of us – guns had to be served and always ready for use. The truth of course was that a gun unfit for service was no gun at all.

Limber gunners in theory were excused duties other than nursemaiding guns but there was never a time when because of the job I was excused those damned guard duties. During the war, though, we never did other fatigues.

A routine soon developed: guard one night, fire picket the next (same, except that one had a pick helve not a rifle), next day cookhouse, then general fatigues and if lucky a day off and then guard again and so on.

At our war site, reveille was at 6 a.m. A whistle would blow us awake as an alarm signal and then, snatching up tins and gasmasks, we would run for the guns. This was followed by PT or PFJ (physical feeble jerks) training, usually conducted by a maniac in shorts, despite weather conditions, who seemed to possess a death wish – for all of us. Then came breakfast and a normal day, if careering around death-dealing guns can be classified as a normal day.

During that fortnight on the war site we all got twenty-four hour leave passes. Maybe the powers that be considered we had been away from mums and dads and girlfriends too long or that perhaps we needed a bath or two. My folk were somewhat put out when I turned up, not only because I was taking time off from my war but because I arrived at a time when they were all in bed. The AckAck had a time schedule twenty-five hours in every day.

While I was beginning to develop into a limber gunner, albeit slowly, I had a section officer who was keen for me to get rid of my stammer. Thus I landed with the job of spotter and telephonist at the command post. I used to wonder what the devil would happen if any enemy plane turned up and I had to raise the alarm. Meanwhile the weather man kept up his attack on our morale. It kept raining and making conditions uncomfortable for all and sundry and things weren't helped when we got called out in the middle of the night at half past two in the bloody morning. With tin hats on and wearing gasmasks we went floundering off to the guns where we spent a half hour tracking aircraft overhead with the aid of searchlights. Then we stood down, went to the cookhouse for soup and bread and then to our fleapits until the alarm whistle blew at the usual time of 6 a.m.

I suppose it might be as well to put the gunsite into its proper place in the order of things; after all it would be the centre of our lives during the years of active service in the field.

Each site consisted of a half battery or troop with four guns ringing a command post comprising spotter, heightfinder, predictor and of course the command control itself with outside phone link and megaphone contact with the guns. The spotter is fairly obvious. It was used to spot an approaching enemy and give the heightfinder a bearing and that crew in turn would give a height to the predictor mob who operated a large box affair which I presume was an early form of computer. In real action this was to prove pretty useless. The predictor crew would fiddle about with dials and knobs and give us a fuse setting number. We would fuse the round, pop it up the spout and bang! Off it would go. As things developed the calling out was replaced by a method whereby the predictor relayed the information directly, thus saving priceless time.

It was all very tidy and neat in theory. The plane ideally should remain at a constant height, constant direction, and then we could shoot it down, providing a cloud did not appear to obscure the view and providing the pilot hadn't decided not to be shot down and hadn't taken evading action. There was one thing none of us had experienced, not even at a firing camp, and that was falling shrapnel from our rounds! It had never been possible to use live ammo inland; the civilians would not have been pleased. It wasn't until the real war started that we realised how much the tin hat contributed to our own well being; without it one felt naked. Jerry did not fly obligingly out to sea in decent firing range but had the un-British habit of zooming all over our field of fire and in particular making us fire at acute angles so that a good deal of our own muck would fall back around our own ears.

At this camp five of us formed the Bundlers, a group dedicated to in-fighting at all times. Anyone of the five could call a Bundle at any time of the day or night and at once we all fell to in a free for all fight with arms, legs and boots going flat out on a friendly killing mission. There was Palmer, who left us very early; Stan Ward who at seventeen had a mission, love the girls, drink as much as possible and have a go at Jerry; there was Mookee, big lumbering, thick headed genial Mookee who volunteered for France and also vanished from our ken early; Fred Smith; and myself.

Fred Smith had been some sort of clerk in civvy street but now it transpired during long conversations I had with him on all manner of topics that after the war he wanted an outdoor life with plenty of exercise, this despite the fact he was supposed to have a weak heart. Supposedly, because in all my army days he was the only one who could hold me down in a wrestling bout, some heart condition he had!

During that Essex rainy season, we, the Bundlers, would amuse ourselves in the evenings, when not working, in the local pubs and we would stagger back to rain-swept and penetrated tents to flop into damp conditions usually around midnight. I was still teetotal though sometimes taking the somewhat unmanly glass of port. The others couldn't see why I tagged along with the boozers but I was tolerated. Young men of course are apt to get their heads down and go off to the land of nod without any trouble. This was important since relieving oneself at night could be fraught with great danger. A sleeper by a tent flap could count himself fortunate in being able to slip out easily but for anyone further in the problems could be immense. First, there was the possibility of treading on somebody's ear or putting an elbow into an unsuspecting groin and then, when the flap was reached, the half aroused and desperate character trying to get out could discover that some fool had secured the tent flap with grannyknots! Life could be hard and dangerous.

One dark and dreary night I roused up and my left arm spread out in the general direction of Mookee but Mookee wasn't there!

Mookee had gone!

Now Mookee *never* roused once his head was down. Once down, that piece of craggy humanity stayed down, turned seemingly into a piece of Lignum Vitae and only a heavy dowsing of Aqua Frigida would rouse him. But there he was gone and the rain belting down outside.

I waited for some time hoping the wanderer would return. I wondered at first whether he had undergone a brainstorm but then rejected the idea since Lignum Vitae was brain free. Eventually I sounded the alarm and roused the others. 'Mookee's gone,' was my warning shout into the inky darkness of the weeping tent. Weeping! It was more than that, there wasn't a dry canvas anywhere. Those Great War tents had had their day, that was sure.

We held a hasty council of war and came to the only conclusion possible: our comrade in arms, or rather our comrade in army shirt, must be found at all cost. A dry Mookee was bad enough but a wet one might well emulate an angry hippopotamus.

We snatched up our rain capes and bundled out into the dirty black morning and spreading out went in search of that lost hippo. We found him in a ditch half lying in water from a bubbling brook and the other half well and truly soaked by Poseidon's downpour. He was not really very happy. He was constantly calling for his mum.

But as was pointed out, his mum wasn't there so he would have to put up with us. And then with a great deal of struggle and universal protest we got the doubly plastered absentee back onto his far from dry bed, though a bit drier than his previous one, and having piled on to him some of our own blankets we went to bed ourselves for half an hour until that cursed whistle blew.

We were all worn out from the night's efforts apart from Mookee who had not only abandoned thoughts of his mum but showed no sign whatsoever of wear or tear. We concluded it might be good for him to spend a few nights in a rainswept bubbling brook.

The next night the jolly-minded Mookee did rouse up in the middle of the night and playfully called 'Bundle', whereupon we all set to and in no time at all the tent was down and not only was that wet but its inmates were even more so. People in neighbouring tents were not amused and we were threatened with extermination.

Then we took off for the firing camp at Watchet in Somerset.

Unloading at the station we sorted ourselves out and marching behind a band we approached the camp beside the seashore. Topping a rise, we could look down on an area of the country which had the camp in the middle of it and right in the centre of the camp was a big brown looking patch which was no doubt the parade ground. Had some fool plonked a slab of Flanders mud there for our practising benefit?

Arriving at the camp we sorted ourselves out, drew bedding, plonked it down on ground sheets which had lain on the weeping ground and went off to dinner. That night we rolled up into our blankets trying to keep everything from flopping over the ground-sheet edges onto the sodden ground. I went off to sleep wondering whether the last campers had been a squadron of ducks.

'Now, Leslie,' I could hear my mother warning me. 'Mind you keep your feet dry and don't catch a cold.' 'Of course not, muvver. Atishoo!'

It wasn't long before the Bundlers decided to go into the village to sample the local brew. Being Somerset it had to be cider and not the ordinary stuff sold as such at home but the real thing, scrumpy at tuppence halfpenny a pint. I had decided that cider could be exempted from the rule of teetotalism and that I could try it. I found it tasted like nothing on earth, possibly it was something the ancient gods of Greece drank, it being somewhat tart but no more dangerous than drinking some sort of unpalatable lemon juice without sugar of any kind.

Into the village pub we marched, as large as life, city slickers who knew all there was to know about drinking and a bit more besides.

'We'll have a pint all round first, then one more and then we'll try the next pub. Right?'

'Right.'

We never got to the next pub.

A couple of old boys sitting on a corner settle as if it and they had been carved together watched us thoughtfully while we were showing off. Then one of them spoke from the depth of his country bumpkinism, 'I'd be a mite careful o' that there scrumpy, if I were you boys,' in a voice of wisdom which we waved aside. One or two had a couple of pints, I think I had one and someone explained to the local yokels that they didn't know what they were talking about and we Londoners could drink anything and to prove the point we were off to the next pub to see if they had a *real* drink.

We never reached the next pub. In fact I doubt if anyone remembered anything more once we hit the fresh air outside.

It was at this camp that we made contact for the first time and the last time with the full X section with its future officers and money no object.

As above mentioned the cookhouse fatigue was a major pain in the neck for all concerned and that included X section, except perhaps that it was even more of a pain to them than to us lot.

When it was the turn of X section to peel the spuds and wash the dirty dishes, some of us went over to have a shufti at the trials and tribulations of our fellow creatures. The characters with the white podgy hands had a general approach to the problem, a panacea for all ills: they one and all offered a fiver to any of the lumpen who would stand in for them and do the fatigue. And a fiver in those days was worth something.

I was happy and indeed somewhat astonished to note that no one accepted any money. All the members of the lower order were happy to forgo the money to watch those podgy hands getting greasier and grubbier. They were happy too to hand out plenty of advice as to how the various jobs should be done.

We never met again after the camp. They probably went on to lead other ranks to death and glory or found places in the seats of power somewhere or other, while we went on to confuse Jerry.

The camp was really an anticlimax after the war site. We did a bit of firing, still on the principles of constant height, speed and direction and no firing with clouds about. We had good food, a sports day in which the 312 or probably X section swept the board. I got much closer to Fred Smith and then we packed up a few days early and we suspected that the powers that were knew a thing or two more than we did. In any case we all packed up on the Friday and went home.

Our war practice was over, the limbering up finished, the real thing was about to begin.

Civvy street was now a strange place. It was no longer my world. A few short weeks had changed me and I suppose all of us. We knew what was going to happen. Any day now the balloon was going up and therefore we no longer belonged to that world we called civvy street. I suppose basically most of us were scared of the future but at least those of us in uniform had weapons to fight with and companions to die with, if ever we thought of such a thing. We also were sure that the civilians would be in the front line. But there again there were differences. Take for example gas masks. We had been sworn in under the Official Secrets Act not to reveal that the civilian gas mask was quite useless and even ours were only good for a few hours; and we all thought that the Nazis would not hesitate to use gas in warfare.

More trenches were being dug, more buildings were being sandbagged, traffic lights were blacked out leaving a mere cross of a slit for use. As if the blacking out of traffic lights could affect the bomb aimers when they turned up! Sticky tape began to cover windows as a precaution against broken glass, more air raid shelters appeared, conscripts were in training, air raid wardens were in demand. It was no longer a question of months or even weeks but days before that balloon went up.

I went along to the Band of Hope but all that was going on was the talk of war and war was not a good breeding ground for temperance. I went and saw Fulham play; I thought it could be about the last time I would see a football match. I took myself up to the Windmill Theatre where they produced very strictly controlled and I suppose tasteful girlie shows. Saw some films, went to the theatre somewhere and helped my old man a bit but my heart was no longer there. After all, if we were going to be bombed to bits what was the point of doing minor repairs to houses?

Everybody was worried and my parents had an extra worry – me. But as I tried to point out, it should be me to do the worrying since I had a tin hat and a dirty big gun to help operate while they had nothing but a possible air raid shelter to cower in. I also already suspected that our attitude would be bless you Jack I'm all right thank you. It was a policy we soon learned to adopt in any action. Put the muck up in the air and keep Jerry off the gunsite and no matter about anything else.

When the Germans bombed Warsaw and attacked Poland, that was it. On 23rd August I heard that some reservists had been called up. Next day I went home after giving a hard day's effort to J. GREEN & SON to find upon reaching the front door that I had no key on me and no one was in. So there I was on that Thursday evening waiting outside the door for a key when a telegram boy parked his bike and approached the main door of our block of flats. I didn't have to guess where he was headed; he was pointing himself straight in my direction. There were not many words on the telegram. It said:

Join immediately.

I packed up and went. At the drill hall I discovered the other Bundlers were there already, fooling about, so I joined in with the cry, 'Bundle!'

Chapter Five

The Warrior goes to War

There was none of the messing about of the 1938 crisis. We were at the drill hall and then Hey Presto! we were gone. The only particular of note occurred while some of us were loading a lorry. A seasoned sergeant who had seen many years at the drill hall was directing the loading and helping with the loading, when he paused, looked up, stared at us young warriors with a knowing eye and said, 'Wait till you get to France, lads. When you do, take my advice, don't shoot until you see the whites of their eyes!'

We young warriors looked at one another. We had had some experience with those X section characters before they had bought their Sam Browne belts but at least, we thought, we could rely on the leadership of the non-commissioned British army officers. But here was one character advising us to wait until we saw the whites of them there eyes and by then we would be standing around a dirty great big 3.7 gun, probably several miles from the nearest seeable enemy! How did one follow a creeping Jerry infantryman with the guns of an AckAck gunsite?

This was indeed going to be an unusual war.

We now found that we had a new war station – Woolwich Common – and we did not have 3.7 guns which we knew a great deal about but 4.5 monsters of which we knew absolutely nothing.

The 4.5 was a big static gun with a larger gun crew than that of the 3.7 and it fired a much heavier round. The 3.7 variety, though weighty, could be picked up and cradled in an arm before being fused and rammed home but if I remember correctly the 4.5 round was well nigh impossible to lift into a loading tray. However, we never had to face that problem in action so that I can happily ignore the whole business and simply deal with the situation around and on the site. The four guns were surrounded by a high wire mesh fence, or rather the entire site was so encircled. Our principal job in those days, apart from gun drill, was spotting for enemy aircraft. But in very short order we found a much better use for the spotters. Woolwich Common was a haven for young lovers and we had a whale of a time spotting them and making sure that their activities, particularly at night, were not of a treasonable nature. Our only complaint was the difficulty of doing our duty during the hours of darkness.

On one occasion I happened to be patrolling the perimeter fence when a totty man on the outside popped up, seemingly from nowhere, and asked if I wanted that old rubbish lying at my feet on my side of the fence.

The totty man did not know of course that I was in the building trade and that in our shed down Brown's yard we had a sack of old brass, used copper and a sack of old lead and that therefore I knew as much about bluey as the next man.

'What rubbish, mate?' I enquired.

'That rubbish darn there, cock.'

'Darn where?'

'Darn there at yer feet. There.' And he pointed to where my boots were plonked.

'Oh, that rubbish!' I was surprised.

'That's it, mate. I mean, you bein' a soldier now, you don't need that rubbish, do yer?'

'No?' I said, 'I certainly don't need it, unless,' (a pause) 'the lead can be turned into bullets.'

'Lead, mate! What lead?' the totty man was overwhelmed with surprise.

'That lead darn there,' I pointed out, 'Darn there by my boots, that lead I'm almost falling over.'

There was quite a pause until the old iron man said, 'But you don't need it now, do yer?'

I agreed I didn't need the lead in its present state but then as it was on my side of the fence and I was responsible on behalf of the government for all the things within sight I couldn't see any solution, could he?

The Totty man changed his tactics. 'How much?'

I considered my responsibility to the government and my duty to the Bundlers and their ever pressing need for refreshments and then decided I could best help the war effort by handing over the lead. I think we agreed a dollar as the price, then handed the lead over to the totty man who departed very satisfied and eager to pass the contribution to the war on to the right place and I continued to patrol the fence, keeping an eye open for marauders and their ilk.

We were billeted in the sports stadium, officers residing in the heights above, no doubt in a bit of hard earned comfort, while we plebs were domiciled on the floor of the stadium itself at the back of the seating area. At that stage of the war we were not allowed to interfere with the sports arena, so to reach the guns we had to snatch up our gas masks and tin hats and belt hell for leather for the guns parked on the common, whenever the alarm sounded.

On 3rd September everyone who was anybody was in the canteen boozing with a radio switched on so that we could keep in touch with what was going on in that big bad world outside. Chamberlain made his well known speech about not having heard from Herr Hitler – we were not a bit surprised as we all knew that Hitler was busy with his army and his air force teaching the Poles a thing or two – so that as from now we were at war with Germany. As someone remarked, 'Here we go again.'

As soon as the announcement ended the air raid sirens sounded and we all had one thought, 'Blimey, the duffy's started already.' And we made our dash for the guns. Maybe the word dash is a bit over doing it. A great many of the TA personnel, to say the least were overweight, many had flat feet, many could only waddle along and most held a glass of beer in the hand on the principle that if Drake could finish his bowls before sorting out the Armada they could finish their beer before showing the Luftwaffe what for.

So there I was with others of my generation standing to on the platform of a big gun, with gas mask and tin hat waiting for the off in the second world war. A bit later I was ordered to stand to on that self same platform while two minutes silence was ordered for the dead of the first world war. My religious convictions took a nose dive and never recovered. After all, the protagonists were supposed to be Christians of some sort or other, even the Germans, so what the devil?

Two minutes silence at eleven a.m. on November the eleventh each year had been the order of things ever since I could remember and now here we were doing it again in '39. So we had our two minutes silence and then got on with the war.

During those army days, particularly the early ones, singing was of great importance to us. At the camp and at the war site we had bawled our heads off and likewise were doing it at Woolwich, it being understood that the curtain could go up at any moment and then a great many of us could be dead or nastily knocked about. So we sang, usually over the beer glasses. There were two kinds of song, the smutty which we sang with great gusto and the others which we sang with great pleasure. We sang 'Rolling Home', 'Quarter-master's Stores', 'The Colonel's Daughter' and dozens of others. Then there was that German officer crossing the Rhine and everlasting parly-vouzing and what about the Siegfried Line? We were still going to hang out our washing on the French Maginot line. That piece of idiocy had been a well-publicised piece of old junk before the war, hailed as the miracle of the age. It was classified as an impregnable wall of defence, stretching from Switzerland to the Belgian frontier which no German could ever breach. It was inconceivable that the Germans would do anything about Switzerland and all their mountains but then it was deemed inconceivable that the Germans might slip round the end of the Maginot line, by attacking Belgium thus outflanking the French defences. That of course is precisely what those confounded Germans did do in 1940.

Sited as we were on the Woolwich Common we were not far from the Woolwich Academy where the Sam Browne brigade did their stuff and also not far from a big RA barracks. As soon as we were settled, arrangements were made for us to go down to the barracks, so many at a time, for a shower. Keeping clean was then and always remained important to us. We had to contend with fleas and bugs but I am happy to remember that I only ever came across lice once during my time in the army.

So, one afternoon a party of us were taken down to the barracks, but we had to wait at an entrance to the huge parade ground because a regular army sergeant major was enthusiastically drilling the not so enthusiastic squad of conscripts. We knew the SM was a regular by the way he walked or rather marched and by the size of his larynx. We were sure his voice could be heard over the Channel by the lads of the British Expeditionary Force.

He marched those unhappy characters here, he marched them there, that sergeant major marched them everywhere.

At one point he halted his victims and going behind each man rapped out smartly, 'haircut, haircut, haircut'. As one of our long-haired brigade remarked, 'Blimey, They're bald already.'

Then, the sergeant major with stick under arm and voice like thunderclaps called the squad into marching action and finally to a halt. Now it was a hot day and those poor baskets had been having a rough time, so rough in fact that one of their number fainted. Two of his comrades were detailed off to dispose of the recumbent figure. The two lads carefully, tenderly, picked up their unconscious compatriot and started to carry him to the safety of the shady wall. The sergeant major halted them with a great 'HALT!' Came a moment's pregnant silence and then we all heard the clearly enunciated command, 'DON'T CARRY HIM THROW HIM,' and the unhappy squaddies (we were sure they were unhappy) paused until the command came in an even greater voice, 'I SAID THROW HIM!' and with a heave and a ho they threw the poor sod into a sunny corner while the drill continued. Our own squad, waiting for a shower, knew just what to do. We silently slunk away, determined to come back another day.

The day after war was declared, a German U-boat torpedoed the British liner *Athenia*. There were two hundred Americans on board.

The Poles were in retreat, Mussolini was told that Hitler didn't need his help and the fighting British were causing us some puzzlement by dropping leaflets on Germany. If the Nazis would do the same to us then possibly it wouldn't be such a bad war. The blackout was a confounded nuisance and the Russians were racing across Poland to get hold of the Soviet loot agreed upon in the Russo-German pact. Cinemas were closed but when the expected holocaust failed to materialise they were reopened.

The cruiser-turned-aircraft-carrier *Courageous* was torpedoed and sunk by a U-boat and the situation became pretty confused all round. There was even talk that the French army had surrounded the Saar valley. But everything would soon sort itself out, the British army had been landing in France for some time and was moving up to the front line while the Saarland was apparently almost deserted.

Volunteers were being called for in the battery to serve overseas. Stan Ward was dead keen to get a bash at Jerry and said I ought to volunteer. He must have twisted my arm or I suffered a brainstorm because I volunteered with him. But, as we were both under age we were both turned down.

On Monday 24th September I got twenty-four hours leave and once again surprised my parents by turning up again so shortly after going off to war.

By December the Russians and the Finns were at it. The Russians had asked for Finnish lands around Leningrad to be ceded to them to help with the defences of that city in the event of war. I believe other lands were offered, situated somewhere else. But the Finns refused and the war was on. We, of course, were subjected to the most monstrous stream of anti-Russian propaganda. The Finns belonged to a tiny country fighting against terrible Red Army odds – a hundred heroes against millions of cowards and of course the Finns were always advancing and Bolshie Russians always retreating. Mark you, the real winner was the Russian winter and it was that which some of us were looking askance at because there was no telling what the powers that were would do to help the heroic Finns against those evil Russians. Indeed the Finns were not just heroic, they were confident of victory and indeed were going ahead planning for the 1940 Olympic Games in Helsinki.

On 30th December I went home on seven days leave after spending a very jolly Christmas on the gunsite, with officers serving the traditional Christmas dinner to other ranks. Various entertainments were organised. This was an aspect of military life much to be appreciated. The capacity for men to entertain themselves seemed endless. In fact it only wanted someone to jangle out a few tunes on an old joanna for a canteen of squaddies to go roaring off into songs both army and decent. Then, as I say, I went on leave and once again my parents raised their eyebrows. 'What, home AGAIN?' This indeed was an unusual kind of war.

But now I had a new interest in getting back home, Kathleen O'Boyle. She was a pretty young Irish lass who worked alongside my mother at the West London hospital in Hammersmith and it was my mother who had introduced us. I was smitten from the start. In army parlance Kathleen was a 'Right Cracker' and once I had got her photograph I was the envy of everybody I showed it to.

Looking back over the years one can recall the delicate pleasure of calf love, the shy approach, the inconsequential talk, the aimless meandering. It was a sort of flashing light on a war-dark background. The truth was that even during the period of the phoney war most of us wondered if we would survive and all of us lived from day to day.

When I started walking out with this 'Cracker' she proudly explained that she had fourteen boyfriends, which statement I countered by pointing out that while I was around she only had one – me.

I then assumed I was in control though I was warned she was boyfriend mad. However we had a right old time going to see love films and sitting in the back row, holding hands on Barnes Common and realising the delights of kissing. That was as far as it ever got and I have always felt happy over that. It was never the real thing and would never have led anywhere but ah! the memories.

In the big world outside the Allies had had a success at sea, the navy had trapped the pocket battleship *Graf Spee* and forced the captain, Lansdorf, to scuttle his ship outside the three mile limit of Montevideo, the captain then nobly committing suicide. The newspapers were reporting the crushing of the Red Army by the noble, gallant, heroic, hard pressed, desperate, victorious Finns and at least two Russian divisions had been wiped out by a handful of Finns, possibly out hunting and fishing, who had stumbled upon them there Reds in the dark.

Early in the new year we moved from Woolwich to Clapham Common, still manning 4.5 guns. For me and many others, the move was extremely popular because it brought us nearer home. In my case all I had to do was walk to a nearby bus stop, hop on to a 37 bus and in next to no time I would be getting off at Quill Bridge on the Upper Richmond road from which place it was a mere trot to home, and 'What, home again!'

By the time we got to Clapham Common I was no longer a telephonist and was no longer frightened to death at the prospect of a stammerer like me being responsible for sounding the alarm. We used to get reports of activity over the coast, warnings of approaching hostiles, though nothing appeared over Woolwich while we were there. One action I do remember. We got the report on the first aircraft shot down over the coast by the RAF and that aircraft turned out to be British.

We spent a cold winter on Clapham Common. There was plenty of mild illness about during that time in those somewhat cold and damp conditions; flu and heavy colds abounded. The

1939, Clapham Common. 'Smudger' Smith. Author, Stan Ward, Cooper.

theory was that what with the flu and the colds and the fuming coke fires in the huts all windows should be flung open during the night time. In consequence, while it has been said that at some time in history Russian soldiers passed through London with snow on their boots, we slept in London with snow on our blankets.

In fact we were gradually hardening up although at the time no one would have thought so.

Being a territorial unit with conscripts gradually being added we were rather a haphazard outfit. The conscripts added to it added colour too when they began to arrive because they turned up not in army greatcoats but in busmen's overcoats, giving the impression that the London transport system was being run down to increase the army. This was a good thing for me since my cavalry bum-freezer was less conspicuous amid that welter of bus and army winter clobber.

I had another reason for hanging on to my warmly lined

overcoat. There was a persistent rumour that someone ought to go and give those poor Finns a pound out. It seemed obvious at the time that there were a lot of trained gunners hanging about on the full pay of fourteen shillings a week and doing nothing much so why should they not be the ones to give a hand out in Finland? Finland of course was next to Russia and Russia was all ice and snow and that brought to mind my bum freezer overcoat.

We had a popular senior sergeant called Wheatley who, one day, got into an argument with some gunner or other whose name I have forgotten. The outcome was a challenge to settle the argument whatever it was with a wrestling match on open ground in full view of the public and at a place where wind and weather had turned the area into an iced caked morass.

When the wrestling bout began there were not two smarter looking RA men than those two. But ere long they both disappeared under a thick coating of slimy, smelly, sticky black mud, ice and water. We cheered them on to greater effort long after the effort was useless since by then neither could get a grip on the other. They were forced to a laughing standstill. Hard by was a water stand pipe with hose attached so they hosed each other down to get the mud off their clothes and then stripped off completely in full view of the public and hosed themselves down until they were red, blue and pink all over. If Jerry could have witnessed that bit of business maybe he would have sued for peace.

We had a section sergeant named Joel who was very far from being popular. He seemed to us to have a wolfish grin, a beady eye and a fanatical desire to put everyone puttable on jankers and force as many as possible to spend endless hours peeling potatoes. I have since come to the conclusion that he was probably much maligned and turned out a useful character under fire.

Now, our gunsite on Clapham Common was surrounded by a fairly low chestnut paling fence with several poorly disguised holes in it for the easy exit and entrance of illegal travellers through them. There was nothing much doing war-wise. There were no raids and only an occasional call out for a practice shoot, therefore the big heavy covers were put on at sunset and left on all night. No one wanted the guns to get dirty or rusty.

During the weekends, parents, friends, relatives, wives and sweethearts would line the fence and a great deal of activity would take place provided no one crossed the line of fencing. At night there was a great deal of activity also, but of a different kind. No doubt there were many meetings with sweethearts and wives but there was also an army of prostitutes. It was then that the holes in the fence were of importance. The fire picket's duty was to continually patrol the fence and keep all personnel from roaming but of course all but the conscientious looked the other way – that is if there were any conscientious pickets. So some would slip away across the common despite the winter climate to spend a half-crown in a time honoured way. Others would nip off home if home was near while still others would pop off down to the pictures. We were somewhat casual warriors. The only real hazard was Joel. He adopted the habit of prowling the fence and would often emerge from swirling mist or deep darkness to pull back both lips in a frightful grin to demand to know what someone thought he was doing.

'Admiring the view, sarge.'

'What, in the pitch dark?'

'It's soothing.'

'Well, go and be soothed somewhere else and not by this fence.'

'Yes, sarge.'

When Joel had moved on a shadow slipped through the gap in the paling. Incidentally I never knew of any hole being closed up all the time we were on that site. There was one young gorgeous redhead who spent a good deal of time at the fence both during the day and at night and I gathered she could be had but it was difficult. I took quite a shine to her for a while but had my nose put out of joint when Wardy passed on the information that Ginger thought I was the slowest lover in creation and did he think I knew the facts of life?

I gave Ginger up.

Stan Ward with his dedication to beer, women and war, was always going through the fence. One night I happened to be in our gun crew's hut, reading before the coke fuming fire, when Stan came through the door, plonked himself down on to his fleapit and heaved a deep sigh of distress.

'What's up?' said I with some concern.

'I'm a failure, that's what's up, a failure.'

A failure at seventeen? That seemed a bit premature. 'What have you failed at?'

'Well, I went through the fence tonight, as you know.'

'Yes I do.'

'I picked up a tart over by the roadway, I gave her half a crown and we went behind a tree. We started all right but then a bloody car came along and the headlights came on! Unusual in the bloody blackout to say the least. Then I saw her face. She was boss eyed! Naturally I couldn't go on and so she got browned off opened her handbag and handed me back one and threepence and said, 'Here take this, you need to build up your strength.' I've never felt such a fool in all my military career.'

One night I was walking along the footpath near the gunsite, a good hunting ground for the local floosies, when one of 'em jumped out from behind a tree and demanded to know if I wanted a naughty girl. I said, no I didn't, she urged me on, but I wasn't interested (what if she was boss eyed?) and so eventually she let rip with some of the plainest and strongest abuse that up to that point I had ever heard. I scarpered as fast as I could.

When it came to guard duties Fred and I were usually on together and often enough Stan was there too. There would be two sentries on the gate with bondooks and one patrolling the fence with a pick handle. We worked out a plan for those duties which was important because the damned thing came round all too often, about every third night. We would opt for the worst spell of duty, two till four a.m. Having relieved the previous lot we would walk about for a bit and then hide our weapons under a pile of brushwood at the gate, which some sensible person had left for our convenience, and then off we would toddle to the all night coffee stall at the Plough. There we would indulge in cups of tea at three halfpence a large cup and large cheese cakes, I think at tuppence halfpenny each. We would then wander back to the gate, pick up our weapons and go call the next three, explaining what a hard life it had become. Funnily enough we were never discovered. No orderly officer or sergeant ever appeared, not even Joel. It seemed that at a certain time of night the AckAck defence of London, or some of it, took itself off to bed and stayed there till morning.

One night however we did nearly come a cropper. Everyone in our hut was out somewhere except me. I was probably bunged up with one of my colds and was staying indoors. Then – suddenly – to my horror, the alarm went off. I rammed on my tin hat, slung on my gas mask and hurtled out into the dark and bitter night, cursing my luck and wondering what the devil I was going to do. The gun was covered by a heavy tarpaulin and there was only me out of a crew, I think, of thirteen.

Ah well! Death or glory. I started to get the cover off.

From the command post the megaphone roared out, 'Hurry up number one gun you are too slow.' Too slow! I was hardly moving. Then one of our crew appeared, we got the cover off and another man appeared.

'Number one gun TRAVERSE you are still too slow.'

We traversed and someone else ran in.

'Elevate number one, ELEVATE. The Germans are coming TONIGHT not tomorrow morning.'

We elevated and got through the motions successfully just as the last of the crew snaked in and that was the Number One in charge of the bloody thing. We decided after that to be a bit more circumspect.

Our social life on the gunsite was going along pretty fairly. It was there that I first came across that entertaining business, the mock trial. We had a character with us called Schembry who had the irritating habit of poking his nose into other people's conversations and making observations when not wanted. He was the sort of unit nuisance, harmless enough and I suppose in some ways endearing. At any rate Fred and I learned to play chess with him though Stan Ward would have nothing to do with such a useless, undrinkable, unwomanly thing as chess even though it could be regarded as a wonderful war game. It was suggested that we should hold a mock trial and Schembry should be brought to justice on account of the fact that he had dropped and smashed a seven pound jar of jam.

It was a hilarious trial with counsels who really knew their stuff, a good deal of mickey-taking of witnesses and the judge, but Schembry was not attacked, he being merely the hub around which things revolved. The high point came when our site commander was put in the witness box and his love life was unveiled for all and sundry to relish.

Somewhat earlier there had been calls for volunteers for overseas and Mookee had disappeared along with Cooper, thus decimating the Bundlers. They went off to France and I recall Mookee coming home with me one day when he was on leave from Flanders Fields and keeping my mother in stitches over his stories of traversing here and elevating there. I never saw him again until after the war when I found him in a very natural element, driving a heavy lorry for the sand and cement firm of Balch's in Putney. With his heavy build, brick red face and jovial air he was where he was born to be.

In February it was rumoured that the Finnish Mannerheim line, a much vaunted defence line, had been breached and much more important for me, Sergeant Dyson came round the huts calling for volunteers to join the 51st AckAck which was bound for foreign parts. He got no takers, especially as I held Wardy back by his pants. After all, as I saw it, Clapham Common was as far as we ought to be. In the afternoon Wheatly came round and told Stan, me and Schembry to report to Stowey House school which was our unit headquarters and where we suffered under the cookhouse fatigue system.

At the school, Captain Graham Green informed us that we were being transferred to the 51st. In Schembry's case they

Author in 1940.

wanted to volunteer him away as he was regarded as something of a nuisance. They volunteered Stan because they knew he wanted to have a go at Jerry and I got the treatment because I was his known buddy. The problem of finding volunteers — solved.

But that left Fred Smith out on a limb, stone cold so to speak, in Clapham. We had a bit of discussion with the captain, volunteering Fred, and Graham Green insisting only three volunteers were needed. In the end he saw reason, made a phone call and then said we could go fetch Gunner Smith. So Stan went back over to our hut for our old cobber. He opened the door and beckoned Smudger who, without a word, or glance behind him, got up and came over to Stowey House.

Down to the MO's. We could never move far in the army without some sort of medical inspection. In this case we were inoculated. It seemed that if anyone was going abroad inoculation was the order of the day. We suspected however that we could be headed for the Isle of Wight or the more distant Isle of Man.

However, the consolation for being jabbed was forty-eight hours of excused duties. My arm became painful and puffy, the only time it was like that and I had many jabs after that. The QM arrived from our Dulwich headquarters to take inventories and then we got the rest of the jab mixture – 75 per cent. How the devil was I going to explain to the folk at home that I was bound for overseas? After all, in this war they had got used to me popping home for a breather.

We got three days embarkation leave and went home. The three of us met up on the leave for a few drinks and one night tried to walk one foot behind the other trying not to fall off the tramlines in and around Tooting Broadway where Stan had his hunting ground.

When we got back to the section everyone was ready for a right old booze up but it had to be short since we had to move that night. The section had a whip-round, and gave the other three a wrist-watch apiece and me a fountain pen and pencil because everyone knew I was always scribbling away at something or other.

Then a night lorry ride to BHQ Wood Hall for another go with the Quartermaster and the last bit of the injections. Then on to Dulwich where we found other volunteers from other batteries assembled and we all got together for another farewell booze up. We carried one character to his billet, so blotto he was, as stiff as a corpse, though, unlike a corpse, he regained his senses later.

On the morning of 17th February we were whisked off to the Duke of York's barracks in Chelsea on ROAC lorries, home of the 51st, TARA. From there on buses to our new outfits. We ended up on the Mitcham Common gunsite not a stone's throw from Clapham Common! We hadn't travelled far on our overseas road.

The weather was cold and there was plenty of snow around. We were convinced that the weatherman was hardening us off for the time, soon, when we would be building our gunsites over there – in Flanders Fields.

On Monday we got allocated to troops. Stan found himself in J or left troop, Fred and I in I or the right troop. We protested at being split on the grounds that we had 'volunteered' together but the powers that were in the 51st were a hard-hearted lot and so we were separated for the rest of the war.

For a time Fred and I were billeted in comfort in a warm school and it was there that we got our third and final jab.

We were then sent to the right troop gunsite at a Norbury sports ground surrounded by suburban houses. It was a sports ground belonging to Barclay's Bank.

Being a Londoner I had no idea where Norbury was, it being a bit further off than our previous sites. We soon discovered that it was not far from Mitcham and near to Croydon, surely a step nearer Flanders Fields.

A week later I found myself on six hours leave and of course I was asked, 'What, home again?' It was hard for them and I suppose hard for me, to understand why we had been inoculated before being stationed at Norbury. Maybe the place was really a swamp and crammed with disease. Or was this really being abroad?

In early March Dutch and Belgian guns opened up on German planes flying across their frontiers. Coming events were casting shadows.

The 51st, we soon discovered, was on stand-by to go overseas. Rumours were flying around that Finland needed a pound out and it was thought we might be part of that assistance. That idea did not appeal to me at all. It was bad enough pondering on the possibility of Flanders mud let alone floundering about in all that northern ice and snow and battered by bleak winds. Despite my bum freezer, that future wasn't looking very bright.

Then it was reported that the British had laid mines in Norwegian waters because the Norwegians were allowing German ships into them. The Norwegians objected but their objections were overruled.

Enter Second Lieutenant Fitzwilliams. He was a well-built character with a big ginger moustache (everything about him was big – appearance and actions larger than life). He had a habit of puffing out his cheeks when talking, and using such phrases as 'oh oh', and 'what what', 'What have we here, TOE JAM?' and was capable of making himself felt even when he was nowhere in sight. In the early days I think we were afraid of him. He was such a damned busybody, poking his nose into everything. He had a bee in his bonnet about winning wars. Victory was not gained on military stomachs but with soldier's feet, thus foot inspections were necessary and numerous. He would have us line up our bare feet and would try to insert his cane between suspect toes in his search for 'toe jam'. Of course he was basically right though it was always a mystery to me why army authorities made so much fuss about externals while ignoring such things as soiled pants and vests. I came to the conclusion eventually that Fitzy was a pretty good section leader, as nutty as they come and braver than most, who probably believed he was the standard-bearer of his class and had to show a good gingerized stiff upper lip to the world. Fitzy was always larger than life and dominated his fellow beings. I think we became fond of him in a strange sort of way.

At Norbury we were still mainly TA with increasing numbers of conscripts and a few regulars (I think) so that it was difficult to tighten discipline; though it was well nigh impossible to slip away for a few hours from a gunsite which was entirely surrounded by suburbia and which boasted only one gate. Fatigues were very onerous at Norbury, there being always not enough men available on various jobs. The major headache was the guard mountings at weekends and particularly on Sundays. Sundays would see the arrival of many relatives and friends plus sweet-hearts so that those guard mountings were carried out under the eyes of the public.

Guard mountings of course, bore no relation to those carried out at the Horse Guards or Buckingham Palace but the RA always seemed to want to compete with those affairs. Fitzy of course was the tyrant of the guard mountings when he was due to take one. There was fear and trembling when it was known that he was 'On' because it was clear he wanted to share his enthusiasms with the uninterested troops and in particular with the general public who flocked to see their own changing of the guard.

Naturally Fitzy took his time with the guard inspection, examining everything that it was possible to examine and in particular he would dally over peering down rifle barrels searching for a speck of dirt while most gunners wished that they had a bullet up the spout and an uncontrollable finger. And all the time he would puff out his cheeks while making observations calculated to induce fear, annoyance, irritation, rage and suicidal tendencies. But the inspection would eventually end and the guard would march off under the leadership of a relieved guard commander.

Then – one Sunday – the inevitable happened; disaster, which we were all expecting to occur sooner or later, struck. The troop was so short of personnel that in desperation they rounded up three men and a guard commander, none of whom had been through the business before! Imagine a warm sunny Sunday afternoon with visitors crowding around in happy expectation having been advised that Fitzy was on display. Of the three men who appeared along with the guard commander, one was known to be a bit simple, the second the scruffiest character on the site putting me well into the shade, the third did not only know nothing about rifle drill but as far as I knew had never seen a bondook before since his only activity to date had been to clean lavatories in a somewhat indifferent manner. One character had forgotten his hat, one had no gaiters and a third had not seen a razor since Christmas. When those folk lined up there was a long pause as Fitzy puffed out his cheeks and then he exploded. Came a further pause as those characters were sent off to collect their bits and pieces and one to get himself a shave. The man without his gaiters did not dress himself in private but brought it with him in his hand, holding it at arm's length as if he was taking it to a dustbin. When instructed to dress himself properly he asked Fitzy to hang on to his rifle while he put the gaiters on – a cardinal sin since no-one was ever supposed to let go of his rifle when on guard duty. In fact, when at last the guard somehow lined up and was ordered to present arms one man offered his weapon to the inspecting officer, while another put his rifle on his wrong shoulder and the third just stood gazing in the direction of Flanders Fields as if possessed of some primeval yearning. There was no doubt about Fitzy's feelings: he wanted to sink into the bowels of the earth while most of us khaki clad bods wanted to be somewhere other than where we then were.

No matter what Fitzy did, how much he talked, lectured, bullied, puffed out his cheeks, said 'Oh Oh,' and 'What What', he never did get any of the three to shoulder arms in any sort of military fashion and the commander of the guard was not much more advanced either. Any other order such as attention, stand at ease, present arms was totally incomprehensible to those three warriors. In the end, in a fit of rage, Fitzy flung his cap to the ground and told the guard to clear off. He wanted another lot found who at least knew what a rifle was even though they didn't know what it was for.

The order came through that our four guns (we now had 3.7 mobiles) should be camouflaged; after all there was a war on and part of the job was to fool the enemy. We had soon got to know those guns with that everlasting gun drill. Fall in, number off one to nine. As I often found myself at number eight which was a difficult number for a stammerer like me to shout out there would be quite a pause as I wrestled the word eight out. I wondered if it would ever help Jerry. It certainly never helped our gun crew.

3.7 Mobile.

'Number off, take post, elevate, traverse, fuse so and so, load, fire.' Over and over again. It could all be done in one's sleep. Ah! That was it. To do it in one's sleep. No matter what else was happening around a gun crew it was always to be, 'Elevate, depress, traverse right, fuse so and so and *fire*.'

But a gun was not much good if it stood out from its sur-roundings like a sore thumb, an easy target for a Stuka dive bomber. Camouflage therefore was the order of the day. Volun-teer painters were called for. We had no idea at the time what it was all about. Some of us got the strange idea that they were short of painters in civvy street and that now, painters were exempt from military service. Baily and I, the usually non-volunteering types – stepped forward. We were told to go get ourselves paint and brushes then proceed to paint guns. The great thing was we were excused all duties apart from guards and we took full advantage of our important position with a determination to make our guns the best painted weapons in the army. It was a splendid time in early spring, the sun was out and we used our skills to the best of our ability though we certainly didn't rush the job. An aircraft was sent up upon completion to see how good the painting was or rather how effective the camouflage was. The report came back that the painting was so artistically done by clearly good painters that they all stood out as perfect targets for any passing enemy plane. So we had to start all over again in that warm sunshine but this time we had to hurt our professional pride by slinging camouflage paint all over the place thus making the guns more or less invisible from the air.

It must have been around this time that I became a limber gunner. The limber gunner in the days of the horse drawn outfits rode the limber where the ammo was stored. In fact he was the bloke who serviced the gun, cleaning, oiling, doing minor repairs and ensuring that it was ready for action at all times. It was therefore a bit of a responsible job. Thus I spent most of my war years in dirty old overalls and dulled, unpolishable greasy boots which were to be the bane of many inspecting officers who could not understand why someone like me, always messing about with oil or grease, could not have shiny toecaps like everyone else.

In early April the Germans invaded Norway and Denmark. The latter was polished off in about twelve hours but the Norwegians put up some sort of resistance; after all, they were not used to being invaded like that. British troops were hastily rushed over to Norway where, it was reported, our lads were giving Jerry a good hiding and the Germans were now falling back somewhere though by that time the whole of southern Norway was in their hands.

As for ourselves, we at last learned we were leaving Norbury and were going overseas. I must say I think we were most keen to move. After all we were young and with all that gun drill pretty fit and Norbury had become something of a bore. At the end of April, having prepared the guns for removal we went on a twenty-four hour leave. 'Not home again surely?' I took care to spend most of it with Kathleen O'Boyle. On our return we handed in three of our four blankets, our bolsters and palliasses and with nothing to do we could wander out of the sports ground at will. That night we slept on floors or chairs, anywhere where there was room. Next morning we paraded in FFMO which now included gas capes as well as gas masks (or respirators to give them their official ranking), water bottles, side packs, haversacks, tin hats, kitbags and field dressings.

First to Waterloo and then by train to Aldershot, that centre of activity for that other peculiar army, the infantry. Here, situated in a very agreeable place under canvas with nothing much to do, Fred and I spent a pleasant enough time playing chess and rowing. But that old enemy of ours the weatherman must have concluded we were having too good a time because the weather changed and the mud appeared. Soon the canteen floor was akin to Flanders Fields and when we turned in at night our groundsheets had a tendency to float.

By this time there were three schools of thought raging as to our destination: France, the East, Norway. Finland was of course a non-starter by then.

In that theatre of war (Norway) the Germans were steadily driving northwards aiming to relieve the town of Narvik which was surrounded by an Allied force. This was a vital centre as Swedish iron ore apparently went through the place. As time passed it became evident that if we couldn't capture and hold Narvik there wouldn't be much point in being in Norway at all.

It was discovered that I had been done out of some rightful leave so I was given a forty-eight hour leave pass and off home I scarpered. It seemed to me that Hitler took advantage of me being on leave because at this point news came through that the Germans had invaded Holland, Belgium and the Duchy of Luxemburg. A great deal of bombing was going on, civilians were taking a hammering and what the devil was the use of the Maginot line threatened by those flanking movements?

I had hardly settled down to my short and hard earned leave when I got a telephone call to go back to Aldershot at once. Though how the devil I got a phone call at that time remains a mystery, ordinary folk in those days not being possessors of such outlandish things.

So, there was nothing more for me to do but to head back to Ash Vale and prepare to meet whatever there was to meet.

I decided not to mention to my parents where I might be going. There was quite enough bad news around without me adding to it, so I left, saying I would see them soon. We didn't hang about in that camp. We packed up, got into our gear and in next to no time we were leaving an empty camp with marquees and tents standing starkly hollow. Entraining at Ash Vale station we piled into carriages made for human beings with normal human being type luggage, so that for quite a while every carriage was the centre of utter chaos and every occupant in danger of damage of one sort or another from the military equipment being swung around.

We stopped for tea and buns at Birmingham and Crewe and next morning found ourselves marching from the station to the docks, if staggering under our loads could be classified as marching. The civilian population of Glasgow gave us plenty of encouragement. The old ladies told us that when we got to wherever we were going we were to give those Germans one for them too. Meanwhile children offered to carry our bags for us even though some of them were no taller than our kitbags.

We boarded the Polish liner *Sobieski*. It had British and French troops aboard with the latter including members of the Foreign Legion. We had a Polish crew, British naval officers and Norwegian guides.

As the tugs fussed us out into the Clyde people on the shore started cheering and as we progressed toward the sea, shipyard workers paused in their labours to give us a cheer and a wave and many mayors of boroughs or whatever they are called in Scotland stood I suppose in an official salute as we went on past.

Then we were out on the open sea under naval escort and our destination was made clear to us – Norway. We were now well and truly on our way to war.

Chapter Six

To Norway and Back

We made quite a discovery about food on board the *Sobieski* and assumed that the Poles had a regular diet of boiled mutton as we did on the ship. At first it was very good, far better than that which we had become used to. But when one gets stewed mutton for every meal the novelty wears a bit thin and one yearns for the simple fare of bully beef and biscuits. We also discovered that the members of the Foreign Legion were quite different to us in their attitude to Jerry; they positively detested the enemy.

We were billeted below decks in bunks and soon discovered why sailors prefer hammocks. The sea was like a mill pond the whole way across the North Sea or whatever sea we were on. If there were waves in that part of the hoggin they never came anywhere near us. Nevertheless men lying in their bunks were seasick. There was little ventilation below, there was no air conditioning and at night for safety's sake we were all battened down apart from those doing guard duties, no one being allowed topside unless on duty. A sensible precaution since some fool would probably show a light and in those days practically all of us smoked.

Fred and I soon found ourselves on guard duties on watch beside a Lewis gun. He and I, by that time, had got into the habit of arguing about anything and it was nothing for us to be nattering on at two or three o'clock in the morning.

One thing did emerge clearly as we got into the region of the Arctic Circle, into the area of no night, only a sort of dimmed daylight, that my old class and geography teacher, 'Maggots', had done a good job, at least on me.

One morning I asked my buddy what he expected to see when

we reached Norway. He thought about it for a bit and then said, 'Mountains, I suppose.'

According to my Mr Madge that was quite possible. 'What sort of houses d'you think?'

'Igloos,' came the instant reply.

'Igloos!'

'Well if there are Eskimos there there has got to be igloos for 'em to live in.'

'Eskimos!' No doubt about it, I was shocked.

'Yeah. Stands to reason where there are igloos there must be Eskimos.'

And there was no way that I could pass on the information, Mr Madge's information, that the people of Norway were rather like us, who lived in houses like us, maybe houses shaped differently but still houses though it would be far more expensive in Norway than in Blighty. If Maggots had despaired of us what the devil would he have made of this Southfields character? It wasn't until we docked at Harstad in the Lofoten Islands that Smudger would admit the possibility of normal human non-Eskimo type human beings living there.

Meanwhile we zigzagged slowly across that wide calm sea scanning the skies, the sea and the horizon with more and more concern as we approached the coast of Norway. We learned that the previous convoy had been hit by Jerry and that there had been many casualties among the Green Howards who had had to swim ashore. Then we were craning our necks looking forward toward the distant horizon. Were we seeing clouds over there or were they mountains? As we drew near the picture resolved itself into a line of snow-capped mountains.

The alarm sounded and we went to our manning stations. No more dozing off, card playing, arguing or fooling about. Serious business was now to hand.

Fred and I grabbed a Lewis gun and went on deck. There was no spare space anywhere. Everywhere was bristling with Lewis guns. Wherever an empty place could be spotted someone had found it. If Jerry turned up he was going to get a reception.

The only space we could find was in the middle of a sun awning which was hardly a good site in which to set up a Lewis gun. But we decided we would have to do what we could in the situation. So we started looking round for a spot on which to park. I nudged my companion, 'Take a gander,' I said, 'Just cast your eye on our possible destiny.' He took a look round.

'What d'you think?'

'What do I think? Tell you this, I don't think much of it.'

I looked around carefully and so did he. We were surrounded by men with Lewis guns, the place was lousy with Lewis guns.

'Where d'you think they are pointing?'

'By the look of it, straight at us.'

'Yeah, that's what I'm thinking. If a flap starts we'll get our heads blown off by our own guns.'

On this point we both agreed and on another point too: it was no place for us. Suicide was not on our agenda. So we climbed down from our position, snatched our gun and went below for a spit and a drag. Any immediate battle would have to start without him and me.

We entered the harbour without a sign of the enemy. He was busy somewhere else. We landed with utmost speed in the knowledge that he had bombed the town just a couple of hours before and we were not in the mood to be caught with our pants down, that is without our guns. So off the boat onto lorries, no bother with any passport control. We soon discovered that if the Norwegians did not want the Germans in their country, neither did they want us and we suspected that they had a point, in so far as neither Germans or British had bothered to take the Norwegians into account in their argument.

We crammed into lorries with the one or two fortunate enough to be at the back of each, describing the scenes of bombed houses and marvelling at how young people were walking about arm in arm in more or less daylight at two o'clock in the morning! The Norwegian girls of course received the wolf whistle treatment. We landed on Friday 17th May and the next morning a Jerry bomber dropped its load on the town, thus being the first

Harstad, Norway, 1990.

enemy action that we had seen. We found ourselves billeted in old barns scattered about quite a small place, hardly big enough to call itself a village and it had but one shop.

We were not fed very royally during the next few days, cooking being somewhat primitive comprising dixies being stuck over trench fires. We were paid in Norwegian currency, in kroner and øre which was highly amusing to us until we discovered how high prices were in Norway. Not that that mattered since there was practically nothing to buy.

But we were hungry and the food was not enough so Fred and I went off to the shop with our Norwegian money to see what we could get. There was a shopkeeper and one or two civvy would-be customers, chatting together, and all gave us either blank or stony looks and were unhelpful, so we pointed to a couple of tins we thought might be useful, held out our hands with the money, the shop keeper helped himself and we left. Finding a decent rock on which to sit we prized open the purchase which looked like a sardine tin. Inside we discovered some small red objects floating in oil. After tossing up to see who was going to do the tasting and so risk being poisoned, Fred gingerly took out an object and popped it into his mouth. He spat the offending creature out with the speed of lightning. I did the same. The things in the tin tasted over sweet and heavily salted. One of us took the tin and its remaining contents and hurled it as far as possible into the surrounding rocks.

The other purchase was in a jar and of course we had no way of knowing what the label said the contents were. I gingerly unscrewed the jar top and offered the contents to Fred. Fred stuck in a thumb and pulled out not a plum but a most powerful tasting paste which reminded us both of latrines long overdue for a clean up. My verdict was the same as his: it was some form of inedible cheese. I screwed the top back on and instead of tossing it away, absent mindedly dropped it into one of my pockets.

Years later I came across a powerful Norwegian cheese called Gamalost which I now relish. That jar we bought must have been just that but possibly a cheese produced when the Danes controlled Norway – or maybe when the Vikings sailed from there. We bought nothing else in Norway.

On Monday several enemy aircraft flew over the town bombing in the early morning and again in the evening; this time an oil dump was blown sky high. The bombing continued and we discovered that the shrapnel from the naval guns in the harbour was more to be feared than the German bombs. Then we were told to keep ourselves hidden during daylight hours since the Germans were not supposed to know we were there! A load of secret anti-aircraft gunners.

Fred and I decided to slip over to J troop to see our old buddy Stan Ward. His lot were billeted in a big barn with a very high timbered roof. We opened the door and met Stan who approached us wearing his usual happy grin.

'What are you sniffing at?' says he. 'Why are you holding your noses?'

We burbled something about the stink but his grin only

broadened as he explained that one could get used to anything if one tried hard enough and he pointed to the rafters. Up there in the height, hanging from the wooden beams were hundreds of drying and rotting fish and the stink, at least for Fred and me, was unbearable. We ran away. We never went there again.

We were issued with an extra special, thick lined ankle length coat said to have been paid for by Lord Nuffield though at that time of the year we had no need for them. One morning some of us were detailed off to do something or other along the harbour wall. Shortly after our arrival and as we were lounging round wondering what we were supposed to do, our leader, Fitzy, appeared, blowing out his cheeks as was his wont and remarking upon the affability of the weather and the need to show our allies the Norwegians how tough their British friends were. He then disappeared to re-emerge later in a pair of bathing trunks. Now I have said that at that point it was not cold enough for the Nuffield coats but we were still wearing our army greatcoats and wondering what a Norwegian winter was like, if this was the Norwegian spring. Fitzy eyed us up and down, suggested we stopped looking like down and out tramps and followed his British example and take the plunge. Then over into the harbour he went, a great white whale, a new Moby Dick, plunging into the keenly blue depths, leaving behind a great many white bubbles.

We all peered over the harbour wall wondering where the great white whale had got to. After a very long time he surfaced, clambered back on land, no longer white but turned a bright blue! He opened his mouth to speak but finding that he could not utter a sound he banged it shut again and with teeth chattering like a Lewis gun, he vanished from sight, never to swim again – as far as we knew.

We were often sent down to the harbour on various missions and the drill was always the same; get down there fast, do your job fast, get out fast. Jerry didn't like us and kept bombing away to prove it.

One day a party went off down to the harbour including a

character called Sandman, a man I was to meet again and again later on. They got involved in an air raid which was somewhat hair raising. Sandman found himself doing a guard duty on a store ship moored alongside a small ammunition vessel. Over came Jerry, down came the bombs, the others dived for shelter but Sandy had none. There was a crunch and an explosion and the next thing our hero knew was that his bondook was wrapped in a neat circle round the ship's rail and he himself was completely and utterly starkers though, to his astonishment, he found he hadn't a scratch on him!

Meanwhile the cookhouse had problems and in fact so did the rest of us. Water was short. We were relying on a mountain stream which already in May was drying up. So we had to move. We took our guns from under cover and went off up a mountainside just out of sight of the harbour though within earshot. We dug ourselves in in a place full of bushes and small trees. It had the unusual name of Death Valley. We worked hard all day, putting the guns in place, laying out ammo, making bunkers, shoving up tents and marquees. The latter puzzled all of us because here we were on a war site exposed to low flying aircraft and yet we had tents and marquees! We toiled all day until the time when it should have been midnight when we had something to eat and then turned in. Only trouble was when turning in we found Death Valley had a tendency to ooze water so that when we flopped down we found our ground sheets afloat. But at that time of the day or night after all our grafting, nobody cared. Then, well before what should have been dawn, we were roused up and told to pack up. The bloody site was in the wrong bloody place! In fact some brass hat had turned up and had condemned the site as being too dangerous. So, as we understood his kind thoughts were for our benefit, we hurried up and broke camp. We worked like beavers to clear the place, knowing it was dangerous to be there at all. I then found myself on the rearguard helping in the final clearing up. Sometime in the afternoon the warning went and almost at once we found out why the place was called Death Valley.

The enemy aircraft swept in low over the area in their bombing run to the town and the naval vessels opened up in defence and it was clear that our site was the very magnet for our own naval flying shrapnel. No danger from enemy planes, plenty from the navy.

There were about twenty of us and as soon as the flap started we scattered in all directions to find shelter behind bushes and stunted trees. I noted that at one time we scattered, then most of us huddled together in a heap behind some useless bushes. Came a short lull then Jerry started up again. This time I dived under a lorry parked on the dirt road, Twinkle Toes, sergeant Jennings, crouched in a somewhat icy, watery ditch while driver Jaques sat in his cab, deciding he was safe enough there and in any case he could get a better view of what was going on from his driving seat.

Suddenly there was a tremendous crash and a cloud of dust and smoke as a naval shell smashed into the road a few yards ahead. Twinkle Toes gave one hell of a yell and rolled over and over in the ditch smothering himself in mud and icy water while

Harstad, Norway, 1990.

clutching at a knee. He'd bought one in the knee cap and was sent back to Blighty. Meanwhile the cab door was flung open, Jaques fell out of it and rolled under the lorry, clutching an arm with his other hand. He sounded annoyed as he said, 'The bastards have got me.' Or rather he bawled into my ear because for quite a while after that shell had landed I was completely deaf. I got his arm out of his coat and asked him for his field dressing which he hadn't got and wasn't interested in. 'All I want', he shouted, 'is a smoke.' So I lit one up and handed it to him. He rolled over onto his back saying, 'That's better.' Then I got out my field dressing and shoved it round the gash in his arm.

When the raid was over it would have been impossible to see 'our bums for dust'. We piled the rest of the gear any old how into the remaining lorry and as soon as the ambulance had come and gone with the wounded we made a very quick strategical withdrawal.

The new site was on some flat land on top of a hill out of sight of Harstad but within earshot and here we proceeded to dig in, learning later that we were the only heavy AckAck troop ever to come into action in Norway.

We built up gun walls, camouflaged the pits with all sorts of local growth and generally got snugged down and soon came into action, sometimes banging away for two hours at a time as Jerry came barging in. The noise of roaring aircraft, crashing guns, naval shell explosions, the shouting of command orders, stumbling over red hot shell cases, breathing smoke, would have sent ordinary citizens round the bend but now that everlasting gun drill was proving its worth. Amid the roar of battle one instinctively did one's job in the knowledge that the more muck we shoved up the less likely it was that Jerry would get to us. We learned that there is no glory in battles. They are grim fearful things and usually a waste of time, energy, life, limb and money.

But war does have its lighter moments without which the participants would go stark staring mad. Take for example those

Nuffield coats which were so warm and cosy. We would be dressed for the dawn, stand to wrapped up to the nines, in jersey, jacket, jerkin, top coat and the Nuffield. Dawn was cold but in no time the weather warmed up and if we started firing we would be far too hampered wearing all that clobber and would have to do strip tease acts as soon as we could. Usually would come a pause, we would get cold, re-dress ourselves, Jerry would find out and come over and we would have to start our discard acts all over again. On off on off on off.

Our first alarm was memorable. The man with the cracked bugle sounded the alarm as Jerry came over at house top height. We could almost see the colour of the pilot's eyes if we had been looking for the colour of the pilot's eyes. But we weren't. As if by some communal instinct everyone ducked out of sight. We were domiciled by a cliff edge and some of us found ourselves hanging there. Now we had with us a regular soldier, s/m Atkins, a small trim man with a neat Ronald Colman moustache. He was a stern disciplinarian though a kindly bloke, always concerned for the welfare of the men around him. On the occasion of our first duffy he was the only man left on the gunsite, or rather the only one visible. He peered around at the empty spaces and called for an immediate return to duty. Some answered the call, some were a bit slow, so pulling out his pistol and waving it about violently, he swore that if we did not return he would shoot the lot of us. So, not liking that idea, we returned and from then on we had a whale of a time letting off at those hostiles. They were, as I have said, only about house top height as they roared over us making for the harbour and while it could be argued we couldn't miss a target at such a height, the fact was that with a 3.7 it was quite difficult to hit a fast moving target when it was more or less at the muzzle end of a gun.

So we did our shoots and had our breaks but through it all, Fitzy, the stickler for army morale, discipline and good clean toes, insisted upon having our kits lined up neatly, each lot outside a tent with the latter's brailing rolled up so that when he had the time he could do his inspecting. He still insisted on toe jam inspections and kept a sharp eye on the sanitary facilities which were of course somewhat crude – a long pole over a trench. He had cause to be a bit concerned since at one time, with a large number of men on the pole, the latter, unable to sustain such a weight, broke, and the squatters ended up all topsy turvy in the trench.

In regard to the kits we of course did not like all that old bull. We had watched, on the voyage over, as boot polish, Brasso, cleaning kit had been tossed with great glee overboard. Fitzy had seen the action too and had made it his business to have plenty of inspection parades, causing queues for the few pieces of cleaning equipment that had not been abandoned.

Jerry, up there in his warplanes, must have had strong feelings about all that old bull as well as us; possibly he had the same problems. At any rate, one day a plane came over and flying as low as he dared he came belting in at us with machine guns blazing. We had to duck but were up as soon as he passed by, swinging after him and then when he had disappeared toward the harbour someone called out, 'Look at that!'

We all turned to look. That obliging Jerry had trained his guns on our rows of kits laid ready for inspection and had machine gunned the bloody lot! In the face of such odds Fitzy gave in. He couldn't take on the British artillery and the German air force as well.

We always knew when a raid was due. The sirens would go off, our bugler would murder his cracked bugle with, 'There's a bomber overhead, there's a bomber overhead.' But we had been forewarned long before those things happened. The only bit of air force at that time in our area of warfare was an old ninety mile an hour Walrus seaplane, no match for the Heinkels and Messerschmidts that were apt to be belting around. So the Walrus would clear off out of it before Jerry arrived on the scene. 'Aye aye, there he goes, here comes Jerry.' Then one day the pilot was a bit slow off the mark and as he rose sedately into the air Jerry came swarming in all round him. By his own account the pilot was never more frightened in his life when he saw what was going on around him. However, frightened or not, he must have decided to have a bash because pressing the trigger, he let fly at something and presto! he bagged one! It was said that when he got ashore from his ancient amphibian he was shaking like a leaf.

One morning we were just about to stand down when the alarm went and in the following silence we heard the faint drone of a number of aircraft coming in up the fjord. It was a much bigger sound than heretofore and also they were coming in from an entirely new direction – the west. There were more of them than usual and we shook hands with each other on the understanding that this time we could be in trouble. Then we heard a great deal of cheering from the town and we wondered if, hearing of our dashing exploits in Norway, Hitler had given in. Then somewhat belatedly we identified them as a squadron of Hurricanes. This was a bit different from the air cover of one old Walrus. We cheered too.

Once again Troop Sergeant Major Atkins was upset. He raved at us. 'How dare you cheer anyone coming in to do our job for us? You should be damned ashamed of yourselves. You cannot call yourselves soldiers, that's for sure. While they are protecting us someone else maybe going through it.'

We shut up and cheered no more.

But from that time on the raids dwindled and died away. Those Hurricanes did a wonderful job while they could but, we understood, they could only use a frozen lake for landing and taking off and when that began to melt they had to quit. But while they were around Jerry kept his nose more or less out of our affairs. During this period I was asked if I would take on a job as cook. There was a shortage of those, so I thought, important people and so took over the tools of the trade: a jack knife to open tins and a stick to stir the contents of dixies. The job meant I was no longer a member of a gun crew and so, when the alarm went, I joined truck drivers, storemen, first-aiders and cooks in diving for cover. In our case the cover was a large Norwegian barn which had all sorts of farming gear on its top floor and it must have been attached to a house because there was a lavatory with a dual seat in it. This puzzled us English barbarians. We wondered if people went to the loo to hold hands or chat socially. The point of this story is that the lower part of the building, the underneath bit, was used for the storage of manure, both the animal and the human variety. In fact in the mass the latter was a large pile, very wide and quite deep. Now in the very early days when the sirens went and the bugler blasted off with his cracked throat choker we would dive under the floor onto the mass of ice-bound manure. One day, however, we shot under the barn only to find ourselves floundering about in a great soggy mass of smelly excrement. The sun, that morning, had been stronger than anyone had dreamed of. In any case there was nowhere else to go, so whether it was warm or cold we still took flying headers underneath that barn. We would re-emerge, scrape off our unwanted additions and carry on with our jack knives and sticks, trusting that the smoke from the trench fires would fumigate the cooks.

As time went by the cooks and for that matter everyone else faced a really serious problem: the water supply was drying up again.

Our diet was far from good. Everything came out of a tin and loose bowels became common place. Then hope rose above our horizon. A naval supply ship was hit and beached just below our cliff-top eyrie. When glasses were turned onto her we discovered that the vessel was without a single person aboard and Presto! there was a large rowing boat beached on the shore! There was but one thought in a good many minds. With Jerry being kept away by the Hurricanes some of us could be spared to go down and investigate the situation. So down the cliff some of us clambered, into the boat and just like a bunch of pirates we swarmed aboard the stricken vessel. The boat was not over safe. It was smothered in oil and walking had to be undertaken with care. Someone found an axe and another character located a big store locker and once the axe had done its work on the lock we burst in to find the place filled with FOOD! We then imitated the actions of the smugglers of old. We took crates of butter and cheese, boxes of tinned hams and above all we took a side of bacon, a real boon. Then with the boat loaded we drove with furious oars to shore. Once ashore we manhandled our treasures up the cliff face much as smugglers of old must have manhandled theirs. And we went back again, happy in our work, happy in the knowledge that we were doing a useful job. But really the whole enterprise was illegal and I suppose could have been categorised as looting.

And soft, we were observed.

The Redcaps had been observing us from their lookout post and soon the blower on the command post was red hot with ringing. Those Redcaps wanted to know what we thought we were doing? They also stated very clearly that they, the military police, would send up a detail to investigate. The command post sounded the alert; not that there was a bomber overhead, but, 'The redcaps are coming, look out look out.' We divided our spoils in half, hiding one lot and leaving the other lot on the tables for the police to inspect. We of course cut the side of bacon in half and waited for the arrival of the Redcaps. Two of 'em drove up in a jeep and explained that they hadn't really been snooping but it had been difficult to avoid seeing us through field glasses. They realised that there was a war on and grub was not too marvellous or plentiful, so while they had to confiscate the goods they thought while they were taking things to the jeep some of the goods on the tables might possibly fall off and in any case we might as well go halves with the bacon! Such an honest bunch of cops!

Honour was satisfied all round and we abandoned the deep yellow cart grease margarine and used butter pats instead, coming to the conclusion that if this was part of navy supply we were in the wrong bit of the armed forces.

Things became quieter and quieter until in the middle of the first week in June, rumour had it that we were about to move. We understood that Narvik had been captured and that we might possibly be moving south. At any rate we all started the business of packing up though this time Smudger was the one to find himself on the rearguard. We probably passed remarks such as, see you in Stavanger or Bergen. Then our party, one of several, began moving down the mountain after being ordered to leave our Nuffield coats behind for the benefit of the local people. A great many men were on the move and as we descended to the town we could see that we were converging on to the harbour and the troops were boarding a destroyer. Were we going south by boat?

Once on board we were soon told we were not southern Norway bound but Blighty! It was said we were going back home because with the fall of Narvik and the wrecking of the iron ore base our job was done. Another opinion was held that Jerry, having won the contest, was giving us the boot.

We were stowed below like sardines but the matelots were a pretty good bunch. They came round with hot cocoa made from those rectangular slabs only seen in naval circles. Once the ship was bunged full the *Delight* whisked us out of the harbour to a damned great mass of a liner called the *Oronsay* which, we were told, had been re-routed from her India run to pick us lot up.

We circled for a couple of days in company with another ship while most of us got more and more nervous. We could see no escort and were on tenterhooks fearing Jerry might knock us about a bit. But eventually the convoy got itself together, the escort turned up and we set off. There were seven transports, nine destroyers, a cruiser and an aircraft carrier.

We were glad to be away. The country had been pretty bleak with too many mountains which had meant not enough flat ground to play football on.

There were still white jacketed stewards aboard *Oronsay* ready to serve out the grub. The first meal was stewed rabbit and do I like stewed rabbit! Having had one great bowl full I wondered about second helpings. I was urged on to be an Oliver Twist and so I asked for more. I ended up with five helpings and the hope that there would be rabbit for every meal!

The passengers were a motley lot. We from Blighty, French

Alpine troops and members of the Foreign Legion. One of the latter had a hatbox which when the contents began to smell was heaved overboard. It was said the owner had taken a shine to a Jerry head!

In the middle of the voyage it was announced that the Italians had entered the war on the side of the Germans. I can still hear the faint chuckling and rude remarks made all round the ship. No one took the Italians seriously, apart from their expertise in ice cream manufacture and their bully boy tactics in Abyssinia; their assistance might do the Germans more harm than good.

Early on Sunday the 9th the convoy was attacked by two U-boats, one being sunk while the other sheered off. Later some Heinkels had a go, losing two to the Fleet Air Arm, and then it was all clear to Blighty. Most of the Alpine troops slept on deck while we more effeminate creatures had cabins which were luxury indeed and to top it all we had nothing to do but sleep, eat, smoke and start again.

Smoking was pretty universal and the army issue was adequate for most of us. I think our weekly ration was seventy cigarettes a week or pipe tobacco plus sixty at a low rate in the NAAFI, so that, apart from the very heavy smokers, no one ever needed to go short of a smoke.

Dunkirk was now in full swing and the British expeditionary force was being pushed back onto the Dunkirk beaches. Our side had not only lost Norway, it was in the process of losing all control over the whole of Western Europe. So that those were pretty grim days for all and sundry with many people considering the war was lost. Though to most of us on that boat that could not be true. We considered that our lads had had a go at Jerry in France and Belgium and we hadn't been afraid of the dog in Norway either. We supposed that in the early days of the war the stage managers hadn't got their act together properly but eventually would. In any case there we were sailing down the west coast of Scotland, passing the Hebrides, entering the Clyde once again, docking and then finding ourselves in a tented camp between Troon and Irvine and what about a spot of leave, eh?

In the convoy we had had some Liberty ships, those welded plodders that the Americans had loaned us, stooging along in our wake. We watched their bows, fascinated as the ships dipped slowly into the waves and just as slowly heaved up again. One could hear the thump of the sea as the waves struck those solid, blunt bows and we, watching from the smoothly gliding *Oronsay*, wondered how anyone could work or even exist on those ever-lasting switchbacks.

In the big tented camp I met up with Fred again, pale and wan and still feeling groggy. He had come back on a Liberty ship! He never wanted to hear the name mentioned ever again. The passage across, he asserted, was diabolical.

He also talked of the rearguard of which he was a part. Apparently as soon as the gunsite had been cleared of most of us the rearguard were told to do as much damage to the guns as possible and then push them over the cliff. Fred said he had been delighted to take part in the destruction of such destructive and useless objects as guns now that his life no longer depended upon them. So he took up a pick and with all the ignorance of a peace time clerk he took an almighty swing at one of the big gun tyres and as the pick hit the tyre so it bounced off and Smudger swung round and round with such force that he landed on his backside. He only tried that caper once. So they removed firing pins and breech blocks and anything that could be moved, toppled the guns over the cliff and departed the way we had earlier gone. According to Smudger they could see Jerry a couple of fields away so no one minded hurrying up. In fact, he said, 'We damn well scurried aboard the destroyer.'

The French declared Paris an open city and the Germans marched in. We were more concerned about leave. Two however refused leave. They said they couldn't face going home since they had had their heads shaven for war purposes and as they were members of the aristocracy they didn't feel able to enter castles or stately homes shaven like convicts. After all, what would the butler say, taking a hat and observing a shaven pate? The rest of us went home.

I got home on Monday 17th June at 7 a.m. in the morning, which was a shade early for the folks residing there and once they had recognised the scruff standing at the door I think it was my mother who said, 'What, home again?' It seemed they thought I had only just left them; meanwhile my brother wanted to know where I had been.

'Norway.'

'Norway?'

'Yeah.'

'Get away, can't have done, didn't have the time.'

Pappy seemed to hold the same opinion though he hadn't a clue where Norway was.

'Well, that's where I've been and I'd be there now but for one thing.'

'What's that?'

'Jerry chased us out.'

But they did not believe me, no they never believed me, until at tea time I produced the jar of Norwegian cheese, now somewhat older than when I had bought it. My old man wouldn't touch it, my mother sniffed at it, my brother, always game for a try, tasted it and then fled to the kitchen sink for some life sustaining water. No one could believe that such awful stuff could be on sale in England so they grudgingly conceded I had been to foreign parts.

Once she realised where her son had been my mother was upset.

But I pointed out, we had been to Norway, had met Jerry and we had come back, we had all come back having learned a bit more about the British enthusiasm for the strategical withdrawal. We had done it again and soon we would have Jerry by the short and curlies.

Perhaps more important: I had come back and as far as I was concerned I would always come back.

I wasn't called the Dodger for nothing.

Chapter Seven

In which Warriors Play at Being Soldiers

I called on my grandparents, had some bread pudding which my grandmother was a dab hand at making, went to the Windmill once, only once because they changed their programme every six weeks and because I couldn't afford too many visits, and had a few outings with Smudger and Stan Ward. We weren't flush enough to paint the town a bright red. At the beginning of the war my pay was fourteen shillings a week of which I sent home three and six though my mother never spent it but banked it so that I got it all back after the war. A married man of course had to send his wife half his pay and often a man would send more leaving himself with the princely sum of three and six a week (17½ pence new money). Not a lot even before the days of everlasting inflation.

That summer of 1940 was a time of fear, uncertainty and a general expectation of invasion. Dunkirk took place with the evacuation – possibly a strategical withdrawal – of most of the British army and some of the French. Paris was declared an open city, the Germans marched in, took over Northern France and began the bombing of England. Raids over London increased and the first casualties occurred. Activity was taking place everywhere as the defences of the country were tightened up. According to our propaganda our bombers were plastering Germany and theirs were certainly having a go at us. The British government offered a merger with France which was turned down. The whereabouts of the French fleet became a cause of mystery and anxiety. The so-called phoney war had become a real one. However in Somaliland the British army was about to sort out the Italians and give us a very necessary victory and Churchill began his series of memorable speeches based on blood, sweat and tears and the 'we shall never surrender' theme.

Back in Scotland we encountered little of that. There, it was the squaddies' war, it being all about keeping one's head down and not volunteering for anything apart from leave, living from day to day and being nearly always broke. Not that that mattered over much. Tents were always open and parcels from home were always shared around with mates and no one need ever go without a smoke. One outstanding thought is always with me: I never came across any theft. The only thing I remember ever losing was my beret and that was in the Middle East. This meant that someone who could avoid a parade gave up his titfer for the time being. When, on one occasion, I left quite a bit of money on my fleapit, Geordie, cleaning up the tents, picked my money up and gave it to me with the advice not to be so careless.

During this period we had plenty of leave, forty-eight hours, seven days and so we were often home, thus bewildering my parents who had come to the conclusion that I was involved in some sort of special war of my own. One time we were informed we could have seven days leave if we paid our own fare! This caused such an uproar that the idea was cancelled.

One day it was decided that everyone ought to have a proper bath so we were transported in open lorries to some pithead baths where there was plenty of soap and hot water. After bathing we hopped back onto the lorries and on the return journey the rain belted down and we all got a damned fine soaking.

We often went into Troon and Irvine and it was at this time that my wound came into its own. During my cook period my jack knife had slipped and I had ended up with a gash in the hand and an arm in a sling. On entering either of the above mentioned towns everyone was under the impression I was one of the wounded heroes from Dunkirk, no one having heard of Norway or in particular Harstad. The Scots who tell stories of their own meanness are in fact a very warm hearted and generous people and I could have spent many days completely blotto on free drinks in pubs. As it was I was not a real drinker but for the sake of the others I would nod sagely when the local folk talked of the horrors of Dunkirk and the infamy of the Germans.

'The lads' wanted my wound to be permanent but even the handiest of bully beef tin wounds must mend sometime and of course mine did.

Then came an official brainwave or Brainstorm. We were temporarily turned into infantry, possibly giving some instructors a job. I suspect if Jerry had discovered it he would have tried his luck on the Ayrshire coast. I never found out if it had any relevance but just prior to our infantry period some of us took a lorry load of ammo to Stirling Castle. On the way back we decided to stop in Glasgow for a look round. In removing the ammo did they want to keep us out of danger? After all, we were now infantry wallahs. We did however get a go on a rifle range. I believe the infantry range was two hundred yards but ours was only one hundred. The powers must have known we were not as keen eyed as your true infantryman.

I remember lying down at the wrong angle and the instructor getting uptight when not only I lay at the wrong angle but aimed the rifle with the wrong eye. Having explained that my right eye was as weak as any kitten's he gave up with the remark that I wouldn't hit an elephant at one yard let alone a target at one hundred. As it was, out of five rounds I notched up two bullseyes and three inners, much to the instructor's disgust. Flukes like that should not happen.

One guy got down on his stomach and fired away but each time got the white disc indicating no recorded shot at all. The target operator on the next one became more and more puzzled as the shooting proceeded. At the end of it he should have only recorded a possible five shots but in this case he recorded ten! What with one thing and another we never went shooting again although we were all passed out as experts with a rifle. This in itself wasn't bad. Every little bit of recorded expertise meant a little bit of extra pay. Then came another brilliant idea: we would go on an infantry battle course somewhere. So off went Fitzy and his merry men. We walked over the course and Fitzy's face became more and more concerned. There were nettings to climb, poles to run along, water to jump over, ropes to swing on and of course he was supposed to demonstrate how it was to be done.

He explained everything carefully while we nodded intelligently and at the end of the explanation period it seemed to be getting late, so we all went home, having passed our ordeal with flying colours!

Then manoeuvres began. We had to surround a wood in the hands of parachute troops. Our section advanced toward the wood, the intention being to capture the villains, then retreat to Dundonel Castle. We were led by the indomitable Fitzy who beckoned us to follow him into a ditch at the roadside so that we would be out of sight of the foe. Down into that muddy ditch jumped our leader. Now it was all right for Fitzy to jump about in dirty ditches; he had a batman to clean up his trousers, socks and shoes. We poor so and so's would have to do our own cleaning. So while our noble leader led the way, splashing energetically through the dirty ditch which seemed to take hours, we walked silently along the road. Our leader never once turned his head to ensure that he was being followed by his stalwart men. As we approached the end of the ditch a wall appeared before us, ideal cover, so our intrepid leader came onto the road, thoroughly happy and covered in his lower parts with Scottish mud, which no doubt is very good mud. At this juncture a vehicle hove in sight and pulled up with a jerk but stopped only long enough to explain that they were the judges and that we had been observed quite clearly from our start position to our present point and therefore that we were all dead. We returned to camp. The only casualty in reality was Fitzy's batman who would have to spend a great deal of time sorting out socks, boots and trousers.

This fighting column business seemed to have been not too successful because the whole idea was changed into something else and we all went back to Gailes Camp.

About a week later a new plan emerged and we went out as an attacking force against parachutists. But just before the off the colonel decided to change the rules and we went from being the attacking force to being the enemy with our particular mob out in front. That decision alone was somewhat risky. Unfortunately, not understanding the infantry rules we got into a hopeless muddle which resulted in one of our sections walking into British army headquarters and capturing every last man inside.

Our section wandered about for a long time rather aimlessly, never making contact with the enemy except on one occasion when we captured six NCOs, who had got lost during the morning operations, which seemed to have had nothing to do with those in the afternoon. In the middle of July it was rumoured that we were either going to a gunsite or to a firing camp. The latter idea sounded to us preposterous. After shooting down six enemy aircraft in Norway what were we going to a firing practice camp for?

On the night before we took off for the firing camp at Burrow Head about a hundred miles away, the air raid sirens sounded, the cracked bugle strangled notes and Bofors guns opened up and someone started shooting off with a Lewis gun while bombs were falling not far off. But those weary veterans, the Bundlers, were too tired to show interest so reaching for their tin hats they turned over and went to sleep again. In the middle of the night at Gailes it was someone else's war not ours.

Next day, sixteen to a lorry, we went off to the firing camp at Burrow Head.

Sunday and Monday were spent banging away with the guns, firing out to sea which was the best place for the guns to be pointing. It meant that the shrapnel from the bursting shells was falling in the water and not all over us as it had been in Norway.

An interesting thing about firing AckAck guns in those days was that the operation was simple and comfortable when the gun barrel was at a low angle. The round was fused, loaded into the loading tray, swung over to the breech and the round rammed home and then banged off. But when the barrel was at an acute angle it became much more difficult to ram a round home. In fact on more than one occasion I have seen a round bounce back out of a breech and hit the deck. Fortunately nothing happened but it was possible for the blasted thing to go off.

Lots were drawn to see when we would go on leave. I drew sometime in August. And then I found myself on a special guard duty somewhere in the country guarding a large country house where presumably something important was going on. We never discovered who or what we were guarding and if the guarded did not know who was guarding them it was probably a good thing. Certainly if there had been a coffee stall handy there might have been a bit of unguarding during the dead of the night.

On the last night of that duty a don R turned up demanding the names of some of the guard including mine. We went on leave the next day.

I arrived home on a Thursday, failed to contact Kathleen O'Boyle the following day and failed again on the Saturday. On the Sunday I went and had a look at the allotment Pappy was renting from the council. It was situated on Putney Common between the Barnes boundary and Putney hospital and was leased out under the slogan 'Dig for Victory'. That year the allotment produced the most enormous carrots that I suspect anyone anywhere had ever seen, though I must confess that for my part the only interest I had in carrots was eating them after they had been sliced and cooked. It was in fact the only year of the giant carrot, after that they shrank into insignificance and eventually were ignored.

On the Monday morning the powers that were were up to their tricks again. I received yet another telegram informing me that all leave was curtailed and that I was to hightail it to the main line station and Glasgow that night. Hallelujah! Pappy came up to Euston with me to see me off and as soon as I was among the lads rumours were flying around that we were headed for the East.

In all that gaggle of khaki clad, eager young men, many happy to have another bash at Jerry, Pappy looked small and shy and out of place. But one had time to reflect on the journey north that he was part of that civilian army that not only had to keep the service people backed up, but might well have to go through far more of a hell than any of us. They were not comforting thoughts.

It was one thing to be part of a gun crew hitting back, reasonably protected from flying old iron and too busy to be scared. It was quite another to be crouching in a slit trench or cowering in an air raid shelter without a tin hat, unable to hit back. My mother was wont to dash from window to window watching searchlights trying to pick up an enemy plane and she would get terribly excited if one appeared like a silver fish in a beam. Her eyes would light up with excitement. Later, however, when the doodlebugs and rockets arrived she became a nervous wreck. If Pappy was a wreck too he was able to keep it to himself.

The next few days saw us doing next to nothing and wondering why we had been recalled. We had had one of those numerous medical parades, had seen how to trap a tank or two with rifles and Molotov cocktails but that was all.

Then on Saturday the other two batteries, the 151 and the 152, pulled out and left us striking camp, pulling down marquees and tents, rolling up blankets and returning all non-personal kit to stores. All we wanted now was tropical kit and we would know where we were off to.

On the Monday, we surmised that the powers that were were at a loss to know what to do with us for they sent us on a three hour route march through the beautiful Scottish countryside. I hobbled into our temporary camp with sore feet. The next day the same powers, still possibly at a loss, not only sent us on the same march but got J troop to tag along also. I crawled back to camp with even sorer feet.

Then on Thursday 8th July J troop went on seven days leave. We would be next.

This was definitely embarkation leave. When I did get home

my mother said, 'What, home again!' I thought it best not to give the reason why.

By the time of that leave the Battle of Britain was hotting up. The coastal areas were under heavy attack and we saw one bomber over our own area.

So, as the war moved towards London I once again set out for Gailes camp. I watched Pappy from the high platform of Putney Bridge station as I waited for the train. He stood below looking small and, I thought, a bit helpless. Events had moved beyond his simple understanding and no doubt, without showing it, he was worrying about his eldest son who might or might not come back some day. I had of course told him I had been on embarkation leave.

We had had one or two enjoyable hours together. I was with him in Putney High Street when he nudged my arm. 'Aren't you supposed to salute him?' he asked, indicating the figure of a somewhat podgy army captain. It was Mrs Belcher's son who had been a failure at running his mother's tobacco and sweetshop but had seemed qualified to walk his wife's little dog out. And there he was, in a captain's uniform and still taking his wife's little doggie out for walkies.

'You should salute him, shouldn't you?'

I said, 'I think I'd sooner salute the dog, he's the one in charge,' and we walked away; there was no power on earth that could make me salute such a character. The thing worrying me was, were there any more captains like that in the British army?

The first thing that happened back at Gailes was a seventeen mile route march through the blasted, silly, Scottish countryside. My blistered feet were worse than ever. Then on Sunday we had an enforced church service followed by tea and cakes at the vicarage and then back to camp.

Then the time came when we drew tropical kit, ever known as KD. There were topees clearly left over from the previous war, heavy headache type things, leg puttees, shorts and shirts and KD slacks. Of course we got togged up. It was carnival time for dozens of white, knobbly knees. From that day to this I can never see an Englishman in tropical shorts without the desire to giggle. There is no other race in the wide world, to my mind, which looks so silly in tropical kit as do the English. Long trousers yes but shorts never! I used to think that Jerry when he met such characters in the desert must have thought he was up against a bunch of scout masters. However, we did, in the end, see Jerry off.

We were all more or less happy to ship abroad although of course, there were misgivings about the possible fate of relatives and friends we were leaving behind. Unlike other wars the civilians were being left behind in what clearly was to become a battle front, while we were sailing away into parts of the world which at that time did not know the clash of modern arms. Unless the business in Eritrea with the Eyties could be called a clash of arms.

On the Saturday evening we had a sing-song in the Salvation Army hut both as a farewell to the people running it and as a goodbye to Gailes camp. We always thought the Salvation Army did a great job during the war. They seemed to bob up in all kinds of unexpected places with tea and buns and although I have no great liking for religion I do still have a very soft spot for those very practical Christians.

On the Monday morning in full marching order we left Gailes camp and entrained for what was to be our port of embarkation – Liverpool. We had the usual crash and bash as we were levered into carriages too small for us even if we had had no kit but impossible with it. But somehow, as usual, we achieved the impossible.

We arrived in Liverpool in the evening and marched from the station to the docks. As before, children, some no higher than our kitbags, wanted to carry them for us, old ladies patted us on arms and shoulders enjoining us to 'Give the buggers one for us as well.' Which was all very morale-boosting, we supposed, but as we had no idea where the devil we were going, such morale-boosting didn't mean all that much. It was true there was fighting in the western desert and in Somaliland but no one considered the Italians worth bothering with. Then of course we could be going to Australia, the Far East or for that matter Timbuctoo. Not that any of us relished the idea of Timbuctoo. The only recreation centre that could possibly be there would be the NAAFI and who the devil wanted to re-create there?

We boarded the twenty-seven thousand ton liner *Dominion Monarch*, launched in 1939. It would be our home for the next six weeks. We lay offshore until the following day when the rest of the convoy hove into sight and then with a naval escort we set off into the unknown.

One character on board pointed out the roof of his house where he lived in Liverpool and the last we saw of England was the top of the Blackpool Tower.

It was the last I was to see of England for a number of years. By the time I did see it again the war would be all but won and the end of it all in sight.

Chapter Eight

Sailing the Ocean Blue

When we sailed from Blighty in September 1940 the bombing of England had started and the London blitz was beginning. We heard of it aboard ship with a great deal of misgiving. In fact the news from London was far more worrying than any U-boat threat to us. We single blokes had plenty to bother about in regard to family and friends but the married men with families could be driven sick. If we had not had those worries I think most of us would have admitted to being happy at the prospect before us. All was now different: the scenery, the food, the billet, the expectations and of course there were few of us who would have been able to travel as passengers on a liner in peace time and a long voyage at that. Such things had been for the wealthy, for those people who could afford the luxury of travel. The working class made do with a short holiday, if it could be afforded, in Blackpool, Southend or maybe Brighton. For many there had been no such thing as an annual holiday and for children there were only such things as school journeys (fairly expensive), country holidays and hop picking.

But there we were sailing the ocean blue.

The *Dominion Monarch* was a whopping great boat which until our arrival had always sailed alone. It was too fast to be unduly bothered by aircraft and a submarine would have to be in the right place at the right time to catch her. We understood too, that she was too fast for any surface raider. (At least that is what members of the crew told us.) But the crew were worried nevertheless. They had got used to travelling fast alone and now here they were for the first time in a six knot convoy going as fast as the slowest ship and hardly ever a sight of the naval escort. We were aboard a fleet of ships plodding, zigzagging, to port and to starboard – everlastingly zigzagging. Some of the sailors at one time said we were very near the American shore though we never discovered whether it was true or not. We were plodding on, over thousands of miles of ocean, not knowing where the hell we were bound for. Some said India, some South Africa, some Singapore. The seamen assured us we were off to Egypt and they were proved right.

As we went further south so the weather turned warmer. Eventually there was nothing for it but to order all personnel into KD and that day all the white, bony knees re-appeared. Naturally, next day the weather turned cold again and we all went around shivering.

Life aboard was not unpleasant. Our main occupation was PT with a few guard duties and lifeboat drills. The latter proved interesting. The seamen had soft collar lifejackets tied to their chests; ours consisted of four pieces of cubed cork in linen shoved round our necks. The sailors pointed out that there was a distinct difference in effect between their soft lifejackets and our cork ones. If they had to abandon ship and jump overboard they could do it any old how but if we tried it with our type of lifejacket we would ram the cork under our chins and the chances were we would all break our necks; it would be like being hanged! So on their advice we would jump into the water holding the cork cube firmly away from our chins, and lord help the absent-minded.

We were issued with hammocks which we slung below decks, finding them extremely comfortable and hard to get out of in the morning, not only because of the danger of overbalancing but because of such unusual comfort.

As the sun got fiercer and the nights warmer we took to taking our hammocks on deck and of course we felt safer up there. Though here there could be no hanging about in the mornings; the crew when told to hose down the deck hosed down the deck regardless of who or what was in the way.

The most popular place in the ship was the canteen where we could drink, smoke, sing 'Roll out the Barrel', 'We'll hang out the washing ...', 'Over the Sea to Skye', 'The Quarter-master's Stores', 'The Colonel's Daughter' and anything else we could think of. There was also a cinema and swimming pool aboard.

Rumour had it that we were going directly to the Cape but then, as we were running short of water, we would have to put into a West African port – Freetown. This we did. Two days out from that port we could smell Africa, the stench of rotting vegetation borne to us on a soft offshore wind.

We entered a huge harbour surrounded by low fertile land and discovered many ships there, for Freetown was a wartime haven for the shipping of the world. It is not possible for me to give a description of Freetown since we were not allowed ashore there on the grounds that plague was rife in the town. So we were confined to the ship, a target for the market traders.

First came the diving boys in their small dugout canoes who would boldly paddle up to the ship and call to us to throw them over our money and that they would then dive for it. A number of pennies were tossed overside and I never saw one that wasn't retrieved. There was no doubt about it, those dusky sons of Africa knew their business. They certainly knew they were worth more than a few mouldy pennies. Indeed they kept asking us to toss overboard 'Glasgow tanners'. 'You throw Glasgow tanner, me dive.' Not many of us could afford such a luxury but some did devise a scheme they thought might be worth the sacrificing of a tanner.

'Come, Johnny, me throw this great big Glasgow tanner over from the other side of ship.' British squaddies always assumed the only way to talk to foreigners was in pidgin English.

'You come other side, Johnny, me throw tanner.'

'Me no dive on other side ship, you wanna me be killed.'

'Come on, Johnny, African man he plenty brave, you dive no?'

'No. Me no dive on other side of the ship, not me.'

The point of it all was that there were sharks on the other side of the ship, because any food discharged overboard was on the other side. One might add that those diving wallahs knew all about the bad language of the British Empire and were never backward in producing it when pointing out that all the soldiers wanted to do in sending them round the other side was, 'You wanna – me up, Johnny?'

Then would arrive the traders of Freetown, usually in much larger canoes than those used by the diving boys. They traded in fruit, oranges, melons, pineapples, dates, furniture and clothing, the last probably made in Britain. It was clear from this of course that they had not met many troopships till then, otherwise they would have left their furniture and clothing at home.

Trading between canoes and ships was supposed to be forbidden but it certainly went on. It was easy to distinguish between the canoes even if it was impossible to sort out the dark faces of the owners of those picturesque vessels. Their names stood out, the *Rodney*, the *Nelson*, the *Hood* and one wag had named his canoe *God Bless the British Empire*. I wondered if the names would be changed if her captain had had dealings with the first truly representative sample of the British people.

It was clear that those men in the canoes loved bargaining. All the time we were in Freetown and while daylight lasted the trading went on. Money or clothing in exchange for fruit or possibly a souvenir or two. The method of trading was ingenious. A double line would be thrown overboard from each canoe with a wicker basket on each line. Into the basket at the canoe end went the fruit, into the basket aboard ship went the money or clothing. At least that was the theory but then we were not middle class tourists. We were hard up squaddies doing business with hard-up natives so that guile soon appeared in the dealing. In fact the whole business became hilarious and a great time was had by all concerned, as the folk at each end of the line would try to cheat the folk at the other end by withdrawing their basket swiftly at the same time as the other basket was withdrawn. Sometimes we lost, sometimes they did and I can vouch for the fact that these bumboat boys (mostly men) knew as much bad language as the diving boys. There was not a cuss word they did not have great experience with and when with orders from above the sailors turned the hosepipes upon the marketeers the air was absolutely blue, though they never, even in the adverse conditions of too much water, seemed to lose their lively sense of humour. They would stand up in their boats dripping ten thousand tons of water, shaking their fists at the hosepipe brigade and then they would roar with laughter, 'You wanner – me up Johnny?'

Sharp, officer-type eyes had of course been watching the situation and no doubt from discreet positions had been trading too but those eyes had been quite able to see all sorts of wearing apparel bunged through portholes into little wicker baskets. At any rate, immediately upon leaving Freetown a kit inspection was called and culprits cornered who had sold off army property for oranges and bananas. This was regarded by one and all as a confounded liberty and what were we fighting for if it wasn't for all kinds of freedom? However it was clear that the flogging off of the clothing of His Majesty's army was not one of them.

While we were in Freetown we heard that Free French forces under a General de Gaulle had tried to take Dakar from the Vichy French but had been repulsed and that our old ship the *Sobieski* had been in that duffy. At the same time we were perturbed by the news from London, which was in the process of being blitzed. There was nothing we could do about it except ponder and worry.

We crossed the line on that voyage, which meant that Father Neptune and his court clambered aboard to do justice to the situation. They brought with them all the paraphernalia for the occasion: buckets, brushes, lather and an abundance of local seaweed. There were plenty of victims to be hauled before his majesty to be lectured, lathered and flung into the pool. The victims were officers of all sorts and sizes including one colonel and none were treated lightly. In fact one character was carried off to the sick bay having sustained an injury as he was flung into the swimming pool. The whole business was rounded off when a particular sergeant major who was unpopular was chased round the ship then dragged before the court where he was duly sentenced before disappearing completely beneath a veritable mountain of lather. Then into the pool he went with some of us wondering whether the force of the throw would take him beyond the confines of the water or even the ship. Most of us kept our heads down, a low profile, innocent expressions on faces and of course most of us were emphatic that we had done it all before.

I suppose the days could become monotonous and it was certainly an uncomfortable time for a person like me who can sweat very easily. But the nights were so absolutely beautiful they were hard to take in. Very few of us had been privileged in the past to see those wonderful blue skies with such a mass of bright twinkling stars dancing for us as they had done for the folk of long ago. Those nights were heralded in by such sunsets that no words of mine can adequately describe them. Those of us who had been to Norway were particularly fortunate in that we had seen the Northern Lights and now here we were in the region of the Southern Cross.

Then we began to peer through chilly mist and rain to glimpse the approaches to Cape Town. When we did at last sight land it was hard to make out features through the drizzling rain coming from a thick grey sky. But eventually tugs took us in tow and nudged us toward a wide quay and we were all amazed as we touched the dockside that here was a harbour deep enough to take the *Dominion Monarch.*

As we docked, coloured dockers were knocking off work and they stopped, or many did, to throw us up beautiful bright red oranges and in return, before long the dockside was carpeted with orange peel.

Smudger was a bit bewildered at first. He had expected another Freetown with natives in dugout canoes and had not expected to see Africans in normal working clothes knocking off work and toddling off home for a meal. 'Ah well!' I reflected once again. There had been something in old 'Maggots' changing his religious lessons into those on geography.

There were hundreds of cars waiting at the dockside, their owners prepared to take anyone off the ship to stay with them in their homes for as long as the visitors had a mind, while the ship remained in port. The hospitality of the people of Cape Town and I suppose the rest of the South African seaboard, was well known. Some people might argue that they had an axe to grind but I believe they were genuinely keen to give more or less all that they had to give.

The pubs however were out of bounds to troops. Prior to our arrival the 6th Aussie division had passed that way on their way north and by all accounts had almost wrecked the place. In Cape Town they had horse drawn cabs rather like open landaus and one of the Aussie tricks had been to unharness the horses and ride them bareback through the town.

Fred, Stan and I decided to decline the hospitality offered and instead went to the pictures. Such enterprise! So we went off to a right modern and extremely large cinema and saw Nelson Eddie and Jeanette MacDonald in a film called 'New Moon'. Inside we discovered that the white or, as I prefer it, the pink skinned people occupied the centre seats while the black and brown folk sat in the two side aisles. This was indeed strange to us and not easily understood.

Then we decided to pay a visit to the top of Table Mountain, that large chunk of land which so dominates the Cape. So next day, while others went off on a conducted tour of the city we took a bus to a place called Kloof Neck, discovering on the way that all buses were free to troops or at least the journeys were. Arriving at Kloof Neck we discovered that we would have to walk four miles to reach the start point for the mountain. Then Hey Presto! At the right moment a South African lady turned up in her heavily laden car and managed to squeeze the four of us inside (though who the fourth man was I can't remember) somehow and off we went. Then having been unloaded at the right place and having given her our heartfelt thanks we walked on to the lower end of the cable car link to the top of the mountain.

The price of the journey to the top was 6s. 6d. (32½ pence new style) but for us in uniform it was three bob: children and soldiers under half price. The wire on which the cable car ran seemed to us to be extremely thin, the journey fearfully slow, but the view as we rose higher and higher was out of this world. The view from the top was awe inspiring, possibly especially so for those of us who had bravely climbed Box Hill in Surrey. Cape Town lay like a toy town below us and we could see houses and hamlets and towns stretching away into the interior to where, in the far distance, rose a range of blue mountains. Beyond the shore lay Table Bay where the waves, coming in to greet the shore, seemed so slow as if they hadn't the energy to roll back into the sea again. Beyond the bay was the great sweep of the Atlantic and the Indian oceans showing the way we had come and the way we were going. We were all silent for a long time.

A bell rang, we assumed indicating that the last car of the day was about to descend but we took no notice; spellbound we sat and watched.

The bell kept ringing, we kept watching. The bell sounded anxious as if it knew that folk were around who would not be summoned by its sound. Eventually the bell gave up and after that we sat for ages throwing stones down a steep cliff which must have been an edge of the gap which appears to divide the mountain top. We wanted to hear the stones hit the bottom but we never did.

Then the lights began to glow in the far below. Soon there were thousands of lights twinkling in mass formation as power was switched on in house, hamlet and town all the way to those far mountains.

The last cable car having long since gone and the bell long given up, we decided to move at last and so began our descent.

We followed what appeared to be a well worn track, holding on to outcrops of rock, tree trunks and bushes. I was undoubtedly the clumsiest of the four and probably on my backside more than on my feet. But none of us were of the stuff mountaineers are made of. Then we heard from afar whistling, whistling of relaxed human beings and the sound came closer and closer. We struggled carefully downwards in the dark towards the whistling until round a bend in the track came a couple of coloured lads with their hands in their pockets walking up! Any mountaineering aspirations melted away into air.

On arrival at the mountain road I discovered that I had worn a large hole in the seat of my trousers. I was no longer fit to be seen – at least from the rear. Once again a car mysteriously appeared and once again the car was loaded more or less to its roof but somehow or other we all squashed in and the young male driver drove us straight down to the *Dominion Monarch*. It was a fortunate thing that we got that lift as we did, I had not relished the idea of walking through Cape Town with a hand over the seat of my pants.

We remained in harbour for a few days then steamed away with pleasant memories and a special one for me since I had bought a pound of pipe tobacco for the ridiculous sum of 3s. 6d.

On the voyage round the Cape we ran into one hell of a swell. The boat began rolling from side to side at such an acute angle sailors turned pale and one said we ought to be turning over any moment now! Thank you! Fred and I were the last to leave our mess deck where the crockery stacked at the end of the tables was smashing to pieces and when the tables themselves started from their floor-holding bolts we decided it was time. We raised our mugs of tea to our mouths, drank, let the mugs go and watched them sail gracefully across the deck space and smash into a bulkhead. 'I think it's about time to go,' Fred said. I agreed and we went like scalded cats.

On deck things looked a damned sight more alarming than down below. There was so much roll on the ship that it was impossible to keep a foothold in the normal way. We had to walk up the steeply rising deck to the opposite rail and then as the boat rolled the other way we had to turn and walk in the opposite direction and this seemed to go on for hours. Up to a certain point we were alarmed but being ignorant of the sea assumed that basically we were all right, when our ideas were shattered by a white-faced sailor. He gave it as his considered opinion that that ship had not been designed to roll at such angles and that by rights we should now be turning turtle! Thank you kindly sir, we said. One thing was clear, he was alarmed himself and that really put the wind up us landlubbers.

However the crisis passed and once we were headed north we knew we were bound for Egypt. Around this time some of the crew came down on to our deck which was the lowest troop deck and started pulling up a hatch. They had come to examine the cargo.

To our consternation we discovered that we had been bivou-acked right on top of our own 3.7 ammunition! One was never really absolutely at one's ease at sea during wartime for obvious reasons, but if we had known that we had been sleeping a few feet above all that ammo we might have been tempted to abandon ship.

Approaching the entrance to the Red Sea with Aden on the one hand and Italian-held Somaliland on the other we had to keep silent particularly at night and of course no light had to be shown, although there were sufficient idiotic smokers to cause ructions.

We were attacked by an Italian bomber but he kept himself discreetly high and when the naval guns opened up he sheered off and dropped his bombs well astern of us. This was decent of him, we thought, as we remembered the ammo down below.

Passing through the straits we steamed up the Red Sea with Egypt on the one hand and Saudi Arabia on the other, brown red hills of sand and rock baking in shimmering heat and no sign of welcome anywhere.

Then at last we dropped anchor at Suez at the southern end of the Suez Canal. We docked at Port Tufik. Our long sea voyage was over. Disembarkation took place rapidly and soon there were just a few of us remaining on board as the rear party. We stayed on board for a couple of days mainly watching the stevedores in their long nightshirts and tarbushes emptying the holds with human labour and cranes and we understood only too well how ships' holds can become pretty foul. Nobody bothered about going ashore to relieve himself and the scratching meanwhile was quite unbelievable. We ourselves of course, being few in number and privileged, had the run of the ship and could choose any cabin we liked and in fact in those two days often changed our cabins just for the hell of it.

Eventually we were taken on board a couple of barges abreast of each other and a tug towed us almost to the entrance of the canal, passing the man responsible for the building of the water-way, the statue of Ferdinand de Lesseps. And thus we came ashore into Egypt. The East was all around us, hot, noisy, dusty and different from anything we had seen so far. Then, we boarded a train and a new phase in our adventures was about to begin.

We may have been a newly arrived, white knobbly-kneed brigade, but we were destined to be the AckAck cover for Wavell's forty thousand, only in fact it wasn't forty thousand, just thirty thousand odd.

But that was somewhere in the future. Before that we had to taste the 'delights' of Cairo, get acclimatized, which included another of those foot wearing route marches, and take part in that great bargaining campaign between British army Greek and Egyptian trading Greek in which the phrase 'give in' was a dirty bit of speech. The Egyptians or Gypos were known by us all as wogs, not too polite a phrase but I should point out that the dock workers who unloaded the *Dominion Monarch* wore arm bands denoting that they were workers on government service – hence WOGS.

Meanwhile here we were, bundling ourselves and all our gear into Egyptian State Railway carriages, roomier than those at home though we soon found the slatted wooden seats were not nearly so comfortable as the upholstered ones on trains in Blighty. We all piled in, the whistle blew or was it a horn? The steam hissed and we slowly moved off into the dusty interior. Egypt here we come!

Chapter Nine

Nile Valley Base Wallah

Almost immediately the fun began. Onto the train, which never seemed to go faster than a lame snail, jumped a local vendor flogging bottles of the local brew. So adept were those vendors at their business that by the time the bottles of beer were being opened at one end of the carriage the beer man was jumping off at the other. The man with the beer certainly moved fast and we soon found out why; the first would-be consumers were spitting the contents of the bottles out pronto. It appeared to be bottled canal water! The British Greeks were outraged, apart from me; I still belonged to the Band of Hope.

Then spritely stepping came another vendor, this time the local fruit merchant with an enormous bunch of bananas, almost as big as himself. He gaily cried his wares as he stood with a welcoming Egyptian smile. 'You like bananas, George? Good, plenty cheap.' One of our number, a gunner of no mean proportions, carefully, gently took the bunch of bananas from our trader friend and waving the lot around asked genially, 'Would anyone like a banana?' Of course we all said, including temperance me, that we loved bananas, some would like at least a dozen. So the big guy began stripping off the fruit and chucking it to all and sundry until there was none left. The vendor had watched the proceedings with growing concern. 'You have banana, George, me have money, George.' The genial middle man nodded happily. 'You want payment, George? George will have payment,' and he thrust the stripped banana stalk at the poor old Gypo and then with a bit of help he threw the poor fellow off the train. British Greek had answered Egyptian Greek and we had no further trading on that journey.

That train was *slow*. The crew seemed to stop it whenever

they felt inclined. On one occasion the engine wheezed to a halt and either the driver or his mate clambered down and wandered off to a nearby village. He was gone for quite a while so we assumed that he had either gone home to have tea with his missus or he was off visiting friends or relatives. How different from the hurry and scurry of our native pastures. And why not? What the devil did it really matter if we got to Cairo at two, three or four o'clock? There was a war on certainly but that wasn't due to end at Christmas, now was it?

The man came back, clambered aboard and off we went to stop again and again as he toddled off for one thing or another. At one point we watched Indians, possibly Sikhs, climb out of carriages and pop along to the engine for hot water! They were doing what we wanted to do, brewing up! What a splendid idea! Let us stop the train somewhere between Peterborough and York, Reading and Swindon, pop along to the engine for hot water and brew up!

The phrase 'brew up,' was on everyone's lips in the Middle East along with that other one: 'Just the job.' At every stop on any journey we ever made, long or short, one hopefully asked the question, 'How about a brew up?' Without that brew up the war would have certainly ground to a halt. I used to argue politics a great deal in those days and I was always positive that any country in the world including the USA was more likely to find itself in a revolutionary situation than Britain. With all our tea breaks there would be no time to man barricades.

In any case I had long since come to the conclusion that my compatriots were a queer bloody lot. I remember all of us being paraded before embarking for our Norwegian campaign and a general came down to give us a fatherly pep talk and wished with all his heart that he could come with us into battle but alas he was now too old for that sort of thing so he was now sadly sending others. Now he had a son who was a captain in our outfit who was no doubt raring to go fight the foe. A few days later his son was transferred to higher things and thus stayed behind!

In due course we reached Cairo and were taken by lorry to an ancient barracks in the centre of the city. The city was all lit up which shook us somewhat, since there was a war on and we had arrived from a blacked-out country and the Italians were encamped on Egyptian territory not all that far off. Would there have been a bit too much skulduggery if the lights had been switched off?

Officially Egypt, being controlled by Britain, was at war or if it were not officially at war, the British held the country and they were officially at war so really, I suppose, it didn't matter if it was official or not.

We went through the city admiring the lights, which I believe were classified as half blacked out, and somewhat thunderstruck by the noise, the eastern smells and the singing from female radio vocalists. It was all hustle and bustle on a warm night, with plenty of stars in the sky.

Then we arrived at a barracks in the centre of the city.

There was an enormous barrack room with iron bedsteads and on each bedstead three flat cushions known as biscuits which constituted the bed mattress. We, the weary travellers, rushed to grab a bed, flinging kit on each, commandeering future comfort and leaving the slower brethren to find some solace on the stone floor. Then stepped forth an old warrior who had been in those parts in times past. He raised a checking hand and in a commanding voice cried, 'Halt!'

'Halt, what for?'

'What for? Just give them beds a tap on the floor and give them biscuits a knock or two as well. Go on, you lot, just do as I say.'

'What's that idiot yapping about?'

'Never mind,' someone said, 'It must be the heat already but we'd better humour him, he may turn violent.'

So we gave the beds a tap on the floor and the biscuits a bang as well and then we all set to to bang a damned sight harder than we had done in the first place because out of the iron bedsteads and biscuits fell hundreds of bugs until the floor was crawling with the lousy things.

That night we all slept out on the open barracks roadway leaving the interior to the much disturbed bugs who we thought could very well have taken their revenge out on us if they had been so minded.

We moved to a large tented camp outside Cairo called El Masa. For a while this became our base from which we made excursions into Cairo on the fast sixty-mile-an-hour trams, usually double carriaged with the conductor in his red tarbush and with his everlastingly blown whistle, standing in the middle of the contraption.

On the first day out of camp we soon realised that we were about the first non-regular soldiers to be there. At the gate where a line of local native boot blacks operated they would ask for our custom, eager to give us a shoeshine. A squaddie would politely be asked if he would like his boots cleaned. Up onto a stool would go a boot and the operator would polish away as if his life depended upon it. Time and again a regular soldier would look at his boots, shake his head and say, 'No good, George, do it again.' The poor old shoe shiner might have to do it a third and a fourth time and often would end up with his box of tricks kicked away as the regular walked away without a thought of payment and laughing his head off. The boot-black was always a 'lazy good-for-nothing bloody wog'.

I could never get my boots properly cleaned myself and could not see anyone else doing any better so I steered clear of the bootboys.

That camp was a vast place which seemed a hive of industry over nothing in particular. Someone in charge had an obsessive view in regard to keeping men occupied, on the theory that idle hands were not to be tolerated, and besides, idle men could sidle into the NAAFI and stay there drinking awful tea and lousy local beer while singing smutty songs to the sound of the old joanna.

In between medical inspections we had to dig holes in the sandy soil in front of our tents, take the tents down, re-erect them in the new holes and then fill in the old tent circles. We did this in 1940 and I found that on my return to El Masa in late 1944 it was still an occupational disease of that camp. We never did get the official reason for this activity and assumed the idea was to keep the ground inside tents fresh and free of vermin. If this was the case then the El Masa tent area must have been the freshest in the world.

Another obsession was marching drill. The camp boasted a very large parade ground, in fact not only large enough to contain the British army but the whole of the German as well. At any rate it seemed like that to us who were constantly slogging it all over the perishing thing. The great mystery was, why toughen us up foot slogging when we were bound to be charging about the countryside in matadors and other vehicles or strictly confined to a gunsite? However, it was always difficult to understand the reasoning emanating from the higher echelons of the army.

On that marching drill business a golden rule was always followed, tallest on the right, shortest on the left. We supposed it looked more impressive that way with the tall in the lead and the shorties up behind. Now me, being one of the tallest, I often found myself in the first three and at times the one on the right and it would be the first three who more or less set the pace. The practice was to yank out all the junior NCOs that could be found who were not on some dodge or other and place them in command of small detachments of men and then for them to shout orders about marching hither and yon, up and down, right turn, left turn and all the rest of it.

Now, we had one bombardier not particularly popular who had an extremely weak voice. On the day in question there he was in charge of our squad and there was I, not only in the front rank but on the right of it, therefore the pacemaker.

The lance jack kept calling out orders and I kept increasing the speed and extending the distance between him and us on the grounds that it was not easy to hear his weak voice.

Time came when we were headed toward the NAAFI so I said to the other two, 'Speed up, cocks, and away we go.' The voice giving those daft commands got fainter and fainter and I am sure we heard a cursing command to bloody well stop. But we kept right on to the end of the road. By now the voice was inaudible, the canteen doors loomed ahead and we marched in, falling ourselves out in true military style as soon as we crossed the threshold. We ordered lousy NAAFI tea and a wad and sat down. Whether the bombardier followed us in or just lost himself I am now unable to recall. I do know we stayed there until tiffin time. Certainly I remember us sitting in the NAAFI comparing the marching techniques of the various squad commanders, and both Fred and I came to the conclusion that while our compatriots were better off with all that drilling, we were even more so sitting quietly sipping ghastly *chai* and thinking.

Eventually we moved from El Masa holding camp to Beni Youseff way out west of the Nile, from which we could just see the tops of the pyramids at El Giza. This was an RA camp where there was no huge parade ground, so no possibility of the irksome mass foot drill. But we were supposed to be hardened off. It was called 'getting acclimatised'. This meant that everyone had to wear the dreaded world war one heavier than lead pith helmet which may have been ideal for tropical Africa but which only seemed to push us into the ground with the weight.

Later they were changed to a much lighter affair, straw coloured and with a flat top, the name of which escapes me. Later still we reverted to the side hat and then came the beret which, while not ideal in sunny climes, having no peak, was much the best headgear save for the one we were always asking for but never got – the Aussie type hat.

Once in an RA camp the gun drill disease soon appeared and we were once again taking post, elevating, traversing, numbering off to the heart's content of all officers concerned.

Fitzy came once again into his own, demanding the careful laying out of kits, tents to be aired, brailings rolled up and feet to be inspected for toe jam. But there was a higher authority than him which decided we had to be hardened off with a route march to the pyramids at El Giza and back, a five mile affair each way. We set off before cockcrow to outwit the Egyptian sun and were led by an imposing figure on a horse. It certainly was not Fitzy who would have disdained such means of transport on the grounds that an AckAck man should be fit enough to march with the best and I can see him saying something like that, puffing out his cheeks as he did so with interspersed sounds such as, 'Humph Humph and Whoosh Whoosh.'

The man on the horse must have been the major. It could not possibly have been the Colonel, 'Mad Mac'. He had replaced our old fuddy duddy of a colonel while in England and MacIntyre was said to have already lost a couple of regiments somewhere or other; whether or not in action was not made clear. No. It must have been the major, who was not known to be an enthusiast in regard to physical activity.

At any rate, all speculation to one side, we set out on our route march to the pyramids and back.

We left in the cool Egyptian dawn to march along dirt roads which ran beside raised water channels bringing precious water from the life-giving Nile, water which was pumped up from the channels by a method as ancient as Egypt itself. It was the Archimedes screw in action. Each device looked like a long slatted barrel and the thing was turned either by a man seemingly in an everlasting squat or by a plodding ever revolving bullock.

We passed scenes which must have been observed over hundreds of years, maybe thousands. I got the feeling that, for all our modern knowhow and fast pace, we were the ones in transit. We were the passers by and the real world was right out there with the static Egyptian *fellah*. How many nations had he and his Middle Eastern compatriots seen off over the years?

If anything looked out of place it was us, especially as the sun rose, as it did with almost malicious speed.

It soon became plain that the local population, men, women and children and possibly the bullocks and the odd donkey, looked at us with wide open mouths. Who were those creatures struggling along the dirt roads like that? And truly it wasn't long before we were straggling along those dusty roads in a most unmilitary manner. The man on the horse was doing fine, no doubt, though possibly perspiring a bit in the sunshine but for the rest of us Dante's Inferno could have hardly been worse. My feet soon got sore and other people suffered too. After all, we were not your young keen infantry wallahs, we were the flat footed standard B more elderly types – at least some of us were elderly. A good many would never see thirty again. At the end of the stagger, it was never a march, officers and men were all in various degrees of bad shape except the man on the horse. In his case it was the horse which suffered.

Reaching the pyramids most of us flopped out using lurid expressions in regard to the pyramids such as, 'If the things belong to Rameses he knows where he can bloody well stuff 'em.' We were certainly not of the tourist class.

But amazingly, not all were physical wrecks. Some did manage to scale the outside of the Great Pyramid, climbing from one giant stone block to another though the apex could not be reached. The tomb builders had covered their limestone with an outer layer of granite; now only a few blocks of granite at the top remained, too smooth for anyone to clamber over.

When we had recovered sufficiently some of us wandered off to have a look at the Sphinx which, until 1924, had been covered to the neck in sand. In that year the government had had the sand cleared away to reveal the temple which lay beneath. We discovered that the Sphinx is much older than the pyramids and that when the French were there with Napoleon their artillery knocked the Sphinx's nose off. Considering the interest Napoleon showed in cultural activities I wondered if that was a yarn put about by the British who were really only interested in trade. As the Sphinx was not floggable they were not particularly concerned with it.

All around the site were the donkey ride merchants and camel ride vendors who had now been forced to change over from trying to extort money from tourists to getting it from the military, a much more difficult task. However, if one understood that there was no seaside, one could imagine oneself at a British holiday resort with donkey rides, refreshment sellers and with the added attraction of sideways chewing camels. Some of our blokes indeed had rides on those flea bitten plodders of the desert.

Me, I hadn't the energy.

Eventually we had recovered strength enough to have a go at a visit into the interior of the Great Pyramid. I think we paid five ackers a head for the dubious privilege of a tour inside, which would be a shilling in old money and five pence in the new.

Groups of us were assembled under the leadership of a native guide and in our turn we clambered up the side of the pyramid past a couple of hefty looking characters, who looked as if they were the local chuckers out of non-paying or awkward guests, to a large hole cut in the side of the structure. The hole was a modern entrance, the original having been concealed by the ancients. Inside we were confronted with a long dark passage-way lit by candles held by the guides. A path led downwards to the Queen's chamber while we struggled upwards along a dark low passage where at times we had to crawl on hands and knees, advancing always toward the top and the King's chamber. I have often wondered what happened in tourist times with the little old ladies and the portly gents. Surely they never went on their hands and knees? Or were they more agile in fact than we?

Finally we reached the great chamber where numerous parties with guides were milling about, the scene lit by a myriad of candles. British voices mixed with those of the guides who were desperately anxious to keep their particular parties together. This guide anxiety was soon shown to be justified. Once inside the chamber a guide would produce a magnesium flare, light it for greater illumination and then demand a further five ackers for the use of same, from reluctant customers who were strongly averse to blackmail.

'Come here, George, you come, I show.'

'Show what, George?'

'Me show you this, very ancient very sacred very important.'

We were gazing into the empty sarcophagus of the king. How thrilling!

'Over there in wall see that hole, that hole for the spirits to come and go.'

'Does he mean booze?'

'Fathead, no.'

'Over that side is hole for food.'

'Who brought the grub, pigeons?'

'How should I know?'

The cultural lesson continued.

'Now me light magnesium flare, show up whole of tomb better, you pay me five piastres,' and whoosh! Before anyone could say the usual Jack Robinson the flare was lit and our guide demanding his money. It may have been our guide's first mistake of the day. At any rate he was going to regret lighting that flare.

With one voice we said, 'We no pay you five ackers, George.'

'You must pay.'

'You lit the thing so you pay. We go now,' and we all dived for the exit led by our two biggest blokes Taffy Powell and Lofty Bale. Down we went helter skelter, bobbing low, crawling, panting, with George the guide hot on our heels calling out to us to stop and pay.

'Honourable thing you pay.'

'Horrible thing we no pay.'

Down and down until the passage flattened out and we approached the exit which was the same as the entrance where the two guardians of fair play stood ready for action. Our guide called upon them to see fair play done in persuading us to cough up our five piastres. We assumed he was calling out in true medieval or Gypo fashion, 'Stop thief.'

The two guardians of justice stood barring our way to safety. Our two leading heavyweights kept right on going and as they met the guardians either Taffy or Lofty pushed the one to one side and hit the other square on the jaw sending him tumbling down off the pyramid and we all jumped to safety. As our guide shook his fist at us we shouted out, 'We no pay, George, you pay,' and carried out a strategical withdrawal.

We all fell in to begin our march back to Beni Youseff, only no one marched any more on a route march, it was more of a mass rout, a kind of strategical withdrawal with nothing strategical about it.

The guns drills went on and the fatigues and the guards and the cookhouse and the gun cleaning.

We had plenty of leave into Cairo. It was always day leave; even if there had been seven days leave where the devil in Egypt would we spend it? None of our kind would have been allowed anywhere near, for example, Shepheard's Hotel. While touching on class I might as well mention the ATS. At the beginning of the war, the ATS were strictly out of bounds for 'us men'. We came to label the women 'officers only, for the use of'.

We had some exciting times getting in and out of Cairo, the only place for us to go. Taxis were usually stationed outside the camp and we were always expected to and did haggle over the fare. We considered the taxi drivers to be robbers; they probably considered us to be the biggest swindlers in creation. Indeed, late at night on return journeys I have often seen more than one fight break out and the poor Gypo was always the loser.

I never did join in those kind of games. I had read some history and had an idea of how the British had been apt to treat colonial peoples and didn't wish to be part of it, even though I kept a sharp eye on old George.

Having settled the price of the fare we would be carted off down to the tram stop where we would board the number ten tram for Cairo, the route passing by the Middle East military headquarters.

The trams were similar to those out of El Masa except that they were slower. They were of the double car type with sometimes a third attached and the conductor was usually to be seen standing in the middle of the set-up in tarbush and with the ever present whistle, when not collecting fares. They were good on fare collection and we never got away with any fiddling though that was hardly necessary since all soldiery travelled at half price. Each car had a small compartment for veiled women marked as either 'Harem' or 'Dame'.

At that time a great deal of Cairo was out of bounds to troops and indeed we did hear that it was quite dangerous to wander off into certain parts of the city, though that probably applied more towards the end of the war than at the beginning. Not that most of us were liable to wander off, not being the museum visiting or archaeological dig types. Our curiosity was, I suppose, divided between the service clubs and the Cairo brothel area.

The Bundlers were now back to their original number of five and so when possible we would all bundle off to town together to the cinema and to the service clubs. The more enlightening establishments for the education of the human kind were not for us. My real cultural life wouldn't begin until much later.

The cinemas were big and air-conditioned and also had sliding roofs. But our best times were had at the various service clubs where all went for food and drink and in the case of the Bundlers, ice cream sundaes which were the most enormous concoctions that any of us had ever seen.

Our favourite was the United Services Club in Ezbekia gardens. The grounds were extensive and pleasant to relax in, especially at night when the stars were out. The lights of Cairo, officially blacked out, shone all around us and the strange city hubbub, the noises off, traffic, whistles, banging, female singing akin to wailing, could make us believe we were surrounded by some sort of fairyland.

Our first purchase would be an ice cream sundae topped with real fruit: melon, orange, grapes, banana, dates and other curious fruits, topped up with a mountain of variegated ice cream. We would order one round but the Bundlers being democratic and plagued with enormous stomachs, one would not be enough. Each of us in his turn would order an ice cream sundae which meant on each visit to the club five sundaes per stomach! Then off to a cinema to see the latest film and back to the club for the evening nosh and more sundaes and certainly the other four would start in on the local brew which was never popular, it being suspected it was either brewed from Nile or canal water.

Foreigners in all countries who came into contact with British troops soon discovered, I am sure, that the British squaddie expected eggs and chips for his meal, garnished of course with other things such as tomatoes, lettuce, cucumber and possibly sausages and pies to make up bulk. But the main dish was always egg and chips.

At the end of an evening spent in such manner we would stagger to the tram stop not through having too much wallop, apart from Stan Ward, but because of over indulged stomachs. At the end of the tram ride the taxis would be waiting in the dark for us and the haggling would begin. As indicated above it was not an uncommon sight to see a local taxi driver flat on his back staring sightless at those gorgeous stars in the heavens above. Though that was usually because of tangling with the regulars. We drove a hard bargain but were never violent.

Perhaps it should be made clear that everyone in Egypt was called George and over the border in Palestine the name was changed and everyone became Johnny. Maybe the Palestine Arab thought himself a cut above the other. If so he was probably right.

A curious fad was the use of the phrase, 'Just the job.' It was used possibly even more than the usual cuss words. I mention it because while it was commonplace among all of us one can hardly use it in a script such as this.

There was a particular place of interest in Cairo known as Berker Street, the street of brothels, its counterpart in Alexandria being the Cages. They were licensed brothels, government-run, army-controlled, we believed. The girls in residence there were kept under strict medical control. They needed to be since they were doing a roaring trade during the war period.

The whore houses were situated over shops and the first thing to be noticed when one ascended the wide stone stairways of the establishments was the smell of urine. Each house had its particular name: Paradise, Blue Moon, Big Kate's and the most famous of them all was Tiger Lil's. Though at this distance of time I am not sure whether it was Tiger Lil in Cairo and the Brown Bomber in Haifa or the other way round.

There was always a large main room where visitors could sit and see what was taking place around them. They could take refreshments there too. The room was there clearly for the buyer to view what was on offer and once the choice was made the couple would disappear into one of the numerous small rooms leading off the hall. A squaddie would often set off for a room amid the cheers and encouragement of his mates or the knowing advice given free by all and sundry. We would watch them as they returned, sometimes with a smirk and sometimes with a hang-dog expression. I amused myself one night by timing them in and out and I swear that the average time of absence was an incredible two minutes! Can I be exaggerating?

The girls were all shapes and sizes, tall, short, thin, fat, all colours of the human race were represented there and also the numerous languages of society were on display among those often very attractive females.

Those ladies had no inhibitions. They would often leave their rooms with nothing at all on and a towel in hand and would go to the wash room to clean up while the lads happily looked on. One night one of the room doors stood wide open and as the lads crowded round, the snores from the naked incumbent were almost deafening. When someone made a coarse remark about the sleeper, the madam said, 'You'd all bloody well snore if you had had as many as she has had today.' I never indulged. I had been well put off by the numerous films we had been made to see, dealing with venereal disease, and many of the illustrations had not been pretty to watch. But then it was, I suppose, fairly easy for a single bloke like me. It was the married men who had the worse problem and I used to feel sorry for them.

Our guns arrived just before Christmas and so we found ourselves busy, with less time to indulge in the delights of Cairo.

We were some of the first amateur soldiers to arrive in Egypt and we soon met with some peculiar customs left behind from the regular army brigade.

We were all used to early morning tea known to us as 'gunfire'. At Beni Youseff the NAAFI personnel, who were all native civilians, had the right to sell any tea left over from the night before. Thus, each morning, a local Egyptian would walk around the tents, or rather two would come round since one was not strong enough to carry the urn. They would cry their wares, '*Chai*, good hot *chai*.' It was of course absolutely foul and almost undrinkable having been well reboiled recently. For some reason which I could never fathom, we always bought the stuff and somehow or other we always managed to drink it. I have often wondered whether any of my compatriots died an early death, cause unknown.

Then there was the shaving business. In my case I was still not close to a razor. In fact I hadn't started using one at that time but of course most men shaved. On our first morning in camp we were roused up with the cry of '*Chai chai*, good hot *chai*.' The man in the bed next to me roused up and slowly rubbed his chin. At first he had a thoughtful look and then that turned to one of alarm as he patted his face. Others rousing up from their deep slumbers were sitting up in their flea pits bemused, bewitched and bewildered.

'Blimey,' someone blurted out, 'I've been shaved while still akip!'

It was soon realised that they had been shaved by person or persons unknown while they were still in the arms of Morpheus, and that this was a regular army custom. It didn't bother the cleanshaven newcomers that they had been cleaned up by professional native barbers. No indeed. What bothered them was the fact that each operation had been carried out with a cut throat razor handled so skilfully that no one had felt a thing!

That practice came to a full stop.

Then there was the business of the blankets.

One morning one or two woke up feeling a bit on the cold side and finding the wooden boards they slept on harder than usual. They soon found out why. They had gone to bed covered with a blanket and sleeping on one. When they woke up feeling cold they had no blankets at all! George the Gypo could creep into a tent in the dead of night, roll a man over onto his side by gently blowing in his ear (so it was said) then after rolling up half the blanket would blow in the other ear and so roll the poor bloke over onto his other side thus releasing the rest of the blanket. The removal of blankets in that way was positively easy. Once again Egyptian Greek had made his appearance and had scored over the British Greek.

The NAAFI as mentioned above was run by civilians. The lighter skinned and presumably better off Egyptians ran the canteens while their blacker brothers were left to do all the dirty work.

We soon found that when we went into the canteen, we with our white knobbly knees were the new boys, the unblooded, the uneducated. There were others recently back from the Western Desert who were almost as brown as the local inhabitants. They were very expansive in their views, opining that the wop (Italian) was not worthy of being fought by members of the British army and that it was only a matter of time before those unmilitary people would jack it in. They explained that the front if there could be such a thing in the Bluey (the Western Desert) was a somewhat fluid thing running somewhere between Sidi Barrani and Mersa Matrouh, with us holding the latter town. The Eyties had come down off the Libyan plateau via the escarpment and were occupying their time by lobbing a shell every two hours into Mersa. No damage was ever done so no one really minded. The only reason why we had made one of our strategical withdrawals was because we just did not have enough men up there, but as soon as Wavell could organise enough squaddies the minor duffy would soon be over.

Nowadays smoking has been in decline for years but in the war years nearly everyone smoked. The pipe tobacco which I often got was quite good usually being popular brands but the cigarettes were a different matter entirely. In the early days the issue was supplied from India and every one of those things had plenty of maggot holes in them. In fact they were really unsmokable though they did get smoked. I supposed that smokers would suffer anything, even old rope coated with tar. Those cigarettes were so bad and the complaints so loud that they were eventually withdrawn and replaced with the infamous Victory V cigarettes which too were not really smokable but they did have the virtue of not having any maggot holes in them. One no longer had to watch the smoke coming out of the sides of a cigarette as if it were a watchman's basket fire.

Christmas day arrived and we crawled out of bed at half past nine for breakfast and then crawled back to bed till dinner time when we were served up with a fair old Christmas dinner: turkey and veg, Christmas pudding, nuts, fruit and beer. We were waited on as was the army custom by officers and NCOs (sergeants) led by that live wire Colonel Mad Mac, against whom we had a question mark because of the said loss of troops in times past. He gave us all a speech advising us to make hay while the Egyptian sun shone, since in a couple of days we would all be getting down to business.

The lads, taking him at his word, took to the bottle with great gusto until the canteen floor was awash with the local lousy brew. I was the only idiot sober. In our tent we had clubbed together to get whisky, beer, soda water and lime juice. The whisky, beer and soda water were for the other nine, the lime juice was for me.

There was an officers versus NCOs football match on Christmas morning and prior to that the NCOs had brought round the morning gunfire which had been pretty good. But on Boxing morning we waited in vain for them to come again so in the end we had to make do with the old 'wog' tea. We didn't bother about breakfast but stayed in bed until ten. The Boxing day fare wasn't bad either: pork and veg, custard and rice. In the evening we went to the pictures.

The next day we resumed normal duties and discovered we were standing by to move. Great bustle and activity around the guns and then our transport arrived. We got up at 4.30 a.m. on Monday 30th December to prepare to move and we moved out of Beni Youseff at half past seven. It was a pretty impressive sight to see the guns on the move with all our accompanying transport.

We headed for Alex and then turned on the road going west to Mersa, stopping around midday for bully beef and bread – the last bread we were to see for a long time. That night we stopped beside the desert road and slept in the ammo lorries and that was far from being comfortable. We breakfasted on hard tack biscuits, a sausage and a mug of *chai*. Well to tell Christmas was over. At dusk we stopped near Mersa and then passed through on 1st January. After Mersa the road petered out and we embarked upon a rough track over which we bumped and bored, often crashing our tin-hatted heads against the roof of the matador on which we were riding, sitting on our ammo.

Around Sidi Barrani we saw signs of war: guns pointing uselessly, wrecked lorries and all around hundreds of petrol tins glinting in the sun. Those petrol cans were interesting. They turned out to be something of a nuisance, easily dented and split and also affected by the heat of the sun. Jerry on the other hand used sensible Jerry cans which it was said could remain unaffected when run over by a tank!

That night we stopped for the usual brew up and to have more corned beef and biscuits. We were a bit surprised to see at night a good many small fires lit for brew-ups but no one bothered in the least about the enemy – the Eyties. In fact he was too busy with his own affairs to bother about our nightly brew ups. We passed through Bug Bug and arrived at the border town of Soullam. Here we were fed on bully beef stew and *chai* of course. Our cooks told us that the Italians bottled up in Bardia lobbed over a couple of shells every hour from a gun known as Bardia Bill but just like the earlier account, as the shells didn't hit anything no one took much notice.

Our meal over we pushed up to the escarpment up which, on a narrow track, we made our way to the Libyan plateau above.

We were given to understand that the place had seen some fighting. Then by-passing a place known as Fort Capuzzo we pushed on to Bardia, a town on the coast a few miles ahead.

Chapter Ten

The Bluey

We had left Egypt behind and were now in Libya. Coming up to the battle zone we were halted within sound of gunfire coming from the direction of Bardia itself. We then proceeded to hang about for some hours for no apparent reason though we suspected our leadership was trying to find out where we were supposed to go. During this time we saw not a sign of the Italian air force. We did see a few of our Gladiator biplane fighters and a Lysander spotting plane but that was all. Some of us whiled away the time looking around the area which had signs of past action scattered all over it. There were all kinds of Italian weaponry: small arms and ammunition, small shells and small, somewhat ancient looking guns that might have seen service in the Boer war. But the really interesting thing about the Italian army gear was that it was nearly all made by Vickers Armstrong.

What the devil were the Italians doing firing all that old junk at us? As it so happened the goods on display were not worth a light but what if the enemy had been supplied with modern lethal equipment? Some of us were asking questions: who had supplied such rubbish and who had profited from the sales thereof? I recalled to mind the story that had gone the rounds at the outbreak of war that three days after the balloon went up, ships loaded with old iron left for Germany!

Behind it all must be a powerful arms sales or organisation and that didn't bode too well for any future peace, now did it?

We moved nearer the town, placed ourselves in a gun position and took a few hours shut-eye. While we were mobile in the desert we would take a pick and shovel and dig ourselves a shallow grave-type hole in which we could doss down. This was known as a bivvy. Fred and I of course shared the same hole. In case anyone imagines digging holes in the desert is a doddle, just bear in mind that the Libyan coastal desert is not soft sand but rock-hard rock. It was partly for protection against flying bits and pieces and partly to allow us at least some warmth, the nights in the desert being extremely cold.

We got our heads down I remember, but it turned into a damned cold night. I shivered, Fred shivered, we all shivered. Did we shiver because of the cold or through fear, or was it both? I remember thinking that if I carried on shivering as I was I would be liable to do myself injury.

During the night came a sound of clanking old iron and then the Seventh Armoured tanks rolled round our site. Those tank characters were a cheerful bunch, laughing, joking, smoking and not bothered one jot about the Eyties just ahead of them. Then, as we lay shivering in the light of breaking dawn one hundred and thirty guns plus those from naval vessels offshore, opened up all at once with one almighty crash. Now, as no one had informed Fred and me that that diapason was going to happen, we both shot several feet into the air and I am sure that I thought our last hour had come. From then on the guns kept pounding away from concealed positions but although they were hidden from sight those damned guns were all around us.

We were stationed across a dirt road. Not far off ran another such road which, for some reason, the enemy seemed to think was important because he kept dropping shells onto it from what appeared his only weapon of reply. As the morning advanced the shelling grew closer and closer to our position until all those not actually on guns or command post were sent away to a safer place. The bursts gradually got nearer until one round did fall uncomfortably close and we all became somewhat apprehensive. Then, in true story book fashion, just as we were expecting the fourpenny one the shelling stopped and we were able to breathe our mutual sighs of relief.

The firing went on well into the morning before it eased off and then we saw the first prisoners coming through, some half dozen Italians led by a squaddie with slung bondook who asked us the way to the cages. As if we would know that! Later the horizon became black as though a low thunder cloud was sitting on it and then it resolved itself into a mass of prisoners headed by a couple of blokes in a Bren gun carrier. The prisoners were either carrying small brown attaché cases or neatly made up bundles containing their personal effects. All looked very clean and certainly not unhappy. We gathered that most of them were glad to be out of it; some went so far as to express dislike for their German allies.

Thousands passed us that day and right in the middle of that vast defeated army came one infantryman with his rifle also slung over his shoulder and looking very pleased with himself. We showed some concern for his situation, demanding to know if he were safe in all that mob, but he only grinned and became more cheerful still and said, 'No trouble at all, they want water which I've got and they had wrist watches which I've got too.' He then produced the watches as proof though how he supplied the water in exchange I never discovered. The last prisoners were around a dozen and they were wandering past us on their own. They too wanted to know where the cages were and not to be made to look too dumb we waved vaguely in the direction of the Bluey behind us. The Italians looked with interest at our guns and one expressed the view that if they had known what they were up against they would have jacked it in the sooner. Ah! What sensible fellows they were!

About this time we heard a tale about the Aussies who had been positioned somewhere around us. The story went that the Aussie infantry, tired of waiting for the barrage to lift, just upped and took off into it. When the Eyties saw the opposition coming at them with fixed bayonets through their own muck and bullets they promptly downed tools and stuck their hands up.

An Aussie dispatch rider tore up to our site at a rate of knots to inform us that Bardia was taken.

The next day the Italian circus put in an appearance. This consisted of a number of planes which flew high to keep out of range of the Bofors guns – well out of range. They were much higher than they needed to be but we assumed the sensible fellows were not taking too many chances. They circled around for a while and then began unloading their wares on the wagon lines of a field artillery unit. We were intended as a surprise for the Eyties and as it turned out we were, because with our 3.7s we could reach him. We reached him so effectively that it was claimed we brought five down. The result was more creditable perhaps than it sounds because when we opened fire one of our four guns jammed up with desert impurities and wouldn't fire. The following day we had orders to move out to cover the HQ of the Seventh Armoured divvy. Halfway through our packing up ready to move, the circus decided to come over again but this time they were not playing ball, they kept themselves at a sensible height; they were not going to be caught again. They need not have worried. We had only twelve rounds of ammo reserved for each gun and when they were expended we were dashing about unloading rounds from the lorries, parked ready to tow us off. By the time we were ready the enemy had unloaded in haste and gone home.

Until 23rd January we didn't do much in particular. We dodged about here and there covering the tank headquarters, an outfit we never saw, though one day their ever popular leader Jock Campbell came over to have a shufti at us and to see what made us tick. He looked a pretty scruffy character and would, no doubt, not have fitted in with our own site leader's idea of military smartness. When Campbell was asked where his tank units were he shook his head. He had no idea where they were. The last he heard of them they were hundreds of miles away somewhere around Benghazi. I believe he was later either killed or taken prisoner. Whichever it was we were upset about it at the time.

We heard plenty of tales about the Seventh Armoured. When we were outside Bardia they were cutting off Tobruk and when we were at Tobruk they were at Derna and beyond. They were said to be not too bothered about maps and were treating the campaign as a bit of a joke. It was said at one time a couple of their tanks stopped at the top of a rise and gazed down at too many enemy tanks but as they began a strategical withdrawal their concern turned to surprise. As soon as the Italians observed our lads at the top of the rise they promptly surrendered.

The only real danger to anyone at this time was from mines which had been scattered all over the place. We did see a few lorries cop it. One blew up on the horizon and another went up with a bang not far from our own moving outfit.

We never saw an enemy plane. There were a few of our bombers and some fighters — Gladiator biplanes and there was a spotter plane sitting over Tobruk aiding the guns, about which the Italians could do nothing. We usually stayed in one spot for twenty-four hours and then poodled off somewhere else. At each halt friends would get together to build a bivouac with pick and shovel out of the rocky desert. With blankets and groundsheets we could make ourselves snug enough even in the cold nights. Each dawn we stood to though nothing ever happened then. When we woke we would find the desert and our groundsheets covered with big white snails which vanished as the sun came up.

About this time mail arrived from Blighty, a very important item in our lives. I received two letters, one of which asked me when I was going on leave again and the letter indicated that they thought I was still defending London in London! They had not yet realised that defending London could mean shooting at Italian planes in Africa! The other letter from Kathleen O'Boyle was private. On one occasion I asked for a 1941 diary to be sent out to me. I received it in 1943. I also received a telegram which took months in coming. The telegram read, 'Listen to Sandy Sunday.' Quite a conundrum until we eventually worked out it meant a character on the radio, Sandy Macpherson, played music requests. I was supposed to listen to a request sent in by my mother for one of my favourite songs, 'The Lost Chord'. But the programme had most certainly gone on air the year before and in any case the nearest radio to us must have been in Cairo and that was in another country!

Smudger received a cracker of a parcel containing chocolates and sweets which we very carefully rationed out to make them last one hell of a time.

Food was of the plainest: corned beef and biscuits, the corned beef served up in many ways. We had it out of small tins and large tins, we had it stewed and fried, rolled and grilled, boiled and sanded and mucked about in all sorts of ways but it always remained bully beef though as someone pointed out, it couldn't have been all that bad, we beat the Germans on it. The biscuits were so designed as to favour the trade of dentistry. Anyone with false teeth certainly had problems unless he took to sucking the biscuits. Then one day came a brilliant, a staggering idea. Boiled rice! A bright idea, a change from bully, but on the day a snag arose. The chuck wagon rolled up as was its wont to within one hundred yards of the gunsite and halted. We hurried over to the wagon but it was difficult to find since a dirty great sand storm had blown up without being invited to the feast. Once a storm arrived it clogged everything, nose, eyes, mouth, got into hair, into vest and pants and prevented any gunnery or for that matter any enemy activity. On this occasion we went over to the wagon, held out our rectangular mess tins and received a dollop of boiled rice. One critic wanted to know if the black things in the rice were some sort of local minute currant only to be told how lucky he was to have meat with his rice – weevils. They were of little concern to us. The sand blowing out of the Sahara was. Indeed, by the time we had scrambled back to our various bivvies the rice had disappeared under a layer of sand. Fred pointed out as he stirred the sand into his rice, 'We could regard the sand as part of a ground nut scheme.' And so we stirred it all up and crunched our way through the unusual concoction. One thing I am able to report: we had no more boiled rice served up to us.

Water was severely rationed to one water bottle full every two days. The trouble was that all water had to be brought up from Soullam by tanker and that made life difficult. But to make matters worse, both our side and the Italians had salted the wells and on top of that the water was heavily chlorinated as if the man in charge had tipped a lorry load of lime into the wells instead of the statutory spoonful. So, drinking the ghastly stuff was not on but of course the same liquid was used for each brew up so that we were doing the impossible, drinking the undrinkable *chai*. We carefully rationed our water though I was lucky in that I still didn't need to shave. We used to give ourselves an all over wash in a shell nose capful of water, the cap being the size of a small cup.

It is interesting to note that it was general practice to keep oneself clean. No vermin trouble for us if we could help it. Sand fleas and bugs were hard to get rid of but lice were not to be tolerated at all. In fact I only ever came across lice once and we dealt with them with the speed of lightning.

The ration lorry came once a day with a few essential stores and some goodies. We were rationed to one packet of cigarettes, one bar of chocolate and one half pint of canned beer. The latter I used to hand over to Smudger; he considered I was completely round the twist in insisting on teetotal principles where good water was impossible to obtain. In the end my resolve weakened and I took to the daily booze and soon wondered why the devil I hadn't done so before.

Two of our number, having been brought up in polite society, went off in search of a lavatory and were gone three days, then were discovered in J Troop having tried to use facilities that were not only not on our site but not on J Troop site either. They were not listed as deserters or absent without leave, just regarded as being bloody balmy. After all there was a vast desert to urinate in without all that tramping about. It was during this time that we really came into contact with Mad Mac the colonel. We knew that he had a bee in his bonnet about AckAck guns. We were about to find out what the bee was.

He considered that a gun like the 3.7 could be used as a field piece and he was desperately anxious to prove how right he was. He must have impressed somebody because one morning he came dashing over to our gunsite bubbling over with his usual

Hingley, author and Mays cleaning 3.7 static with a piassava brush.

enthusiasm but more excited than usual. Incidentally his batman told us that all the dashing about in shorts early mornings was bull. He used to change out of battle dress before leaping out of the jeep.

His plan was to go ahead and act as a spotter for the guns which would be taken forward to a decent firing position and brought into action. Much to the disgust of the crew, the number four gun was chosen for the trial shoot. We speculated much on how it would fare since it was well known that the ever popular number one, Sergeant MacEwan, was somewhat deaf, being, for us, a bit on the elderly side. We of course, happily waved the chosen gun crew goodbye, congratulating them on having the honour of suffering in such a great cause.

At the end of the day the colonel came roaring back, bubbling over with excitement, assuring all and sundry that the shoot had exceeded his wildest dreams. We had visions of him being made a major general there and then on that very desert spot upon which he was standing or dancing. On the return of the gun and its crew there were numerous raised eyebrows, a few sneers and quite a number of ribald remarks. It seemed they had fired about a hundred rounds at an enemy pillbox and had actually knocked one corner of it off. Someone opined that if Jerry found out about our current shooting ability he might well take over the desert campaign himself and leave his ally to mess about with Somaliland. It must have been a costly exercise. We never heard any more about Mad Mac's idea.

It was about this time that Fitzy made his famous ride for our supper. It was in this wise. The circus put in an appearance one afternoon and just as we were in the middle of bashing away at him an awful cry came from the command post. It was Fitzy bawling through his megaphone for us to 'Cease Firing!' Somewhat astonished at such an order when the enemy was floating about in the sky, we waited in expectation. Then came an almighty shout from the man in the command post. 'Barry T, Barry T, bring the jeep, the jeep man, the jeep, the jeep.'

Barry T, no doubt somewhat alarmed at such a call at such a time, drove up to the command post and Fitzy, calling on his driver not to stop but keep going, leapt aboard and as he did so he yanked his pistol from its holster and called out in a fierce voice, 'After it, after it.' And away they went, racing madly across the desert until lost in the hazy distance.

'Now what was that all about?' someone asked. No one seemed to know. All we could see was the Eytie circus fooling about in the sky dropping bombs where they didn't seem to be doing any harm. Perhaps they too were puzzling over our intrepid leader shouting in triumph. 'We've got it, we've got it, we have got it!'

Got what?

They had rushed off in pursuit of a roebuck which our leader had shot with his revolver. That night we all had a splendid supper, dining on fresh roebuck, and our leader wasn't such a bad thing after all.

Fred and I spent much time discussing all sorts of topics. We would reflect upon what the war was all about and what we would do when we had finished off Jerry and his allies, for we had no doubts about winning the war. We British might be all kinds of things but one thing was sure, along with the Anzacs and the Gurkhas we made the best soldiers and Jerry was going to find out sooner or later how true that assertion was.

There were plenty of unpleasant things to consider apart from war itself. In Egypt we had noticed the very rich fleetingly and the majority poor a great deal. We had seen black-clothed old-looking mothers with babies in arms with big black flies crawling around the babies' eyes. We knew that meant trachoma. The Egyptian peasant would spend a lifetime of drudgery keeping a small plot of land watered by means of that ancient Archimedian screw. We hoped we were not fighting to preserve that way of life but that we would see a general improvement for everyone when this damned war was over.

Prior to the capture of Tobruk we found ourselves with plenty of time on our hands and one day some bright spark suggested we should get ourselves a bit of education, since our senior Sergeant Westcott had been a west country schoolteacher back in civvy street. To this suggestion he readily agreed. At the appointed time Fred and I, Fred West and Coxy with all the others, gathered around for the first lesson. Knowing what a bright lot we were, Westcott suggested we leave out such things as algebra and equations and concentrate our formidable minds on decimal arithmetic. But in a short space of time we were transferred to the fractions department of that newly created university of the desert. Soon though our teacher was shaking his head in sad dismay and he took us to the simple sum seminar. In the end he had us all saying our tables in chorus, not excluding twice one are two. I think he told us that in civvy street the authorities might well have doubts about letting us into an infants' school.

An ammunition dump had gone up in Tobruk and a great pall of smoke hung over the town. As soon as it fell we moved in toward Tobruk, crossing El Adem aerodrome with bomb stacks dotted around and with some burnt out aircraft. There were plenty of prisoners floating about. In fact they were all over the place, sometimes in small groups, sometimes in hundreds, often led by their own officers. British escorts seemed to be a bit thin on the ground.

There was a perfectly good tarmac road into the town. At dusk we pulled off it to wait for daylight before proceeding. It was too dangerous to move about in the dark with so many mines uncleared. There was also the possibility of the booby trap. It was not uncommon to discover innocent looking objects wired and the infantry claimed they had discovered corpses so wired.

Then we moved into Tobruk.

Chapter Eleven

Tobruk

There were plenty of shrapnel marks to be seen on most of the buildings which were flat roofed and white to the gaze. The harbour was small and seemed to be filled with sunken shipping. We passed a fine looking hospital though the native quarter looked somewhat dilapidated. The Italians seemed to have had no more regard for the native population than the British. I wondered, as I had wondered in Norway, whether the local population had said, 'A plague on both your houses.' We went through the town to a peninsula between the harbour and the sea. As we looked south the harbour was on our left; to the right, the sea. The town was out of sight but as we were soon to learn, very much there.

We dropped our guns into position on the peninsula where we had a far-reaching view and soon discovered we were there to stay as the town's defence. We decided it would be a nice change to settle for a bit especially in a place where it seemed the war was over!

No one took much notice of the fact that a couple of German Panzer divisions had landed at Tripoli. Tripoli was a thousand miles away. No one could conceive that such a small cloud could turn into a mighty whirlwind.

Having established we were now permanent, we set to under the enthusiastic leadership of Fitzy to make our site a worthy place to live in. We scrounged hundreds of Italian ammunition boxes but with less enthusiasm we filled them with parts of the local scenery lying about that sandy rock-strewn landscape. As it turned out it was a damned good job we built solid gunpit and command post walls. Without such defences we would not have lasted very long.

We assumed that over in J Troop they were doing the same thing. We assumed because none of us ever got over there to see for ourselves apart from possibly officers and don Rs. We also built a solid pit for Lewis and his Lewis gun and made a first aid post for that seemingly cold-blooded fish the medical orderly, who turned out to be as calm as any mill pond during enemy action. He was slow of speech, wore thick lensed glasses and though we called him the butcher, he was a comforting sort of customer. Incidentally we never saw Wardy again, even though he wasn't far away, until we returned to Blighty.

We in the number one crew built a hut along the seaward wall of our gunpit, where we could lounge in comparative comfort when having nothing to do. Then another idea germinated, based on the Fitzwilliams attitude toward hygiene. We were taken with the idea – a row of hygienic latrines. We were greatly helped in the construction business when we discovered an abandoned woodyard in the town which we ransacked for our building projects. The latrines rose as a majestic row of half doored cubicles, the end one for use of officers but which from the off Fitzy considered to be his own private domain. On the official opening day, someone found a length of white tape which was run across the row of latrines and a pair of scissors were produced for the occasion. It always amazed me the way in which things turned up for special events such as that one. Then with due solemnity the Master appeared and after a short speech, with much puffing out of cheeks he cut the tape and declared the vital offices open. We then insisted that he should do the honours and be the first to experience the delights of our up-to-date building programme. This he did and we received a running appraisal of the delights of modern plumbing. The new lavatories did help to keep at bay those ghastly Middle East flies which seemed to be capable of dive bombing attacks on human beings, but they also presented a problem for all of us when on latrine cleaning fatigue. The method of transport was to line the filled buckets up and run a long pole through the handles then, lifting the buckets away, we would go to the sea wherein to deposit the contents. The trouble was the roughness of the terrain between the gunsite and the sea. Both Fred and I would end up usually deluged with the contents of the buckets, no matter how carefully we trod. We developed the technique of walking gingerly down to the sea and then walking straight in up to our necks, thus cleansing the buckets and ourselves at the same time. If we were clothed it didn't matter in the warmth of the desert though often enough we took our clothes off before the start of the exercise.

Italian hand grenades were not regarded as lethal but they could take off an arm or a leg or do other damage. Then one day while Fred and I were on the beach a couple of lorry loads of Aussies came careering along and as the first one shot past an Aussie yelled out, 'There ya are, Pommy, have a bang bang,' and the next instant an Eytie hand grenade was lobbed in our direction and went off bang. As the other lorry shot past over came another hand grenade and off it went with yet another bang. Fred and I didn't wait for a third; we took off into the sea as fast as our legs could carry us. It was the first experience we had of that disease of the Middle East known as being 'sun touched'. As the years went by it became more and more apparent that most of us were suffering from that particular complaint.

We pondered the question of allies and wondered whether the Australians had declared war on Pommy land since the Italians had turned out to be not worth bothering with.

It is possible that by this time in our adventures our leader had been promoted to maybe lieutenant, because a new character joined us in a junior capacity, who was rather plump, perhaps podgy is the word, and who seemed to want to be a lap dog to our Fitzy. We got the impression that he was over eager to please and therefore a bit of a pain in the neck. At any rate we assumed that Fitzy and Atkins must have got together to get him employed somewhere else, where he wouldn't get under their feet. They made him chief scrounging officer so that he spent much of his time away from the site.

One day he came tearing over to the command post in the

jeep shouting as he came, 'Mr Fitz, Mr Fitz, I've got it, I've got it.' The jeep crashed to a halt in front of a bunch of curious gunners.

'I've got it, I've got it. Come round the back and have a look, Mr Fitz.' We all moved round to the back of the jeep, really curious. After all, by this time we were all hardened scroungers. In the back of the jeep was curled the most enormous and certainly the thickest coil of rope we had ever seen. We immediately concluded that it was a bit of naval string but it looked long enough and thick enough to hold the *Queen Mary* in position no matter the size of the storm.

Out puffed those cheeks and out came the 'Humph Humph' and the enquiry as to what it was for. To which the little fat man thought it might come in useful. Useful, but for what? The nearest ship was away in the harbour and there were none on our gunsite. It wouldn't even help with a barrage balloon; the weight of the rope would prevent such a balloon taking off. So the rope was dumped and as far as I know it is still there, unless nomad camel herders have used it since for tethering their camels.

Meanwhile Fitzy continued his ruthless war against flies, fleas and toe jam. One of his weapons in this merciless war was the Flit gun. One daily chore, therefore, was for a man to take charge of the Flit gun, load it and keep it firing at every fly in sight. No fly was allowed time to settle. It must be attacked on sight, no messing.

My turn came and away I went with the official Flit gun, into our billet, into other folk's quarters, into the Lewis gun pit, into the first aid dugout to aggravate the butcher and then on to the command post, into which I stepped with the Flit gun at the ready.

'Ah ah,' says Fitzy, or words to that effect. 'The most important man in our society, the Flit gun operator.' Or he may have said, 'The man with the fly Terror weapon.' Whatever he did say, he made it perfectly clear that I was to proceed with the attack without interference from either TSM Atkins or himself.

'Blast away, blast away,' roared our leader. 'Blast away.' And at that point a big fly, as if in pure devilment, landed squarely on the nose of that very neat and soldierly figure, TSM Atkins. I halted in mid pump and looked at Fitzy who allowed a broad grin to appear on his heavily moustached face. He noted my dilemma but roared with the greatest enthusiasm, 'Attack, attack the enemy on all fronts and no quarter.' Or words to that effect. With that encouragement ringing in my ears I let the fly on Atkin's nose get a full blast from a mighty carronading and it, the nose, disappeared behind a wall of disinfecting mist. I did not find out what happened to the fly. I could see that the sergeant major didn't like it 'for giving a kind of a roar ...' but he checked himself and smiled somewhat bleakly at the command post in general and even more bleakly at me.

Fitzy was delighted that one of his gunners had such an accurate aim and he was sure that the fly was dead. Atkins followed me outside and muttered something about he would see me later. Me, I beat it back to the safety of our gunpit.

The Italians had left behind them plenty of food including canned macaroni, stews and above all tuna fish. There were also canned tomatoes but it was the tuna fish which we had the most of. We found ourselves with so much of that damned tuna fish with its firm flesh and oily taste that I have never been able to face the stuff since. It was infinitely worse than good old horrible corned beef which I might nibble at today if there was nothing else around.

Drink had of course been a problem in the desert but it ended with the capture of Tobruk because the Eyties left behind them an enormous supply of Vichy water which we likened to soda water. So, from the time of its capture until it ran out, if it did run out, we were supplied with tea made with Vichy water. Sometimes it was used on its own and a good time was had by all – yuk!

The other commodity our friends the enemy left behind was tobacco, cigarettes and cigars. The officer issue was just about smokable but for the rest – yuk! The lower rank cigarette tobacco was so coarse, the contents so dry that the stuff would drop out of the papers almost at a touch. The cheroots looked like little twisted adders and that was what they tasted like. In fact we considered we were facing much more certain death when choking on those things than when facing their original owners. The signs of our danger were everywhere, the growing sounds of coughing.

However we soon found a use for them. We would stack the cigarettes and cigars into piles and play cards with them as stakes in the sure knowledge that everyone played desperately to lose.

The other bit of smoking history concerns King Farouk of Egypt, who, we were given to understand, was a German sympathiser and who, in our view, demonstrated his sympathy by sending up to every man in the Bluey a packet of gold-tipped Egyptian cigarettes to commemorate our glorious victory in the desert and for liberating his country. I never met any one of those hard bitten smokers who could take more than a couple of puffs at a gold-tipped Egyptian cigarette.

About a week later the ration lorry rolled up with boxes and boxes of gold-tipped Egyptian cigarettes. Hundreds of packets

Presumably Jerry 88.

were handed over to us card-playing and somewhat reckless gamblers. There seemed nothing else that could be done with them. Unless of course they could be handed over to the Italian prisoners who might possibly be able to handle them. This idea was probably turned down because it contravened the Geneva convention, and the Eyties were saved.

Farouk's star waned even further. Why the devil hadn't he plucked up courage and bought us a few packets of Players?

For a few weeks we had narry a sight of an enemy plane. Our forces took Bomba, Derna, Benghazi, sweeping westward. The forward troops were so far away they might as well have been cavorting on the moon as far as we were concerned. In fact one of our number, Sandham, got so browned off he applied for a transfer and got one to a bomb disposal squad. Later some of our blokes saw Sandy sitting over a hole in a Tobruk street with his legs dangling down into it. The conversation went something like this;

'Watcha, Sandy.'

'Watcha.'

'What's the idea sitting over that hole?'

'Keeping an eye on my mate.'

'Whereabouts is he?'

'Down the hole, where d'you think?'

Sandy carelessly swung his legs to and fro. He smiled his well-known dreamy smile.

'What's he doing down the hole?'

'Defusing a bomb.'

He was still smiling happily as the rest hurriedly drew back to a safe distance. After all, it had been Sandy who had been involved with a bomb in Norway. Someone said, 'Y'know I reckon Sandy's bloody nuts,' and they all moved on.

One day we received the information that our forces had evacuated Benghazi but not to worry: this was a traditional strategical withdrawal and all would be well. We then learned we were withdrawing faster and faster, luring the enemy into the usual well laid trap. We on our gunsite were not so sure.

In fact we were becoming somewhat apprehensive at the thought that the war was not leaving us behind. It was coming towards us. Hallelujah!

> The one five three in the firing line,
> The one five one behind 'em
> But when they looked for the one five two
> Buggered if they could find 'em.

Up till then we had heard a few mines explode, a couple of ships had gone down in the harbour and the only dead body we had seen had been that of an Italian bobbing up and down on the seashore, with bloated body, eyeless and with a face eaten away. He had been shot behind the ear.

Then, one evening, when most of us, including the plane spotters, were standing around admiring the beautiful evening, just before stand-to, someone pointed to three aircraft flying low from the East. We noticed little fairy lights racing landwards from the aircraft. Someone remarked how pretty they were. Another character, possibly a bit brighter, thought they might be tracer bullets. But objections were raised on two counts: one, Jerry was nowhere near us, two, he was in the west, so how could he fly from the east? In any case weren't those planes Blenheims? Then someone followed the Blenheim idea through with the reasonable theory that there were three of ours playing about!

In fact it had been Jerry shooting up the harbour. He had come and gone without too much notice being taken of him. Certainly the AckAck defences did the gentlemanly thing and practically ignored the fellow.

A few nights later came the first air attack.

It was dusk when they came in, low and swiftly, like angry bees, and began dropping their muck all round us. He started something that night that was to continue for a long time – months – ten and a half months of everlasting battle.

We all stood to an hour each side of dawn and dusk. The dawn was never disturbed and we concluded that the enemy liked his early morning lie in and breakfast in bed. The dusk stand-to was always to be a busy one. But that first heavy night raid was the one to be remembered, vividly, for a long time and even now, after so many years, the memory of it has hardly faded.

Instruments at night were not much good and the usual method of working, developed early on, was to send up a box barrage and hope those bandits were caught in the middle of it all. The traverser would traverse, the elevator elevate, the fuse setter would be poised to fuse the first round in and the loaders would be holding rounds at the ready. Fused, into the tray would go the round, over would slam the tray, the rammer ram the round home, the breech would slam shut as the tray was yanked back. The number five would bang down the firing lever and crash would go the gun.

The loading tray had been introduced to speed the action up and in theory at any rate, do away with trouble when ramming home by hand. It was also designed to prevent a round from falling back out of the breech, although I did experience a number of rounds falling out of the breech when the tray operator was a bit too quick for the sliding breech to close. Fortunately on those occasions nothing happened. The round, happily, fell to the ground without the striking pin being touched.

On our first night shoot I happened to be the number two loader which meant I followed immediately after the first round was on its way. I had to put the nose of the round into the fuse setter so that the correct fuse could be set on the fuse ring and then I had to withdraw the round and roll it into the loading tray. Now, in all our everlasting gun drills no one had ever thought about gun flashes at night. We had had some exercises but no night firing and in any case during peacetime it would have been unthinkable to disturb the civilian neighbours. On that first night shoot in action the gun went off with a crash, there came a blinding flash and I, going in with the second round, was momentarily blinded. I wobbled about in the dark for a bit trying to find the fuse setter, being urged by all and sundry to '– hurry up' and 'What's up, dodger, can't you find the – hole?' or 'Hey Dodger, the bloody gun's over here.'

Eventually I got the thing right and we continued with our firing with an occasional round missing the fuse setter and thus being sent heavenwards unfused with results to be related later.

At this stage of the proceedings, while we were dicing with death, things were taking place beyond the confines of Tobruk which were to affect our lives for some time to come. Our army, carrying on normally, heroically and efficiently, had been busily strategically withdrawing eastwards with Rommel's Panzer divisions happily harrying from behind. The general opinion was that a great mistake had been made in withdrawing the seventh armoured from the Bluey and replacing it with the second armoured, which, we understood, had been equipped in large part with captured Eytie armoured vehicles. No doubt the second had done its best but it had been no match for the Panzers with their tiger tanks and 88 millimetre guns stuck on them. So that it was a sigh of relief that we heard the Seventh was racing up from the delta to deal with that idiot Rommel.

We were all playing cards in our recently built luxury hotel type bivvy when someone said, 'Just a minute, listen.'

We listened for a while and then someone said, 'Sounds like thunder.'

'Never heard of thunder round these parts before,' someone thoughtfully put in.

'That's not thunder.'

'No?'

'No, that's bloody gunfire.'

We listened, noting that minute by minute the sound was creeping nearer and nearer, coming from Bomba in the west. Then someone, I think it was Smudger, started to grumble about too much attention being paid to noises off and not enough to the game in hand. So we returned our attention to the cards though cocking ears in the direction from which the sounds were coming and all the time those sounds were creeping nearer and nearer.

Later, we took ourselves outside for a shufti and listen as the noise of the tank battle drew nearer and nearer. We were all of the opinion that when the Seventh Armoured arrived the noise of the battle would soon begin to roll west again. But it didn't.

Then one of our don R's came tearing up and leapt off his bike in great excitement.

'What's up, tosh?' someone asked, 'What's the news from HQ?'

'HQ,' he said, 'I couldn't get to it.'

'You couldn't what?' Surely he was drunk on some form of tarted up Vichy water. 'Listen, I got just out of town on the Bomba road and got stopped dead in my tracks. Strung across the road was a field battery and they were kneeling with rounds in their hands. Someone wanted to know where I thought I was going and I said, 'To our HQ,' and he said, 'Well you're going in the wrong direction, mate, there's nothing out there between us and Jerry.' So I skiddaddled back here. Jesus!' Though no one could quite figure out what the latter had to do with the situation.

And now the sound of gunfire was very near, in fact it was more or less parallel with us. Then came the order, 'Troop will be ready to move in half an hour.' We didn't need telling why and in fact we were ready to move in ten minutes, gun pit entrances widened, guns limbered up, tin hats on bonces and Hey ho! for the Nile Delta. But as we were doing all this the sound of the duffy was moving rapidly eastward. In consequence of that the next order was, 'As you were.' We were to put the guns back in position. We weren't pulling out after all. Jerry had unsportingly cut us off and we had no way of getting off our peninsula, let alone out of the town. The only people liable to take leave of absence would be able bodied swimmers. It was a long way to Alex. I couldn't swim so I would have to stay. So we set to, and tidy the gunsite was the next objective. Meanwhile the noise of the tank battle faded eastward and in due course came silence. Jerry and the Seventh Armoured had taken their battle eastward to the Egyptian border. The Tobruk garrison was the only bit of the Allied army left in Libya.

Having finished our chores, had our stand-to and eaten some Italian food, we got the cards out.

It was at this point that the right note was struck. By common consent we agreed that Jerry might have the whole of Libya but we had Tobruk. He was going to have to be satisfied with his share of the loot and no matter what he did he wasn't going to get any of our bit. And so it turned out in the end.

From that point on our officer in charge of scrounging must have come into his own, because as the siege unfolded our gunsite bristled more and more with all sorts of weapons, Bredas, Spandau, Brens, Lewis guns and I doubt if anyone would have been at all surprised if some bod had turned up with Greek fire. This sort of light weapon cover soon showed itself to be absolutely vital. Jerry announced he was coming in after the 'Rats of Tobruk' and as the battle developed it became clear that his aim was to knock out the defences, the air defences, so that he could send in paratroops.

All around us were Bofors guns, the crews of which we came to admire a great deal. They quickly developed techniques which we, with our heavy guns, could not emulate.

Jerry was never far away after the town was surrounded. For a short while Hurricanes operated from El Adem and then when we lost that they used the escarpment on the other side of the harbour. We used to watch them take off and land and they did their job with great zeal and with our whole-hearted support until Jerry forced them to abandon the site. From then on the Germans controlled the sky over Tobruk. Once the Hurricanes had been forced away the dive bombers could operate and it was with them that the Bofors crews developed a pretty effective technique.

With the Hurricanes gone and the Luftwaffe only two minutes flying time away we were in for one hell of a time and the Stuka dive bombers were just the kiddies to indulge us. They would swarm over us, peel off and dive for us with their screamers going full blast in an endeavour to frighten the living daylights out of us. No doubt they did but that everlasting gun drill now

Bofors light AckAck.

proved its worth for we could work the guns without too much thought as to what Jerry was up to.

Down they would come screaming, some peeling off to attack J Troop, the others hell bent to give us what for and as he came down more or less vertically the Bofors would hold their fire until one of the nasty creatures flattened out to drop his load of egg fruit. At that point he was vulnerable and a sitting duck; the guns could bring him down. It must have taken a good deal of cool nerve to stand waiting as a deadly Stuka came directly at you but stand and wait they did.

The night tactic was a shade different. To start with it involved searchlights. Now when they first appeared we played merry hell about them. In fact we wanted them out of it, considering them to be positively dangerous and indeed on the side of the enemy. When they switched on and started searching for the attackers they really lit up our gunsite so effectively, so we thought, that Jerry could not possibly miss us. The last thing we wanted was for him to see us silhouetted amid all that electric light. But they too earned our praise as they became more and more effective.

Over would come the Stukas, on would go the beams and a beam would catch a bandit and follow him down. The trick was to hold the beam on him until he flattened out and then Bingo! Switch off the light and into the deck he would go, blinded by the sudden darkness. The trouble was that Jerry would counter by firing his guns at the light as he came down and that wasn't very funny.

The pace of proceedings rapidly increased until life became pretty hectic. All sorts of things happened which cannot be set down in any sort of order. It is not possible to sort out anything from such a frantic blur.

An early casualty was our number one gun living quarters built so lovingly with ammo boxes and timber. We knew of course that we had to avoid shooting at a low angle over the roof but in the excitement of trying to hit planes diving all over the place it was difficult to do so. Jerry of course didn't help. He seemed positively to enjoy low angle flights so that in consequence we blew our abode over. We rebuilt it when possible several times but it always got the Jerry building treatment until eventually we had to give up and live like tramps. But the greatest tragedy, and the one which must have broken Fitzy's heart, was when we blasted his pride and joy, the latrines, to kingdom come because that idiot Jerry flew too near the horizon.

Our time was fully occupied day and night. We would stand to each dawn, shivering in the cold, but he never came then. He got into the habit of attacking us at breakfast time and it seemed to us that each time we changed breakfast time he got to know about it and would nip in while we were about to have it. We began to suspect that he had a breakfast-hating spy planted among us. We didn't think it funny having to go on firing maybe for a couple of hours or so when we had been forced to miss our breakfast.

The firing could continue for hours, and the hot shell cases would pile up round the base of the guns; we would have to kick them out of the way and heave 'em with our ammo gloved hands out of the pits. Thus we found out why we had those heavy ammo boots and we appreciated them. A gunpit was not a place for delicately shod feet. Maybe there would be a lull while Jerry had his elevenses, then over he would come again until possibly tiffin time, then a lull until the time for the afternoon bout. Our nights were pretty well occupied too. The difference then was that we didn't have to think about tea breaks.

During the daytime raids the sky would be almost blotted out with bursting shells and exploding bombs. The noise is quite impossible to describe. The most remarkable thing about all those weeks and months was that no one was wounded or killed except me and of course I wasn't killed. Certainly the terrain helped in that respect. There were no flying bricks and concrete slabs and glass flying about but just the muck from the desert. The desert could be helpful. When a sandstorm blew up we could relax for a bit, He wouldn't be chancing his arm in a sandstorm. We did have cause for alarm on one sandstorming occasion when out of the yellow thick, stifling haze, a German army spotter plane appeared. This usually meant the German army wasn't far away and we wondered if the idiot had broken through the perimeter defences. As it happened nothing followed and we assumed the pilot had got lost.

One night we could hear a plane buzzing about overhead and the box barrage was duly delivered. A little later the pilot broke the silence to ask what the hell was going on since he was on our side and would we kindly stop messing about. When asked to give the recognition signal for the night he said he couldn't remember it, so he was told that that was his hard luck and we carried on with the box barrage. The which tale brings us back to the question of those rounds banged off, fused at safe.

An AckAck shell will burst at the position in the sky set on the fuse by the fuse setter. If the round was sent up unfused, that is at zero safe, then it would not explode until it hit the deck. Thus it was essential to send the rounds up properly fused.

As explained above, we did have trouble on our first night shoot in finding the fuse setter, at least I did, so that one or two went off in the wrong manner. Then we got into the habit of by-passing the fuse setter if the flash blinded the leading loader. In other words we got a bit sloppy. Then one night the phone on the command post rang and the following conversation took place.

'Yes?'

'Is that I Troop?'

'Of course it is, who else could it be?'

'Well now, can you tell us how far Jerry is supposed to be from us?'

A bit of head scratching and thoughtful command post calculation and the reply:

'We think about nine miles away as the crow flies.'

'Then he's not within shelling distance?'

'Hardly, why?'

'WHY? Because if the enemy isn't somebody bloody well is.'

We supposed our telephonist gave some noncommittal answer and then hung up. Meanwhile we continued to blast away. A little later someone yelled, 'Listen. That wasn't a bomb going off.'

We listened, the other three gun crews listened, the command post listened and sure enough we heard several distinct whines of approaching shells.

Someone swore an oath. 'Christ, Jerry must have broken through after all.'

One or two shell bursts came very close indeed and caused our command post to communicate with J Troop command post with all possible speed.

'Someone,' J Troop was informed, 'is shelling us.'

'We know.'

'You know?'

'Yes we do and when some bloody idiot stops shelling us we'll do likewise.'

No more unfused rounds went up after that.

Meanwhile as already indicated a mighty army of weapons had been built up around us so that the site absolutely bristled away with them and they barked and rattled and kept low flying aircraft away from us. It was site policy to keep Jerry out. We didn't care where else he went as long as he didn't drop anything on us. He never did succeed in putting a gun out of action though time and time again he went close. As I have mentioned before, the one on number four gun was the ever popular Sergeant Macwilliams. He was never rattled by the noise, flying splinters and bits of desert but remained always calm though we knew that this condition was helped by his deafness. One day we were banging away with great gusto until Jerry sheered of for a meal or something and the command post megaphone bawled 'CEASE FIRE' and the number four gun went bang.

'Cease firing,' from the megaphone and bang went the number four gun.

'Sergeant Mac, cease firing,' and off bang went the gun again.

By this time we all thought that Fitzy must be doing a jig up and down the command post and then his voice came roaring through that megaphone, 'NUMBER FOUR GUN STOP BLOODY WELL FIRING,' and again the gun went off.

Someone must have told the sergeant that everyone else had stopped firing and that he was wanted by the command post because the firing did stop and in reply to a further shout from the command post sergeant Williams called out, 'What?'

When the Panzers did break through the perimeter defences and were said to be approaching our site through the town and were to be expected at any minute, Mac was put in charge of our anti-tank defences. He was handed a Boyes anti-tank rifle and told to place himself in a strategical position so that he could keep any advancing Panzer division at bay. He calmly picked up the rifle and walked off. We wondered if it had been the right choice since, as he was deaf, he might not be able to hear the clanking approach of tanks.

However, his services were never needed; the hole in the perimeter was sealed off. The Aussies and other Allied troops were never going to let Jerry through. The general opinion was, 'Bugger Jerry. He's not as good as us anyway. He can stay out.' An enemy plane came down doing a pancake landing not so far from us and then we watched as a load of infantry started running to the plane with weapons at the ready. One got the impression that they, the infantry, were bent on doing the pilot a mischief. Fitzy called for Barry T and the jeep and away raced our leader, waving his pistol around in an authoritative manner, bent on seeing fair play. In this he succeeded and the pilot was taken prisoner.

It was this very same leader who made himself famous with his personal attack on the Luftwaffe. One day when some Heinkels were flying over us and well out of reach of the 3.7s, he yanked out his pistol and blazing away at the aircraft yelled, 'I'll get you, I'll get you,' or words to that effect. I suppose it was another case of that sun-touched business that became common with us in the Middle East.

Gun barrels became a problem.

In peacetime gun-barrel bores were supposed to last around five hundred rounds before being changed. Immediately when war broke out that figure was doubled and then of course in a place like Tobruk the number was far exceeded. In fact it was pretty nigh impossible to strip a gun down and change a barrel at the height of the siege. Then again barrels were in short supply. We did have one turn up which was left lying on the ground all the time I was there, simply because there was no time in which to change a barrel. In consequence our range got shorter and shorter and the Heinschel spotting plane came lower and lower. All the pilot had to do was sit just above our ceiling and chat to his mates at base.

No doubt many people have seen the Charlie Chaplin film in which a large shell flops out of the muzzle of a big gun and falls only a few yards away. This is what began to happen to our guns as the siege progressed. They were beginning to flop out of the muzzles before I left and after I had gone one barrel split like a peeled banana. Fortunately and surprisingly no one was injured or killed. I never found out how the barrel changing was managed but of course it did happen.

We had a Sergeant Head who upon seeing an ammo lorry ablaze sprang aboard and heaved the boxes clear. For this he received the MM. In regard to medals I was given to understand that a number of medals were awarded to the unit and they all went into a hat. After all, when a bunch of characters are holed up as we were, how can anyone be selected for special mention or medals?

We were there in Tobruk, of course, as the air defence of the town and harbour which none of us ever wanted to visit. The gunsites in the early stages at least were the prime targets but the town and harbour got the hammering. We didn't. At least with a gun we could hit back but those poor blighters down there had to just sit and take it. There were wrecked ships in the harbour and one, partly submerged, was used as a gun platform. I think it was the destroyer *Daisy* which had hit a mine and sunk in two minutes. We could see the fire and hear the shouting though we were unable to see the ship itself. Each hospital ship which arrived either got damaged or ran aground and in the end they were withdrawn and the wounded were taken out on destroyers.

There were two hospitals in town, one a general, the other a field hospital. One day six Stukas came over, peeled off into sets of three, and then each group proceeded to bomb one of the two hospitals, causing casualties. Naturally we were outraged, through a rumour got around that some bright spark had placed an ordnance depot between the two hospitals and that was what Jerry was after. On top of that it was said he was accusing us of bringing non-medical supplies on the hospital ships. Another report circulated that much earlier, before the siege began, some of our squaddies had brought in a bunch of prisoners who had been handed over to an Aussie escort to take east. The Aussies, so the story ran, returned a bit too quickly and when tackled about it merely shrugged.

The siege was to last ten and a half months until a relieving force broke through and met a defending force breaking out. Long before that, however, I had left the place. I left after being wounded on Easter Monday. As far as I know I was the only one to cop anything in my unit.

We had had a hell of a night, more or less at it all the way through. I have a vivid memory of dusk and the alarm sounding, the sirens and our cracked bugle. By that time the offensive had been built up and there were far more planes coming over than in the early days. I remember clearly the command post megaphone announcing a large number of hostiles approaching. Then fifty were announced, then seventy, then eighty, a hundred, and a hundred plus and then the megaphone gave up. We just had time to shake hands all round, considering that this raid must be our lot. Then they were there all over the bloody place. The sky in darkening dusk was full of diving planes, gun bursts, tracer bullets and bursting bombs and the noise was stupendous. Gunnery theory had gone out of the window long ago. Instruments were of no use at night and equally useless in daylight with Jerry dancing about all over the sky. Those German pilots never intended to oblige us by adopting the constant height, constant speed and constant direction theory. With all their diving about it was impossible to train instruments upon them. So we adopted gun control in which a gun covered a section of the sky and then once the plane was in the gun site, we would follow it and hope to hit it, with the gun number one calling what he thought would be the right fuse. We may not have brought many planes down but we certainly kept them away from us.

A common enough situation would develop as our gun lined up on a diving plane. A shot might be fired and then someone might yell, 'Look behind you, guv'nor,' as another plane came roaring in from behind, so that the gun would be swung or more or less flung round to meet the new menace and so it would go on for hour after hour until Jerry got browned off and jiggered off. Or maybe he ran out of ammo. The Italian pilots had kept at a respectable distance but not that damned fool Jerry. He became positively reckless. But we kept beating him off.

Tobruk

On Easter Monday we had had a busy night, had had our dawn stand to, had just stood down ready for breakfast when he came again and we hadn't even had time to take our overcoats off, let alone have breakfast. But in a way it was a blessing because it had been a particularly cold night and the renewed action warmed everyone up until the sun appeared.

Well there it was, Jerry buzzing about, us banging away, the bombs bursting and the light guns rattling, sand spilling up everywhere and of course all the time most of us, though busy, had that gut feeling of getting nastily damaged. Then one bomb came down too close to our parapet wall for comfort. Up went a great pall of smoke mingled with sand and rock and bits of old iron.

Now that morning I was operating the fuse setter which entailed a good deal of right arm work. During a slight pause I felt my arm getting stiff and then as we renewed operations it got stiffer and stiffer. Then came another lull and I had time to have a shufti at what was happening to my arm. There it was, as plain as a pike staff, a rent in my right overcoat sleeve. No question about it, I had copped something. And soon I was unable to operate the setter handle.

It didn't take long for the word to get round. Our first casualty. Dodger had been hit! What was more the Dodger could no longer operate the gun. He would have to go over to the Butcher in his cubby hole, for a field dressing and perhaps a comforting cuddle.

The first aid man with the thick lensed glasses and mournful mien was only too happy to have a customer. First thing he proposed was to cut my overcoat sleeve away. Ruin my beautiful bum freezer! No way. I got my coat off without the help of his coat-removing implements. He dressed the wound which turned out to be a fair old gash and gave it as his opinion that I would have to go in to the field hospital. To which I replied in my best cowardly manner that I would sooner die first to which he replied that if that was my wish it was no problem since all I had to do was to stand out in the open for a few minutes.

When Jerry turned up again that man went calmly about his work, very happy with his non-paying customer and quite unperturbed by all the racket going on around him. I have forgotten his name. I wish I could remember it.

When he had finished dressing the wound the Bombardier Butcher said I had better stay with him since I was useless on a gun in my state of health, to which I replied that he might feel snug in his little billet but to me it seemed like a death trap and I was about to move out.

'Where the devil d'you think you're going?'

I took a shufti round and indicated the Lewis gun pit where gunner Lewis and his mates held sway.

'In there.'

'What, in there?'

'Yeah, in there.' I said I thought it was much safer than where I then was.

'You can't go in there.'

'Why not?'

We were now bawling our heads off to be heard above the racket.

'The place is full up already. It's crawling with cooks and vehicle drivers not to mention a don R or two.'

Full up or not there was going to have to be room for one more bod and that was me. When the next lull came I nipped out of the dugout and hopped over to the Lewis gun pit where I fell over a number of recumbent figures sheltering from the storm outside. Having nothing to do in particular they were trying to mind their own business.

Lewis was a cheerful character and full of welcome.

'What d'you want, Dodger? We ain't got an inch of space to let, you can see it's all taken up.'

'I haven't come for a doss down, Lewis, I've come to give a helping hand.'

'Helping hand! What the hell's the good of you with one flipper in a sling?'

But I was determined to give them my help. It was a selfish

idea, I wanted to keep my mind off what was going on outside the pit.

'Well now,' I said, 'Up till now my left hand has been pretty useless. I wasn't able to pick up a mug till quite recently. Must have been some trouble when I was a kid.'

Lewis looked intrigued, so did his mate or at least I thought they did.

Lewis cocked his head at me and then at his mate. 'You'd better nip over to the command post, Harry, and ask them to tell Jerry to hang on a bit, Dodger's about to tell us his life story.'

Funny man, I thought. I explained that if I kept active it would stop my arm from getting any stiffer but if that was no good I could exercise my left hand and force it to work. So I wanted to have a go.

'Have a go at what?'

'Loading the Lewis gun pans.'

Lewis was not impressed. He didn't think that one of those heavy gunners had the finesse for helping out with his Lewis gun, besides he'd got a mate, hadn't he? I pointed out that I had no intention of butting in and spoiling beautiful team work but if his mate loaded the pans with live ammo I could shove in the tracer and thus speed things up a bit. Lewis expressed his doubts but eventually agreed so we started in on the new plan and when Jerry turned up we found that it worked pretty well. Lewis was able to fire away shouting and laughing and threatening the enemy, though as will soon be revealed, the Germans didn't think much of Lewis the Lewis gunner.

During one bout of fierce activity an aircraft which had swept in had dropped his load and then came right across the site at no more than roof top height. He was an absolute sitting duck flying very low, at a constant height, constant speed and would we believe it a constant direction! Had the pilot gone dotty? Or was the pilot contemptuous of the opposition?

Lewis was furious and made his feelings plain, shouting, 'I'll get you, you –, so help me you son of a bitch, I'll – get you.'

As that pilot flew leisurely by he turned his face in our direction and putting his thumb to his nose, waggled his fingers at Lewis. Lewis was so flabbergasted he stopped firing and all of us crouching in the pit, commented on the confounded cheek of that damned Jerry basket.

Then came another lull and at once we noted that the number one gun was silent. There was no sign of life. Was the crew in trouble? We yelled to them but there was no answer. Were they all dead? Had our luck run out at last?

We called again, 'Number one gun, are you all right?'

After a while a tin hat appeared above the parapet wall followed by another and another until our anxiety was allayed. We counted the full number.

Lewis' mate called out to say how pleased we were that they were all safe and of sound mind. Then a voice called out, 'We are all right but no thanks to you lousy lot.'

'Why, what's up?'

'The next time you fire that bloody gun of yours turn it on the bloody enemy not us. We are supposed to be on your side, Lewis, or didn't you know?'

From then on when anything flew very low Lewis would stop firing and content himself with posturing at the enemy with his fingers, giving an unusual type of Victory V sign.

Our butcher with the big pebble glasses didn't like the look of my arm.

He said, 'Everything up here turns septic y'know ...'

Yes I did know and I didn't like the thought either.

'It means the hospital sooner or later. Best to go now.'

'What, into Tobruk?'

'Get it stitched up. Yes. Better go now.'

'I'll go tomorrow.'

'No, now.'

So I was driven into the town trembling with fear. Everyone was worried. Fitzy was very concerned indeed. He didn't like the idea of one of his gunners being incarcerated in that hell hole.

I was seen to by a naval surgeon and all the time he was sewing my arm up I could look out onto the harbour. That was enough to put the wind up a fit man, let alone one that was unfit.

The surgeon gave me a glass of brandy and suggested I turn my head away. I may have sounded brave to him but as far as I was concerned it would be much more nerve-wracking looking out into that harbour with all its wreckage than watching him with his needle and thread. Besides, as I pointed out, it was my arm and I wanted to know what was going on.

He had just started sewing when there came the sound of a thump as if something heavy had fallen somewhere in the room. The surgeon said, 'What the devil was that?'

I said, peering round, 'It's the driver, he's passed out. I think he wants some brandy.'

The surgeon looked grim. 'The brandy is for patients and staff [I'm sure he added staff]. No one else. I'll soon fix him.'

He stopped work on my arm, picked up a bucket half full of water and threw the water over the prostrate figure of the driver. The latter swiftly recovered.

We returned to the gunsite without incident, where I continued in my elected job as tracer bullet loader but each time the Butcher saw my arm he would sorrowfully shake his head and mutter, 'It's going, yes it is, it's going all right.' To which I would make the obvious enquiry as to the meaning of 'going'. He would smile grimly and murmur, 'Septic. Everything round here turns septic.'

When the MO turned up and took a shufti at the arm he frowned, looked unhappy and said, 'Septic.' But he added an even more unpleasant word, 'Hospital.' That meant Tobruk where the enemy bombed hospitals. I wasn't happy. No one was happy. Fitzy was very unhappy at the idea of a Tobruk hospital for one of his gunners. He huffed and puffed and went, 'Humph Humph.'

But in the end I had to go and ended up in the general hospital, where I was informed that along with most of the occupants, who were mostly Aussies, I would be evacuated to Alex on the next hospital ship!

My period of fear now truly began. I wasn't the only one, all the others were afraid as well. This was because every night and day for weeks the town had been blitzed. There hadn't been much let up during that time. So we sat on our beds nervously smoking, swearing and eating – young men always eat.

The day passed and no raiders came and the night passed and no raiders came. The hospital ship was reported to be in the harbour and we were to be ready to move. We clambered into old Eytie buses; the stretcher cases were manhandled in by the hobbling and those with damaged flippers. We moved through the town, tension growing all the time. Still no air raid. It was but a short ride to the harbour though it seemed like ten thousand miles to all of us. We got out of the lorries and were shocked and dismayed to see such a huge hospital ship in such a small harbour! No wonder such ships had been hit and beached. They could hardly be missed, even by a pebble spectacle wearing German pilot.

We were all rapidly turning into nervous wrecks. And where the devil was Jerry all this time? Such absence was unheard of.

On the dockside we noticed what appeared to be a huge cave which seemed a very handy place to be in and we all instinctively moved towards it. But we were called back. We were destined for that huge monster of a boat blocking out the view of most of the harbour water. We were cajoled into ship's boats and the reasonably fit were told to row them over to the ship. This was duly done. We all somehow or other clambered aboard and discovered the place was out of this world, clean white sheets, comfortable beds, decent meals and very considerate and attentive hospital ship staff. Both these and the crew were Indian and we appreciated all of them. After all, it was a big ship in a little harbour and they went about their business without means of defending themselves. But we, the cause of them being there, were not at all calm and far from happy. Dusk began to fall and still there was no raid and He hadn't missed a dusk for weeks, apart from the night before. But nothing happened.

Then those damned fool Indians turned on all the lights on

the ship! We were lit up like Blackpool or Southend at the height of the summer season! We set up a howl of protest. 'Put those bloody lights out.' The Aussies were particularly vocal. After all, they had got in the habit of crawling about in the front line in the pitch darkness. Light was deadly.

The lights remained on. According to the Geneva Convention hospital ships must be clearly marked and lit up at night.

But what about the rumour that Jerry accused us of carrying war material in our hospital ships?

No one slept that night. At least none of the sick or wounded did. We had a quiet night and dawn broke slowly, oh so very slowly, and still he didn't come. Did he know that Gunner Green was on board?

We began slipping out of the harbour slowly, silently, like a huge ghostly whale, a target no one could miss. We cleared the harbour and it dropped from sight and no bombers came. What I did not know at the time and what possibly Jerry did was that the lads on our gunsite insisted on manning the guns whilst Dodger was in the harbour. At least that's what I was told when I met up with them again in Palestine. So I left Tobruk with instructions from Smudger Smith to send him up some sweets.

There were a number of different nationals on the ship including a bunch of Gurkhas, the only non pink skin soldiers allowed into a British army canteen, and for good reason. They were really the number one soldiers. In discussing the merits and demerits of soldiering a Johnny Gurkha smilingly (they seemed to be always smiling) covered a half of one of his thumb nails with a finger. 'British soldier that much better than Gurkha.' I assured him that he needn't be so polite but he only smiled.

I was with a group of Aussies when we got chatting to a Gurkha, trying to get him to draw his *kukri*, the short stabbing knife they always carried, but he kept politely declining. Eventually the Gurkha explained that they only drew them to use on somebody but if one of the Aussies would care to let him nick the said Aussie somewhere and so draw blood, he would happily take his *kukri* out.

There were no takers. It wasn't, they explained to Johnny Gurkha, that they were afraid but they knew that in the local atmosphere even the teeny weeny cut turned septic. So the matter was dropped.

On that ship I found one Aussie who actually felt sorry for the Germans. He said he started feeling that way after an experience he had had with a Gurkha.

'I was out on the perimeter wire listening out,' he began, 'It was pitch dark and I couldn't see a damned thing. I kept myself strictly to myself and was scarcely breathing. I could hear Jerry talking ahead of me but I felt pretty secure, a part of the local landscape. Remember, it was pitch dark and no moon. Then as I lay there, minding my own damned business, a hand slid round my neck and fingers felt my collar badge. I had no means of identification on me apart from my identity disc. A voice, a mere bloody whisper, said "Aussie – good." The hand went and I heard no other sound. So I slid off back to our lines and got hold of our bloke and told him not to send me out there any bloody more."Don't try because I just won't go." What's more I never did. I used to lie awake at night wondering what would have happened if I hadn't had that shoulder badge on.'

We could understand his feelings especially as it was said that the Gurkhas, to prove that they had been busy, collected German ears. Some, it was said, had little bags of 'em.

On the boat I got yarning with an Aussie who was as usual broke and he asked for a loan of ten ackers which in my expansive manner I obliged him with. He said he wasn't sure whether or not he would be able to repay me at present but if I liked to call at his place any time he'd gladly cough up.

'Where d'you live?'

'Perth, cobber, Perth.'

I still haven't got that debt repaid after fifty years.

We arrived without incident at the port of Alex from which place I was taken to the fifteenth general hospital in Cairo. Just beyond the railings of the hospital grounds, well within sight, was a native village built entirely of rusty petrol cans. The human beings went in and out of their homes, along with cats, dogs, donkeys, bullocks or any other animal which took a fancy to do so.

In the hospital a story circulated to the effect that an Egyptian AckAck unit had been formed and stationed at Mersa, until it was discovered that whenever the enemy flew in the gunners fired in the opposite direction, afraid of upsetting the Germans, who, they thought, would soon take over their country. It was also said that tanks had been called in to surround King Farouk in his palace because it had been discovered he was trying to do a bunk to Jerry. One thing was certain, after that free hand-out of Egyptian gold-tipped cigarettes which were unsmokable, Farouk's popularity with us lot was well below zero.

I remember nothing of the hospital except that I wore hospital blues for the first time and felt a bit superior to others in normal KD.

Then I was shipped off to the convalescent camp at Nathanya in Palestine and my desert days were done.

Chapter Twelve

Nathanya

Arriving at the Suez Canal we had to disembark from the Egyptian state train, to cross over the canal in some barge or other and then get on a Palestine train, there being no bridge at that time. The local folk, whom we referred to as usual as Wogs, just as the Italians were Wops or Eyties, and the Germans Jerries, tried to earn themselves a few ackers by carrying our kits for us. We British were alerkifik about it but the Aussies, and there were quite a few of them, worked themselves up into right old paddies. In fact some of them turned positively nasty, yelling abuse at the poor *fellaheen* and then came one helluva commotion in the darkness; some Aussies started effing and blinding; one produced a revolver and in next to no time he was taking potshots at the locals and calling them all the bastards under the sun.

The locals took off. Evidently discretion was the better part of valour.

'What's up digger? You gorn mad or something?'

'Those bastards led Jerry through paths in the salt flats around Benghazi, that's what they did and we lost a lot of cobbers through that, the bastards.'

And the revolver went bang bang once more. It didn't seem to matter that Benghazi was over a thousand miles away and in another country where the people were not Egyptians. Those Aussies were just mad with all native personnel. Nobody ever stopped to consider that the Germans, the Italians and us lot were making war against each other in countries which didn't belong to them and where they really had no business to be.

We boarded the Palestine train and I found myself in a carriage facing an old bloke who, I reflected, might well have joined the army at the start of the Boer war.

While we were waiting for the train to move off a native vendor came by along the platform flogging oranges for cigarettes. I bought twenty large Jaffa oranges for ten Victory V cigarettes, to me a great bargain. Soon afterwards we heard a commotion going on on the platform. That poor old vendor was in dead trouble with the military police and a short time later one of them came along poking his head through carriage windows asking if anyone had been buying oranges. I said I had and of course had got enough oranges to prove it. So the Redcap said, 'Here, have your money back,' and he tossed into my lap twenty Players cigarettes, regarded as an elite in smoking. The vendor had certainly suffered painfully; I had done extremely well. The train started to trundle off and I settled down to make a pig of myself with those whacking great Jaffa oranges. With only five remaining I suddenly remembered my manners and offered an orange to the Ancient Pistol. He smiled amiably and declined the offer.

'What's up, don't you like oranges?'

'Yes, I like 'em, but not at this time of the year.'

'Why's that?'

He smiled even more. 'If you take a look inside each orange and I mean each, you will find that everyone of 'em is full of little white things. They are known as worms. This is the back end of the season, they all have worms so I never touch 'em.'

I peeled the next orange and had a shufti inside and sure enough, there were the little white things as described. I grinned back at him. 'Well, having eaten fifteen oranges I don't suppose the other five will matter much will it?' To this he agreed and so I ate the rest.

It was my first experience of the fruits of the Holy Land.

Having disposed of the oranges and the old Pistol not being inclined to talk, I sat musing over the this and that. I wondered what this new country would be like. It was bound to be different. For one thing I would get more pay since Egypt was classified as a 'home station' which meant a lower rate of pay. Also, the country had a large and influential Jewish population. I wondered how different the native Arab would be and was to find that in the main the local character was on an entirely different plane. But for Egyptian George, the Cairo street vendor, most of us had a soft spot.

I remember a day when a character with a tray of goods confronted me with his beaming smile and knowing look. He was a street seller of razor blades, packets of razor blades. We had been warned to be wary of those sons of trade who had been at pains to imbibe the heady wine of capitalist enterprise. They were said to be skilled in the art of wrapping old rusty blades into new looking packets and passing things off as the real Macoy.

I noted that George had on his tray a packet of Blue Gillette which I had begun to use. The trick was to ignore what you really wanted and concentrate on bargaining for something you didn't want. So, after haggling for about fifteen minutes for something I did not want and had no intention of buying, I switched my attention to the Blue Gillette. My new found friend George became ecstatic over the 'very lovely blades, George.'

'You have good taste, George, very good taste, these very good blades, give very good shave, many times very good shave, last for ever.'

'How much?'

'For you, twenty piastres.'

I called him a blue pencil clifti wallah and walked away. He followed hard on my heels. 'How much you give, George? How much you give, eh?'

I looked at him sternly. 'They are worth one acker and no more.'

He laughed. 'You wanna rob me, George, eh?'

I didn't say so but that was the general idea though with a character like him it might prove a bit difficult.

He said, 'Fifteen.'

I walked on and he followed. 'Twelve?'

I sneered at him, 'Robber.'

'No no, me no robber, me man of business, ten.'

'One.'

'Seven.'

'One.'

'Six?'

'Not on your Nellie.'

'On my what?'

'English expression for no dice.'

'Look George, me I have family to keep. Times are hard, war on. Five.'

I kept walking, he turned away, stopped, looked back at me, then came hurrying back.

He held out the packet of blades to me. 'All right, George,' he said. 'You hard man. I say four piastres.'

I smiled upon him a truly British smile. 'You've come down to meet me I'll come up to meet you, one and a half ackers. That's my final offer.'

As he thrust the packet of razor blades into my hand he said, 'Here, George, you take razor blade, Inglesi soldier good but you very hard man, my family starve.'

I paid him the money and we parted company. I was of the opinion I had got myself a bargain especially as at that time I shaved hardly twice a week and as it turned out the razor blades were genuine, none of your doctored packets. That incident was a far cry from being served with tea at a service club by Lady Wavell, wife of one of the two most popular generals in the Middle East – Wavell and the German commander Rommel.

Nathanya con camp was a big place with huts, iron bedsteads, biscuits and all clean and comfortable, a sort of home from home. The food, as far as memory serves, was no worse than usual and therefore bearable.

We had to appear before an MO once a week to see how we were faring. The first such appearance was crucial. One was asked, 'Can you play football? Can you play a musical instrument?' The answer given was important. If it was negative you were passed in as an ordinary cove but if the answer to one or both of the two questions was in the affirmative, then you became a special case. The bandsmen in that camp were the best there were and most had been there for years still as con patients recovering from something or other, some like my Ancient Pistol having been there since Noah came ashore in his ark. As for the footballers, well well well! There was more than one football team in the place but the number one team was the real McCoy. Nearly all the footballers that were in the Nathanya team in 1941 were still in the team when I returned there in 1944. It soon became apparent that a soldier with footballing talent was permanently sick in Nathanya. In fact, it was said that any one with ability to play football was unlikely to leave the camp alive! There was a visiting football team which travelled around the Middle East, called the Wanderers, and they comprised professional footballers of a high degree of talent. The only time they were ever known to be defeated was when the invalids of the Nathanya football team played them. The Wanderers did not stand a dog's chance. I ought to point out that we the audience, who were domiciled by the way in a pukka football stand, always sided with the defeated, the always defeated visiting team. On one memorable occasion the opposing side scored a one-nil victory which sent us, the audience, into raptures of applause. The visiting team was an Arab one who played football in bare feet. The trouble was that the Arabs were so fast on their bare feet that the local team could not catch them and so, with our cheers echoing and re-echoing around Palestine, the Arabs ran out winners at one goal to nil. Then there was the memorable occasion of the game against the matelots from a destroyer in Haifa harbour. The captain phoned to say he had heard that the con camp had a football team and he thought that perhaps it would be about the right mark for his matelot lads, long confined to the ship and anxious to give their legs a bit of a stretch.

Of course the con camp football team would be only too pleased to oblige.

In due course the matelots arrived and turned out, some in boots, some in slippers, one or two with football kit but mostly in long trousers and other such duds. We the audience were expecting to see the third team turn out but the first team of long established thugs ran onto the pitch and in so doing absolutely bowled the fans over.

The game ran its course; the home side scored nine goals while we yelled at them to stand still and let the sailors get a goal, which in the end they did, thus giving us a final score of nine goals to one.

We booed the home side and cheered the naval ratings as the latter either collapsed where they stood or staggered to the front of the stand so that they could hold themselves from falling over with utter exhaustion. One or two were even gently carried off. One matelot leaned against the stand rail and looked up at us with utter bewilderment.

'If that team is made up of convalescent geysers what the bloody 'ell are the fit ones like?'

You will recall that in my innocence as a recruit to the TA I had carelessly advised the clerk filling in the particulars to please himself what he put my religion down as. In consequence I became lumbered with doses of Church of England church parades. When asked my occupation I hadn't quite decided how I could class myself but on balance, since in my youth it was much superior to be a white collared worker than a mere manual bod, I decided I had been a builder's clerk and so for all time in the army I would be a builder's clerk. I could of course have said I had been a builder's labourer, an unofficial apprentice, a keeper of my daddy's books, a compiler of accounts or even an ex-pawnbroker's assistant. Instead I said I was a builder's clerk. Such snobbery!

However it didn't do me much good. The powers that were at the camp sorted out jobs for new arrivals and so, taking one look at my record, told me to report to the office where I was made junior clerk writing out some sort of card index.

The only trouble was, and as a matter of fact still is, I had difficulty in reading my own handwriting and if that was so with me it was much more the case with the RSM and his minions. My experience was, for much of my army life, that the authorities didn't have much of a clue what was going on, but it was clear even to the dimmest wit that an orderly room depending on unreadable script could only lead to chaos and anarchy.

After a week I was taken off the job and given one in the open air assisting another Ancient Pistol who was really ancient, he being well turned forty.

Someone suggested I had been offered the job as a punishment for not being able to write decently. Another character assured me he would sooner volunteer for the Russian front than work with *that* tyrant. A number of Pistol's former assistants were produced to affirm that the man was really a *tyrant*, a bull, a country oaf, a work-happy crazy nut who would not only work all day but all night too if only enough light could be supplied to do so.

But in the end it had to be my choice as a non-football playing, non-instrument-blowing very run of the mill con camp inmate. It was made clear to me that I could take part in the democratic process and either work as a slave to the Ancient Pistol or be returned to base camp in Cairo. The trouble was that base camp business. As a B2 man I would not be able to return to my own unit. The Powers that were had got fed up with lower grade men returning to their units and then falling sick again. On the other hand, if I returned to base I could be sent anywhere within the Middle East command and we had a suspicion that that could mean 'up the Bluey to another outfit other than one's own.'

I was constantly advised not to work with that 'nut', out there flogging himself sillier by the minute in the sun. I took a stroll round to size up the situation, to take a quiet shufti. He was a well built sunburned heavy jowled man with large muscles, quick movement and no desire whatever to stop for a meal. He just worked. No one ever approached him, no one called out to him and in the canteen he always sat alone.

I made up my mind. At the next medical I would ask to be returned to my unit and hope that they would ignore the business of being B2. Perhaps they would break the rules for me!

The MO asked me how I felt. I said I felt my unit needed me. He looked at my record and must have decided that anyone asking to go back to the Bluey when he was in lovely Nathanya was a bit sun-touched. Having thought that, he could only conclude a person a bit touched would be a great danger to others in the desert but a great help to another sun touched character – the local landscape gardener.

I got the job and was told to give Pistol a helping hand.

The next day I went.

I have never been able to remember that man's name but it had to be a simple country one like Tom or Dan only it should have been 'Ole Tom' or 'Ole Dan'. But then I supposed he would have had to have less energy and a clay pipe stuck in his mouth. But alas, he was bung full of energy and didn't smoke. The reason for not smoking revealed a real country trait; he wasn't mean, just very very very careful, only allowing coins to escape from his purse stealthily. So I call him Tom along with other, less endearing, names.

I found this man to be no natterer. He guarded his words as he guarded his purse, let things leave his mouth as if it would be difficult to get them back again. I soon discovered that apart from the war in the Western Desert, this particular job upon which we were engaged was the most important thing then taking place anywhere. I don't think he meant only the Middle East either.

The most important thing about it was its urgency. Thus it was that I came to spend most of my waking hours with him on this important exercise. We had picks and shovels and wheelbarrows, crowbars and any other instruments which could aid us in our task to take up all the largest pieces of well-dug in boulder we could find and put them somewhere else. In civilian life this Tom had been a landscape gardener and it seemed to me that he was not only bent on landscaping the semi-desert of the con camp but the rest of Palestine as well.

We dug up boulders and heaved and tugged them from point *a* to point *b* sometimes with the aid of a wheelbarrow. We carried them into position which gradually formed themselves into garden shapes which could be identified as flowerbeds as soon as sandy soil was thrown into them. The sand of course was filled with scorpions and always buzzing around were those confounded big black flies with the pincer-like jaws. I was soon as brown as my master and as physically fit. Gradually I came to see his vision. He wanted to create a Kew Gardens out of the wasteland. He had been hard at it for a very long time and had had many unwilling assistants. I must have become the first 'willing' assistant because I began to share his vision and to understand that it was much better to create a garden than to spend one's time trying to blow other folk to bits.

But he was a hard task master. He never wanted to stop even in the middle of the day. Meal times were necessary nuisances to be got quickly out of the way and sleeping hours were an absolute waste of time.

I kept pace with him for something like three months, not far off four, I fancy, until I began to get browned off, especially when everyone began to regard me as just as potty as my master. As soon as one garden was finished he was on to the next creation. The job was clearly limitless since he did not appreciate that the main gates meant the end of the camp jurisdiction and the end of our gardening territory. We began to have rows. Then we would spend hours together without saying a word to each other. In the end I decided enough was enough, admitted defeat and asked to be taken off the Grand Design. This should mean a return to base but by that time I didn't care. I had proved I could keep pace with the old tyrant and I didn't want to prove anything else, such as dying for a cause.

I was taken off the job, someone in authority admitting that that Ancient Pistol was a bit difficult. But he claimed that it would be more difficult for me back at base, so how would I like to set up in business on my own? Me, a landscape gardener in my own army right? It was explained they were about to extend the camp, going to make it a few miles longer and wider and how would I like to landscape it all? Anyway I had better, since I was still not fit enough to be returned to base! So I found myself with picks and shovels and a wheelbarrow starting in on virgin soil and expected to upturn it even though the huts in the area were all empty and for some weeks I became a rival landscape gardener and toiled on in the heat of the day and in the evening though with a little less enthusiasm than the diabolical Tom.

Then a rumour circulated that there was to be a general clear out apart from footballers and musical instrument wielders.

I was neither so I went back to Egypt. Tom wasn't either but what the devil could be done with him except that which he was already doing?

I must confess I had learned a great deal during those landscaping days; it is difficult not to learn from an eager beaver keen on his job.

Back at El Masa the same old rules applied. Tent occupants were required to dig holes nearby, take down the tents and re-erect them in the new holes and fill in the old ones.

I did make a formal request to return to my unit and was formally told to bugger off, no B2 men were ever required in the Bluey. So that was that. I'll be honest, I was disappointed that I couldn't get back to Smudger and the boys but not unhappy at the thought of avoiding the drudgery of digging bivvies, emptying soil buckets and fly-swatting sergeant major noses. After all, I had become used to huts, iron bedsteads and canteens which sold lousy *chai*. I was in fact, turning into a right old base wallah.

It wasn't long before I got my marching orders: report to the school of AckAck and CD in Palestine forthwith. It was a new unit being formed a few miles south of the port of Haifa. I took up my belongings and the army's too and I went.

Chapter Thirteen

School Days for a Warrior

So, in October 1941 I joined this new unit. CD stood for coastal defence but as I never recall doing any of that I cannot comment on same.

In the distance to the north rose the Lebanese mountains and behind them reared the snow capped peaks of Syria; to the west, the ever moving sea. Of that sea it was said that the water was only calm for six days of the year. To the south, Tel Aviv, Jaffa, the Sinai Desert, the canal and Egypt. Of course the vital link was the canal, the lifeline to India which the Germans were so anxious to cut. That was why we were there. In the past year Jerry had done his best to carry out his design, having taken Greece and got Rommel and his Afrika Korps charging down to Egypt from Benghazi. Rommel was now pushed back westwards and the Free French held Lebanon. Jerry had taken on the Russians and was pushing them eastwards and all was doom and gloom despite our small successes. I was almost alone in believing that the Russians would hold back the Germans, most people having been indoctrinated in the belief that such a horrible monster as a Communist state must have feet of clay. It was but a matter of time before the collapse and a short time at that.

No one seemed to understand that Hitler was no Napoleon. The latter, a military genius, had failed in his attempt to conquer Russia. What a military genius could not do a character like Hitler could not do either. What of course he could and did do, was to maim and destroy on a vast scale.

Japan had also been active in the attack on Pearl Harbour and the countries of the Far East. At one stage they seemed unstoppable. But there again, a pause to stop and think showed that the Japanese industrial output could never match the American in the long term. So, when I toddled off to the school of AckAck I was just as sure of victory as I had been in Tobruk.

The newly formed school was divided into two sections, the school itself which was situated between the Carmel hills and the Haifa-Tel Aviv road, and the gunpark which was sited more or less on the beach west of the Tel Aviv road. This consisted of a large hut and a number of store tents. The personnel comprised six limber gunners, one bombardier and a cook. Our rations were delivered to us every twenty-four hours and consisted of nothing much, especially nothing much in the way of bread which was rationed to a half of a small loaf per man per twenty-four hours. But though we were naturally always very peckish, being young, we managed pretty well and in particular were careful to take only our fair share of the bread. Our cook as a person I recall not at all, but I do remember that as a cook he had certain unusual ideas.

Cooking itself was largely beyond him but much worse was his attitude toward that sacred ritual tea brewing. There was no such thing as warming the pot. He would put the tea in the pot and pour the water in whenever it occurred to him to do so. It never mattered to him if the water had boiled at five p.m. and he was making tea at seven p.m. – in would go the water even if the latter were stone cold.

We loved our cook.

I became very friendly with our twenty-year-old bombardier, with a Ronald Colman moustache and a pleasant and happy nature. He had only recently been married and was the father of a baby he had never seen. He stayed with us several months until he was discovered to be A1 whereupon he was shipped away to a more active front. We were sorry to see him go.

I can only remember three of the others, including Sullivan, a delightful South London character who adopted a mongrel dog called Flossie and who (Sullivan not the dog) was one of the most amiable men I have ever met. He was always good company. He disliked the war, did not think much of soldiering but never complained except for one thing. He would sometimes mull

Author and Sullivan (Sully), School of AckAck on Palestine coast opposite Athlit.

ruefully over the fact that when he was engaged sexually with his wife she would on many occasions insist on reading *Peg's Paper*. He was never able to understand it and nor were we.

Then there was Sully's mate Whitehouse. It was a long time before I took to him. I remember him because one day when Rommel and company had reached Alamein he came bustling into his tent and began hastily packing up his gear. When I asked him what he thought he was doing and where he thought he was going he was quick to respond, 'I'm off.'

'Off! Where to?'

'Anywhere, I don't care as long as it's out of here.'

'Yeah, yeah, but what's it all about?'

'Jerry's reached within sixty miles of Cairo, hasn't he?'

'Yeah.'

'Well I'm not going to be taken a bloody prisoner for nobody.'

'Yeah but, the front is in Egypt, we're in Palestine.'

'No matter, those Panzers can move.'

'But they are over four hundred miles away!'

'No matter.' And he kept packing.

Needless to say he didn't go and in fact he was a very good gunner, and I might add at this point I cannot remember anyone whom I disliked for long. We all have our faults but most of us can get along well enough with our neighbours.

The third one I remember was 'Fangs' King, so called because he had only one tooth in his head and that was in the middle of his top jaw. Fangy was a great character, rather elderly as far as most of us were concerned, who never as far as I recall had a bad word for anyone and who would go out of his way to do a favour. He had a problem. He had a bad stutter and like most folk with a speech impediment, loved to talk. In talking he would, in trying to get his words out, push himself steadily backwards. I, of course, had a stammer, but not anywhere near as bad as Fangy's impediment.

Now, we used to have a night guard on the gunpark. This was manned by people from the school and we also took our turn, though as limber gunners we were supposed to be excused.

One night I picked up a rifle and sauntered off down the gunpark to join up with my companion on guard duty, Fangy. Now here was a 'how d'ye do'.

First, Fangy, who was about half my size, clutched an enormously long Italian rifle which was longer than himself and for which there was no ammunition. Secondly, I was holding an Italian Mountain rifle or cavalry bondook which was about half the length of Fangy and which also had no supply of ammunition. I looked at Fangy, I tried to look at myself without going cross-eyed, I looked out to sea and then looked again at my companion.

'You know something?' I said, without too much stammer.

'No, what?' asked Fangy with a great deal of difficulty and with a movement backward.

'We are the defence of this coast as far as the eye can see and we are expecting an invasion.'

'Are we?'

'Yes we are.' And we strolled up and down along the dark deserted beach with the waves whacking against the shore. Presently we stopped and Fangs King began to utter one of his difficult to get out conversation pieces. While speaking he kept moving back with me in close attendance until the sea was lapping at his boots but still he kept talking and walking backwards until he gave an extra thrust to get a word out and fell back into the sea. I heaved him to his feet giving the opinion that it was a Fangy ploy to fool the Germans. Dear old Fangy, that did not stop his animated talk and I carried on listening, not being anxious to get worked up into the same pitch of excitement.

The night guard consisted of six men and an NCO, never a sergeant, and in the seven months we were on Kayat beach no duty officer had ever turned up to take a shufti at proceedings, thus the night guard was a pretty easy-going affair. But the easiest guard of all was when an old soldier bombardier was in charge. Sam – I can't recall his surname. I do recall he was a well made figure, red faced, red nosed, full of army tales that went back into the dawn of military history out of which he himself had obviously come. He was a regular and an ex-farrier which was not surprising since somehow he exuded horses; he looked an ostler. He could make even the gloomiest character smile and his fund of stories would keep us all in high spirits until late into an evening.

He had a unique approach to the matter of guard duties, especially during our winter months which, people might be surprised to know, could be very cold. Certainly we needed our overcoats at night and often our jerkins too. First he would ensure that the two sentries going on duty would have a hot drink and those coming off would get the same. Then round about ten o'clock, he would go to the hut door and call to the sentries to come in, it was bed-time! The sentries would, in true military style, obey the last order and return to the hut. Then the guard and its commander would undress, climb onto their blankets laid out on tables and before long the only sound inside the hut would be the heavy breathing of the members of the guard and the stentorian snores of the erstwhile horse doctor. Come the morning they would rise and shine, get dressed, have a hot drink and wait for transport back to the school. If Jerry tried a landing from then on he would have to face the combined might of six limber gunners, one cook and one NCO.

Then one night with the ex-farrier in charge it happened. We limber gunners lived in a smallish room at the end of the hut and so were disturbed by strange noises off. The door of the large end of the hut had been thrust open and an irate if squeaky voice was ordering the guard to 'TURN OUT!' The guard sleepily dropped off its tables and began to dress in a somewhat sluggish manner. The orderly officer, for that was who it was, kept urging them to turn out; the guard commander kept cursing stupid orderly officers who should know better, while trying to get a leg into a pair of long johns. He was still trying to get into the other leg when all of them were assembled outside, that is to say all the guard and the orderly officer. The latter made an abortive attempt to inspect the nondescript assembly, but after a while placed the guard on open arrest and especially the guard commander. Then he left. The guard commander then led his men back into the hut where they all climbed back into their fleapits with the old warrior assuring his men that 'that stupid sod won't come back here tonight.' And indeed he didn't and nor did any other orderly officer appear at any time in the future.

Our Sam was under open arrest but wasn't a bit perturbed. 'I'm too old for those idiots up at school. I was soldiering when they were in nappies and in any case know too much about *their* activities for their own good.' Nothing more was heard of the open arrest bit though our old codger never took another guard duty on the gunpark. He was probably protected by Major Ferry who would hear nothing bad about 'my limber gunners' and we presumed he would hear 'nothing wrong about *his* guard commander'. In the spring of the year I heard that our battery was out of the Bluey after a spell of fourteen months up there. So it came as no surprise when Major Ferry informed us that we were going to be visited by an expert on gun control, a certain Captain Fitzwilliams who had perfected the technique in the siege of Tobruk!

Now, our 3.7 mobile guncrew, including me at times, had become so expert at potting at a towed sleeve in a ten degree arc that invariably the number one had to call out 'Ammunition expended' long before the order 'Cease firing.' This proved far too expensive and a bit pointless when we kept on bringing the sleeve down. So they shoved us onto the instruments and the OCTU and officers' training classes onto the guns. We were not too good on the instruments and they were usually hopeless on the guns. But it saved a bit of money, we supposed, so that was all right.

Then one morning Fitzy jauntered down and started explaining the technique of shooting down diving aircraft coming in at all angles. He crouched behind the gun, ordering, elevation and traversing and guessing at the right fuses but all to no avail. He got nowhere near the sleeve. This must have put him out a bit because he had spotted me in the gun crew, had blown out his cheeks, puffed and huffed, twirled his whiskers and had said, 'Well

well well, humph humph, with Gunner Green in the crew and myself how can we miss?' But he missed all right. Then Major Ferry, who must have had the strongest sense of humour in the Middle East, suggested that 'his' crew might have a go. And so we did. Our young bombardier with the Ronald Colman moustache and young baby he had never seen, crouched behind the breech, said, 'Elevate, traverse, fuse four, fire.' And damn us all if we didn't bring that sleeve down with our one and only shot!

Fitzy puffed and huffed, twirled his moustache, went 'Humph humph' and left.

My buddy with the film star moustache being A1 and therefore fighting fit had to leave and was replaced by a young man who had ambitions. He wanted to be an officer and started off life with us by acting like a bad one. That ambition ended when, in an interview for an OCTU course, he was asked if he had independent means. He hadn't. He returned to us full of melancholy and still with only one stripe, an unpaid, unwanted, unloved lance jack.

A crisis loomed when our new leader decided that polite voluntary bread rationing might be a very good thing for the rest of us but not for him. We received a ration of a half of a small loaf of bread per man per twenty-four hours. We had always jogged along on the principle that everyone played fair. Our new leader did not appreciate the word 'fair'. He thought that was a word to describe the colour of a person's hair. So at the first meal which he attended he whopped into a loaf, saw that off with no trouble and then carved into the next one with great gusto, his policy seeming to be every man for himself. 'You big heap native work on empty stomach, me big white chief rest on a full one.'

The rest of us quickly took up the principles of democracy and agreed that in future we would cut each loaf in half on arrival so that each man, regardless of race, colour or creed, would get his proper share. Our hero protested that we were a bunch of selfish idiots and that it was a silly idea not worth any consideration and how could he repel a 'German attack on a ration of bread that size?' But we ignored the opposition and shared out the bread. At our next meal one half loaf disappeared faster than it would have done if a kite hawk had fancied it. The rest of us dillied and dallied over our bread, tightened our belts and contrived to build up for ourselves reserves of stale bread which we left exposed to big footed flies and hungry looking lance jack eyes. But with jack knives at the ready no unauthorised gaze dared stray in the direction of even a small hard crust. Soon the hunger of lance bombardier youth was overcome and we returned to our normal routine. Indeed, our new leader became a responsible and likeable gunner type.

Over the main road was St Luke's camp, a NAAFI and a cinema run by civilians who charged high prices for mostly low budget films. Us lumpen proletariat at the front were charged thirty mils, the sergeants in the middle forty and the Sam Browne brigade at the back fifty mils. Thus was democracy shared out. Jewish and Arab civilians were often in the audiences but the devil only knows what they paid.

It was in the St Luke's canteen I got talking to a squaddie who told how he pulled his trousers on one day and felt something nip him sharply in the backside. He whipped off his trousers, shook them, and a young black scorpion fell out of them. The fact that it was young was a help because it was understood that fully grown ones were deadly. He had the bite serviced with iodine and he lived to fight another day.

It was in this canteen that a load of civilians in somewhat down-trodden order turned up and bought up nearly all the goods on sale – one character buying twenty-five sandwiches presumably for absent friends and not for himself. They turned out to be Greeks who had escaped from the Germans and who had come to join the Greek army. The gist of their story was that the Germans had outnumbered the Greeks by four to one so that the odds had been too great. Sad for the Greeks since before the arrival of Jerry they had chased the Italians all over the place. It was a salutary reminder for us, meeting the Greeks, that there were many people beside ourselves fighting the Germans.

Gunner Green's War (1938–1946)

It was at our camp on the beach that we came into contact with members of the Palestine police. We usually met them at night when we were doing our night guard bit and they were doing their night patrol, a much longer stint. They always patrolled in pairs and were never happy with their lot since their patrol lasted all night, ten p.m. to five a.m., barbarous hours as far as we were concerned. They were quite pick-outable even in the dark and with their dark blue uniforms since they wore the distinctive kaftan type Russian hat. They had come from all over Europe, having in many cases fled from the Nazi terror. They came from many walks of life and when hearing of their experiences one was brought up sharply to understand that so-called civilizing influences can often be skin deep.

We came across one or two who were very anti-Russian in outlook and that was understandable since they could claim rough treatment from the Russians. But by that time, with the Soviet Union losing millions of her citizens in the defence of the country against the invading Germans, we were all staunch supporters of 'Old Joe and his mob'. So we would defend our allies with great vigour.

People in the mass can be easily persuaded by their rulers to think the way the rulers want them to think. Since the Russian revolution the rulers of the west and north of Europe had always had a fear and hatred of the new Russian state. Thus, just before the war when the Russians were anxious to form an alliance against fascism, the British government answered the call by sending a minor official, Sir Herbert Strang, on a slow boat to Moscow. The Germans didn't hang about, they sent their chief negotiator Ribbentrop by fast plane to do a quick deal with the Russians who themselves had to look to their own future. That meant of course that the 'evil Soviet Union' could be vilified. But of course when Jerry invaded the Soviet Union in 1941 the Russians became our splendid allies. It was a dead cert that as soon as the war was over and won our rulers would go back to vilifying 'our Splendid Allies'.

And as we all know that is what they did.

We watched fishermen on the shore with their cone-shaped nets fishing with poor results usually, though they were full of determination, not least so an old man with one leg. Then there was the scruffy old character who used to drive even scruffier looking cattle along the seashore and it was noticeable how much smaller the cowpats were in comparison with those big fat squadgy ones one was likely to step into in Blighty.

We paid several visits to Jewish kibbutz settlements and learned much. At one, for example, we came across cattle in stalls suffering from foot and mouth disease. It was explained to us that in our country such cattle were killed off but there they were being cured. Then we visited one settlement with thirty thousand white chickens. We tried to find a coloured one but couldn't. Then we visited a settlement that had been moved back a bit from the original site near the seashore because that original place had become silted up with sand. They had had to move and begin all over again. At another place we attended a concert with very fine artistes performing on stage and were told, when we couldn't understand why there was no applause, that everyone knew the performers were good so there was no need to do any clapping. Of course we found ourselves at one time bloated out after every meal of roast chicken, roast potatoes and Yorkshire pud or some similar dish. This was at a time when we suffered on corned beef and biscuits, lousy bread, spinney and soya link sausages. Who was winning this war anyway?

It always struck me as peculiar that we, the ordinary British squaddies, would run the Jews down like mad but be perfectly happy to spend a leave in a Jewish settlement but, although we got on well with Johnny Arab, would never dream of having a leave in an Arab village.

I soon came to the conclusion that Jew and Arab could live side by side simply because of mutual benefits and it seemed to me that the trouble was stirred up from beyond the Palestine borders. I had the impression that there was just as much hostility between the kibbutzim and the ordinary city Jew who was as keen a capitalist as anyone else.

We also were told in no uncertain terms that as soon as we had quit the country the Jews would settle the Arab question once and for all and we certainly believed them.

It was round about this time that Sullivan joined us. He had been called up, given his bit of training, had come out to the Middle East and had landed up with that great fighting force, the limber gunners of Khayat beach. He had left Britain with all its wartime shortages and could not remember the last time he had had an egg. He would not believe us when we explained that while the local chickens were somewhat smaller than the Blighty variety and that therefore the eggs were smaller too; there was no shortage of eggs. He could have as many eggs as his stomach desired in our favourite Haifa café, the Ring.

As he wouldn't believe us we decided to take him in to the Ring Café to prove our point. We sent a messenger ahead to let the owner know of our intentions and to get a table ready. In due course a bunch of us turned up at the Ring ready for action.

I ought to mention that the Palestine cafés were always spotlessly clean, free from flies and free from all cooking smells as well. We sat ourselves down and then urged Sully to order as many eggs as he wished. Though he was reminded that whatever he ordered he would have to pay for and not us. In the end he got a bit peeved and said, 'All right you sons of bitches [he included the waiter in that remark], fetch me thirty bloody eggs and stop all your rabbiting.

The waiter nodded and left and in a surprisingly short time he returned with a large plate containing thirty fried eggs garnished with lettuce, tomatoes and things.

Sully's face showed disbelief and then it clouded a bit when we insisted on him eating all that he had ordered. In fact he did so and assured us he could have eaten more if he wasn't such a polite sort of bloke.

No matter what country the British squaddie was in during the war the café owners always knew what he wanted – eggs and chips. Fish and chips were of course not part of foreign menus, at least the type we were used to, a tuppenny and a pen'orth, wrapped in newspaper and well salted and vinegared after being fried in dripping. Some drivers asserted that a couple of civvy Britons stranded in the country at the outbreak of war had set up in the fish and chip business somewhere between Haifa and Tel Aviv and the fish and chips were 'cracking', 'just the job'. Though I never found the place myself.

Mark you, we did sometimes have a change. It was in Tel Aviv that I made the acquaintance of hamburgers, big fat, hot rolls, stuffed with hamburger meat and onions. Expensive at twenty five ackers a touch (around 33 pence new money) but what the hell; one can only live once and after hogging down a few of them we could have brought the whole German army to a standstill. I cannot say the same about the modern concoctions; who knows what the hell goes into them.

In those early days on Khayat beach we had a young Arab who did odd jobs for us, mending clothes and cutting hair while he took our washing home to be laundered by his mother, and very well done it was too. They lived in a house in the Arab village of Athlit on the far side of the Haifa road. Johnny had his complaints. His bread ration was very small, less than ours, so we used to give him some of ours to take home, and his income was very low. His biggest complaint however was that no one wanted to visit his home. We pointed out that Arab villagers were not famous for giving a welcome to the likes of us but he assured us we would be perfectly safe as long as we understood that the local bints were strictly virginal and not for us. So a couple of the lads paid Johnny and his mother a social call which made Johnny very happy and when they left Johnny's mum was clearly over the moon. They discovered that while the village in its externals might look like a council refuse dump with many dogs always on the prowl, internally one could have eaten a meal off the floor of the house and everywhere inside shone in bright cleanliness.

It would be wrong to imply that there were no Arab prostitutes. One turned up offering herself for half a crown a time (15 pence). Compare this with the price of a hamburger! The lads settled her in an ammo tent on the gun park and lined themselves up. I suppose understandably the most eager were the married men. For one thing I was too immersed in my reading and in writing my verses and for another I couldn't see much romance in having it off with a prostitute on a load of ammunition boxes. Then of course we were always being reminded by literature and with slides and films of the dangers of venereal diseases. Such warnings never seemed to bother many men though they frightened the life out of me. In fact a special tent was set up when we moved to our new site containing free issues of the well known preventatives.

Later on we had one regular soldier who joined us and got quite bothered when faced with the prospect of being upgraded to A1 and therefore entitled to the honour of going to a battle front. So he decided to go into Haifa and get himself a 'dose'. So into Haifa he went and believe it or not he did get himself poxed up.

> You've gotta be bright and merry
> and go and chase after Jerry.
> Now truly I find,
> I'm not inclined
> To chase after a desert fox.
> So, if you don't mind,
> I'll go for a grind
> and get me a dose of pox.

The rest of us came to the conclusion we would opt for the battle front.

On Monday 12th April 1942 the first phase of my sojourn at the ME School of AckAck and the mysterious CD came to an end when we moved a few miles south along the coast to our new school, still being built, opposite to the village of El Tira.

We would no longer be in sight of those far northern mountains nor be able to look out over the large expanse of Haifa bay, with the harbour looking so very small inside it. But we would still be in view of the Carmel hills, the long road and the

Author, School of AckAck

sea nearer too to the underwater remains of ancient Caesarea. I had examined the Roman water supply pipe which ran from the hills to the sea, with its internal glazed white tiles, and had been given to understand that the pipe was still serviceable. And I wondered if that will be said of our modern pipework two thousand years from now. Doubtful.

But above all, I could still watch those magnificent sunsets which could burst across the evening skies with racing chariots, huge flocks of flying fantasies, glorious gardens of giant flower blooms, armies enrolled for eternity, and then see the ringing down of the curtain when the sky changed from blood red, to orange, blues of every shade and then the gentle greys turning into night.

What more could anyone want apart from one's ticket home?

The people at the school had moved a week earlier than we did. We moved on Sunday 12th April, cursing the powers that be who had insisted on us moving on what was supposed to be a rest day. We loaded our gear onto lorries and we perched on the top of one of them all in our working dungarees, unwashed, unshaven and looking as if we had emerged from a swamp or a rubbish tip. By this time our number had increased to ten and we always seemed to have enough work for twice that number.

And so we moved off, nursemaids to a load of guns, and funnily enough we enjoyed the job. We must have been in the true line of artillery men who cared for their guns to such effect that they often died for them. Human beings are peculiar things. One ought not to have affection for guns which after all are death-dealing horrors. For a time we had to sleep and mess at the new school and travel each day to the gunpark a mile and a half away on the seashore and we complained because the arrangement meant we could get less work done! But until the builders and plumbers had finished their work we could not really live on the gunpark.

A few days later I learned that the 153 battery was resting a few miles down the coast. They had entered Tobruk on 23rd January 1941 and had stayed there until the garrison had been relieved months later and then they had remained in the Bluey doing a stint of fourteen months. I thought they deserved a visit from me. Soon after reaching the new school the weather changed; summer had arrived. I noted that the summer out there arrived on a certain day in April and took itself off on a certain day in October. So we put our battle dresses away and got out the KD.

Because we were situated in an olive grove we were the targets for every insect known to man. When evening approached on would go KD slacks and shirts with sleeves buttoned down and none of us would forget to turn our boots upside down and give 'em a knock. Scorpions seemed to have a partiality for army boots.

Having the chance to get out for a bit one Saturday morning soon after getting to our new site, Tiffy Hills and I set off down the Haifa road in the direction of the 153 battery. A light lorry pulled up beside us and its driver, an army captain, offered us a lift and we, being gunners and not used to walking, gladly accepted and hopped in. When we stopped by the battery site our new friend offered us cigarettes which we sociably accepted and in return we put him right when he asked if we knew of a good place in which he could stay in Haifa. He then drove off with a wave of his hand and we walked up the short road to the camp.

We met a number of the lads along the road and had quite a chat to Section Officer Townsend who directed us toward Smudger and Co. and he pointed out that as they had only just arrived on the site everything was upside down. So was Smudger Smith. He was standing on his hands in the middle of camp doing a slow somersault. As I stood over him as he lay prone on the ground after his exertion, he caught sight of me and his mouth promptly fell open, thus causing him to be speechless. I must have appeared to him as one of those desert Arabs who had the habit of appearing suddenly from nowhere and who seemed just as suddenly to disappear.

'How goes it?' I enquired politely.

He replied with a question of his own, 'Why didn't you send me those damned sweets you promised me?'

Sweets, I had to point out, were bad for the teeth. 'And I have always been concerned about your health, as you know,' and from then on, much to the enjoyment of Fred West, Coxy and others we were plunged into our usual heated arguments. My own dental history had been fraught from childhood onwards. In fact during my army days I had from time to time been ordered to attend a dentist but as the reputation of those military gentleman ranged from 'butcher' to 'savage torturer' I always avoided them, not attending a dentist until well after the war when I was forced into it by the condition of my somewhat neglected molars.

Some of the old gang were floating about though many were away scrounging for the benefit of the unit.

We were quite a bunch gathered into one tent: Fred West, Potter, Squibs Squires and Coxy. We spent a great deal of time yarning about the old times, naturally, as such veterans young or old usually do. Photos were produced taken during the siege of Tobruk; the old gunsite, the road Jerry built round the perimeter when he failed to take the town, and pictures of the battered town itself. (It should be remembered that Tobruk had been the most heavily attacked town, up to that time, of the war.) They told how they had manned the guns permanently the whole time the hospital ship had been in the harbour with me in it and had only stood down when the ship had steamed out of sight on its way to Alex.

They talked about the guns and how they had managed with them during the siege. Two barrels had been delivered but it had been a very long time before a barrel could be changed. Jerry was apt to interfere if he spotted a gun with its barrel on the deck. They spoke a great deal of the Aussies whom they held in high esteem, of days and nights of continuous bombing when sleep was difficult to get but for me the great thing was that, no matter the difficulties, humour always seemed to bubble through.

It must be remembered that most of them were ex-Saturday night soldiers, with a sprinkling of conscripts. They had been clerks, building workers, shop assistants and none high in their jobs since they were at the time mostly in their teens. It was those characters who had fought Jerry to a standstill at Tobruk. So great had the resistance been that Rommel had ordered a road to be built round the outside of the town.

There were no chairs in their canteen and only lousy Palestine beer but never the less we got stuck into that, I surprising Fred and the rest with my new found ability to engage in heavy swilling. The drinks kept coming, we kept drinking, Squibs still insisting on calling me Cabbage, I insisting I would rejoin the unit, which was because of my medical category now impossible, and Fred arguing I was much better off where I was and who the hell wanted in fact to go with them among the muck and bullets? An idiot perhaps. Squibs kept on trying to calm us down as Fred and I got more and more heated trying to make ourselves heard over the caller in Housey Housey.

Their canteen was closed at eleven o'clock that night and we got thrown out. So we staggered off into the night air. I never did find out what part Tiffy Hills played. I suspected that he had kept himself to himself and, obliging character that he was, had sat or stood throughout the long day and evening, playing the part of a true guest and drinking everything set before him.

Once outside Fred kept on going round and round in wobbly circles shouting all sorts of incomprehensible remarks while Squibs with his orderly mind kept making arrangements for more jolly meetings during their stay in Palestine.

Then Fred wobbled off somewhere, probably to his tent, and we saw him no more. Bombardier Squires also disappeared, probably going in search of a notebook in which to record the dates of our future meetings, which left Tiffy Hills and myself and some unknown character who had attached himself to our party during the evening. He showed us the way out which was a vital piece of work since neither Tiffy Hills or myself could have possibly reached any exit in the condition in which we now found ourselves. Having indicated the way out the stranger turned back and I watched him disappear into the canteen marquee. I wondered what his position in the outfit was. Could he have been the canteen manager who had been over liberal and had now gone to check his losses? Was he a quiet drinker with a key to the cellar? Or had he merely lost his way and was following an instinctive trail back to the canteen? Another question to remain for ever unanswered; how could anyone rush back, if that was what he was doing, to that store with all its gut rot booze? But I soon forgot that knotty problem. In no time at all Tiffy Hills and I were lost!

We staggered off along the Haifa road as merry as any English drunkards on any English road. By the time we had tottered on for a mile or so we were no longer tipsy or merry. Deciding we had missed our turning to the gunpark we retraced our steps until we found ourselves once again in line with the 153 gunsite. So we started off again, this time in the right direction and on arrival at our own place we booked in at the guard room at two-thirty in the morning, after which we toddled off to bed to sleep the sleep of the dead until 6 a.m.

It had been some day and for a one-time teetotaller I had put away an awful lot of that hellfire brew. One thing it did reveal, I had a reasonably large stomach with a cast iron lining which could enable me to outdrink most.

I said I would look up Stan Ward who was somewhere around in J Troop but I never did find him though I must confess I didn't look very hard, my spare time being taken up with a number of outings into Haifa with Smudger and company.

I never caught up with Stan Ward until we were all back in Blighty and that was possibly because of the way in which an AckAck unit was organised. The regiment was divided into three batteries, each battery into two troops, in our case I and J known as left and right troops. In the case of our battery in Tobruk J Troop was situated on the other side of the town and we never saw anyone from them apart perhaps for a don R or stray officer. As for the other batteries, well, one was somewhere in the delta and the other, the 151, got itself captured in Crete.

We were given to understand that when the paratroopers started tumbling out of the sky, 151 battery gave a good account of itself and probably could have finished Jerry off on their own but – and it was a very big but – the only people who had small arms were officers with their revolvers, so that once the airborne troops had landed, a 3.7 gunsite was a sitting duck. The net result was that the whole damned bunch was taken prisoner.

Mark you, none of us were issued with rifles until the war was over and then they were handed out, we believed, so that we could play nursemaids to refugees of one sort or another.

The early days at the new school were not particularly pleasant. On the old site we had been on the gunpark, a small group happily working as and when we liked and usually full of the joys of spring no matter the season of the year. Here it was different. We were billeted at the school, had to attend 6.30 a.m. roll call and then go down to the gunpark until breakfast and then back again until tiffin and if I was duty limber gunner not till 14.30. Then back again until around 1900 hours when we knocked off for the day. This was the routine because the gunpark was still being laid out and built by the civvy engineers.

For the limber gunners Saturdays and Sundays were regarded as normal working days but we were never excused other duties. In consequence of this we would find ourselves on guard duties every third day. Not that we ever indulged in any such bull as guard mounting. When it was my turn I would wash the grease and dirt off me, go and collect my bondook and do my stint, if an early turn, before I took off my overalls.

I was probably one of the scruffiest soldiers in the Middle East. At one time there was a craze for muster parades and my boots would be conspicuous for their absence of shine. The section officer might suggest I get some polish on them, the adjutant, following, would demand polish, the colonel, if he happened to turn up would just nod. Then the day arrived when the adjutant seemed to turn purple and I got the distinct impression he was about to explode but the colonel calmed him down, explaining that they were Green's boots and what else could he expect? From then on not only my boots but my whole person was ignored on a muster parade. It was not that I ever set out to be bolshie over such matters. It was just how I was. In any case such parades were not the things to be over bothered about. But I was never meant to be neat and tidy and no matter how much I tried I could never match up to the silly standards the authorities set. I remember one time in Germany when I had become a member of that self opinionated, over-zealous bull outfit, the tenth medium regiment. They also loved muster parades. I tried for ages to make my kit look ship-shape and Bristol fashion and I had plenty of help from my hoppos but they all gave up in the end and once again the inspecting powers that were thought it prudent to ignore the kit of Gunner Green.

Meanwhile, back in Palestine, the colonel kept on complaining about the dirty state of vehicles and gear in general and that faults must be remedied. He never seemed to comprehend that we lived in a dry climate where a road could be a natural dust bowl in summer and that very dust with only the slightest of breezes could surge up in high glee from a road and attack anything which looked remotely clean or for that matter, remotely dirty.

Now and again Jerry would come over and drop a few bombs around Haifa but I cannot recall any damage being done. Mark you, he had every incentive to duffy up the area. There were big oil storage tanks by the docks and an oil pipe line coming in from somewhere inland. But he always appeared to us to be half hearted and we usually spent a bit of time in slit trenches for no real reason as far as we could see. We sometimes wondered if he was not happy about bombing the place because he was hoping to capture it for himself.

We thought things had improved when the colonel offered to supply us nightly with a lorry into the nearby British army ordnance depot. But then as he wanted to charge us eight ackers a head for the privilege we declined the offer.

That character was replaced by another one who showed how sensible a man he was by ordering the limber gunners to reside on the gunpark.

One night I was doing my guard stint leaning against the outside wall of the sentry box. It was a night which ought to have been reasonably cool but it wasn't. We had concluded during the day that the temperature had been 199 in the shade or thereabouts and rising, that our blood was boiling and we were about to all burst into flames. At all events it had been damned hot so I was taking advantage of a bit of cooling off at two in the morning and was thus busily day dreaming at night with eyes firmly fixed on closed eyelids and allowing the gunpark to guard itself. Unnoticed by me, the stars were their usual brilliant selves and except for an occasional howl from a pye-dog over in the Carmel hills, all was quiet.

I mulled over the questions of the local harvest, so different from those in our own country. For a start, at the end of April the corn was ripe and gathered in. It seemed only a couple of weeks ago that I had watched the little green shoots sprouting and growing apace. As far as the eye could see, corn, with here and there standing out in the bright moonlight, dark patches of vegetables. It was possible to believe that both crops had come to a mutual agreement not to trespass on one another's territory.

At the appropriate time the harvesters would appear from the village of El Tira, said to be the most dangerous bed of intrigue in the entire country, the head of a family astride his donkey leading his wives and children out to work, the latter walking. Then the gathering would begin: sir, astride his donkey as operational director, no doubt tired after his donkey ride, while his wives, relatives and children would spread out in a line to scythe down the crop, scenes like this having been observed since way before biblical times.

One Sunday afternoon I took a leisurely stroll along the seashore towards the ancient ruined pile that stood on a promontory jutting out into the sea. I assumed it to be an old Roman town or fortress or something important to its builders. I assumed it to be Roman since Rome played such a significant part in the history of the area but of course it could have been a Saracen stronghold or Crusader castle. At any rate I approached it with my imagination going full blast in the heat. But that heat beat me. I had to slow up and eventually stop and turn back to the smoothness of the Haifa road. From the gunpark the distance had not seemed all that great but in that burning sun it was far too far away. In any case, in walking along the shore, the sun had burnt my right leg, right arm and right cheek and I was about to boil and of course the burnings could be categorised as self inflicted wounds which of course they were. Although of course I would have tried to hold the sun responsible. I turned away before the halfway stage, and paused to roll a cigarette and study the lie of the land.

The ruin rose up from the waters like a colossus, impressive, dominating, to demonstrate that the ancient world still had the power to overawe. I couldn't help wondering whether our time would produce anything so enduring as that old pile, a pile which had withstood the ravages of time but also the marauding armies of many nations in those long centuries since it had risen upon the seashore.

I looked inland from the white beach, the rocky shore across the road to the fertile strip of land which ran parallel to the hills, where the corn was ripe and the vegetables green. I walked homeward, passing a square, squat, flat roofed white Arab house. The women who were outside fled as I approached, a scraggy dog barked furiously and I passed by.

How old was that house? How many generations had been born and had died there? This was an old land where time meant nothing. How many nations had passed by? What marching troops had tramped along this road? I began to see and hear the soldiers marching this way and that, south to Egypt and the Nile, north to Syria, to Persia, to the high plains of Anatolia and beyond into the cold northern steppes. Egyptians, Assyrians, Romans, Turks, Jews, Arabs. I could hear them all swearing, cursing the place in their own languages.

Now this land was enduring Britons, Aussies, Americans and Africans, and even Chinese military were to put in an appearance. And the reason for them being there had nothing to do with the native population who probably only wanted to be left in peace. I got back to the road near an internment camp where at a bus stop I met up with some of our lads and we all went back to base together.

There were two Alsatian dogs who kept each other company, two dogs we assumed had been police dogs. They would turn up at our gunpark every few months or so. They would only appear at guard mounting time, would lie themselves down by the guard post and there would remain all night without making a sound or taking any refreshment whatsoever. While they stood guard the human character could sleep as long as he had a mind to. We assumed the two dogs had set themselves up as a guard patrol and that they visited the various camps along the Haifa road giving each camp a turn with their expertise.

It was early morning and all was quiet and the sentry, which was me, had dozed off pleasantly enough inside the sentry box, when suddenly both dogs moved and they moved faster than any greyhound had ever moved. One moment they were there minding their own business, the next they were gone minding somebody else's.

I called the guard commander and we trotted over to the area of the cookhouse where the dogs had gone. Nearby was stacked a pile of lorry tyres and near to that on the wire fence was a large piece of what could be identified as torn Arab trousers. No humans in sight, nothing stolen and the dogs had gone.

On returning to the guard house there were the two dogs lying perfectly still as if sound asleep and I was thankful I hadn't been an Arab trying to nick a few more army tyres. When dawn broke the two dogs rose, shook themselves, probably, in their own way said good morning, and then they walked off down the gunpark road.

The Palestine buses were run by the Egged company. We understood that they and other things had been organised by an Australian called Spinney left over from the first world war. It was also said that the reason why local matches would flare up, then go out, on being struck was because this character had bought up and used old army huts that had been fire proofed! Be that as it may Spinney was immortalised in the hall of ill fame by the Spinney sausage. No one who served in Palestine as I did, will ever be able to expunge from memory, thoughts on the Spinney sausage.

We had a long period of agony of alternative breakfasts. One morning we would be landed with a couple of long, narrow very wrinkled sausages which tasted reasonable at first but soon had stamped on them, 'Throw me into the swill bin.' This we did although we were given to understand by the pig swill man that the pigs didn't like them either.

At the alternative breakfast we were regaled with a big fat inviting looking soya link sausage which tasted reasonable for the first few mornings but they too inevitably found their way into the swill bin. I can only imagine that if the pigs accepted the soya link, as the British soldier got leaner and leaner so the Palestine pig got fatter and fatter.

Not far away from us was an internment camp, where refugees

from all over Europe were housed, sometimes being held for over a year. Some managed to slip away but most remained mewed up until the authorities gave them permission to settle in the country. We supposed it was a real problem in a situation where the mandatory power, Great Britain, had promised to help the Jews and had at the same time sworn to help the Arabs when neither party wanted each other there at all. The refugees from Europe kept arriving, deserving sanctuary, but their appearance upset the Arabs and possibly upset some of the long established Jews as well.

In consequence the authorities were in an impasse, or in our language they were right up the creek.

Both the Jews and the Arabs knew that the authorities were unable to cope and both sides were actively preparing for a showdown as soon as the war ended and the mandatory power moved out.

The living quarters within the camp appeared to be very good with clean huts and absolutely beautiful gardens. So well did the place look to us that at one point we asked if we might possibly swap places with the inmates, their hole seeming to be a better hole than ours was.

The one jarring note was to see a British born Palestine policeman patrolling the main gate with his rifle. He explained that from noon till five p.m. the two sexes were allowed to mingle. He also explained that there were twenty children in the camp, six of whom had known parents while in the other cases the parentage was being looked into. The men of the camp had volunteered for the army but had been turned down, possibly because of the fear of spies and saboteurs.

On the day some of us were chatting to the internment camp guard, one of our blokes nipped across the road to a Jewish army cookhouse to see if there was a chance of a cup of *chai*. All he got in reply to his enquiry was that *chai* was for soldiers only. Our friend was somewhat taken aback but recovered sufficiently to say, 'What d'you think I am, a sodding nursemaid?' But he got no tea.

It was in the merry month of May that I went down once again with that merry complaining sand fly fever. I had it in Tobruk and again in November of '41 and then again in May of '42. In other words I was getting a dose of the damned thing every six months. What I did not know was that I would get it every six months for years after the end of the war. I believed then as I do now that it wasn't sand fly but malaria, the difference being that sand fly was not pensionable.

I was ordered to bed by the MO and put on a diet of dry toast with biscuits and tea. I had been in the army long enough to forget about the diet and in any case there is no way in which anyone can enjoy food with a bout of fever no matter what that fever is called. So I just sank onto my fleapit but it turned out to be a lousy idea. I ached all over and the fact that I slept on three bed boards which over a long period grew to the shape of my body did not help. Then again, as soon as one sweated under a mossy net the net was soon cast aside and then one had to face the onslaught of fleas, bugs and flies and keep a sharp eye open for any lurking scorpion, all of which creatures seemed to understand that there was a weakened human being lying wide open to a concerted attack.

Even Jerry heard about my attack because he organised a raid on Haifa. Illness or no illness I led the way into a handy slit trench until Jerry had dropped a few bombs way off his target, the oil tanks. Then we returned to our beds. I might add that the reader would not regard me as a coward leaping for safety; the truth was it was better in the slit trench. The fleas and bugs and flies had no conception of what a slit trench was for and so never used one. This incident reminded me of the time in Tobruk when Fred and I first discovered old Eytie dugouts. Inside one of them there seemed to be a big black moving cloud which aroused his curiosity but not mine. He went in to investigate and disappeared for a time in the cloud. When he emerged he was covered in the cloud which turned out to be a mass of fleas left behind by their owners, the Italians. Smudger headed straight for a bath, up to his cranium in the sea.

The BSM, who had hardly spoken to me in the past, became quite concerned about my health, advising me to take it easy, rest up, don't overdo it and hurry up and get well. I soon discovered this was no new found sense of humanity, but that he was desperately short of men to do guard duties! I became sorry for the poor distracted creature and my bed was so hard and my back ached so much I told the MO I was feeling fine and went back to work and the sentry box where I was better off.

In May someone decided that there was a real threat of German invasion or at least a diversion to take pressure off himself elsewhere. It seemed that our school authorities were working on the theory that the German High Command was working on a theory of its own, planning to attack the school of AckAck from the sea and the beach. We in the lower ranks got the idea that a Jerry attack from the sea might be a bit difficult since we still had a navy and in any case we considered that if we were the German High Command we would send in airborne troops and drop them in the Carmel Hills, thus giving themselves control of the heights overlooking the plain below. However we were not asked for our opinion. Instead we were kept busy digging fifteen gunpits round our camp to house our weaponry which may have included a Lewis and a Bren gun, our four guard-duty Lee Enfield rifles and eight Italian ditto of ancient date and doubtful ammunition supply.

I came to the conclusion that if Jerry did attack the school, the staff would be handed the rifles so that they could have turns in taking potshots at the advancing enemy. This I was sure would be a decisive act because it would take the enemy so much by surprise that he would become bemused and demoralised. Over at the school itself they organised a couple of test alarms when something like three hundred Germans had landed. Needless to say the school was victorious, having defeated the foe with consummate ease.

On the gunpark the guns had to be manned. This meant that when the alarm sounded we would all dash for the lorries, which would whip us along the mile to the guns which we could then uncover (we limber gunners never allowed the guns to be uncovered at night; sea air was apt to turn metal rusty very quickly), and bring them into action. I happened to be on the gunpark when the old man turned up in full colonel splendour and sounded the alarm. Down the road dashed the trucks, onto the guns swept the crews but one gun was put down between two tall sheds, making a view of the sky somewhat difficult. This, naturally, upset the colonel but he showed a great deal of patience as he waited for the gun to be taken up and resited in a more suitable place. When the gun was finally settled it was discovered that the ammunition was nowhere near it, it having been left lying in the original position. Nevertheless the enemy was decisively defeated and everyone was very pleased except the limber gunners who had to clean the guns up afterwards.

While we at the school were doing our bit toward the war effort the real duffy was taking place way up in the Western Desert. This was the time, at the end of May and the beginning of June, when Rommel and Co had defeated our forces under Ritchie and had beaten them back to some forty miles south of Tobruk. This was the time of Bir Hakheim, held by the Free French and the Indian Brigade, the Knightsbridge box and the devil's cauldron held by the enemy. This was the time of bitter fighting and fluctuating fortunes, the fall of Tobruk and the strategical withdrawal into Egypt, to Alamein. It was a grim time, the death toll was mounting and mounting and it seemed that there could be no end to the deadly devastation.

I was having my own personal problem in the form of spots. In the end I got so many spots, particularly under the armpits, that the MO became alarmed, said I had scabies and ordered me into the Casualty Clearing Station in Haifa. To this I was duly taken in a 15 cwt truck and dumped at the door clutching my regulation hospital kit, two blankets, water bottle, gas mask and tin hat. Inside the building I took note of the fact that a side of the hospital was a part of the harbour wall and as an unemployed gunner without a gun, I took immediate alarm at the thought of finding that fool Jerry had discovered I was *hors de combat* and fit to be bombed at along with the Haifa storage tanks. The hospital MO when he saw my spots laughed his head off and pondered on the question as to why someone in his profession could not tell the difference between scabies and a heat rash. He then told me to jigger off back to wherever I had come from. So then I found myself outside the hospital in an area known as Bat Galim, walking along a road leading vaguely south, carrying my two blankets, haversack, water bottle, gasmask and tin hat.

Then the air raid siren went off.

I had come to dislike towns where bombs were likely to fall but I could not run for cover along with dozens of Arabs for two reasons. One, I was supposed to be a battle hardened soldier and running would be somewhat infra dig, and two, I was surrounded by all that bloody kit, sweating like a pig (if a pig sweats) and so couldn't run anyway. So I walked on, hoping to get a lift back to camp when hey ho! the same truck which had taken me into the CCS pulled up beside me and so leaping aboard I was whisked back to camp.

On the Monday following I had to report sick again (it wasn't possible to go sick on a Sunday) much to the surprise of our Polish MO, the one who had difficulty in sorting out different types of spots. He prescribed calamine lotion which the medical orderly promptly vetoed, giving me instead a special concoction of his own which did the trick, causing my spots to take themselves off, hopefully in the direction of Jerry where they might possibly turn into German measles.

In July someone came up with a very bright idea. A certain number of limber gunners would have to attend each Saturday morning muster parade. (This smacked of adjutant ideas, not the colonel's.) Covered in muck and grease all week we now had to join the school lads who spent their time dolled up. After the muster, of course, we would be kindly allowed back to our oil grease and muck. I happened to be on the first parade, with a couple of other unfortunates, so we downed tools long before our usual time and cleaned up. On the parade I daresay I stood out like the proverbial sore thumb with my greasy sun helmet and even greasier boots.

The parade sergeant ordered open march and then took a turn round the section, ignoring the greasy pith helmet and unpolishable boots. The orderly officer ordered open march and then, inspecting me, said, with great venom, 'Your helmet is filthy and your boots are unpolished.' He was a newly commissioned one pipper who, when he was a cadet, training on our predictor, called out, 'Fuze ten thousand.' (I think the fuze scale went up to about ten or twelve, something like that.) To this order the sergeant major IG (Instructor of Gunnery) called out in no small voice, 'Now we'll give the bloody Japanese what for.' And this character was all boiled up about my pith helmet and boots! The one pipper then ordered close order march and we waited for the higher brass. The adjutant gave open order march, came round and informed me that my pith helmet was greasy and my boots unpolished. When the old man turned up he said nothing. His mind was probably on much more important things than a greasy pith helmet and unpolished boots, such as counter-attacking an enemy invasion.

Having been dismissed, we three limber gunners decided that if they wanted us to be clean we had better learn the habits of the section and decided not to return to work until Monday morning. Until then we had regarded Saturday and Sundays as normal working days.

Soon after that episode another vital order in connection with the supreme war effort appeared on the notice board. The order said that six great-coat buttons should be shown when kits were laid out for inspection. In consequence of this order anyone going out in an overcoat would reveal six brightly polished buttons while the others would appear as dirty black horrible blobs on the coat.

Perhaps this is the moment in time to mention my overcoat but before that I should refer to that other interesting object, the army blanket. We had our issue of blankets, the number of which could vary from one to three and perhaps under some circumstances four. I had an issue of blankets when I first arrived at the school but it was over two years before anyone thought about having them fumigated. They were never washed officially.

Before the war, in my cavalry days, I had been issued with a 'British warm' cavalry coat, known as a bum freezer. This was a very thick, fleecy lined coat which came down to just about the bottom of my bottom and was ideal for riding horses in cold weather, and which made the most splendid blanket. Everyone else in the British army, or at least everyone I ever met, had been issued with the long, unlined, miserable looking infantry greatcoat. This meant that in winter when I was standing out like a sore thumb with a greasy helmet and unpolishable boots I was also standing out like a sore thumb because of my unusual overcoat.

Not that this ever seemed to cause a problem. Time after time I was ordered to change my winter warm for a proper overcoat and time after time I managed to sidestep the issue until at the end of the war the poor old thing was actually falling to pieces, giving the general impression that I was some down and out somehow mixed up with the military and so, with much sorrow, I was forced to change it for a very poor substitute.

In July they attached a searchlight troop to the school, which we all resented including our colonel, who even ordered the searchlight captain off our gunpark. We all had the fear that the lights showed the guns up clearly to the enemy, in fact showed the guns more clearly to him than they showed him up to us. Thus the lights were always subjects of booing, although experience had shown me that searchlight crews could be a damned brave lot.

A number of minor incidents occurred in August. My old mate Perks bought a chattie from one of the civilian workers and I, naturally, wanted one too. Those earthenware pots being un-glazed kept water wonderfully cool and were in that regard far superior to the army issue water bottle. The only thing was, of course, the earthenware bottle was easily broken. I tried out Perk's chattie. The idea was to raise the mouth of the bottle to one's own orifice and then without lips touching the neck, pour the contents down the throttle. I nearly choked myself to death in the effort to take a drink but nevertheless I bought one, filled it and then hung it out in the sun to cool. In the evening I dashed up to the tent to take a long cool drink. Nothing doing. The blasted thing had a hole in its bottom!

In October of the previous year while we were on the old gunpark a civvy worker gave us a brown mongrel puppy which we named Flossie. Everyone took a fancy to the yappy, somewhat dim brained animal, everyone from the colonel downward. Then we moved to the new site where Flossie got into the habit of dashing hither and yon and inevitably attracted some of the wild dogs which roamed in packs across the Carmel hills and sometimes got into the camp. The number of dogs coming in increased and the damned things began to ignore us completely as they went after Flossie. What with this and the discovery of camel ticks on Flossie, it was with great regret that we agreed Flossie

Front Row: *Author, Whitehouse, Flossie the Dog.*
Back Row: *Unknown.*

had to go. She was taken beyond the static 3.7 gun pit walls, tied up, and a Captain Cole produced his revolver and shot Flossie. Whereupon she set up a great yapping and yowling, broke away from her moorings and ran for cover to our tent where she curled up and died.

From that day forth we had no more dogs; we stuck to self-contained self-controlled independent cats.

At the end of the month I took my first seven days leave since leaving Blighty. I decided that as I had enough money put by I would head for Tel Aviv and Jerusalem. I had ten pounds saved up, or in Palestine terms ten thousand mils to splash out with. Three others decided to do the same, Perksy, Sheriff Sprang and a squaddie called Berry. We got the Egged express to Tel Aviv – a journey of about seventy miles. The fare was 340 mils which, if a thousand equalled a pound must have been 6s. 6d. old style money and 32½ p new style.

The road to the seaside town of Tel Aviv runs along the plain between Carmel and the sea until the hills turn away to the east to merge with the hills of Judea. It was at that point that the orange grove country began, the groves stretching on away to Hadera and then on again from Petah Tikvah to Tel Aviv.

I may as well confess I became well acquainted with the orange groves of Palestine. Nothing better in my book than to wander through an orange grove during the season from September to May, picking and choosing oranges the size of which is never seen in Blighty. One could pick an orange, taste it and throw it away if it wasn't just so. And of course as the season went on so the oranges changed from unripe green to mushy orange. If we brought oranges they worked out at a farthing each but we rarely paid good money for them.

The groves would be carpeted with bright orange because with the war on there was no export market for what seemed to us to be the major export of the area. It always seemed such a pity, such a tragedy that the world was burning up in gunsmoke while the worthwhile produce of the earth was allowed to rot. It was just one small scene in the panoramic play of man, a

Tel Aviv 1942–3. Bombadier Perks, 'Sheriff' Sprang, Author, Berry.

creature extremely creative and also vastly destructive. The older I have become the more evidence is produced that the destructive power of the human being is accelerating, and that not only are we heading for a global disaster but there is no power on earth capable of stopping it.

After reporting in at the town major's office we began wandering around the town in search for somewhere to stay. Then the sheriff suddenly thought of the Hotel Joseph in which he had stayed the year before.

Joseph himself had gone round to the town major's office possibly in search of army clients, so we saw a man who called himself the manager who explained that he had been in the Austrian army during the first world war and how would we like this top room; yes we would. So we had the top room with four beds in it on the fourth floor of the Hotel Joseph. The price per bed with breakfast was listed at the town major's office as 200 mils per head per day. But the manager, if in fact he was the manager, suggested 250 mils a day.

'I know it is 200 mils but [flinging his arms wide from time
to time and emphasising points by forming a thumb and finger
into an o and flourishing the o in our direction] but – if you
want plenty bread – plenty jam – plenty tea – plenty butter –
plenty everything – two hundred and fifty mils – that not plenty
that very modest – plenty modest.' I cannot remember whether
we paid the extra but we probably did on the grounds that the
self-styled manager made a very good comedian.

Palestine had three holy days a week: the Moslem Friday, the
Jewish Saturday and the Christian Sunday and we of course
argued that it ought to be our duty to support all three, thus
making a reasonable weekend.

On the first day we made our way to the beach and the Aussie
club. The beach was crowded with Jewish holiday makers and
there wasn't a great deal of difference between that holiday beach
and any of the popular resorts in Blighty. Everything was there,
the ice cream man, the side shows, the donkey man, the beach
balls, the sunbathers, the swimmers. The holiday makers themselves were not quite the same; they were darker skinned in the
main while the men were far more hirsute.

There was in fact a difference which only became manifest
with the passing of time. One began to notice that despite the
holiday atmosphere there was an air of sadness hanging over
the place. Children might play without concern as children will
anywhere but the adults who had come from all parts of occupied
Europe carried their cares openly with them. I got the impression
they felt themselves strangers in a land which was theirs now
but which harboured dark dangers. One could only guess at the
things some of them had suffered and guess at what tragedy
they had left behind them.

On the Sunday morning we took a rowing boat out onto the
little Yakon river with me steering so well that we struck the
central support of a stone bridge, so we abandoned rowing and
occupied ourselves with knocking off small hard green oranges
from the private groves on the river bank.

But our true vocation while on leave in Tel Aviv was drinking cold Aussie beer and smoking Aussie cigarettes, I believe known as Black and White, and Aussie tobacco. Aussie drinking hours were a bit peculiar and meant we had to do our heavy drinking as soon as possible in the afternoon then rush inside the club for a hearty nosh. The order of the day after last drinks was to totter back to the fourth floor of the Hotel Joseph and flop out till the evening. Thence into a café for a meal, to a cinema and so back to a café for a late nosh. Then we would occupy the late evening with drinking cheap port and, at the same time, sitting outside the café to watch the girls go by.

One morning we set off for Jerusalem in an Egged bus, fare 240 mils, and arrived at the place two hours later, having travelled a winding twisting road through the hills of Judea, down several sharp bends known as the Seven Sisters, knowing that it was unsafe to travel in the area at night when Arab marauders stalked abroad. Having booked in at the town major's office we fixed up digs at the YMCA by the old city wall near St David's street. The sheriff and Berry didn't go much on Jerusalem, considering it a bit too ancient for them, so they stayed one night for 180 mils and then headed back for the bright lights of the Aussie club in Tel Aviv. Perks and I went off to Bethlehem and Jericho and the Dead Sea. We joined a party from the YMCA and were taken down to old Jericho in a number of taxis. On arrival we found the place very hot, the area very barren and that the high sheer cliffs looked down upon us as if we were unwanted intruders. The guide gathered us all together on a large bare mound, pointed to the distance, said that that haze over there was the Dead Sea which was so salt one could not drown in it and the mound we were on was the site of old Jericho. Whereupon one somewhat overheated and perspiring squaddie burst out with, 'D'you mean you've brought us all down here to this poxy mound just to tell us there's nothing here?'

The guide pointed out that up yonder was the Mount of Temptation where Jesus had been tempted but the only answer he got was, 'Let's bugger off back to Jerusalem.' 'This is the

hottest place on earth,' explained the guide with great enthusiasm, not of course shared by us. It was indeed hot and I wondered
if the ancient inhabitants of old Jericho had been consumed by
heat, thus explaining the lack of people. Someone said, 'I don't
care if it's the hottest place in the universe, let's get out of here.'
And someone added, 'Wot, no beer?' and another added, 'No
dancing girls either.' But the guide was not to be put off, 'This
place most historic up there ...' But everyone had had enough
and we climbed wearily back into the taxi and were taken back
to Jerusalem. The guide would have to wait for the return of
the tourist mob; we needed a cool beer in a decent services club.

Back in Jerusalem Sid Perks and I wandered about the old
town with its mass of hurrying humanity, the donkeys, the shady
open fronted shops and the everlasting noise of traffic and human
voices. We returned to the place several times and took part in
what was known as 'your pilgrimage to the Holy Land'.

On the following Monday morning I reported sick, my varicose veins having got worse so that my leg wasn't looking too
healthy with those damned desert sores refusing to heal up. The
MO pulled a face, then gave me his favourite cure-all, two
Aspros and two days bed down. Having just come back from
leave and due for an immediate guard duty I didn't think it was
right to pull sickness so I ignored the order and took my turn
on guard. This nobility didn't help my leg. The sores would
not go away. They would dry up and then break out again. Our
orderly Taffy Ross was getting browned off with it all. Then,
one day, when he was dressing my leg, the new, young and
enthusiastic MO who had replaced the droll Pole, turned up,
pulled a face and said things like, 'Tut Tut' and 'Dear oh dear
oh dear oh dear,' the result of which found me in hospital, first
in the 53rd General in Haifa and then next day by bus to the
32nd in Nazareth. Nazareth was an Arab town surrounded by
hills and I have pleasant memories of the local children rushing
out of school as noisy and as boisterous as any children anywhere.

I remember, too, the Polish children in army uniform. Seemingly all Polish nationals, irrespective of sex or age, were put into the Polish army as soon as they turned up in the country.

In the hospital I found myself sitting on a bed in a ward which contained five other beds with occupants. All servicemen of course and all smoking like chimneys. I was offered a smoke at once. The room was full of smoke and the noise was somewhat hearty. The wounded were almost all from the Bluey. Some badly, some lightly hit, some with a leg or an arm gone missing but the scene was like a rollicking roaring beer garden. In other wards were other squaddies, naval men and Brylcreme bods from the RAF plus a couple of German prisoners. After a couple of hours a sister came into the mêlée to tell me I was supposed to be in bed, not messing about smoking, dancing and generally making a nuisance of myself.

Next day there was a right old ruckus when a couple of patients in our ward got uptight about the two Germans down the corridor. One produced a revolver, called in the sister and promised to 'Shoot those buggers if you don't get 'em out of here.' She laughed and told him not to be silly, whereupon he hopped out of bed minus one leg and his mate followed him minus something too and they headed for the door. At that moment an MO appeared wanting to know what was up and the buddy of the revolver-waving herbert said, 'We are on our way to shoot those damned Jerry baskets, so get out of the way.'

'You can't do that.'

'No? If you don't get 'em out of it they'll be dead.' The German prisoners were shifted. This was another aspect of the war. We with our guns had not been all that close to the enemy, unlike infantrymen who had come up against booby traps and dead bodies wired up along with unsuspected objects.

Someone got the idea of a football match down the corridor between the armless and the legless. It was bedlam while it lasted and I never found out who won, probably no one.

After a few days I was moved from surgical to a building next door which was called the Tarasancta school or something like that and was said to be built over the site where Joseph and

Mary with Jesus were supposed to have stayed after their return from Bethlehem. I was never quite sure about those historical assertions. After all, we were told of two mangers in Bethlehem and invited to see two sites of the Holy Cross in Jerusalem. All we knew was that despite the war the tourist trade seemed to be doing all right, though with the tourists mainly of the military kind it possibly might not be financially booming.

One day one of Africa's dark sons came over to me and by signs and guttural sounds indicated that he wanted to write home to his mum and would I lend him my brand new fountain pen, thank you very much. No one can spend a great deal of his time talking about internationalism, socialism, universal understanding and co-operation and then refuse to oblige a fellow comrade-in-arms, even though that comrade was one of the East Africans and therefore not allowed to bear arms in case they did the wrong things with them, such as turning them against the pink-skinned benefactors, who were kindly allowing East Africans to work and die for them in the war effort.

So I loaned him my new fountain pen and the ink to go with it and borrowed someone else's pen so that I could carry on with my own writing.

It was painful to watch our coloured brother's efforts to ruin my pen. He seemed to use the nib as a dagger with which to attack the paper and it was clear that he hadn't written many letters home to his mum. A small price to pay, I supposed, for international co-operation and understanding.

On Thursday 17th December I was discharged from the hospital and along with many other squaddies boarded the bus taking us back to our various units. I was put down at the top of the gunpark road just as the colonel drove up. So I was driven in style down to the gunpark where upon arrival I was unable to open the door, so the colonel hopped out and opened it for me. I had arrived in grand style and turned up before a grinning and appreciative audience of lesser gunner fraternity. Our new colonel since his arrival had made sweeping changes such as limber gunners domiciled on the gunpark, free lorry rides several times a week and a much improved diet. And naturally the place was in an uproar with the return of the Dodger chauffeur-driven by a full-blooded colonel who even opened the door for his distinguished passenger.

Meanwhile the war was still going on. Rommel was in retreat after Alamein, the Russians knocking the guts out of the Germans and all kinds of nasty things were taking place in the Far East. And we were still having our own local troubles. Sergeant Brookhouse went into Haifa and got beaten up by some Aussies. Recently a British squaddie had been kicked to death by some Aussies and local Tommies were going into town, armed, in search of the kickers. Rumour had it that the offenders had been found and dispatched.

It must have been around this time that the first Americans were seen in Haifa. The story went that there was a big scruffy looking Aussie with collar open, hat at back of his head and cigarette in mouth, leaning against a shop doorway in Kingsway when a jeep drew up beside the curb of the wide pavement with a number of Yanks aboard. One of the occupants of the jeep leaned out and addressed himself to the Aussie, saying, 'You can put your gun away, Aussie, we're here.'

The Aussie lounged up from his reclining position, lounged over to the jeep, pulled the American head towards him, hit him on the jaw, thrust it back into the bosom of the jeep and without a word returned to his relaxed posture in the doorway. The Yanks drove off and I must add it was the kind of story we liked to hear. The men of the Aussie ninth division expressed an universal opinion that they were going back home for two reasons: (1) to sort out those bloody Yanks carrying on with our Sheilas and (2) to sort out those little Nip bastards.

During that autumn we had been sharply aware that while life was by and large something of a comedy it had its tragedies too. We had a Gunner Beaver, a genial character who could be relied upon to be the life and soul of any party. In fact I had a photograph of him mounting guard with nothing on but his tin hat and holding his Italian bondook. I stuck it into an album and forgot about it. It was only when two maiden aunts of mine started to have the giggles when looking through my album that I realised that the photo was still there. I hastily removed it. No use going round causing maiden aunts to get the giggles.

Now, this Harry Beaver reported sick, not feeling so good. But our Polish type MO didn't seem at all impressed. We kept making the Beaver go sick and the MO kept throwing him out until in the end that same 'medical man' threatened to run him as a malingerer if he put in another appearance and so Harry stopped going sick. A week later he died of a rare form of malaria. He was buried with full military honours and the firing party took great pains to get themselves smartened up for the occasion and no doubt at all we saw him off in style. I have photos of the Beaver farewell which I have kept and do still possess – somewhere.

Soon after that incident we found ourselves with a new MO.

The camp site in the olive grove where the school hung out was not a healthy place. The civvy REs would shake their heads when the camp site came up in conversation and murmur, 'Musquash, musquash.'

It must have been about this time that we began to get a bit

Funeral of Harry (Ginger) Beaver.

bolshie. For one thing, Perksy and I found ourselves named for the muster parade even though our gun had been firing and needed attention, needed in fact to be got ready for the next day's shoot. So we decided to give the stupid muster parade a miss and get on with getting the 3.7 ready. The section officer, the adjutant and the colonel demanded to know where we were. We said we had been working. They said we should have told them where we were, we said they should have phoned and asked us and we could have told 'em. We never heard any more about it and I suspect the colonel left soon after that anyway.

Then there was the business of the tent floor. The olive grove was a splendid breeding ground for scorpions, bugs, fleas and mosquitos. We soon got the scorpions and bugs under control but the mongol horde type fleas were a different matter. They seemed to leap out of the sandy floor in mighty droves as if driven berserk by the smell of human blood. They were certainly fond of me. I counted forty flea bites on my upper arm one bright and sunny afternoon.

And then Gunner Whitehouse had a bright idea. 'Why not,' he suggested, 'concrete the tent floor?' Brilliant thinking! No sooner suggested than acted upon. The civvy REs had been working on the gunpark for months and were at that time busy, or should I say engaged, in building a concrete ammunition dump. We decided that they would never miss a few bags of cement so we carted a few up to our tent, went along the gunpark road where they were using chippings, sand and tar to surface the road and relieved the engineers of some of their road chippings and sand. We laid the floor in our spare time, sometimes in daylight but usually at night by the light of oil lamps. Naturally other tent dwellers became curious and began to investigate the activities taking place in and around our tent. In consequence the REs lost a lot more material. But there was no come-back. They may have put the blame on nasty thieving Arabs (though Arab workers always seemed to us to have difficulty in lifting a shovel let alone a bag of cement). Then again, what would have been the point in raising a shindig?

Once concrete is usefully laid you can't unconcrete it without some difficulty and the army was paying for it anyway and in any case the powers that were were too busy with army bull to notice concreted tent floors. In the end we came to the conclusion that the sand and cement were never missed by the engineers. The only one who might have raised his eyebrows was the sergeant major who often found something new in our tent. One thing was certain, the fleas were not amused and went away.

I have mentioned that Colonel Rope replaced Frith or Firth and soon made changes. Our section officer, sensing the new climate, daringly laid on a nightly liberty truck to the 2 British Army Ordnance Depot down the Haifa road. The unsociable adjutant immediately cancelled it whereupon the new colonel came to the rescue and had it laid on again. But he could not help us with the rain. I woke up in the middle of the night on the first Sunday in October to the sound of tiny raindrops on the tent roof. The morning clouds looked so ominous that Tiffy Hills, Perksy and I went off to the gunpark in a hurry. We had got the recoil system of one of the 3.7s stripped down and we did not want that lot going rusty. We were just in time. When the rain came the heavens opened, visibility was pretty well zero and the gunpark was soon a vast sea of sticky mud. All right for Jerry parachutists to jump into but no good to us. Down fell the rain. The thunder crashed, the lightning flashed and gone was sunny Palestine.

A week later the colonel decided the limber gunners should be where the guns were, on the gunpark. Bully for him. But we thought it must be the adjutant's brainwave that we should sleep in the gunstore while all kits should be lined up each morning outside ready for inspection. We decided he must be ex-cavalry or an infantry wallah or just plain nuts.

But the weather came to our rescue when it decided to turn lousy again. The rain came down as heavily as before, turning the gunpark and the area around the gun stores into another sea of mud. Our exposed kits turned each into a right soggy mess which we left to deteriorate for anyone on an inspecting mission to inspect.

The rain didn't help the cook who had to operate from open trench fires which did not respond kindly to the heavy rainfall. The rain lost control of itself and belted down for days until walking about was like treading in heavy glue. One thing was certain, the colonel might pop round but the adjutant in his dainty bootees would never besmear them with our mud. Now and again the rain would take a breather, the sun would take over, dry the mud, lure us into a sense of false security and then Wallop! Down it would all come again. No wonder crops would hurl themselves out of the ground.

The colonel insisted that there should be three men on night guard but he didn't mind if we had a total of six or nine men. We took a vote and decided on six men three hours on three hours off. Then I found myself on guard in the middle of the searchlight park. I wandered about that night for a bit because there was no rain. But then that damned weather man must have heard me moving about because the heavens opened and down came the pawnee. In just five minutes the mud appeared. I took shelter under a searchlight cover and surveyed with some gloom the partly ploughed-up field I must traverse to get back to the guard house. When I was due off I started out and it took me quite some time to cross that mess of mudage.

I had to stop a couple of times to get my wind back and at one stop, fortunately, I came to an outcrop of rock on which I was able to scrape my boots, thus relieving myself of the dead weight of glutinous mud.

The big circular area in the gunpark must have hardened its bottom because eventually the winter weather of the country produced a permanent lake upon which one could easily have floated a flat bottomed boat.

In the middle of November we were all cheered up with the news that Tobruk had again fallen into our hands and this time we were confident we would not lose it. Meanwhile the Germans were going on the defensive around Stalingrad and though things were still grim we could look for brighter days ahead.

On Christmas eve Tiffy Hills and the Dodger went into Haifa. I wanted to get myself a replacement pen and diary. I got the pen but not the diary, so I made do by buying a couple of thick writing notebooks, one of which has long been lost and the other only recently found, thus leaving me with the horrible task of trying to think of what occurred in one of the six month periods. In the evening the Tiffy and myself set up our drinking arrangements: four bottles of lousy Gold Star beer (15 mils a bottle), one bottle muscatel 150 mils, one of sherry at 130 mils and one bottle of port (price no longer known). We saw the booze off and then turned in.

Christmas day we had dinner at the school, soup, pork and mashed potatoes, chicken and vegetables, followed by Christmas pudding. By tradition officers and NCOs served the repast and they all did the job pretty well, the colonel not afraid to do his bit. They even went so far as to relieve the duty policeman on the gunpark gate with two officers, thus demonstrating how important the duty bod was.

Everyone was a bit canned before lunch and were certainly positively canned in the afternoon as the condition of the canteen revealed on Boxing morning. By early evening it was all quiet on the school of AckAck; everyone was asleep.

I might add that it was customary for the Scots to do the guards and fatigues over Christmas while we obliged the Scots over New Year, though that rule never seemed to prevent either party from joining in.

I ended that year on an unusual note.

I received a message over the phone that I was wanted at the school office. No explanation was given which I suggested was a bit thoughtless since it could have been bad news from home. As it was it was bad news enough that I had to see the adjutant who had long since taken a strong dislike to my greasy hat and unpolished boots.

I considered he must be waiting for me with plenty of nasty

thoughts if not a shot-gun. However, his first remarks almost bowled me over. A good job it did not, I thought at the time; he could have had me for anything like that, possibly he could have called it insubordination. Instead of a cold expression on his pallid face and a pursing of his thin lips he offered me congratulations!

Congratulations!

I was dumbfounded. Speechless!

However, it 'was just the job' to see for the first time, perhaps for the very first time in his whole life, on the adjutant's face just a flicker of a smile. He went on to say he was congratulating me for being awarded the Commander-in-Chief's car! Now like most of my contemporaries I thought a great deal of General or Field Marshal Wavell; we considering him to be one of the two best generals around at the time, the other one being Rommel. But I found it difficult to believe that Wavell was rewarding my admiration by presenting me with his car. In any case if it was an army car it was WD property, not his to give away. Then the adjutant went on very kindly and thoughtfully to ask me if I would like it sent to the school or would I sooner have it sent home?

What the devil would I do with the Commander-in-Chief's car in Palestine? For one thing I couldn't drive and even if I could afford to pay a chauffeur, would the powers that were agree to it? Too complicated, so I said I would have it sent home.

The gunpark was agog with speculation over the affair. Had I met Wavell? Was he a secret uncle? Was I therefore a disguised lord incognito in the ranks or was I just rank? 'And in any case,' one sourpuss pointed out, no doubt full of jealousy, 'what's the good of any general's car? The way they rush around in useless circles the bloody thing is most certainly clapped out.'

'Yeah, that's right. Why don't you wire your uncle and tell him to keep the bloody thing?'

Eventually the truth dawned upon all of us. I hadn't been awarded the C in C's car at all. I had been awarded the

Commander-in-Chief's CARD, a mention in despatches and that seemed to everyone a damned sight more useless than a clapped out general's car.

I did eventually get the car/card business sorted out. It had to do with that time in Tobruk when I got shrapnel in the arm and had been reluctant to leave the gun and then helped in the Lewis gun pit. That was all a question of not wishing to leave the bits of shelter the pits supplied and expose myself to flying old iron. It was the kind of attitude anyone of the mob would have adopted.

And so that year ended.

Meanwhile the First Army which had landed in North Africa was driving Jerry eastward while the 8th Army under Montgomery was driving him steadily westward far away from Egypt and the Nile delta. At the same time the Russian Red army was remorselessly advancing, driving the Germans out of Russia.

We often came across some of the long distance army lorry drivers ferrying supplies north to the Russians. They would unload somewhere on the Persian border and then head south again. All of them could tell more or less the same story. The Russians could never quite understand our blokes and their attitude to the war. On the Russian side they would be working day and night in their war effort while on our side come four o'clock or thereabouts our lads would knock off for the day. War effort for them did not carry on into the darkness of night.

There was a thing called the Army Comforts fund and one day we all had to take part in it. We were all lined up or gathered around officially before or around a box which contained jolly comforts for the troops. Everyone had to put his hand into the box without peeking and then had to withdraw the hand, clutching whatever he had been able to get hold of. In went my hand when my turn came round and out it came, clutching a small tin of fish paste. What luxury! Investigation revealed that the tin was so small there was barely space enough for the price tag which boldly showed the figure of ONE PENNY. How we wondered, had they managed to squeeze such an amount in to so small a tin? Then again we wondered, why did anyone bother?

In the middle of January all travel to Haifa was stopped owing to an outbreak of bubonic plague. Needless to say the powers that were had no trouble in enforcing the ban. We amused ourselves at home until the all clear sounded.

Tiffy Hills had two pet subjects, engines and figures. And he was not the man to accompany on a jaunt to a cinema when, for example, a film was being shown involving air fights between German and Allied aircraft. He could tell any aero engine by the sound it made. It was no fun to be told in the middle of a gripping, nail biting sequence that the Heinkels and the Spitfires, the Messerschmidts and the Wellingtons were all powered by, for example, Rolls Royce Merlin steam roller engines made in Britain.

Then he set up a question: if a star is 200 hundred light years away from earth what is that distance in statute miles? According to Tiffy Hills the answer was one hundred and seventy three billion, eight hundred and eight thousand, eight hundred million. Or to put it another way, 173,808,800,000,000 and who was I to argue?

So, how long would it take a space ship travelling at 1,000 miles per hour (1,000 miles an hour? How slow!) to reach the star which is two hundred light years distant? The answer is said to be, one hundred and thirty five million, forty six thousand, six hundred and thirty six (13,546,636) years. Anyone, according to Hills, considering such a journey should take with him plenty of Aussie beer and certainly no lousy Gold Star and plenty of bread and cheese but if he went via ... at this point I threw Tiffy Hills out of the billet.

One of the innovations introduced by the new broom was a canteen on the gunpark, which was a good idea since more and more people were being domiciled there besides limber gunners. This proved a great success despite a shortage of beer and an abundance of boot polish which was never applied successfully to my boots.

Once the canteen was taken over by one 'Betty' Bedford, the place began to look up and in a very short while we could discuss ways and means of sharing out the profit. All canteen profits were by law to be shared out among the dwellers on the gunpark. So at one canteen meeting some bright spark suggested that we should all get a new pair of swimming trunks apiece. This was agreed, but time rolled by and nothing was done because a number of lads wanted other things. Sullivan for example wanted whist drives, not swimming trunks, though how one purchased whist drives was never fully explained. The arguments increased, some wanting this and some wanting that and so nothing got decided. I cannot recall the outcome but I daresay we compromised and the money was shared out. Hurray for democracy.

Chapter Fourteen

Promotions and Other Things

With the expansion of the school and the increase in personnel on the gun park from around eight to something like sixty, promotions were necessary and so stripes were handed out. No one could work out how stripes were awarded but in fact, in the main they made little difference to anybody because by that time we had become a closely knit community with a very happy atmosphere.

Bedford was given a stripe as canteen manager, Sullivan got one because he was the expert on generators, Nicholson knew all about gun drill. Jack Fell was made a sergeant, a promotion which caused Jack a great deal of puzzlement. Another one given one tape was 'Doodlebug' Floyd, the only one capable of taking heights, a situation which caused us to wonder what would happen if he disappeared. Tiffy Hills was given a couple. In his case he had real knowledge of guns and his promotion was inevitable. So was the termination of our close friendship. I had warned him that as soon as he started the climb up the promotion steps I would ditch him on the grounds that our paths would diverge. I threw him over and threw in my lot with the rest of the lads, entering one of the tents to begin one of the most enjoyable experiences of my existence. Others received stripes which we thought were drawn out of a hat, so many people got them. In course of time my limber gunning buddy Sid Perks got a stripe. Some said he got the promotion through chat while I did the work. What really mattered was that we went on working amicably together despite one or two upsets which will in due course be related. But before discussing these minor hiccups in our relationship, I ought to try and throw some light on the reason why I never got one of those damned silly stripes.

It could have been because of my speech impediment. After all it could be a bit difficult if someone like me had to give an order on parade and nothing came out of the mouthpiece. But it was generally assumed I was a bit too bolshie. After all, Harry Withers, my partner in bolshieism, had been a master tailor in civvy street, employing staff, and was a pretty astute character but his crime no doubt was that he had the *Daily Worker* sent out to him regularly and we supposed it was not the done thing in the British army to have a *Daily Worker*ized NCO. However I hope to show that in our outfit at least, power did not lie with the NCOs.

The day after Sid got his third stripe he took me by the arm in our static 3.7 gunpit and said, 'Just a minute, Dodger.'

I at once informed him that NCOs were not supposed to handle gunners, that the seizing of my arm was tantamount to an assault and I could of course run him. He ignored my information and said, 'Look, I might have these three stripes up but I want us to carry on as we have always done, mucking in with the work and of course going out together.'

I said it was OK by me. Then he added, 'But – er – if an officer turns up I think you ought to call me sergeant.'

Looking back I can see I must have been a bit bolshie really. I invited the speaker to step round to the front of the pit underneath the gun barrel so that the pit wall hid us from any one happening to be looking in our direction. I then took him by the elbow, explaining that while a sergeant mustn't touch a gunner I could see no reason why I shouldn't touch a sergeant. I then waved my fist under his nose and said in plain language that if I ever heard such nonsense in future I would flatten him. No idle threat since I was far bigger that he was. He expressed surprise at the violent reaction but said, 'That's all right, let's carry on as usual.' Which we did. This was in fact an example of the local attitude; we knew the army had to have NCOs but we all got on with our jobs without the need for overseers.

The time did come however, when officialdom at the school decided there was not enough discipline on the gunpark so they sent us down Sergeant Major 'Pip' Pernell, a genial character who soon became a popular figure around the place though as a disciplinarian he was a dead loss.

One of his first actions was to call a muster parade and from it detail clearing up fatigues. The limber gunners excused themselves as of right: the heavy gun team had to practise gun drill and the Bofors teams declared that they had to do the same. Others had special jobs to go to; for example Sully had to do his generators, Yorky had to do the canteen, Doodle had to do his heights, the boiler man had to stoke his fires and the sweeper upper had to do his sweeper upping. When all was said and done Pip was left with two men for his blitz on the camp because of the expected arrival of royalty or some general or other. One of these promptly said he was reporting sick which left only one other. The other one looked at Pip, looked at the camp, observed the work list in the sergeant major's hand and said, 'If you think I am a camel or a donkey and liable to do all the work you've got down on that list, you've got another think coming.' He then dismissed himself and disappeared into his tent in high dudgeon.

Sometime later we sat in our tent admiring the way in which our sergeant major was busy cleaning up the camp.

Gun Drill (with predictor on left).

We were expecting a visitation from some general and Pip got himself a brainwave. The brainwave was in two stages. First, he went round the central part of the gunpark which could turn into a pond in minutes, and whitewashed all the boulders thrusting themselves up through the stony soil into the light of day, until the place looked like a small sea of miniature icebergs. We all admired his handiwork especially that part of it in which he got whitewash on himself. Some got so enthusiastic that they went out and helped him, which I suppose is a sign of good leadership. Then came his second brainwave. He went out into the local countryside and dug up hundreds of the local plant which looked for all the world like 'Aunt Agatha's Aspidistra' and replanted them all over our gunsite. Once we were informed of the nature of the plants Pip found that he had plenty of enthusiastic support, which highly delighted him; after all it was another sign of good leadership. We became so enthusiastic that in no time at all the empty quarter looked like a newly planted jungle badly needing a good watering. And Pip beamed with joy and satisfaction. Then we introduced him to a local civvy worker who was a known dab hand at the horticultural business.

'What d'you think of this?' asked Pip with understandable pride as he swept his arm in an arc embracing the new found jungle.

'Interesting,' admitted the local horticulturist.

'What are the plants called?' put in someone carefully.

The expert told us the name in English and Latin.

Pip was duly impressed, especially with the Latin, and weren't we all!

'Have you got any in your garden?' someone questioned politely.

'No I haven't,' answered our horticulturist and there was a trace of indignation in his voice.

It must have been Sheriff Sprang who said, 'And why not, you Eastern dude land grubber?'

Or words to that effect.

Our local man looked round with a wan smile.

'No one would ever grow them in a garden simply because they are the commonest weed in the country.'

There had to be a hasty rethink of the plant life of our domain although the white icebergs had to remain, which didn't help Pip once the word got around that the visiting general couldn't stand bullshit. Though whether drooping weeds over white-washed boulders could be categorised as 'bull' was a moot point.

Then came the last episode in the disciplinary ploy. A muster parade was called. The lance jack 'Doodlebug' came into our tent, and said we had to go on parade. He was invited to stand against one of the two tent poles and we tied him firmly to it. The orderly sergeant came looking for the orderly bombardier and found him in our tent. We invited the newcomer to go stand against the other tent pole which he very obligingly did. So we tied him up and then amused ourselves by giving them cigarettes to puff at without their hands being free. Ere long, as expected, Pip hove in sight searching for his missing NCOs. He found them in our tent. He sat down on a bed and, contemplating the situation, said, 'What the devil do I do now?'

It was suggested that we told our leader, our section officer that we were all too busy to attend his silly muster parade.

'What about releasing them, eh?'

'No.'

'Oh!'

The section officer appeared, approaching purposefully with stick under arm, searching for our sergeant major.

'Sergeant major ... sergeant major ...'. But there was never an answer. Then more urgently, 'Sergeant major where are you?'

Pip rose from the bed and went to the tent flap and looked out. 'I'm over here.'

'What about the muster parade, sergeant major; we're late as it is.'

Pip took care of the situation. 'It seems everyone is very busy right now, tied up, so to speak and so perhaps we had better cancel the parade.'

'Very good, sergeant major.' And away went the section officer perfectly happily, so that by that time it must have been the 'black mamba' because at the age of twenty-four he was writing his memoirs and wanted as much time to himself as possible. Pip had no more trouble with us after that. We made his life as easy as possible and he became one of the happy band.

In fact on the day that the general was due we obligingly turned out on quite an unpleasant wet and windy day, organised the mobile guns along the gunpark road for some reason possibly only known to Pip himself, and even donned our greatcoats, though this caused a problem since some buttons were highly polished and some black and covered with fungus. We stood about for hours and no general came. In the end we all stood down and had to have an issue of rum because of the hardship caused by the weather. The general did turn up a few days later when no one was looking.

In that other war things were going reasonably well. The First Army was on its way east, the Eighth Army going west, the Russians rolling the Nazis back, though the unfunny, un-lovely, unromantic war against the Japs was causing problems.

As summer struck we tossed aside battledress and donned KD shirts and shorts and handed in our gumboots. The next day the sun took itself off, winter came back, down came the rain. We all shivered and got wet feet.

I lost my diary notes and kept no record again till 1945, though I never could stop scribbling. I turned out improbable short stories, not too well constructed verse and unstageable plays which demanded hostile armies to meet on stage with air battles taking place above a bewildered audience. I certainly had a pile of the stuff and had it with me, ever growing, in Germany. There one day I left my magnum opus tied up in brown paper on my bed, not realising that I was no longer living among honest soldiers in the Middle East. Some idiot knocked the lot off. Maybe someone thought it was a parcel from Blighty or maybe it was a hard-up Jerry. The only consolation I had, if that were so, was to imagine the expression on the looter's face when he opened the parcel and found not treasure trove but a bundle of old and not too clean papers in a foreign language. And so from now on in these pages it's reliance on memory all the way – and that can be a bit dodgy.

In March the light guns were taken off to the staff college in Sarafand for a demonstration. Then it was our turn to have a go with a heavy gun.

The night before we set out for the college the wind had blown, the rain had belted down and prospects for the morrow had seemed none too rosy. But undaunted, we set out at 7.30 a.m. to cover the ninety miles or so to Sarafand. The gun crew and I were tucked up snugly in the back of the matador, with our number one, Sgt. Howcroft, up front with the driver – poor weather-beaten devils! The rain just belted down as we travelled south following the coast.

From El Tira to Benjamina was about thirty miles. The site was in the midst of orange groves at the point where the Carmel hills turn east to meet the hills of Galilee. From that point the road ran through land rich with orange groves, lemons and grapefruit. Hadera was a large settlement and a main stopping point for the buses running between Tel Aviv and Haifa. Incidentally, buses did not run after 6 p.m.; there was too much danger from marauding Arabs. Arriving at Bethlid we stopped at the café there for a couple of wads and a cup of *chai.*

There was supposed to be a café in the area run by a couple of civvy Britons who had been trapped in the country when war broke out. They were an enterprising pair and organised a fish and chip shop which of course did a roaring trade with passing squaddies as customers.

Our stop was at the crossroads where one road turned right for the settlement of Nathanya, known as an American settlement and a rich one, where our convalescent camp was situated, while the other road went left to Bethleed and the railway station.

We finished our tea and wads (cost price 40 mils) and then we pushed on for Petah Tikvah, about fifteen miles from Tel Aviv. We passed a left turning which some of the lads said we should have taken, since it by-passed Tel Aviv which we were supposed to avoid. No one wanted a large gun flopping about in the traffic of the town. But Bombardier Philips, who had made the journey recently, was sure the turn was further on. Thus we found ourselves where we should not have been, mixed up with the traffic of Tel Aviv. By this time Howcroft was all at sea, so to speak. Eventually our number one hit upon a bright idea. Now that we were clearly lost, ask a policeman. So we stopped in a busy street and asked one the way. He turned out to be unable to speak English. But Howcroft was a persistent cove. We kept stopping and asking every policeman we came across, but none of them spoke English. In the end we encountered three squaddies who said they could show us the way. Howcroft squeezed them into the front of the matador between him and the driver and the three guides proceeded to give him precise instructions. The only trouble was they were all different.

But we made it in the end.

After the demo we all set off for home and this time we were led by Major Palmer in his jeep. On the way the jeep driver ran into a runaway horse but Todhunter the lorry driver proved a resourceful fellow, so that we drove into camp with Toddy at the wheel of the matador, towing the 3.7 gun to which was tied and therefore bringing up the rear, the somewhat battered jeep.

The next day a party set out for Sarafand again, this time to attend a point to point race meeting. They got back at midnight mostly broke and complaining of having no luck and also beefing that while there were plenty of ATS about they were for 'Officers only'. Comments were made about the number of ground sheets lying around in secluded corners and one story went that there had been a somewhat ancient brigadier tottering about on the arm of a bint who must have been well into her teens.

Sid Perks was of the opinion that a good many of the above officers had never had it so damned good and the last thing they wanted was for the war to end. Everyone of course was incensed over the monopoly officers appeared to have over service women. We were even told of an RAMC ranker who was punished by his CO for going out with a nursing sister.

Soon after this my old buddy Howcroft left the unit. I had first met him at the El Masa base camp where he had suggested I might try and join him at the school. He was something of a rebel and in consequence fell out with the then section officer Holley and so asked for a transfer. Holley left, Howcroft became section sergeant, happy with his lot. But the die was cast. His transfer came through and away he went.

It was at El Masa that I met a really interesting character I knew as Jack. Jack was a bit long in the tooth to a person like me, he being in his thirties. He had dark hair, sported a Ronald Colman moustache, looked a dashing character and it turned out that he was just that.

Before the war he had been engaged to a girl who understood that Jack had itchy feet. In the end she said she thought he ought to satisfy his bent and go off a-wandering and she would wait for him to come back. So off he went to Australia where he got a job riding fences on a sheep farm in the outback. Having learned the art of horse riding he would spend around three months on the job and then take himself on leave to the nearest town about a hundred miles away where he would blow all his wages and return to the sheep station dead broke. After a while, getting browned off with such a lonely life, he jacked it in and headed for Hong Kong where he knew he had a cousin living. So off he went through the islands, New Guinea, Celibes, Sarawak, Borneo, Philippines until he reached Hong Kong. He contacted his cousin and asked him to get him a job, any job, washing up would do. His cousin said there were no jobs in Hong Kong for the likes of Jack apart from one in the Hong Kong police so Jack signed up for that. The consequence was he found himself aboard police boats in pursuit of smugglers and often shinning up the sides of Chinese junks, cutlass in mouth, as a member of a police boarding party – or so he said.

This went on for some months until he found, to his surprise, that after some years away he was feeling homesick. So he resigned, went back to Blighty, married his girl and they took a country pub with roses round the door, cows in the meadow, lovers in the haystacks and ole men drinking scrumpy.

Then war broke out.

His wife could see he was getting restless and his feet were itchy so in the end she told him that he had better go and enlist which he did with all speed. Thus it was that after a spell in the Bluey chasing Italians and Germans he was able to sit and yarn about his past and swear that once back in Blighty he would go a-wandering no more. But I have often wondered about that.

The cinema had played a very important role in civvy life. It had been usual to line up outside a cinema and wait for an available seat. The cinema continued to play an important part in army life. It was a must for anyone on leave to visit a cinema, particularly in the Middle East with its grand cinemas with sliding roofs to let fresh air in. Sometimes they did show films at the school and one night Mayes and I toddled up there to see a film, having no wish to join in the housey-housey game in the gunpark canteen. The film was so ancient it kept breaking down until it broke down altogether. So we left and went back to the gunpark. Mayes decided to join in the housey-housey and I went to our tent to get my writing materials out. Later, deciding I needed a drink and a packet of biscuits, I went to the canteen where I found Arthur Mayes very happy, having won ten bob. I was so impressed I decided to take a hand and damn me if I did not win ten bob too!

But it was really the 2 BOD where we went for the pictures. The depot was a couple of miles along the Haifa road but it was quicker to cross the fields to it. The Sheriff and I often went there though many of our poor worn out mates would only go if a lorry was laid on. The films were of all sorts from the latest 'Gone With The Wind' to a very old peculiar film such as the 'Dark Eyes of London'. This film starred Bela Lugosi, a specialist in horror films, who spent his time urging elderly factory workers apparently making lavatory paper to 'Hurry Hurry Hurry' and then going into a room with flashing electrical gear to strike a well-bound man blind, deaf and dumb and then, opening some big doors, flinging the poor basket into the Thames. After closing the doors he rushed back to his raised platform in the factory to urge the elderly lavatory paper workers to 'Hurry Hurry Hurry'.

With minds like ours the Sheriff and I enjoyed such lousy films.

It was possible to tell the kind of film that had been shown, at the end of an evening, by the way oranges had been used. If there were piles of orange peel along the chair rows then it had been an absorbing film such as a cowboy or adventure thing. But if the film had been no good the orange peel would be situated at the foot of the screen and the screen itself almost awash with orange juice.

It was there that the sheriff and I went to see a film called 'The Adventures of Red Barry', an old bit of mayhem which had started life as a weekly serial but had been put together to be shown as a full length film. Red Barry indulged in all sorts of mighty deeds such as knocking out twenty-five hefty crooks, diving into a harbour, climbing through a secret door in a bridge pillar, knocking out a half dozen secret agents who were radioing secret information to other criminals, diving out of the pillar, swimming to the surface where more crooks emptied something like four hundred tons of coal from a wharf onto the noble Barry's head. Having shaken the wet coal dust out of his hair he sprang ashore, knocking out all the crooks. Then he jumped into an aircraft and from it into a motor boat, guided the motor boat to shore after knocking out the crew, then leapt out of the boat just before it blew up. At one stage he drove onto an airfield, knocked out a lot more villains and then started looking for an airship. He placed his hand above his eyes and gazed keenly into the distance. Meanwhile the airship as it slowly descended had caught fire and was burning merrily. Now when it was only two feet from the top of Red Barry's head, the audience (including me) started yelling, 'Look above you, you silly sod, look above you.' But he never did and the screen went blank at the end of that episode, followed by a new bit tacked on. To the sheriff and me it seemed as if that damned film had gone on for hours and hours and the audience which at first had made little piles of orange peel now began to bombard the screen. We left, wondering why the devil we had sat so long. Then a few weeks later we noticed that the film was being shown again, surely not by popular request? So we went around the gunpark telling everyone what a marvellous film it was and something never never to be missed. As I suppose we were regarded as something of film experts nearly all our gunpark comrades decided to take a shufti at the film.

So off we all went.

It soon became evident to my companion and me that our more discerning brothers in arms were not too happy and as Red Barry rushed on so the audience began to hiss dire threats and the Sheriff and I decided to beat a retreat. We got to the exit just in time, just as the lights were going up, and we took off at speed for home and safety. Soon we could see what appeared to be a lynch mob hurtling after us. We took the short cut across the fields and both of us, not showing a morsel of fear, tore straight into and out of a patch of very nasty camel thorn. Our pursuers eased up and circled round leaving us to take the shocks and other things that man is heir to. We calculated that by the time that tobacco smoking lot reached the tent they would be too far gone to deal out revenge for being lured into seeing 'The Adventures of Red Barry'. And so it proved. We all turned in, worn out but we were never allowed to forget Red Barry.

Throughout the winter season when low cloud formations were common we could often watch small whirlwinds winding about out at sea like wiggling black snakes which stretched from the bottom of the clouds to the surface of the sea. It was always fascinating to watch.

I had gone down with a very bad fluey cold and I had been given a couple of days bed down plus the usual Aspros. My temperature was rather high at the time, around the 104 mark, so off I went to bed. In the afternoon the other tent dwellers, either to keep me company or because they too felt in need of a rest, came in and laying themselves wearily down began yarning in the usual way, each man telling his own story at the same time as the others were telling theirs.

Our idyll was suddenly shattered by the approaching sound of ten thousand steam rollers bearing down upon us at a colossal rate. I had never heard anything like it and it was more terrifying than anything I had heard in Tobruk. I turned deathly pale; everyone turned deathly pale. I was scared stiff, so was everyone else. What the devil! A great wind came at us, the tent brailing ripped up, and the tent took off and blew away, leaving us marooned amid our scattered kits and me, with my bare backside, hot with fever, sticking up into the wind like an enquiring weather vane. All the tents were down, pieces of corrugated iron were tossing about in search of victims and a Bofors lorry went three or four feet into the air and came down again. We had been hit by a whirlwind that had savaged out of the sea, wrecked

After the whirlwind

our camp then torn into the Carmel hills where it dissipated itself. Sid Perks kept his cool and took photos.

At the school we developed an uneasy relationship with the air force. In the early days they helped us out by putting a plane up towing a sleeve. We had fun with it. In fact we got so adept at the game that we often shot the sleeve down when we were not supposed to and often would get too close to the towing aircraft, much to the concern of the pilot who often gave his opinion as to AckAck personnel.

But usually we fired out to sea on a ten degree arc without a sleeve. We were of course limited to firing out to sea because there would have been a rumpus from the civilians if we had done anything else. The idea was that the officers and the trainee students manned the instruments while we manned the guns. They of course were usually dead slow at their job while our lot, being expert, were fast – probably the fastest in the Middle East. The result was that quite often no firing could take place because the instrument operators couldn't get on target in time. But if they did it was odds on we could bang off the rounds fast enough for our number one to gleefully roar, 'Ammunition expended.'

This of course would never do so we were switched round: gunners on instruments, officers and their ilk on guns: result, chaos and failure. Then to help us out a bit the air force sent us over a Fairey Fulmer for us to practise on, particularly the Bofors bods. The plane crew overdid their zooming and diving, overworking the engine, which packed up and the pilot had to make a pancake landing in a nearby cornfield. The crew were unhurt, the plane only slightly damaged. It was us lot on the ground that got the worst of it, we had to guard the bloody thing.

On my first stint I got so cold I decided to hole up in the cockpit out of the draught and I had a jolly time training the weaponry on the village of El Tira. Next day someone passed on the word not to touch the instruments on any account – the guns were still loaded! 'To think,' I thought, 'I could have started an Arab war!'

The incident did not end there. The powers that were decided it would be impolitic to move the plane until the harvest had been gathered in; it could upset someone. We wondered how the Germans would have approached such a problem. We suspected there was another reason. There was only one rescue unit and that was in Beirut in Lebanon in another country. So, we had to guard the pesky thing for a month, not that anyone ever went near it apart from us guards.

A night shoot was arranged with the aid of searchlights and a Wellington bomber and everyone was having fun tracking the bomber and pretending to shoot it down when it suddenly veered off course and went straight into Mount Carmel. The following week we had another night shoot and again the Wimpy came down. A third was sent up and unbelievable as it may seem, that too hit the deck. When some of the air force wallahs offered to take us up for a ride to see what it was like under fire there were no takers; circumstances make cowards of us all.

One day a gaggle of Hurricanes rose up from behind Mount Carmel, just like a swarm of bees. They flew all over the place as if all the pilots were sozzled. Two collided and down to earth they came. A little later one of the pilots came over to help us out with our training programme and proceeded to demonstrate how no AckAck gun on earth could catch him. He zoomed and dived, twisted, turned, banked to left and right and then coming across the sea low, too low, he ripped over us, banked toward the sea, tipped his wing which touched the water and in he went. Our strongest swimmer went in after him with a lifeline but it was too late. When his brother paid us a visit later he said his brother had been a bit of a maniac. We agreed.

The usual gang of us went on leave to Tel Aviv to do the usual things, with the Hotel Joseph as our base. As usual we were going to see all the films in town. But my hoppo Sergeant Perks said he couldn't stand that idiot Gary Cooper. Righto, we said, we'd leave him and his film till last. This we did. Then we decided to go and see the hated film actor, suggesting Sid Perks stay away. But complaining and swearing, he came. I thought

Gary Cooper was a tough fighting man fit for the AckAck while Perksy had long since regarded him as a twit.

But Perksy paid and came with the rest of us up into the circle, grumbling all the way. The film unfolded, my companion, who had insisted on sitting next to his chum, swore, grumbled, swore, fell asleep, swore, snored, woke up, swore and grumbled and it was clear he did not like Gary Cooper. The film ended and down the stairs we went and came out at the front of the cinema where all kinds of military gentlemen were milling about, colonels, majors, captains, two pippers, one pippers, all sorts of NCOs and a variety of civilians. Still my buddy complained. How could we have wasted our time and more importantly, his, seeing such an idiot as Gary Cooper?

I could stand it no longer. My patience was exhausted. I took my old mate by the shoulder, turned him round to face his old cobber and than I hit him squarely on his jaw and he fell over amid all that milling brass.

He lay flat on his back for a bit and then slowly sat up rubbing his chin.

He looked completely bewildered. 'What did you do that for?' he enquired quite politely. What a brainless question.

'Why? Because you don't like Gary Cooper and kept on saying so, that's why.'

'Oh.'

As he got to his feet I looked round for the Sheriff and Berry but they had taken off into the deepest of dark shadows and were peering at us from a distant and safe corner. They had no wish to be associated with a lunatic limber gunner who went around hitting officers on the chin even if they were only the non-commissioned variety.

In the early days of the war punishment for striking an officer was severe though stopping short of the death penalty. As the war went on views changed and such villainy could place one in front of a psychiatrist and one could end up behind the wire of a mental institution, on the grounds I suppose, that no sane man would dream of striking a superior officer, commissioned or no.

Perksy got to his feet and we slowly walked away, me still glaring at him as we went in search of the troops which had fled the field. Sid could not understand why I should get so uptight about that bloke Gary Cooper! Wasn't as if he could act! Not one of the milling crowd there assembled did anything about our little fracas. Either they were all blind or it was now the accepted thing for a gunner to knock down a sergeant, particularly in public. It was all in the day's work and of no consequence.

After Berry and the Sheriff had recovered from their respective shocks we all toddled off to a café for wine and a look at the passing bints and Perksy didn't seem much the worse for wear. Sprangy came to the conclusion that the officer types had been so taken up with their preserves, the ATS, that they never saw us. Sidney Perks decided that they had all become so browned off with watching that idiot Cooper, they couldn't care less what happened from then on and would have probably jacked it all in if Jerry had suddenly appeared.

I must record that our newly promoted Sergeant Perks never bore me any malice and we went on working together just as before, and if memory serves me correctly he carried on disliking Gary Cooper.

It should be noted that brute force is not always the answer. In fact it seldom is.

I should have known better. I had had some experience of what could happen if one fell foul of military law.

One of our blokes did hit a sergeant and was hauled before a psychiatrist and then found himself behind 'the wire' of the mental side of a hospital. Mark you, the climate must have had a bit to do with it and eventually everyone decided that all of us in some way or another were a bit sun-touched.

On one occasion when I was in hospital there was a squaddie in the next bed to me in with a surgical problem like the rest of us. The day before he was due out the MO noticed what most of us had long observed, that this particular character had a tic over one eye. This was a nervous condition which interested the MO. So, this new friend of mine was sent off to see the local psychopath or whatever he was officially called. When the bloke came back he was quite a bit put out because he had been told to gather his gear and take himself off to another part of the establishment. He found himself on the wrong side of the 'wire'. When he came to see me a few days later he assured me that if he stayed where he was for any length of time he would be as nutty as some of his new found companions already were. Me, I remembered my impediment of speech and took precautions. From that time on until I was discharged I abandoned the impediment whenever one of the hospital staff turned up.

Despite our pagan attitude toward religion we did do the rounds of the holy places. After all, it was true that we would probably not get the chance again and even if it became possible after the war there would be no such thing as free trips to those places.

The mosque of Omar in Jerusalem turned out to be a very beautiful building when we paid it a visit. At least it looked that way inside. Like most of the great buildings in the area the inside was more impressive than the outside.

Before entering the mosque you had to remove your footwear unless you happened to be in uniform. In our case we were allowed to keep our boots on our feet and the problem was got round by us visitors pulling goloshes or huge slippers over our clonking great army boots. We were a bit ungainly but satisfied protocol.

This state of affairs had been brought about sometime in the past. When soldiers went into the mosque leaving their boots outside they returned to find their footwear missing! And of course a military man without his boots is not worth his pay.

Once inside the mosque we had a history lesson, being told that it was on the rock inside the mosque – thus its other name, the Dome of the Rock – that Abraham was prepared to sacrifice his son Isaac. Indeed we were shown a channel in the rock where the blood of sacrifice was allowed to drain away in those days of early Jewish ritual. It was from this rock, Moslems claim, that Mohammed ascended into heaven mounted on his winged steed. The crusaders erected an altar here when they converted the mosque into the Templus Domini for Christian use. Even we barbarian type British squaddies were left breathless when viewing the interior which was covered in magnificent gold work which the guides assured us was priceless. Two rows of columns ran round the wall while old beautiful carpets covered the floor, each, we were told, worth £5,000. We were impressed not only with the value but the way in which the local guides put a monetary value on everything.

One must remove one's footwear before entering the mosque and rightly so. We decided that if any of us owned a £500 carpet let alone one valued at £5,000 we would not allow anyone in sweaty socks to walk over it let alone anyone in army boots. We naturally took in all the sights: the church of All Nations, the Garden of Gethsemane, which disappointed us because it looked so small and was full of old gnarled olive trees, the thirteen stages of the cross along the Via Dolorosa, the Wailing Wall, the church of the Holy Sepulchre and not forgetting the old town itself with its David's gate, Damascus gate, Dung gate and the Golden gate, closed until Christ should come again.

Sounds a bit like a tourist brochure but then we were tourists, though the keepers of those holy places insisted upon calling us pilgrims.

A party of us got to the main door of the Holy Sepulchre a bit early to find it well and truly locked. We were fooling about when an Arab rode up, dismounted from his bike and leaned it against a handy holy wall. He was carrying an enormous key over one shoulder. It was the largest mobile key I had ever seen, that any of us had ever seen. Naturally, we were all curious. Why should an Arab Moslem, for that was what he was, be in charge of a key to a Christian church? It seemed to us to be plainly potty.

'Why you got key to a Christian church, Johnny?' The inevitable talk in broken English had begun. 'You Arab, you Moslem, why you got key?'

'Me Moslem, me not Christian.'

'Then why, Johnny, you have key to Christian church?'

Johnny gave a good natured grin, happy no doubt that he had a job. 'Me hold key, Christians fight over who has key.'

'Fight each other!'

'Sure, they fight plenty fight, plenty punched noses, plenty blood – blood everywhere. They no agree who hold key so me – I hold key. Plenty blood – blood everywhere – so Moslem hold key – everybody happy.' He grinned and opened the door with the huge key and we all toddled off inside.

There were five Christian sects sharing the church and the territory of each was carefully designated and woe betide the one who crossed the line. The churches as far as I can recall were Catholic, Greek Orthodox, Coptic, Armenian and, I hope I am right, Abyssinian. I did learn that one of the churches was chucked out of the body of the church and so took up its abode on the roof! Where as far as I know it still remains. We ourselves were unable to sort out who was who; they all seemed to have adopted the same dress, black gowns, tall black hats, and all sported long black beards, thus getting themselves labelled by us with the somewhat crude name of shag nasties. All of them when on guard duty held silver salvers ready to accept baksheesh which was something very hard to extract from us northern barbarians and particularly difficult from such people as Sprang and me.

We began our tour of the church in a none too auspicious manner, the sheriff stumbling over a black clad old woman prostrate at prayer who certainly did not take too kindly to having army boots stuck into her ribs.

We came to an altar before which could be seen a hole in the floor lined with either brass or gold. Neither of us having had much of the former and even less of the latter could really tell the difference. The little black bearded priest (all the priests seemed little to us) waved his collecting plate in front of our noses as he explained in excellent English that the hole was the sacred place which had held the base of the true cross. But both of us declined the opportunity of adding to the local fund-raising scheme and walked or started walking away.

The little priest was full of indignation and determination. 'But you must give alms.'

'Must?' questioned my companion, 'Must?'

'You are on pilgrimage and must put in.'

The Sheriff was getting quite peeved. 'There is no must about it. I won't because I don't have a mind to.'

'I insist,' said our friendly priest. 'As a pilgrim ...'

'I don't bloody well want to, so wrap up.' And I expected our Sheriff to begin to threaten the little man with a pistol whipping or an invitation to a necktie party not far from Boothill.

The priest then said, no doubt eying his empty plate. 'Then do it for the poor.'

The Sheriff looked at the priest, convinced that the latter was somewhat demented.

'Do it for the poor! Then you'd better start giving us something, we are bloody well poor enough. So – off.'

We then beat a retreat or, to put it in the correct military manner, we made a strategic withdrawal.

We came to the Holy Sepulchre itself, a tiny room only large enough for a priest with plate half extended and two pilgrims in army boots. Into the Holiest of Holy places we went, ducking our heads low as we entered, not out of reverence but because of the low doorway. The priest inside with plate, speaking English, invited us to touch the tomb, the most holy place, where, according to Christian tradition, Christ had been laid after being taken down from the cross. In regard to the hole in the floor I had told the priest that I would not stick my mitt into it in case there was a scorpion wandering about inside it but in regard to the tomb I could see no reason for refusing to touch it. After all it would please the priest, raise his hopes in regard to baksheesh and would do no particular harm to me. So I touched it.

In the case of the cowboy from Eastbourne, his dander was up. No way was he ever going to touch the top of that tomb. He dug his fists firmly into his pockets and shook his head.

'You are on pilgrimage; you *must* touch the tomb of our Lord.'

It sounded rather like an order and the Sheriff glared at the priest. 'I am on leave, *not* on pilgrimage and I will not touch your damned tomb.'

The priest's dander was also up. 'You bloody well will.'

'I bloody well won't.'

'Yes you ...'

I ducked out of that holy place, leaving them to it, but also aware that by taking that particular action I would be avoiding that menacing alms plate.

The Sheriff emerged still with his hands in his pockets.

'You didn't?'

'Of course I didn't put anything in his damned plate. He nearly knocked my bloody teeth out with it.'

He wouldn't listen when I suggested that the church was hard up and that the outside was all shored up with scaffolding and might need money for repairs. As far as he was concerned they could take the shoring away and let the poxy place fall down.

As our visit drew to a close we were invited by other priests to gather round a table so that we could pay five ackers and get a piece of the true rock set in wax plus a certificate to say we had done our pilgrimage. Sid and I must have got our bits and pieces early because while we were waiting for the rest of our party the plainsman from Southern England decided he desperately needed a smoke. I did point out that quite reasonably smoking was not allowed but by that time there was no way in which my old mate was going to be law abiding. He lit a cigarette but did agree that he would be discreet which I supposed was something.

So, there he was taking a quick puff and then hiding the cigarette behind him in truly military spit and a drag style, while I watched somewhat apprehensively, knowing how much bother we must already have been.

As indicated the priests seemed to have been built on a small scale while Sid Sprang was quite tall. He took a puff and then put his cigarette behind him and then took another puff until presently, noticing an unusual smell, I asked him if he could smell burning. He sniffed a bit and then agreed. We turned

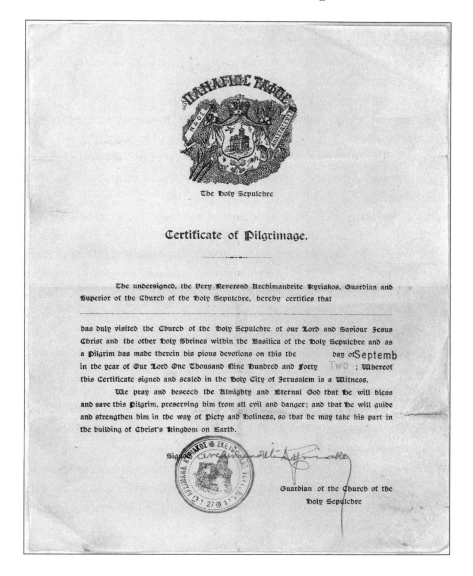

The Holy Sepulchre

Certificate of Pilgrimage.

The undersigned, the Very Reverend Archimandrite Kyriakos, Guardian and Superior of the Church of the Holy Sepulchre, hereby certifies that

has duly visited the Church of the Holy Sepulchre of our Lord and Saviour Jesus Christ and the other Holy Shrines within the Basilica of the Holy Sepulchre and as a Pilgrim has made therein his pious devotions on this the day of Septemb in the year of Our Lord One Thousand Nine Hundred and Forty Two ; Whereof this Certificate signed and sealed in the Holy City of Jerusalem is a Witness.

We pray and beseech the Almighty and Eternal God that He will bless and save this Pilgrim, preserving him from all evil and danger; and that He will guide and strengthen him in the way of Piety and Holiness, so that he may take his part in the building of Christ's Kingdom on Earth.

Signed

Guardian of the Church of the Holy Sepulchre

around and there behind us jumping up and down and clutching his beard was a priest clearly trying to put a fire out. This time the Sheriff had no pride, no desire to argue. He took off clear out of the church with me hot-foot behind him.

Our next bit of sightseeing took us along the Via Dolorosa to see the thirteen stages of the cross. We were in a party organised by the YMCA and our guide was a very studious, serious minded young man dead keen on his job. He was a Christian Arab who did his best to impart to us some of his enthusiasm and devotion to his faith. He little realised into what stony ground he was scattering his seed.

He started off by explaining that he had been born in Texas and that he preferred that place to Palestine and then he began his enthusiastic guiding as we went along. He was a very good guide and knew his stuff much better than he could have known his audience. At each stop we would all gather while he explained what had to be explained, going through the history of each sacred building that had been built on one of the thirteen sites. Most of us agreed that the commercialisation of the stages had been very thorough. But by the halfway mark the folk were getting restless. The sun was hot, the streets were noisy, there were too many people trying to flog us souvenirs and things we might want but could not afford. So gradually the guide's audience began to disappear.

Round about the ninth stage someone called out, 'All right, Johnny, we go now, thank you very much.'

'Go, go where?'

'NAAFI, we go to NAAFI, Johnny, we thirsty.' Pidgin English was always used in such circumstances even if the person addressed could speak the lingo better than we could.

'You cannot go yet, you're still on pilgrimage, you must stay.'

One or two swore, someone told him where he could go and we all staggered off to the NAAFI, no doubt leaving poor Johnny wondering what sort of Christians he had been dealing with. We waved politely because he had done his best. It wasn't his fault we were what we were. But confound it all, here we all were, mostly against our will, messing about in someone else's country, caught up in a war caused by idiots and fortune makers not to mention maniacs and we were convinced that the 'Enemy' felt just the same as we did. The Pope had blessed Italian soldiers, German soldiers, and as soon as we took Rome he would bless Allied troops too. We also understood Rome abounded in brothels. We didn't know much about the other religions but considered that there couldn't be much difference in any of them. And I truly believe I am expressing the view of most of the squaddies out there at that time. We went to Bethlehem, saw the things to see, and left.

Chapter Fifteen

Pictures from a Life

In Hospital

I went into hospital a number of times while in the Middle East, either for some sort of fever or more often with desert sores. The visits were always made pleasant by the hospital staff. One such visit I remember very well. There are those who, like St Paul on the road to Damascus, experience a vision and thereafter become addicted to religion. I had some sort of vision in regard to music.

Before the war when radio was king, whenever a chamber music concert was announced I would be the first to rush to the radio and switch it off. It was alien music. I had been brought up with the music hall, light entertainment, the popular song. Then I found myself in hospital somewhere in Palestine. One day it was announced that that evening there would be a gramophone concert in the grounds. I hadn't got anything much to do so I decided to go. After all, if I couldn't stand the stuff I could always hobble away.

So I went.

The big wind-up gramophone was placed in the middle of an ancient olive grove where ten million crickets were in conference, the stars glittered a diamond pattern in the sky and the moon rose. It was night time in fairy land.

Then the music began. It was the perfect setting for a conversion. The music was Tchaikovsky's Pathétique symphony and as the sound of it stole out into the night it seemed to gradually embrace the magnificence of those natural surroundings and I was hooked. The olive grove was my Damascus road and I have been a constant convert ever since.

At first in that hospital I was confined to bed, so was a kind of captive. I was a captive audience when the specialist came bouncing along with a deferential body of students to whom he explained something about my leg. 'Now here's a case of kill or cure, where a patient can die or make a good recovery.' And he bounced off while I muttered something like, 'Ta very much.'

The expert was utterly wrong: I neither died nor made a perfect recovery. I still have to keep a sharp eye on my varicose veins in the left leg and keep little spots, when they appear, under control. One day I am sure I shall be plunged into real trouble. This somehow or another brings me to the subject of chess.

Opposite me was a young man in bed playing chess with an up patient, i.e. one who could wander about, and he was clearly no match of the man in the bed. Indeed it was clear that he was about one remove from a person unable to play chess. After the walking patient had toddled off I made the mistake of mentioning I could play chess. A silly statement, since the degree of playing ability is as wide as the Pacific Ocean.

However my opposite bed number was clearly delighted, as I thought, to have someone to play with. In fact he was delighted to have yet another victim to torture. We played a game which he won, another which he won and another which he won. We played before and after breakfast, before and after tiffin, before and after the evening meal, before and after supper – he even had a torch which could be used after lights out. It didn't help to discover that I was bed ridden but he in fact became a walking patient the day after our first game!

He was a fanatic. I was a trapped idiot.

We played in such manner for days on end, long dreary days in which I never won a game, he was that good and I was that hopeless.

Then one day by pure accident I got him checkmated.

He went spare. He tried to analyse where he had gone wrong, what I had done which I hadn't done before. He consulted books on chess, talked of consulting the Delphic Oracle and I am sure he was on the verge of baying at the moon.

I was only able to escape the games which continued unabated after my sole victory when I became walking wounded and could go hide myself behind a local bush in the grounds or crawl behind some lavatory tank or other.

But you know, some of us never learn. Years later my step-son Andrew came to stay with us for a few days when he was either eight or nine years of age. I played him five games of chess and he won 'em all.

I have never played since.

The Folk

It was not all smiles and sunshine. At one time we had near enough half the married men down with family problems. Wives often took off with other men. This never surprised me though it always shook the husbands, even though the regular customers at the local brothels were married men. Women with menfolk away for years had to cope with a great many problems: raising children, rationing, making ends meet, bombing, looking after less fortunate relatives and friends. Hardly surprising that many strayed from that straight and narrow path laid down for them.

One of our number received a letter from a neighbour of his, a woman who explained that his wife had upped and left the kids playing in the street, walking off with some bloke or other. She, the neighbour, was looking after the kids.

He never got any compassionate leave and slowly went round the twist with worry. We watched him day after day, walking up and down the gunpark and as time passed he would walk longer walks and talk more and more to himself until eventually he just kept walking and talking to himself all day long and into the night until he was taken away.

Then there was my great partner in political polemic Harry Withers, who was never popular with the powers that watched caringly over us. How could he be popular with that power when he was in regular receipt of the *Daily Worker*! We might be for the time being allied with those Bolshevik Russkies through no fault of our own but to have a sympathiser floating about in the army!

It wasn't just that he had these Bolshie tendencies but being a master tailor he ought to have known better.

Harry was a great believer in freedom and equality. 'How can you lot rant on about what your wives are doing in England when you frequent brothels yourselves?' He would carry on, 'What's good for the gander is also good for the goose?' Thus would he stand up for women's rights.

Then, late in 1944 he learned that his own wife had walked out on him. I reminded him of his public attitude toward such things. But the walking out didn't unduly upset Harry. He was much more put out to learn that his wife had walked off with a bloke in cloth cap and muffler!

'I wouldn't mind,' he was apt to remark, 'if only he wore a collar and tie – but a muffler!' And he never did get over the indignity of a master tailor's wife walking off with a low-brow dog in cloth cap and muffler.

Every army unit had its Irishmen. We were always astonished in Blighty when the Irishmen living in the South of Ireland went home (they had to go home in mufti) on leave and came back to us again. We figured if it had been us we would have stayed there out of the way. But they always returned. And so I gave up trying to understand the Irish. But I came to appreciate the Romans. They were the only people to take a shufti at the Irish and then leave them strictly alone. Our own particular Paddy was, all week, a quiet, pleasant happy-go-lucky hard worker who could not be faulted. But when the weekend arrived!

At first he would go off to Haifa for beer and a fight and would roll back to our place blotto unless he had been thrown into gaol by the Redcaps. Time after time before the tent floors were concreted he would lose his false teeth and we would spend a great deal of time searching for them in the somewhat murky sand. In the end we made him hand his teeth to his mate while he went off to indulge in his chosen hobby in Haifa.

One day he sallied off as usual and got involved in a café with Yanks who gave him free beer. Then he spotted a group of hulking Aussies in a far corner. Now Paddy knew all about the Aussies and how much they disliked the Yanks so he proceeded to raise his voice in fierce argument with his new American friends until the noise he was making reached the large flapping ears of the Aussies, one of whom lumbered over to where the Yanks were minding their own business and said, 'What's up, Pommy, these bastards bothering you?'

Paddy's answer was to the point, 'They won't let me drink me beer in peace.'

The Aussie said they'd see about that and called over his mates with a wave of his hand and in no time at all there was a right old mêlée taking place. Tables upset, chairs overturned, bottles and glasses flying, fists flailing, curses stringing and Aussie hitting Yank, Yank hitting Aussie and Paddy hitting all of 'em. Soon the Snowdrops arrived and joined in, Aussie Redcaps got wind of the affair and flung themselves into the fracas and Redcaps and Snowdrops were soon chucking each other out while Paddy was trying to chuck them all out. The battle raged for some time until British Redcaps arrived led by some pink faced young officer who tried to calm things down and spoil the fun. Once again Paddy was bailed out of the jug but with some wonderful memories.

Then there was that Geordie character who graduated from being the British army's most smoked boiler man to the British army's most incompetent cook. Most of us could not understand his Geordie language and we wondered if they could understand each other in their own land. I ought to point out that it was Geordie who, before he was elevated to stoking, was the camp tent sweeper-upper, who found my money lying loose on my bed and put it to one side for me and who advised me to be more careful.

When the gunpark cook house was established a couple of field boilers were set up and Geordie got the better job of keeping them properly maintained and fired and he did a good job too.

The only thing was it was hard to distinguish between the hard black bulk of the boilers and the hard black body of the stoker, who must have concluded early on that while he was stoker there was no point in washing. He became a kind of dry, greased wraith slipping in and out of great puffs of swirling boiler smoke.

Then for some strange reason it was decided that the stoker should become a cook. This was possibly a grim decision by that higher authority beset almost permanently with the problem of finding people willing to cook. We assumed that when Geordie was approached, not understanding what was what he just nodded, so that he could get back to his boilers.

He was sent off on a month's cookery course and on his return we rubbed our hands, figuratively speaking, in great expectations. What would Geordie the ex boiler man produce? The question was vital since up to that time we had not been overwhelmed by first class cuisine.

We from our tent were the first in line for breakfast on his first morning and we took our bread and fried eggs and went into the mess marquee and as usual by the time we were settled the eggs were less than lukewarm. Then one by one we took a turn at the eggs and immediately gave up in disgust. We decided by universal consent that our new cook had fried the eggs in paraffin!

We called forth the orderly officer who took a long time turning up so that by the time he did so our eggs were very cold and very congealed. We made our protest and he did a bit of tasting and decided that while there might be a bit of a tang the eggs were not too bad really. He did go and have a word with Geordie but we knew that without an interpreter nothing would be understood. That left us to decide what to do with the eggs, eat them or throw them in the swill bin. I must confess I agonised over mine for a long time.

Geordie was not pleased with us and indicated his displeasure with his somewhat loud and violent language. We gathered that he concluded with, 'Wait till the next meal.' Was that a promise or a threat?

The next meal was tiffin, a light meal served up during the middle of the day and which might consist of a piece of triangular wrapped cheese, half an onion and a small slice of bread or hard tack biscuits. There must have been other forms of tiffin which I cannot remember, such as a lonely pilchard on a tin plate.

When evening came round, then it was time for the big meal and so we went off to the cookhouse in great expectation. There, Geordie proudly flopped onto each plate a large dollop of something which looked like a pink pile of coconut. In fact it turned out to be salmon and rice mixed. The only thing was, as we soon discovered, Geordie had sugared the rice and well salted the salmon. There was no point in calling the orderly officer: either he would pass it as fit for human consumption or he would taste enough of it to give himself a meal. Then again we asked ourselves, where the devil had all that sugar come from? Normally we never tasted sugar except in tea on guard duty.

We took the law into our own hands and chased the cook clear out of the camp and the next day he returned to his stoking, smothering the place with soot.

Our outfit was not addicted to sport. We had one or two early instances of that sort of thing which put us off for the duration. First, in the very early days we had a school football team which soon earned the reputation of never winning. They would lose by the odd goal or two and victory always eluded them. Then one day, like a prairie fire, word got round that someone had joined the school who had been a pro in the football third division and not only that, he was a full back!

Ah! Ah! No more defeats by the odd goal or two and now maybe a win or two from time to time.

So he was put into the team and we all went along in great anticipation and lo and behold! Our team lost 9 goals to 1. It was suggested that the full back should be immediately repatriated to Blighty, particularly to the third division. And he didn't have a very long stay at the school of AckAck.

The game of cricket will always be associated in my mind with our first canteen manager, Canada. He had been on a visit to England when war broke out and had then joined the army despite the fact that he had a rupture. This intrigued us because he was given the job of canteen manager which meant among other things messing about with crates of beer and he himself always proudly said he had a double rupture, single ones were for the English. He was the man who produced, from God knew where, a half sack of chestnuts. But as he said he would have to charge the equivalent of a shilling each for them he was told to eat them himself, which he probably did.

He had a guitar which he was always fiddling with and could never get tuned to his satisfaction. Gradually he got more and more browned off with the thing until one evening he got so annoyed he took the guitar and wrapped it round a tent post. Then of course he discovered that he had nothing to fiddle about with or swear at. So he found a tea chest and proceeded to make himself a new guitar. When he had finished the job no one would have been able to distinguish it from any other instrument, he did such an excellent job.

One day we decided to have a cricket match, thinking that maybe we could form a side that could take on other unit teams. Canada said he didn't know what cricket was, which caused a great deal of disgust in the ranks. So we set up a wicket, gave him a bat and told him all he had to do was to hit the ball and when he had hit it hard enough he could run to the bowler's end of the pitch and thus score a run. If he ran back he would score two and so on.

He went in and holding the bat proceeded to hit every ball that was bowled at him. At last, the heat beginning to cause a strain amongst the bowlers, the latter changed from bowling to flinging and then hurling the ball at Canada, not at the bat. But it made no difference, he kept hitting the balls and he was clearly becoming more and more puzzled. 'What happens next?' he wanted to know. We told him when he was out someone else would have a turn. When he had scored seventy-five runs he flung the bat down pointing out that he couldn't see any point in this game called cricket. Nor could we and we never broached the subject again.

I suppose I can say that the Sheriff, Sid Sprang, was one of our main characters though I would have to admit we had quite a lot of main characters. He was a citizen from Eastbourne and all the time I knew him his usual language was film cowboy talk, which everyone encouraged, such as 'Howdy hombre?' or 'Shucks son, go fetch them there shootin' irons o'yourn,' and 'Hit the trail dude, you ain't welcome in these parts.' Then again, 'Any more talk of gun toting and you'll sure wind up in boothill.'

One day the sheriff complained bitterly at the lack of a horse. How could a real live Westerner like him exist without an old cayuss? It was a problem which engaged the public attention of our old Western town citizenry for quite a while. The only horses we had seen in the country had been those ridden by officers now and again. One of those horses we remembered very well. Perksy and I were on the night guard, he as the guard commander and me standing leaning against the sentry box while he and I chatted. It was very early morning and nothing much to be concerned about until we noticed movement in the distance. It was a rider on a horse, an officer riding on a horse. Avoiding the gunpark gate the rider put the horse to the fence and both sailed over it as if they were competing in horse trials. It was an unpopular instructor of gunnery playing silly billy.

I aimed the rifle at the nasty fellow and pulled the trigger and informed the guard commander that the intruder was officially shot. He couldn't be shot for real, we not being allowed to put bullets up the spout; possibly the powers that were considered that such action would be too dangerous.

Our unloved intruder rode over to the 3.7 static, dismounted, went into the gun pit, jumped onto the loading platform, removed the firing pin mechanism and then clambered aboard his offending nag. I trained my bondook on the silly idiot and shot him a second time. Perksy and I agreed he, the guard commander, would phone the school to report that a captain IG had ridden down to the gunpark on a horse and stolen a firing mechanism

Static 3.7 with Hingley and author.

and so had been shot both coming and going and if he approached the site in the proper manner he would have been challenged correctly. Now it so happened that the man in charge of the gunpark and its limber gunners was Major Ferry, who considered that the said limber gunners could do no wrong. In consequence that nasty piece of work the horseman, when he got back to school in triumph as he thought, found himself with a flea in his ear and within days he was gone. Probably transferred to the front where he could chance his arm with a horse and try taking mechanisms from Jerry guns rather than from ours.

So, horses were in short supply. However, in true army style someone came on to the gunpark leading a horse! Where it hailed from we never discovered but what was more startling was that it was no ordinary officer-type hack but a fully grown *cart horse!* We had never seen one in Palestine before and were never to see one again. We all stood dumbfounded, unusual amongst us lot. The Sheriff spread his feet wide, placed his hands on his hips just about where his six shooter should have been and said, 'Dang my hide and bust my boots if my old cayuss ain't turned up.' Now at the time of the year when the horse incident took place the centre of the gunpark surrounded by the circular road was like a lake created by the winter rains. The horse was slowly brought along the road and presented to his new master, the wild mustang rider of the plains, who, gingerly touching the horse's flank, said 'Dang my hide but he sure is a purty critter, I'm gonna be right proud of him.' The wild Westerner kept on babbling away until someone said, 'Cut the dude talk, Sheriff, and git aboard that there critter.'

But of course our very own home bred cowboy had no idea how to climb aboard a horse and knew still less how to do so with neither stirrups nor a saddle. 'Tain't many of us cowpokes what climb aboard bare backed hosses, it's usually only them there redskins what has a mind to do that.'

But the time for dissertation was over and so with a push and a shove and a heave and a ho, we got the Sheriff up onto the horse's back while urging the rider to take hold of the creature's massive shaggy mane. The horse, no doubt entering into the spirit of the thing, gave himself a little shake from side to side with the result that the rider or would-be rider fell off. The Sheriff from his prone position looked up sorrowfully at his late mount. 'Dang my hide, hombres, if he ain't a wild mustang.'

After some effort we got the lawman back up onto the horse again, enjoining him, this time to 'hold onto the bloody mane.' This at last he did and then one of our number gave the horse a tap on his rump and off he trotted in a leisurely manner with his rider clinging on for all he was worth and singing a prairie cattle song until the horse, still entering into the spirit of the thing, stopped as it were at an emergency stop. The Sheriff, not waiting to argue, shot straight over the horse's head and ended all ends up in the middle of our inland sea. The horse seemed to us to be actually guffawing until he was led away out of sight and we saw him no more. The Sheriff decided he would stay a land based lawman having had too much contact with air and horses.

Damn your eyes and damn your boots,
You coyotes have been in cahoots,
Just ain't right I can't think
For me to end up in the drink.

Well perhaps he didn't say that but them words are sure better'n than them nasty blue words he did spit out though it don't matter since there weren't no females about.

The day came when the powers that were wanted to make up another lance jack. So the Sheriff was called into our section officer's poky little office and told that he was it. But the Sheriff firmly rejected the idea. Who ever heard of a Sheriff wearing an unpaid stripe on his arm and a tin star on his chest? The idea was ludicrous. The section officer insisted, the Sheriff refused and the argument got heated. I know, I was listening at the door.

'You can't refuse.'

'Can't I?'

'No you can't.'

'I do.'

'You can't. It's an order.'

'I turn it down forthwith.'

'I could run you for this.'

'Run what you like but count me out.' And so it went on.

In the end a compromise solution was reached. The Sheriff agreed to accept the stripe provided that everyone understood he would never give anyone an order and would never put anyone on a fizzer. With that agreement he reluctantly accepted the stripe and had to face a barrage of comment as the striped cowboy later on.

Sandham walked into our tent one day when the Sheriff was minding his own business and shaving, using a mirror hanging from one of the two tent poles. Sandham stopped in front of the sheriff and said, 'Sheriff, your clothes look almighty tatty, you should get 'em changed.' He then went behind Sid and slowly ripped the latter's shirt right off his back. The Sheriff said not a word as he slowly put his razor down and then, turning the unresisting Sandham about face, ripped the latter's shirt from his back. He then picked up his razor and went on shaving. Sandham, in silence, responded by producing a jack knife and with it proceeding the cut the lawman's braces in twain. He then removed the Sheriff's trousers and ripped them to pieces. Again the Sheriff refrained from speech but put his razor down and destroyed Sandham's trousers, borrowing the latter's jack knife to do so. They ended up the pair of them, standing in the tent stark naked. Sid went on shaving, Sandham picked up his ruined clothing and walked off without uttering a word. I do not remember what happened when Sandham took his ruined clobber to the stores but in the Sheriff's case he returned with a pair of KD slacks at least a foot too long for his long legs. We said he would have to get our master tailor to alter them but he was emphatic in his reply. 'This is how they've issued them to me, this is how I'll wear them.' And indeed he did.

I must say that he was something of an embarrassment when we went into Haifa; he was always falling over his trousers. At one point we were passing some officer or other and the Sheriff as he gave one of his sloppy salutes staggered over his trouser bottoms and nearly pitched into the astonished officer who gave a quick return salute and hastily moved on. He didn't want to be involved with a bombardier in over-long trousers. But there again, it must have been a part of that condition into which we all fell sooner or later − being a bit sun touched.

Soon after that a parade was called and the section officer enquired from the duty sergeant after the whereabouts of the duty bombardier. Why wasn't he on parade? The sergeant called out to the Sheriff who was still in his tent and the latter called back, 'Wait a bit, I'm not ready yet, I gotta lock up the calaboose.' There was a long pause until the missing person appeared in his recently issued over-long trousers, falling over them three times between the tent and the parading troops.

The section officer, a caring man, suggested politely that it would be better if one of his majesty's bombardiers, even though he was unpaid, would get his trousers seen to. But the Sheriff said, 'They issued me with these and if that's what they want, if that's how they think I should dress, who am I to argue?'

In the end he was forced to compromise. It just wasn't the done thing for one of his majesty's soldiers to walk about in public in trousers so long that he constantly fell over the things. So, he turned the legs up so that he had two distinctly visible turnups about a foot long.

Eventually we persuaded him to take his trousers to our master tailor but that was after we had brow-beaten that unwilling master craftsman into submitting to the will and bondage of the gunpark launderers.

Which brings us to another two characters, Lofty Bale and Tich Robinson. Lofty Bale was the biggest bloke in our outfit apart from Taffy Powell. He was a genial character, never known to get upset, who could neither read nor write but who was always willing to work. It was he who came to me one day saying, 'Look here, Dodger, here's a letter from my bird, will you read it to me?'

This of course I did and it proved to be quite a decent letter, full of goodwill towards her boyfriend Lofty. I said he had better answer it and he nodded agreement. Some weeks later when I asked him about replying to the letter he just grinned saying how could he, he wasn't a writer of letters or anything else. But I kept pestering him to reply so that a few days later I sat with him in his tent, opened up one of my numerous writing pads and said to him, 'Right, Lofty, let's begin the letter to the girlfriend.'

'The what?'

'Never mind, let's just start.'

We sat for some time in silence until I nudged him to see if he were still awake.

He was but quite speechless.

'Right Lofty, let's begin.'

'I don't know what to say.'

I started to write the letter for him. When I paused for a think he said he thought I ought to let him know what I was letting

Back Row: *Author, 'Lofty' Bayle, Mays, Unknown.*
Front Row: *Hingley (Hung Low), Sergeant Perks, 'Tich' Robinson.*

him in for. So I started to read what I had written out to him.
'My darling ...'

'My what?'

'My darling.'

'I can't say a soppy thing like that.'

'Why not? She's your bird isn't she?'

'I know that but she'd think I was crackers starting off like
that.'

'All right, I'll cross out darling and put dear so and so.'

Having agreed he allowed me to continue thus; 'My dear so
and so as I sit here at the entrance to our tent I look out ...'

'I'm not looking out of my tent, I'm flopped out on my fleapit.'

'All right,' I said, 'I'll cross it out and put down "as I lie here
in my flea pit".'

I carried on, 'My dear so and so as I lie here on my flea pit I can see the moon coming over the mountain, as the sun sinks slowly in the west leaving the sky in a blaze of golden light ...'

'I can't send her that, Dodger, no way can I send her that.'

But I determined to get my way and so continued with a letter that perhaps only a would-be poet could have written. I made him put his cross at the end of the letter and walked him to the post box and watched the letter disappear. The sequel to all my efforts – he never heard from his girlfriend again. Letters were censored and I thought our section officer sometimes gave Lofty a queer look.

Tich Robinson was of a much smaller build than his pal Lofty, possibly half his size, but Tich though small, was tough and wiry and also always cheerful and impossible to upset. He was proud of the fact that before the war he had been a bricklayer's hod carrier. This had made him strong and he had a power of endurance greater than the rest of us. To most he was an old man, in his late thirties, but even as an 'old man' he was more energetic than most and he always showed a lively interest in the girls. So much interest that he finally embarrassed Lofty so much the latter positively refused to go out with him any more.

'It was like this,' explained Lofty, with great indignation. 'We were walking along a main drag in Haifa, me happily looking at the world in general but minding my own business but this idiot here,' indicating Tich, 'kept eyeing the girls up and down, stopping and staring at 'em, turning round, passing remarks, and generally making a poppy show of himself. Some were good looking Jewesses and Arab bints while some were in uniform. Made no difference who they were. Then we came up behind a really classy chassis in a flowered frock who looked pretty good from the back let alone the front. And then Tich here comes up close behind this handsome piece as bold as you like and says, "I could really DO YOU, that I could." Lofty was well into his tale now. 'The girl stopped dead in her tracks, turned round, looked straight at Tich and said in a voice that matched her classy chassis, "BUT YOU WON T GET THE CHANCE." And I just

Author and
'Tich' Robinson
(hod-carrier).

shrunk though Tich only grinned. So me and him, we are not going out together any more and that's a fact.' The joke was that Tich was quite incapable of hurting or taking advantage of anyone.

Gypsy was a member of the Harry Withers, Lofty, Tich tent and was our only pure bred gypsy. Somehow he looked just as everyone supposed a gypsy should look. He was dark complexioned and never seemed to have done anything about washing himself though I am sure he did. Now, this Gypsy had a habit of picking up pieces of scrap wood and carving odd shapes and figures out of them. It seemed he had to be constantly employed with his hands. He would sit carving away for hours not saying much but always a part of the company. Then, one day, while carving away his knife slipped and it jabbed savagely into his private parts and severely cut that part known as his 'John Thomas'.

Now when any of us 'goys' damaged ourselves the wound would always turn septic. So, when Gypsy ended up with his heap of trouble we estimated at least a few hospital visits. But he merely laughed, found himself a piece of dirty old rag and wrapped it round the offended and unhappy part. We rolled up. Here was a future court martial case, a self inflicted wound. But Gypsy assured us that it would soon heal up and damn me if it didn't!

The sun, as I have said, played a vital role in the creation of character while we were domiciled in Palestine. The heat made us do things we would never even have thought of elsewhere. One cannot imagine, for example, anyone in uniform in Blighty refusing to shorten his trousers and ending up with trouser turn ups roughly one foot long and getting away with it. Then what about Doodlebug? He was not the most reliable of lance jacks in that he was so fond of his sleep that at times it was almost impossible to wake him up. One day he lay contentedly breathing slowly and loudly, oblivious to all the world. So one of our number had a brainwave. The result was we lifted Doodle and his bed out of the tent and placed the lot right in the heat of the sun. We were pretty well exhausted and certainly sweaty by the time we had done. Then we piled onto Doodle twenty blankets and waited for results. All that happened was that our victim roused up, muttered something about it getting a bit warmer and went back to sleep again.

Taffy Powell was one of the heavyweights of the outfit. He and Lofty Bale were the big pair with myself third. But when we needed brawn it was to those two that we turned.

Both were right heavy boozers and Taffy, whether drunk or sober, was a true Welshman in that he knew how to talk. His great yarn was that he had hanging up in his room in his mother's house in London, fourteen suits. That made Taffy a liar. No one believed him, especially me. I had had one suit when the war broke out. While I was away my mother loaned the suit to the son of a great friend of hers. The son, in my suit, went to a dance hall in Putney, a bomb came down and took the son and my suit to kingdom come. I with no suit could not believe that anyone of Taffy's age could have fourteen. Yes, indeed he was a liar and so we all agreed.

We had a series of young officers, second lieutenants who were put in charge of the gunpark. On the whole they were not a bad bunch and indeed some were very good as far as we were concerned. They were the ones with the policy of live and let live. They left us alone to get on with our work while we left them to their own devices such as writing their memoirs. The adjutant though seemed to be our mortal enemy. When he turned up he brought with him an aura of old bull, seemingly searching for trouble, expecting people in greasy overalls to look like guardsmen waiting to do a turn at Buckingham Palace. He wasn't very popular. The colonel would bustle in and bustle out again, his head possibly full of night shoots and plans to repulse any number of enemy landings. The officers we came into contact with mostly were the instructors of gunnery from sergeant majors to captains, the efficiency usually declining with the rise in rank. But more of them anon.

Chapter Sixteen

Tales from a Life

It must not be supposed that we were a jolly bunch of layabout soldiers lucky in our billet and far from the frontiers of war. In fact most of us worked hard and indeed, when I look back, I am astonished how hard we limber gunners did work. Sometimes we downed tools when the authority upset us with its stupid bull but in the main we kept at it, Sundays being no exceptions. The underlying rule of course was to keep the guns serviced and ready for action at all times. After all a gun is useless if it cannot fire when called upon to do so. Then again we were a gunnery school and a student course could be expected to appear at any time of day or night. Though night work was not too popular, since everyone concerned was in favour of his sleep. There would be student courses, refresher courses, courses for foreign students and then there were special occasions when demonstrations took place, as for example when the Chinese delegation turned up.

Our bugbear was the sea air which could turn bright metal rusty in next to no time, causing over-zealous and somewhat ignorant of weather conditions captains IG to become irate or positively threatening in their behaviour towards the hard working work force.

We never worked as individuals but always in teams, so that no one ever sloped off or vanished into Haifa with work undone. In fact evening passes were never issued, only long leave ones, and I believe we were the only unit in the area who had this set-up. So I must emphasise that whatever we did, whatever tricks we got up to, nothing was ever allowed to interfere with the maintenance of the guns.

Gunner Green's War (1938–1946)

Tale One: The Laundry

Every unit had its own dhobi wallahs, civilian characters who did the laundry and the mending of clothes and where necessary the tailoring of uniforms. Though when it came to the latter Harry Withers the master tailor would laugh his distinguished tailor's head off. Indeed the work of the local launderers left much to be desired. As time went by things got worse. Clothes were returned in worse condition than they were taken and sometimes it would be asserted that the clothing had passed through a mud bath or stain-producing machine. Gradually individuals took over doing their own laundry. After all it merely meant a quick rub through at least with shirts and underclothes and hanging out to dry, a process which would usually take less than half an hour to complete.

One day Tich Robinson observed to his mate Lofty Bale that as neither of them were avid book readers they might usefully occupy their idle moments with a bit of dhobi wallahing for a small fee. Lofty was enthusiastic and so the pair of them set themselves up as the Gunpark Laundry Inc. The business thrived. The washing blossomed in such manner that before long the tent of Tich and Lofty vanished underneath a mountain of washing. Soon the other inmates of the tented laundry were drawn into the business whether they wanted to or not. They simply had to help out if they wanted to get to the safety of their own fleapits. And soon the personnel at the school cottoned on and were sending their dhobi to the tent.

Then someone turned up with an ironing board and another keen worker discovered a charcoal iron so that life in and around the tent became hectic. The work would go on until late of an evening. If one entered the laundry tent one had to brush aside drying washing, hanging pants and vests, old trousers and drying shirts until speculation began as to whether the inmates would be liable to contract rheumatism, arthritis, flu or pneumonia. But the work rolled on.

I often visited Harry Withers for consultations on the way to construct our local political activity and to talk of things in general and we would often have to talk through wet washing or move out of harm's way. Then the beady eyes of the entrepreneurs turned toward our Harry. Here were a pair of idle hands and skilled hands at that, lying idle amid all that glorious activity. Harry insisted on his citizen's rights as a master tailor and refused to downgrade himself into a dhobi wallah. He would come over to our tent, moving furtively to escape the attention of beady eyes, and discuss with me the future of Socialism, the meaning of the Red Flag, the triumphs of the Soviet Union, the disgusting ethics of capitalism but on no account would he demean himself by washing other people's clothing, be those people Socialists or Capitalists or nothing in particular.

The rest of his tent hoppoes began to put pressure on the rebel. Either he cooperated or he would be evicted on the grounds of not paying his way and he would have to sleep in the open since no other tent would be allowed to house a traitor to the cause of cleanliness. No one cared about godliness but cleanliness was another matter. The first world war had produced a load of lice; so far our war had produced none. Then, a solution was suggested.

'Why not, Harry, use your skills as a master tailor and do the sewing and mending?'

'Do the *what?*'

'The sewing Harry, the sewing.'

'The *sewing!* You mean stitching those smelly old clothes?'

'Smelly Harry! Smelly! They will be laundered before you touch 'em, won't they?'

'As a master tailor I cannot lower my standards.'

'Then Harry, we are afraid we will have to throw you out, we can't have idle hands.'

'When I was in business I used to employ women at low rates to do that sort of thing.'

Someone then pointed out that in that case he should have been ashamed of himself, a professed Socialist, exploiting the labour of poor women and making huge profits out of 'em.

'Profits! I had to watch them like a hawk, otherwise they would just natter.'

'Harry, we will supply the needles and thread.'

Of course he had no choice and so there he used to sit when official work was done and often before 6 a.m., stitching away with nose averted but with a needle flying and I would go and discuss with him the glories of manual labour, especially when payment was in the region of a halfpenny an hour (old style) which was never paid because all money went into a general comforts fund.

Business kept on booming and the laundry lines kept increasing until parades were somewhat difficult to organise. Forage parties were organised to search for charcoal. The section officer soon sent in his laundry and other officers followed suit on the understanding that they paid an officer rate. Then came the crowning moment when the colonel sent his washing to be done. Our camp was now in danger of being transformed from an active gunsite into a laundry factory!

It could not last. It didn't.

The civilian dhobi wallahs suddenly found themselves without any business at all. They would sit gloomily all day gazing out from their deserted, silent premises apparently faced with slow death by starvation.

They went to the old man and complained. He, of course, had no option but to stop sending his laundry down to the gunpark factory. He told his officers they would have to stop also and advised our launderers to ease up. After all, there was a higher authority than himself. He did of course sternly advise the dhobi wallahs to pull their socks up if they had any and do their work properly. So indeed they did and in due course everyone was happy or nearly so because the local launderers, for some reason, could never match the spick and span turn out of the Gunpark Laundry Inc.

Tale Two: Sully

Sullivan the generator man was a very genial Londoner, who could sometimes lose his raspberry or blow his top, though such outbursts never lasted long. He was a true civilian, called up and shoved into the army where he showed a dogged disrespect for all authority and a deep devotion toward all generators. His was a kindly nature and it was he who looked after the dog Flossie in the early days. But Sully could certainly fly off the handle. On one occasion he fell out with one of the sergeants, someone sent in from outside and not one of the true school gunpark fraternity. Sully reckoned the sergeant had 'got it in for him' and if that character didn't soon stop needling him, Sully, the latter would certainly plonk him one. That of course was a course of action fraught with danger since striking sergeants no longer carried a fifty year hard labour sentence but possibly a stay behind the wire of a military mental institution. The situation got worse and it was clear plonking time had arrived. A solution came when a light AckAck mob camped a little way down the Haifa road waiting for transport overseas. Sully asked for a transfer, an exchange was effected and he went off to join his new outfit.

So Sully disappeared and we heard nothing from him for months until his old mate Whitehouse received a letter from him. Sully with his new unit had boarded a boat which took them as part of an invading force to the islands of Cos and Leros. When the ship docked, according to Sully, the Germans were waiting for them and in consequence poor old Sullivan found himself a prisoner of war, sending out letters: at least, one to us from somewhere in Europe.

Tale Three: Bathing Picket

Our own made-up NCOs were OK but now and again we got one from outside who could cause problems. Sully's NCO was one and I had a problem with a regular bombardier who soon turned out to be too big for his boots.

The sea was usually far from placid. In fact it was reckoned that we had only six days of really calm water a year. Therefore when bathing was the order of the day a bathing picket was essential. A bathing picket usually consisted of a number of men some of whom, like me, couldn't swim or could hardly swim, headed by a bombardier or lance jack. As usual we limber gunners were excused the duty but since there were never enough men to go round we always took our turn, sort of detailed volunteers. We usually finished the job we were doing and then with bathing trunks on and towel in hand would wander down to the beach, the beach of course being only yards away from the gunpits. On one occasion I arrived, as usual, a bit late, with towel and trunks at the ready and was immediately accosted by the regular bombardier, red faced, angry and bawling his head off to the effect that I had disobeyed an order, was late, was not allowed to please myself when I turned up for duty and in consequence of my insubordination I could consider myself on a charge or in other words under open arrest.

I sat down with the lads who had been witnesses to the above event and we all rolled round the sand in high glee and everyone expressed the opinion that we could look forward to a bit of sport now that the Dodger was on a 'Fizzer'.

I should make it clear that by this time Harry and I were a team of, I suppose, barrack room lawyers, leaders of public opinion, social activities consultants whom sensible section officers, seeking a quiet life, would negotiate with. We were I suppose a sort of military trade union committee. Keep this committee happy and everyone was happy and then the idiot bombardier stuck his regular army oar in. For the rest of the day the bombardier concerned was either derided, laughed at or told to go jump in the hoggin and stop breathing.

Next day I was marched into the section officer's tiny office and he, poor fellow, was somewhat startled when told that I was there on a charge of insubordination. The section officer looked at Bombardier Bailey, then looked at me, then turning to the bombardier said, 'You can't do that, this is *Green*.'

He then politely told me to leave and stepping outside I listened at the door while our official leader tore Bailey off several strips, told him not to be an idiot particularly where bathing pickets were concerned and what the devil did it matter if some hard working limber gunner was a bit late for a bloody bathing picket and for god's sake clear off and don't be so bloody silly.

This did not meet with the approval of the said non-commissioned officer who, we suspected, would bide his time and make another onslaught on our freedom.

It came soon, the vicious attack on democracy.

Our canteen was a marquee rigged up by this time with electric light and it was the duty bombardier's job to turn the canteen lights out at 11 p.m. Bombardier Bailey did just that, one dark and stormy night. It was the custom to give a warning of the switch-off and the was never any hurry apart from the speed of Bailey, a right regular soldier without too much upstairs. Bailey went and someone switched the lights on again. Bailey returned swearing he would have someone's guts for garters and switched the lights off again. It was supposed that he thought he was in the infantry or dealing with a bunch of newly arrived conscripts. The lights were again switched on and the idiot returned to do his bit and at the same time to announce that everyone in the canteen was on a charge, a fizzer. This time, as the darkness switched on, someone hit Bailey with a bottle and then most of them left the marquee, walking all over the prostrate bombardier in doing so. It was said that he was trod on good and hard that dark stormy night.

Everyone proceeded to turn in and listen as the wretched bombardier went crawling past groaning, bewailing his lot and calling for the section officer. Arriving at the door of the higher official he opened it to confront our leader with his battered and bloodied figure. The section officer by all accounts was utterly astonished at the sight confronting him. No doubt he was somewhat taken aback to learn that Bailey had been attacked, that everyone in the canteen was on a charge which would have to be one of attempted murder.

His advice to the wounded man was to get himself cleaned up and go to bed. After all, the gunpark laddoes were a gently kindly bunch. A few days later the bombardier was posted away and we saw him no more.

Tale Four: Sandham

Mad Sandy became bored. He could not stand the slow peaceful life of the school of AckAck. He applied to join the Palestine police and was accepted, so transferred to that somewhat reactionary organisation (at least some of us thought so). He then discovered that, having signed on for seven years, he would be mucking about in a war-torn Palestine long after the rest of us had gone home. He would be mixed up with a civil war between Arab and Jew of which Sandy could understand little and wouldn't want to understand. One day he came to announce he was now the Haifa police chief's driver. It was a change from one of his duties – policing the brothels of Haifa. From time to time he had turned up with goods for sale; he would hold a sale of ladies' underwear and other kinds of female knick-knacks which he accumulated on his non-fee paying visits to the establishments of those ladies.

As soon as he got his new job he abandoned his sales and instead would recount tales of the activities of the Palestine police, happy that he himself was not obliged to go around waving a pistol in front of native noses, knocking about and locking 'em up on the least pretext.

Now, all he had to do was to drive the man in charge of it all around in a jeep. By 1944 trouble was hotting up, bombs were bouncing about in all sorts of places and the Palestine police were a prime target. It wasn't just Johnny Arab, the Jewish population led by Haganah were getting worked up. Word got around that the civvy workers, Jews, were making rifle bolts not destined for the British army; at the same time at a BOD, one of our lorry drivers, pulled in with a load of weaponry, popped into the office to get his papers signed, came out and found his lorry had disappeared along with its cargo. Yes indeed it was all hotting up and we were eagerly talking about going back to Blighty. We had had enough of one war and were not keen to get mixed up in another.

Sandy appeared one day looking pale and nervous, quite clearly not relishing the idea of leaving our peaceful domain for the ups and downs of the civilian world beyond. The night before, Sandy's boss had told him he wouldn't be needing his driver in the morning. He would take the jeep out himself and Sandy could go take the day off. Now Sandy's official duty that morning was to go down to the garage and take the jeep out ready for action. That morning the chief himself took the garage key, unlocked the door and boom! Up he went with garage and jeep in a cloud of bomb explosive, thus leaving a vacancy for a police chief. Sandy didn't like the situation one little bit and when we came to mull it all over neither did we.

Tale Five: When Christmas Comes

Whenever I have cause to contemplate Christmas, one Christmas comes to mind.

Our tent, like the others, had clubbed together and had bought a great deal of drink of all kinds, except whisky which was the prerogative of the Sam Browne belt brigade, and of course the local beer which was only drunk when in dire need. During a five day period Taffy Powell and Lofty Bale had gone on steadily drinking, being more or less sozzled throughout that period. One night, one of our lads came into the tent demanding a bottle of booze, liquor preferably, for his friend, a local worker then at the main gate. The only trouble was his friend hadn't contributed toward the forthcoming Christmas booze up and was therefore not entitled to a sniff, let alone a whole bottle. Now that year I was the guardian of our liquor store because I was on the water wagon in the belief that alcohol didn't help my desert sores any. I said the answer to his request was no. I was accused of all kinds of things, racism, meanness, spite, cussedness, especially toward his dear friend. As he departed he turned at the entrance to the tent and wagged a finger in my direction and said, 'Taffy and Lofty said it would be all right.'

I said I didn't care if the C in C said it would be all right. 'Your friend is not on.' I pointed out that Taffy and Lofty were only part owners of the alcohol supply. His friend could have my share but since I wasn't clear what was my share, that wasn't on either.

'I'm gonna tell 'em what you said and in their state they are likely to mash you into some sort of horrible pulp.' He then left, muttering something about international cooperation and similar long worded phrases such as 'You stinking basket.' He left me with a bit of a nervous twitch. After all, I did have a bad leg and both the aforementioned were bigger than me and that could make matters difficult.

So I waited with some concern for their arrival. In due course they appeared but by then they had drunk themselves utterly sober and both agreed I had done the right thing. They rolled into their fleapits and the guardian of the communal drink breathed easy once again.

The night of the booze-up arrived. We settled down in a circle, me with my lemonade bottle, they with the rich flavoured and highly coloured traditional bottles of happiness. Fangs King was not in the circle since he was in bed and due to do a stint on guard duty that very night. But he was not to be excluded from the festivities. The laws of democracy demanded he be included for his share.

We had gin, rum, vermouth, Cointreau and anything else one can think of. The pouring out began, everyone receiving a good tot in his mug. Fangs was roused up for his share.

'Here y'are Fangy, get a load of this.'

'What's this red stuff?'

'Never mind, Fangy boy, drink up.'

Fangy did as he was bid, said, 'That was nice,' and went off to sleep again.

Round went the next bottle and Fangs was duly roused. 'Here Fangy, have a drink.'

'What's this green stuff?'

'Never mind what it is, drink up.' This he duly did.

The next drink which was some sort of orange colour really impressed Fangy. He said it was nice and he had always like the colour blue.

He turned over with a happy smile. Thus did the drink go round and round for a long time and always Fangs King got that which was his due. He began to sing happy songs in his sleep and then had to be raised to a sitting position and helped to drain his mug each time it was filled. Thus Gunner King became inebriated, probably for the first and the last time in his life and he knew absolutely nothing at all about it. He was a happily singing fast asleep contented drunk.

Then the guard commander turned up and we gave him a drink; after all it was cold outside. He wanted to know where Fangy was, which the guard commander had a right to know.

Someone pointed to the man in question who was clearly incapable of sitting up in bed let alone standing a guard duty.

'What the hell do I do now?' asked the bombardier of no one in particular. Someone poured him out a drink and he took it to steady his nerves.

'What if some twit of an orderly officer turns up, eh? What about that, eh?'

'Here, have another drink. It'll clear your head, you'll be able to think better.'

Then someone had a bright idea. 'Why don't you do his guard for him?'

'Have another drink.'

'If any fool turns up you can pretend to be Fangs King and say the guard commander has been taken short.'

The guard commander thought for a bit, took another drink, nodded his head and tottered out into the ghastly night air. We carried on with our session and Fangs carried on drinking, singing, sleeping and waving his arms about as if he were being bothered by those big black stuka-like flies which abounded by day.

The Sheriff got an invite to the sergeants' mess. He emerged from that den of iniquity with a pint glass in his hand; he was beaming all over his wild western face. 'These yer hombres [indicating a few sergeants] ain't so bad after all.' He raised the glass on high. It looked as if those devils with stripes had filled the glass with mud. In fact they had concocted an outsized cocktail the size of a ten ton bomb.

'Down the hatch,' cries Sprangy and down it went in one great draught.

Now the Sheriff was no drinker. One glass of two per cent beer and he was gone. He beamed at us with a big wild western grin and then went crashing to the floor. He was lost to the world for three days and I knew all about it since his bed was next to mine and he kept up a monotonous singsong as he tapped his stomach with his hand. Then one night he wanted to relieve himself without any possibility of him reaching the tent exit. He stood up and loomed over me full of relieving menace. 'Sheriff,' I called in some desperation, 'Them Injuns is a-coming in right behind you, about turn and *fire*.'

He did and Doodlebug who lay on the other side of our western hero, got it full in the ear. He promptly sat up in bed with a jerk.

'The tent's sprung a leak,' he yelled. Sheriff fell back onto his fleapit and I said, 'Can't have, 'tain't rainin'.'

'That's funny, I'm sure I'm wet,' and he went back to sleep, blissfully unaware that the Sheriff was continuing with the tribal song of the Dingaway Indians.

Tale Six: The Dodger Takes a Drink

I had been a staunch teetotaller until we had been some time in the Bluey but even after that I was never one for heavy drinking. I did find I had either a very large stomach or one made of cast iron because apart from being a bit garrulous I could never seem to get drunk on beer. I found I could outdrink most. It was with this knowledge that I approached our somewhat elderly regular soldier who eyed the rest of us with contempt when it came to drinking. According to him he could drink anyone under the table and as far as he was concerned neither Lofty or Taffy had the stomachs to go with their bulk. So I decided to test my new found cast iron stomach against his. The old codger had never thought of me as a drinker so he agreed to a drinking match pint for pint quite willingly.

So there we sat that evening drinking pint for pint until we had reached double figures at which point the old codger put down his unfinished glass and said, 'I quit.' We both toddled off to bed and we heard no more sneering remarks about those kids who thought they could drink.

Then one night the canteen manager 'working man' suddenly decided that he hadn't bought me a drink for a long time and he was ready to put that omission right.

This was quite a pleasurable surprise because he was not over keen to lash out with his money. So we took on board a few lousy gold star beers, a few shorts and split a half bottle of port between us. The bottle of port would have cost around twenty-five pence a bottle. After the last drink I said goodnight to Worky and anyone else within earshot, made for the loo and went off to bed, being quietly sick on the way. Number one rule in drinking, never mix drinks. It was the last time I did so.

Next morning someone wanted to know what had happened to my compass the night before.

'Compass? What compass?'

My interlocutor gave me a quizzical look. 'Last night, Dodger, you circumnavigated the canteen three times before you found the door and stumbled through it.'

So much for my ego.

Tale Seven: Geordie

While on the subject of drink I might as well mention our

ex-cook, the Geordie. He took to drinking heavily in the canteen, usually on his own and would usually end up calling in a loud voice for his dear mum – at least that is what it sounded like. It was of course well nigh impossible to follow his conversation when sober let alone when he was half seas over. We wondered if the humiliation of being a demoted cook had turned his brain or whether sometime in the distant past he had been thwarted in love. Not, we thought, impossible, where speech was more or less unintelligible. As the nights went by his cries of lamentation became louder and more prolonged. At last we could stand his racket no longer, especially when, after chucking out time, he would sit and bay the moon or call to the wild dogs of Carmel.

We delegated the task of sorting him out to Lofty Bale and Taffy, they being our two biggest heavyweights. So they proceeded one night to the canteen where Geordie was in full cry, lifted him off his feet and frog-marched him outside, telling him to wrap up and get to bed. Geordie responded by setting up his usual paean to the moon and at the same time began a heart-rending call for his mum.

The avengers stood him up, warned him, he called for his mum, they hit him, first on one side of the jaw then on the other. Each time they took a poke at him he went down to the ground but each time he got up again and called for his mum and each time the call became louder until the noise became quite deafening. But no matter how hard Geordie was struck he always got up and either called for his mum or bayed the moon. He was so hard he could not be knocked out. No amount of hitting seemed to bother that granite jaw. In fact it was each attacking fist that was beginning to suffer when there came a sudden intervention.

Our section officer – the Black Mamba – appeared, disturbed at such a late hour when, no doubt, he had been concentrating his mind on his memoirs.

He arrived on the scene to announce that after lights out all good soldiers should be tucked up in bed. He was told that everyone agreed with him except Geordie and he was being made agreeable – everyone hoped. Then the miscreant was hit on the jaw again and again. But he kept bouncing up, noisier than ever. Then Lofty drew back his fist or was it Taffy? The Black Mamba remonstrated and was told to keep out of it: it was a private affair or rather, as it was artillery business, a gunner's affair. But the Mamba was resolute and stepped between the Geordie and the oncoming fist. In consequence he went down first followed by the mummy caller who sprawled across the officer in charge before once again staggering to his feet. When Mamba regained his feet he was told that he had been warned not to interfere.

The Black Mamba however explained that it was his duty to keep law and order. If everyone would go quietly off to bed he would escort Geordie to his bunk and see that he caused no more trouble. So everyone cut away and our section officer took our Geordie to his tent (Geordie's tent), took his boots off (Geordie's) and put him (Geordie) to bed. There was hope for British army Sam Browne belters yet.

Tale Eight: Gamesmanship and Gunner Marks

We were never the energetic types when it came to games, there were too many flat footed, short-sighted, smoke winded types and pot-bellied soldiers for that sort of thing. Our games were therefore of a gentler kind, drawn from army welfare: cards, dominoes, draughts and Monopoly. Gambling was not allowed but that didn't matter. It was done just the same, though not on the scale of the Aussies. In fact cards were always in use, the most popular card game being solo which I always avoided since it seemed to me the game was for fanatics not card players. But there was one card game I did play – sevens. Then one day I realised that over a period of time I had lost a couple of quid so I dropped out of the card school in haste. It was too heavy a loss for me.

I watched and watched until I had got the game sorted out

and then I rejoined the card school and had such a long string of successes that damn me if they didn't change the game to solo. My winning way ended abruptly.

Saturday nights a few of us devoted to Monopoly at a half crown a corner. Winnings were pretty well even until the day that Gunner Marks took a hand. He announced quite positively that in his opinion the Monopoly set was not the monopoly of a few but the property of all and as he wanted to send some money home to his mum he thought it was about time he joined in with the Monopoly players. So, as was his right, firmly affirmed, he joined in the games.

He duly won the games and sent his winnings, ten bob, home to his old mum who lived in the east end of London. The following Saturday he won again and so he did the next Saturday. I thought at the time that his winning ways were the answer he was giving to the Dodger who was always defending the Jews. He was showing me that he could look after himself, thank you. I recall that at one time I was busy defending the Jews against Johnny Arab when Marks came up to me and said, in no uncertain terms, that neither he or his fellow Jews needed my assistance, they could all get along nicely without it, thank you. I thought it a bit off but continued with my self-appointed defence of the Jews just the same.

The Marksian Saturday night collection for his poor old mum in the east end of London got a bit monotonous, so we decided to do something about the situation.

I dropped out of the game and took the bank.

As time passed our friend demonstrated his flair for capitalist enterprise and began to scoop the pool. So, I began organising working class resistance and led the fight back by passing money under the table to those in desperate need of it. But still, relentlessly, Midas kept cleaning up until – well – it may have been Arthur Mayes or Hung Low Hingley, I forget which, but someone whispered, 'Hey Dodger, pass me some money quick.'

I was feeling about the Monopoly box underneath the table in desperation but had to whisper back, 'I can't.'

'Watcha mean CAN'T?'

'What I say, can't, Marxey's got it.'

'What, all of it?'

'Yep, all of it and the rate he's going on he'll have the box and all.'

It was true. He had all the houses, all the hotels, all the cards, all the money and the others would have to apply to enter the workhouse.

Marks rose to go very satisfied no doubt at the thought of a happy mum. There was a gentle smile on his face. 'Y'know,' he said, 'Cheats never prosper.'

We never played again, we were no match for the real capitalist be he Jew or Gentile.

Chapter Seventeen

Cultural Warriors

The Newspaper

Some time in the October of 1943 an idea occurred which was to cause a stir, particularly in the mind of the sheriff. Whether it was the idea of Thomas, our then section officer, mine own or that of the master tailor Harry Withers, I shall now never know. I do know that second lieutenant Thomas was enthusiastic and managed to get the blessing of the colonel. The idea was that we should run our own newspaper on the gunpark. We aimed to keep the flag of Liberty, Fraternity and Equality waving over our army base. After all, we were supposed to be fighting Fascism, weren't we? Freedom was the order of the day, wasn't it? Yes, it was.

There was one important stipulation made: nothing derogatory should be said about any officer. This meant a drastic cut before we had even started. However we set to.

Me, I was inspired by the thought that my old headmaster had urged my parents to get me into Fleet Street. Now here I was helping to launch a newspaper and in the army to boot!

I wrote most of the articles in the first number and set down most of the ancient jokes. The Sheriff supported me in my aspirations but cowboys had never been famous for their literary acumen, while Harry Withers considered that journalistic prowess was not part of the equipment of a master tailor. I did get an article from one of the Norfolk farmers' sons, which was so long and boring that I was convinced the only person who could possibly have read it right through was the editor. I am sure that the author of the article didn't read it right through either since he seemed to get lost somewhere after the third page. However, observing the rule in regard to freedom of the press and because we had nothing else with which to fill the pages, in it went.

Our section officer approved the draft and to the school it went.

Three months later we were still making enquiries about the whereabouts of our newspaper and getting no response whatsoever from the school.

So we sent our delegate, the Sheriff, to make a few enquiries and he was promptly thrown out of the office by the chief clerk, who said he knew nothing about any newspaper and what was more he didn't want to know about it – 'Now get out.'

Charming! Then a clerkly sergeant told the Sheriff to clear off and the Sheriff, being a true son of the west, started cussing. The RSM, overhearing the remarks of the irate ambassador from the gunpark and not appreciating the idea behind Equality, Liberty and Fraternity, gave him a right old dressing down and more or less threw him in front of the new adjutant who in earlier times had been our section officer. The latter wanted to know, why he, Sprang, did not salute an officer when both were properly dressed and then told our courier to go outside, come in again and do the right thing.

By the time the Sheriff got back to me I was a hound dawg, they at the school were bloodthirsty scalp huntin' injuns and as far as the paper was concerned it could go and stuff itself up the nearest gallows tree.

Eventually everyone calmed down and we did run two issues but the enthusiasm for a democratic press in our outfit was so diminished that we called it a day and turned our attention to other and perhaps finer things. Not least of these would be determination to resist authority in all its forms and I must admit we got rather good at it.

The Library

One day I was called into the gunpark office by our newly

appointed section officer — we had quite a turnover in them at one time. He was very affable and after passing some pleasantries wanted to know what I thought the lads would most like to do in their leisure time. He went on to explain that he had the men's welfare at heart and he himself wanted to be, so to speak, the captain of a happy ship. I was somewhat taken aback, first because he seemed to think he was in the navy and second because even the lowly paid unwanted lance jack had more official power than any limber gunner and I told him so.

The new man only smiled and explained that he had been given to understand that I did have some influence in the camp. Being a modest sort of fellow I deprecated the suggestion by the flapping of both hands and then made it plain that the 'lads' had a favourite pastime which they all thoroughly enjoyed and I thought if they could continue as heretofore everyone would be happy.

'And what is their favourite pastime?' I noticed he didn't include me. Flattery?

'Blanket pressing.'

He looked puzzled and I suspected that he had some vision of everyone being energetic doing a sort of mass bedding cleaning. At any rate it was clear that blanket pressing had not been in his training schedule.

'What would that be — blanket pressing?'

I explained in simple language which he could understand that it meant lying on one's fleapit as long as humanly possible. But he didn't mean that sort of thing; such inertia could lead to all sorts of conditions of men including inertia, boredom and stunted mental growth. I explained that my hoppos didn't mind those kind of complaints providing they could sleep them all off.

He went on to explain some of his ideas and as he did so I began to warm to the man. What he had in mind was some sort of intellectual uplift, some effortful exercise destined to keep the lads mentally alive and an attempt to fit everyone for an eventual return to civvy street. That may have seemed a long way off at the time but we all knew it would be possible some day. The only trouble seemed to be that some folk were already having a fair old time and so the end of the war could be delayed a bit. I gave the matter some thought and then after a while a splendid idea struck me a mighty blow and I let it emerge. 'How about a library?'

He was immediately enthusiastic and there was no doubt about it, the idea was absolutely brilliant. We could combine a certain amount of blanket pressing with intellectual uplift.

Harry wasn't over-enthusiastic. Although he was a staunch advocate of Socialism he wasn't too sure that a highly educated and over-read proletariat was a good thing for the forthcoming revolution and the mounting of barricades. The manning of barricades would be made difficult enough with all the statutory tea breaks but with revolutionary bods sitting behind barricades reading *Lady Chatterley's Lover* and *The Well of Loneliness*, resistance to the Capitalist onslaught might be totally muted. Besides if the idea caught on among women what would happen to master tailors if needlewomen started to get too bolshie? Socialism was something to be nurtured with care, a plant to be tenderly nursed into a great flowering life.

However he agreed to give me his support by pointing out that there were quite a lot of intellectual books such as *Lady Chatterley's Lover, The Well of Loneliness*, and *No Orchids for Miss Blandish*. The last was a real winner. Everyone had heard of *No Orchids*, even Lofty Bale who couldn't read.

The first thing to do was to go into Haifa with a truck to the army welfare, which supplied a box of forty-eight books per unit per period on request. Funnily enough I had long since discovered that the army library in Haifa contained books banned or at least unobtainable in Blighty, the first two named above being prime examples.

I took a box of books out of the army welfare department and carried them back by lorry in triumph to the gunpark. Some of the lads, Harry, Mayes, Hung Low, the Sheriff, Doodlebug and Fangy, gathered around in great expectation as I opened the box. There, inside, were forty-eight second hand books. Then as we began our examination the truth dawned on all of us. People do not discard their favourite books but usually dispense with books they have no further use for. In that case of forty-eight books were six copies of John Bunyan's *Pilgrim's Progress*. Hardly the kind of masterpiece to set the lads along an intellectual road or for that matter hardly a book to cause anyone to fly to the barricades. There were no *Chatterleys*, *Wells* or *Blandishes*. The lads retreated in disgust to their flea pits leaving me with my thoughts which soon crystallized. I would get a pen and pad, start a library list, get everyone to borrow a book at three ackers a go per week so that I could build a float to *buy* books.

There was no enthusiasm for my brilliant idea. The Dodger could go read the six copies of *Pilgrim's* bloody *Progress* himself at no charge at all. But I was not to be denied. If democracy was to survive books had to be read and they had to be made to multiply.

I went round the tents and handed out the books to forty-eight 'readers'. They were full of protest, especially when I demanded a payment of three ackers a time for each book received, a demand to sign for the book and a warning that a fine would be imposed if the book was not returned on time. There were of course a number of unsolicited remarks such as, 'I thought we were fighting dictators?', 'Who the hell is John Bunyan?' and 'Who cares a sod about that geyser *Pilgrim's Progress*,' and 'Who's got *No Orchids?*' But I was able to brush such remarks aside, pointing out that in this case Dodger knew best and anyway if *No Orchids* was in demand, with the library money collected we could buy a copy – possibly charging double for such a popular piece of cultural literature.

Everyone paid up and everyone kept paying up until I was able to go into Haifa buying books. Eventually and pretty soon we had to build library shelves in cupboards in the canteen, which I took care to keep locked. No sneak reading in our library. I had of course taken the precaution of getting the section officer to agree to a fee. He had been a bit dubious at first. After all, as he quite rightly pointed out, the books were lent freely by the army library. But I was able to point out that if all the boxes of books lent by the army library to local units were like our one and especially if they contained six copies of *Pilgrim's Progress* we would never get our blokes to read and thereby raise their cultural outlook. The only way for us modern Pilgrims to Progress was to get the lads to pay so that they had a financial stake in the business and could at the same time read the kind of things they wanted to read. With some reluctance our leader agreed.

My next democratic move was to insist that everyone must take out a book whether he read it or not. 'I've had bloody *Pilgrim's Progress* three times running.'

'What does it matter?'

'What d'you mean what does it matter?'

'You never read it, do you?'

'But it costs me money.'

'All for the cause and the cause is great.'

We carried on and I was able to build the library. It was painful in the beginning, painful extracting money from everyone but it gradually got under way until I was able to get a truck to take me into Haifa so that I could visit the bookshops and buy what I needed. This move was a good one because it meant that some of the readers could nip onto the truck for a visit to Haifa.

The demand for blue books was somewhat high but I was able to satisfy all tastes in that particular branch of literature until the demand began to change. It began to be realised there was more to life than blue books so that in a short time I was being asked for other types of reading, not excluding that under the heading of 'classics'. I even had a demand for something on philosophy. Even Lofty Bale became restless. We had to move on from *The Well of Loneliness, Lady Chat, No Orchids* and *Hopalong Cassidy Rides Again.* Lofty kept beefing about his own loneliness in being the only non-reader. He felt out of things.

Since he paid for a book a week whether he could read it or

not I felt we had a duty towards him and promised to start him on picture books and then easy to read words, books containing cat, mat, fog and dog. Then came the day when our section officer complained that the only thing his men seemed to do was read books, all right in their own time no doubt but in working time he thought it a bit off; after all there was a war on.

It became necessary to raise the cultural standards. Such things as *Hopalong Cassidy Rides Again* and the latest whodunit could be read while working but it would be more difficult with Charlie Dickens or that bloke Thackeray, so I went to our section officer and asked him for a truck into Tel Aviv.

'Tel Aviv?'

'Tel Aviv, yeah.'

'Whatever for? Y'know it's fifty miles away don't you?'

'Books.'

'Books!' He almost choked.

'Yes, you see we need more and more.'

'What's wrong with Haifa? Plenty of bookshops there, I know, I've seen 'em.'

'We need to strengthen our vision, increase our range, broaden our minds,' or words to that effect. 'Besides I have got more or less all I can in Haifa, it has to be Tel Aviv, an intellectual necessity.'

He wasn't too sure about a truck for that distance for books. After all it *was* the British army and not the British Library. However we did get the truck and I was amazed at the number of book enthusiasts that climbed aboard that first truck. Were they so eager for new books that they couldn't wait until I returned with them?

As for me I hardly read one of our own library books though I paid in my money. I used to get my books from the army library in Haifa. It may sound surprising but it was from that library that I borrowed *Das Kapital* and John Stuart Mill's *First Principles*. I remember battling through the former with a wet towel round my head, having demanded, as far as possible, deathly silence from those nearest to me. The *Principles* I can still see in front of me, a large tome with fifteen hundred pages of small print and that is all I do remember about it.

Withers was astonished at all the brain strain. He assured me that he had met many Communists in his time but in all his experience he had never met one, let alone a character like me, who had read *Das Kapital.* Funnily enough, in after years when I met many Communist party members, I never came across one either.

One morning I had that book and one about the French Revolution on my bed when the orderly sergeant walked through and noting my books passed some unnecessary remarks in answer to which I pointed out that when the revolution came the first people to be sorted out would be nosey sergeants.

Came a day when I was utterly shattered.

I walked through one of the tents and there was 'Fulham' sitting on his bed and surrounded by half a dozen paperbacks and reading one of them.

'What's this?' I demanded, knowing, as I did, every book in the expanding library. 'What are you reading?'

The villain first of all adopted an air of innocence and then turned bolshie.

'These are my books, I've just got them in a parcel from Blighty.'

'Are you intending to set up a rival library?'

'Of course not. I'm just acting normally in reading my own books that's all.'

I picked up the books, all paperbacks, lying on his bed and gently eased the one he was reading out of his hand.

'Hey what d'you think you're doing?'

'You should know by now that all books belong to the library which is communal, therefore for the benefit of all including you.'

'But those books in your fists are mine.'

'Well really, Fulham, *were* yours because you have either loaned 'em or made a gift of them to the public library.'

He pointed to the one he had been reading. 'But I'm halfway through that bloody book.'

'No reason why you shouldn't finish it.'

'Oh well, Dodger, that's very decent of you I'm sure. Thank you very much for allowing me to finish my own book.'

'Providing you pay the usual library fee.'

He paid up and after I had registered the book he got it back – for a week.

One day we set off for Tel Aviv on a book foraging expedition, loaded with book enthusiasts in the truck or enthusiasts for something, when we rumbled past an infantryman loaded down with his gear and plodding steadily down the road. He was not only all geared up but carried his bondook as well. We yelled to our driver to pull up, and we called to the infantry wallah to chuck his gear into the back of the lorry and he himself hop aboard.

He shook his head. 'Thanks,' he said, 'but I can't.'

'Can't!' That was amazing, a free lift and it was being turned down!

'What d'you mean can't?'

'I'm reporting sick.'

'You can ride to the MO can't you?'

'Not really. I've just come down from the border [sixty miles away] and I gotta get to ...'

'Well, hop in.'

'I'm under orders to walk there.' And we left him stolidly marching to his sick bay. It was beyond us. Once again we were reminded that there must be two British armies, them and ours.

By the time I left Palestine at the end of 1944 we had 750 books and a well read clientèle. I was pleased with my efforts and life in general when I handed the keys of the cupboards over to Harry. It had been an experience I would never forget.

Religion

When my brother and I were sent off to the Wesleyan church Sunday school in Gwendolyn Avenue, Putney it was to get us out of the parental hair for a few hours. I became something of a star pupil in course of time but somehow failed to get involved by seeing 'the Light'. I daresay under the influence of the public speaker Burns and the gradual breakdown of peace, the double dealings of politicians and the inability of churches to stand up to fascism, I built up a wall of cynicism which grew and grew.

When asked for my religion when joining the TA I made the mistake of advising the clerk to put down anything he liked. He promptly shoved me down as Church of England and I soon discovered that one couldn't change one's religion when there was a war on. My mistake hit me in the face as soon as war broke out. Catholics, Free Church folk and Jews could walk to their place of worship; we others, the majority, were marched to ours, being carefully watched to prevent anyone from escaping.

I found that in the main the Church of England clergy were somewhat elderly and usually very boring and they had a tendency to drone on.

Once in the Middle East we discovered that the clergy were a lively enough lot who were mostly Free Church. One day in Tobruk an Aussie Free Church man turned up, dropped his altar cloth over a pile of ammunition boxes, gathered us around and began his service. We had just started murdering 'Onward Christian Soldiers' when our bugler appeared with his cracked bugle and began blasting off 'There's a bomber overhead, there's a bomber overhead.' The sirens started up and our singing tailed off. Did we carry on singing or did we dash off to take post?

The padre solved this problem. 'Right lads,' he said with his Aussie matter of factness, 'we'll adjourn the service and you go give those Jerry bastards hell and then we'll carry on where we leave off.'

And off we all dashed. A long time later when Jerry had had enough we returned to the ammunition boxes and altar cloth and finished 'Onward Christian Soldiers'. At the school we had a series of Church of England padres of the drone type. We were always paraded and directed into the hut where the service took place. On one occasion I happened to sit next to the school sergeant major and as he sat down he was muttering about the service. He hoped the effing thing would soon be over and it was all a lot of effing cobblers.

I had often had discussions with men of the cloth in which I had argued that they had a right old number, having officer privileges and conditions and provided with in the main an unwilling flock and for this, in return, they saved our souls! I believed the shepherd should be in the middle of his flock not residing in the *big* house. One day a Free Church man arrived and wanted to have a word or two with the Dodger!

He had been told he ought to have a talk with me since I had some influence among the plebs. He wanted ideas so I gave him one: why must we always be driven to church like cattle to slaughter? Wouldn't it be better for him and us if we went to his services under our own steam? No coercion. He thought it a good idea but he also thought the colonel would not agree. But he said he would speak to the old man about it. I said if he could get the church parades knocked off for one month I would guarantee a full house and after that he would be on his own and up to him.

And so it turned out. He got the colonel to agree and I told the lads there would be no more church parades. 'Hurray!' everyone shouted. 'But you will all have to volunteer to attend each Sunday for a month.' Loud and prolonged booing. 'In the name of democracy thy will be done; me, Lofty and Taffy will bring up the rear and gawd help the backsliders.'

Now that padre had a full house for a month and he was a damned good bloke and ran some pretty handsome services which were 'just the job'. At the end of the month, I am always happy to recall, he kept most of his congregation including me. The numbers only started falling away when he left. We never had another church parade.

I daresay there are people who will take a dim view of my approach but ... in Europe it was so called Christian against Christian and Christian against Jew. Indeed it was in Europe that the rumpus had started. The Pope had blessed Italian troops,

German troops and then blow me down if he didn't bless the Allied troops! No doubt if the Japs had got that far he would have blessed them too.

Chapter Eighteen

Other Matters and the Aussies

No history of my sojourn at the school of AckAck would be complete if I failed to mention those doughty warriors from Down Under, the Aussies. But before that there are a few things to be cleared up, not least the part that Harry Withers played in our activities.

He was a slightly built man with quick movements and a ready tongue, a guy who could be nothing else but the life and soul of his surroundings. He was a 'B' man and classified as having a nervous condition and was therefore excused guards, heavy fatigues, driving a vehicle and, despite the fact that he was a gunner in the RA, excused guns. As someone pointed out, for all the good he was officially, why didn't he just hold his breath? However, the army being what it was, Harry did guard duties and fatigues and had the special job of driving a Bofors truck with Bofors gun at night. Further, when we needed a light truck to take some of us into Haifa it was Harry who usually got the job. He wasn't too bad in daylight but at night! Having got the truck we would frogmarch Harry into it and force him into the driving seat and then off we'd go. Always an erratic drive down the gunpark road but we all helped out on the main drag. One of us would sit on one front mudguard, someone on the other and each would call directions to Harry at the steering wheel. 'Over a bit Harry, right hand down, mind the ditch, look out Harry, nearly off the road.' I might add we never did have an accident though some of us came near to it with our raucous laughter as we wobbled from side to side.

Palestine was the land of the Jaffa orange and in wartime, unable to export the fruit, the orange groves would have massive carpets of fruit during the season and if one nipped into a grove one could select fruit at will, discarding those not to one's taste and never of course picking those small ones seen in Britain. If anyone bothered to buy them they worked out at a farthing each. I remember at Nathanya one day they brought in a tip-up truck loaded with oranges and tipped the fruit onto the ground. Arming ourselves with as many as we could carry, a group of us adjourned to our hut where, dividing our forces, we proceeded to have a right old battle hurling oranges at each other.

One day it was decided that as it was known that the sheriff and I were partial to oranges, an orange eating contest would be staged to see who was the orange king. Two sacks of oranges were produced, one for me, one for him and thus supplied, the sheriff and I set about eating our way through the sacks of oranges.

Half way through the proceedings we paused to partake of a large tomato sandwich each. I have never been able to understand the reason for this unless it was because only having eaten half a sack of oranges apiece we were feeling a bit peckish. Eventually the sheriff gave in and I was duly declared the orange king. To mark my success and to prove what a pig I was I proceeded to eat half a dozen more oranges than the sheriff had consumed.

A few days later it was decided that having got themselves Royalty in the shape of an orange king they, 'the lads', ought to establish a melon king also. So one night some of us went crawling across the Arab melon fields in search of sugar melons. We had to operate thus because the Arab owners liked to sit in the middle of their melon patches with shotguns which they liked to blast off at the first opportunity. We never could get hold of water melons, they seemed to be something a bit special. We crawled about until we had collected a half dozen fair sized melons and then we headed back to our tent and the melon contest.

After two melons I gave up and Sprangy became melon king.

Next day I had difficulty in getting off my fleapit. Fact is, I didn't get off it for three days – I had acquired a dose of colic.

Needless to say there was no reporting sick that time. The

powers that were did not approve of their personnel going sick
with Melonitis. I came to the conclusion that someone must have
informed Pip Purnell that I had gone on a three-day book-buying
orgy because nothing was ever said about my missing presence.

A Chinese military delegation was expected soon so the gun
teams were kept hard at it, gun drilling until the whole business
became tiresome and ridiculous. It was soon clear that mutiny
was in the air. The Bofors crew were not too badly off with
their light gun and ammo but our lot with the heavy gear were
suffering painfully. So an idea was thrust forward, 'Why don't
you lot all go sick?' After all, it was the absolute right of a
soldier to go sick if he felt he needed to. In consequence the
heavy gun crew went sick – all nine of 'em.

The impossible happened. No one came back. Some went to
hospital, others had periods of 'bed down' and the Chinese
delegation was due on the morrow!

Panic stations. Would we please not start our sick period until
after the Chinese had been and gone? Please help us out, won't
you?

But the MO's word was law in matters of sickness.

Please consider the situation. We had. No more stupid gun
drill for a start. Who cared about those Nationalist Chinese
anyway?

'Please.'

'Under certain conditions.'

'Any conditions.'

With many concessions agreed the sick folk tottered back to
the gun and postponed their illnesses until the following day.

One day when co-operating with an OCTU class (Officer Cadet
Training Unit) we were engaged on a firing run when a round
got jammed up the spout. The drill laid down was specific,
withdraw to a safe distance and wait two minutes. It was a safety
rule we had quickly abandoned in Tobruk simply because there
had been no time for such antics. After two minutes someone
should take the piasaba pole with a brass cone at the end and
gently, very gently, try and push the offending object out of the

breech. Another member of the crew should then walk the thing away to a place of safety.

On this occasion neither the gunnery instructor nor his students appeared anxious to see if the laid-down drill worked. So I said to Perksy, 'You go stand by breech, me go muzzle end and me shift naughty round Chinese fashion velly klick.'

Round to the muzzle end I went and shoving the piasaba pole down the barrel gave it a gentle push and nothing happened. I pushed a bit harder but still nothing happened. Oh dear! I gave it an almighty shove but nothing happened. I then banged at the offending round several times.

'Any sign of it moving?' I yelled to my partner. 'No,' he said quite calmly. So I gave a few more bangs and then the offending object slid into Sidney's hands. I nipped round to the breech end and took the round from him walked it off onto surrounding rocks with my buddy in close attendance and laid the offending object down. Then we walked away somewhat relieved.

Back at the entrance to the pit we paused to take a shufti round the place. There was not a soul in sight; everyone had legged it, not only out of the gunpit but out of the gunpark as well.

A Captain IG turned up outside our gunpit workshop demanding a live high explosive round which we gave him and which he locked into our vice. He then asked for a hacksaw which we gave him. Then damn me if he didn't start sawing through the HE end of the round. Perksy tapped him on the shoulder. 'What do you think you are doing?'

The expert was quite happy to explain. 'I am sawing this thing in half so that I can show my course the inside of it.'

Sidney undid the vice. 'Shell cutting is not permitted inside the gunpit, SIR.' He strongly stressed the sir. We suggested he take it to the right place, the Tiffy's shop, where disasters and explosions might be allowed. Off he went full of enthusiasm to the newly appointed QM artificer. We waited for the explosion, not from the round but from the QM. Then we heard the roaring sound of that man's voice. 'Take that bloody thing out of here and don't fetch it back and DON'T YOU come in here again EVER.'

Many of those IGs came out from Blighty and many of them brought with them nasty Blighty ways commonly referred to as bullshit.

A certain captain IG seemed to take an instant dislike to me and made no bones about complaining. One day he came storming into the gunpit, picked up a thick rubber ring with a hole in the middle and told me I was too slack, the rubber should be in its rightful place on the gun. Being a very conscientious limber gunner I invited him to show me where it went and Perksy came too to enjoy the fun. The captain then took me and the rubber round the gun, trying the offending object on every protruding piece of metal upon which the rubber might fit. Having failed to find a home for the thing I politely took the rubber from the irate Sam Browner and placed it where it belonged, on one of the two holding spikes of an ammunition box!

Sidney Perks was upset on my behalf. 'I think,' he opined, 'he really is going to have it in for you from now on.'

Words of wisdom, words of truth, and so I braced myself for the attack.

The next day he arrived with his cadet force beautifully togged up in clean bright summer KD and in front of all he berated me for being a lazy, tired, good for nothing, useless, dirty dog. The barrel slide was rusty, the bearings were dry, there wasn't enough oil around to make a gnat slip over and if I didn't get the oil can out my feet would never again touch the floor. I could only think that he had been told of my influences at work on the gunpark and had decided to take that damned Bolshie type down a peg or two.

After they had all gone I got the oil can out.

My partner was quite intrigued with what I was about to do.

I explained briefly that a certain idiot had complained about the lack of oil so I would unhesitatingly give him some. I oiled everything in sight, barrel slide, barrel, working parts, non-working parts and I even oiled the ramming handle and the elevator and traverser seats. If he wanted oil he could certainly have it; after all we had a good supply of the stuff.

Of course all the other lads got to know of it, we made sure they did. The Dodger was at war with a captain of artillery industry, a Gunnery instructor.

I suppose I had a grudge against those people who wanted everyone to be at everlasting gun drill. They themselves never rushed back and forth, to and fro, but made others work at it. When I had been a member of the mobile 3.7 crew I had got pretty browned off with that blessed drilling so I had slowed up. I wasn't keen on dashing about putting the damned thing in and out of action, pulling down heavy gun legs and hammering home heavy holding spikes. The idea had been to get the time down to something like a minute or a minute and a half. By the time I had finished the time was up to seven minutes! This no doubt would have suited Jerry but not our powers that were, so I came off the gun team more or less classified as a hindrance.

Now here was one of the torturers trying to do the dirty on me. It just wouldn't do.

The next morning he arrived with his shining cadets, looked at the barrel slide, grunted and began teaching. But it wasn't long before he was rubbing his oily hands on his uniform and the cadets soon followed suit until spots of oil were appearing in all sorts of places on uniforms including head gear. We thought the IG was about to burst, he became so choleric. 'Look at all this oil,' he more or less screamed. 'Look at *me* and look at *them*.'

I looked. They certainly appeared somewhat oil stained.

'What the devil's the idea?'

'You said oil everything, SIR.'

He stormed off to the school but got no joy out of our Major Ferry. A short while later our irate IG disappeared from the scene. We hoped he had been seconded to that Chinese Nationalist mob.

Yorkie Smailes or, to give him his rank, Sergeant Major Instructor of Gunnery Smailes, was the most popular IG amongst us. He was genial, clear in his explanations and certainly knew everything there was to know about a 3.7 gun. He once stripped one down to its base ring with only one large screw-driver.

His name will be forever linked with the Aussies.

Throughout my time in the Middle East I came across the Aussies on many occasions. Early on in our school days we had some of them on a course and they used to sit together at the end of the mess marquee while we sat at the other. They used to watch our meals with interest and were particularly puzzled at the sight of large tins of our 'oleomargarine'. It was a thick yellow substance which not only looked like old fashioned axle grease but tasted like it.

One day an Aussie came over to us and explained that they had never had the chance to taste our kind of English butter and could they try some? Could they do an exchange? The Aussie promptly slapped a pound of Aussie butter on our table. We in turn offered him our entire stock of 'oleomargarine'. He declined, only taking a spoonful. In fact they only sampled our ghastly rubbish and soon gave it back. We all knew very well why they did it. They wanted to help us out without hurting our feelings. It was one of those open-handed gestures one came to expect from those characters from down under.

On one occasion some of us had to go off to a big Aussie camp, probably for some demonstration or other. At that camp was an immense marquee, probably the biggest I had seen anywhere. It was full to bursting with Aussies grouped round tables and gambling. Everybody was at it and it seemed that all ranks had joined in. It would have come as no surprise to find one of their generals indulging in what appeared to be a national craze.

So it was that whenever we had some of them on our gunpark on some course or other, at every available opportunity out would come the cards and away they would go. It didn't matter if there were no tables; they would bunch around and squat on their haunches. At those times they were lost to the world.

One day while some of our Australian friends were busy at their national sport one of our white-kneed officers came into view with his little cane under his arm, observed what our allies were doing and told them to cease forthwith. Gambling on British army territory was verboten.

He expressed his point of view several times and several times was ignored. In the end one Aussie told him to buzz off and go play soldiering somewhere else and not bugger about when serious business was afoot. Our young man was very annoyed and strode off in search of their own officer, a captain no less. The latter arrived, hardly distinguishable from his own rank and file, hands in pockets, collar undone, no tie, hat on back of his head and doing the Aussie slouch. Our young man pointed to the offending group with his little cane and said that they were all acting in an illegal manner, in an insubordinate manner, and must be stopped forthwith.

The captain first peered over a couple of shoulders and then moved closer, then more or less absent mindedly he put his hand in his pocket, drew out a note and flung it onto the money lying on the ground in the centre of the circle. He started to bend his knees to line himself up with the other blokes and our Sam Browne belter demanded to know what he thought he was doing. The captain waved our gallant man away but the latter persisted so the captain with some irritation turned to the second lieutenant and said, 'Why don't you bugger off, mate, can't you see I'm busy?'

Our man marched off, chin up, cane under arm and disappeared from sight, not to return for the remainder of the day.

Some bright spark got round to the idea that the Aussies should not bring their own rations with them but should partake of the refreshments supplied to the British soldiers by the British army.

So, at midday it was tiffin time and we all retired to the mess marquee and waited for tiffin. It turned up on time all right. Not surprisingly really, since it was one of our commonest meals and did not over-stress the cooks, consisting of a few hard tack biscuits, half an onion and one of those silver paper wrapped triangular cheeses, usually found in a round box and which would not have made much of a meal for a healthy mouse.

One Aussie peered at the scrumptious repast and said, 'What's this – starters?'

'Starters?' One of our lads looked puzzled. 'Starters?'

'Yep, what you begin with, a kind of taster.'

'No, no.' There was general laughter. 'That's it mate, that's the midday meal, that's real tiffin that is.'

'You must be joking,' an Aussie suggested.

'You got an orderly officer?'

'Yeah.'

'We suggest you call him. This grub is a right humdinger.'

Very soon the orderly sergeant appeared and one of our allies said, 'Who are you?'

He said, 'I'm the orderly sergeant, you sent for me.'

There was general down-under laughter and one said, 'We sent for the orderly officer not his dog, you go fetch him.' The sergeant made a strategical withdrawal; he was one of us and had no intention of getting involved in food matters with our visitors. There was a long pause before the orderly officer appeared. He was of the same breed as the young man with the cane. He marched in with that instrument under his arm, his Ronald Colman moustache neatly trimmed, his eyes flashing fire in his pink English face.

'What is the complaint?' he asked.

One of the Aussies stood up with a plate in his hand, bulging with hard tack biscuits, half an onion and a triangular cheese.

'What is this?' he asked.

'Tiffin.' Our officer seemed a bit surprised. Surely everyone knew that.

Then the Aussie said, 'Tiffin!' He looked at the food carefully, holding the plate somewhat away from him. 'Is this supposed to be food?' He seemed surprised that anyone should imagine it to be food.

Our Sam Browne belter bristled up no end. 'It certainly is food and I can tell you that that is the same ration that we get in the officers mess and I can also assure you that I like it.'

'You like it?' The Aussie was amazed. 'How can you like such a trifle?'

'Yes, I do like it a great deal.'

'In that case,' said our Aussie friend, 'If you like it so bloody much you can bloody well have mine.' And without more ado he flung the plate of goodies at our officer with one mighty throw, causing the latter to stagger backwards. Someone yelled, 'You can eat that since you like it and meantime send us in some bloody grub.'

Our orderly officer fled hotfoot away and food was wheeled in on the double. We came to the conclusion they must have emptied the cookhouse, the foodstore, all the tea chests and sugar bags in one swift thrust. We had a fair old blow out and future tiffins improved after that.

Sid Perks had to spend a good bit of time at a nearby Digger camp where he fed like a fighting cock and drank plenty of that fine old brew, Aussie beer. One night he was gathered into a band of down-under brothers and hustled into Haifa where the bunch of them after a few drinks got hold of an Arab taxi driver asking him to take them to a cabaret and not a brothel. He suggested the usual places but they wouldn't have any of that. They wanted a real Arab dive where the real shows took place. At first he shook his head but eventually agreed to take them to a place he often went to himself. Arriving at a building in some dark area of a village beyond Haifa he stopped his taxi and told them to wait until he returned.

Into the somewhat shadowy building he went, to emerge a little later to say that OK, they could go in, but they would have to sit at the back of the hall and remain perfectly quiet. 'No Aussie capers if you please.' And he passed his hand significantly across his throat. They went in and Perksy said they did keep quiet, ogling at the performances of the girls on the stage and then, as advised, they left quietly. Perksy thought they left in an uncharacteristic Aussie way because they were overcome by what they had seen.

And that is all the information anyone is going to get out of me on that subject. The only thing I was sorry about was that my old mate went and not me.

At times on the various courses given at the school the students would be taken into a classroom or lecture hall and given a run down on some artillery subject or other. On one occasion the Aussie contingent had come up against one of our class-bound snotty moustached, toffee nosed know-it-all RSM IGs who seemed to regard them as either dumb schoolboys or lowbrowed provincials or both. Soon there was tension between them. In the classroom they all sat waiting to see who was going to teach them something when lo! in walked that horrible creep no one had time for. And he started off on the wrong foot by stating that they should stand to attention upon entry of the chief centurion. That did it. Clearly a riot was imminent. Someone heaved a chair at the big head of the IG and he, not being built for action at a battle station, took off. Everyone waited patiently if not quietly until lo! who should step in but Yorkie Smailes, hat on back of head, cane in pocket, shirt open, hands in pocket and cigarette drooping from mouth. In fact he looked very much like the average Aussie.

He said, 'I hear you've been having a bit of trouble lately. Well, I don't aim to look for trouble, but if it is wanted I am willing to volunteer to take my coat off and step outside to take on anyone, provided it is one at a time, not all you lot in one heap.'

He had established rapport immediately and from then on in the eyes of our allies he could do no wrong. He also clearly established the fact that it is possible to get more out of people by a reasonable and pleasant approach than by bullying. As for the cause of the trouble, we never saw him again and we speculated as to whether he had been dispatched to some front or other to exercise his talents on the enemy.

When the Ninth Australian Division was getting ready to return to Australia, those we met, when not concentrating on gambling, were considering what they were going to do when they got back home. As one of them put it, 'We're going back home to finish two wars. First we're going to sort out those Yankee bastards who've been having it off with our Sheilas and then we are goin' to do over those little Nip bastards.' I know not what happened with the American Allies in Australia but we all knew that the Australians certainly, alongside others, sorted out the Japanese.

A good many of us bods who fought in the war alongside Australians, New Zealanders, Canadians, Indians, Gurkhas and other folk from around the world, remember that, and we also remember what the Japanese did. As for the Americans, they got a reputation which stuck: 'Over-sexed, over-paid and over here.'

Chapter Nineteen

War Weary Warriors

By 1944 most of us could be described as sun touched, witness Sandy and the Sheriff tearing each other's clothes off and the business of the laundry. Then there was the case of Ellison our gate man.

At night the gate was guarded with men and rifles; during the day it was the unarmed Ellison who was in charge of the gate. His job was to keep an eye on things, opening and closing the pole gate when required to do so. Ellison was a simple soul without too much ambition and I suppose the ideal man to operate a simple pole gate. No doubt he would have been unregarded by me if he hadn't earned the right to be in my hall of fame over the business of the colonel's visit.

I was at the gate one day when Ellison suddenly said to me, 'Dodger, I'm fed up with this job.' This took me utterly by surprise since I had come to believe Ellison had very few thoughts indeed and that the gate job enabled him, throughout the day, to spread out what few he did have.

'Oh!' I said, in a voice full of expression.

'Yeah, fed up.'

'Oh,' I repeated intelligently.

'I've been doing this job for years.'

I tried cheering him up. 'It's a very important job, manning this gate.'

'No it's not. At any rate I'm not opening that gate any more. Not for anybody.'

'Nobody?'

'Nobody. Just nobody.'

'The colonel's due here soon, is he included?'

'Everybody's included, the king and all.'

A little later I nodded up the road. 'Here comes the old man.'
'Sod him. He can open the gate himself and that's final.'

The colonel drew up in front of the gate, opened a window, poked his head out and passed the time of day as was his wont, expecting the usual service. Ellison ignored the polite remarks and told the colonel if he wanted to come in he would have to raise the pole himself; he, Ellison, had had enough of doing that. The gentlemanly colonel alighted from his car, raised the bar and, getting back into the vehicle, drove on through. Ellison was soon standing in front of the bonnet. He was standing no nonsense from anyone, 'Don't forget to shut the gate.'

The colonel without demur got out of his car and closed the gate and then once more passing the time of day, drove on. He must have realised something like sun-touchiness was about or maybe he was a bit suntouched himself.

My young brother Victor was a sergeant in the Hampshires who were resting somewhere near Nathanya in between bouts of muck and bullets which they seemed to indulge in. Harry and I took off to find him. I was given to understand that I could claim a younger brother if I so wished into my unit. We never saw him. We were told he had gone ahead with an advance party and maybe it was just as well, because if I had been him I would have told me where to get off. So Harry and I started back for the school. We got a lift up to the main Haifa – Tel-Aviv road with a bus load of Greeks, the driver being the most talkative and expressive character in a bus load of talkative and expressive characters. He seemed to spend more time facing the rear nattering to his mates than looking where he was going. I shut my eyes and Harry shivered and we both hoped for the best. Sometimes we were on the grass verge and at others narrowly missing oncoming heavy lorries and at one time he braked so hard we spun right round and began the journey back to Nathanya.

We wobbled off that bus and hoped for a lift on the long haul back to camp. We got one for about half a mile, then it was shanks pony all the way because after 6 p.m. no public transport was ever on the road. We never met up with an army vehicle either, with the result that Harry and I had to walk more miles than I care to remember, I sometimes dancing round the sagging Harry to keep his spirits up. We were not helped either by the thought that wild dog packs were in the hills and bandits were not unknown. However we staggered into camp in the early hours of the morning. Harry was indignant at the silence, thinking the lads ought to have sent out a search party, so he insisted on pulling his tent down. Someone yelled, 'Whirlwind,' another, 'Germans.' A third thought it was a bunch of enemy parachute troops that had got lost. Harry and I narrowly escaped with our lives.

One bright sunny day we were called on parade by one of the Sam Browne belt brigade who explained to us how it would be a good thing if we could see our way clear to take out shares in a company as a help to us all after the war was over. It could of course be a help to the adjutant or the colonel or someone like them who seemed to own the company or who had large shareholdings in it. Harry and I were in the rear row and every one instinctively looked round at us. I grinned broadly, Harry gravely shook his head and when all were asked to step forward who were interested, nobody moved.

On another occasion we were all paraded and it was suggested that we might donate one day's pay toward building an RA centre in London for use after the war. We were asked to consider it. We considered it. It didn't take much considering. For one thing a great many of the lads didn't live in London, a point soon noted by the two Norfolk farmers' sons who couldn't be persuaded to spend anything in our local canteen, let alone be expected to fork out for a train fare to London to spend money on things they neither needed or wanted. In any case who were likely to benefit? The lowly, underpaid artisan and labouring classes and perhaps a few master tailors maybe, or the ex-officer bods with rolled brollies, bowler hats and sandwiches in brief cases, trotting back and forth to their city offices? There was no response from us plebs.

The third attack on our pockets was the most serious.

On that parade it was pointed out that it would be the height of patriotism to take out war bonds. We were dismissed to think about it.

It did not take a genius to point out that now the powers that were were not only expecting us to fight the bloody war but expecting us to pay for it as well! Since married men had to pay over half their wages to their wives, then they had to live on the other half, it seemed a bit off to be asked to help out the war profiteers and others who no doubt were building nice little nest eggs for their old age.

There were no takers at the recalled parade.

A little later a selected few of us were told to report to the lecture hall at the school. We knew what it would be about; we had our fifth column up there. Then Lofty Bale paid Harry and me a visit.

'Look,' he said. 'I agree with what's been said about taking out war bonds and all that but as you know I can't save a damned thing. I'm always skint.'

This was true. Money burnt holes in his pockets and if he couldn't spend it on himself he spent it on others.

'Maybe if I took out war bonds I might have some dough at the end of the war.'

'Yes,' we agreed and Lofty was allowed then and there to volunteer for war bonds.

In the lecture hall we found quite an array of Sam Browne belters beside the paymaster who pointed out we had been called there, we happy few, we band of brothers, because it was known that we had plenty of lolly and therefore could afford war bonds. This did not apply to Lofty who had not been invited for obvious reasons. Then a pleasant-faced young officer stood up at the back and announced, one presumed to break the deadly silence, that it was known that there were pernicious influences at work on the gunpark, influence which could easily wreck the war effort, etc., etc. Withers looked at me, I looked at Withers and quite a number of brothers in arms looked at us and Lofty fidgeted. Speeches were made, urges were urged and then we were told we could go but all those who wished to take out war bonds should remain.

Lofty looked so out of place amid all those Sam Browne belters. As for the rest of us, we headed for the canteen to spend our hard-earned fortunes before someone else got hold of another bright idea.

As the new year of 1945 approached, attention became more and more focused on the question of what was going to happen when the war ended. Jerry was being pushed back, squeezed on all sides by the Allies into an ever shrinking box of resistance in Germany itself. Jerry seemed bent on fighting to the bitter end, forced into this attitude by the Allies who were insisting on unconditional surrender. Certainly the Nazis would be shown no mercy – we hoped – and they were still in charge of affairs in Germany. At any rate it was only a matter of time before the war in Europe ended and then the full force of the Allied war effort could be turned against Japan.

By the end of 1944 I was a real old army sweat, a senior gunner, a chief librarian, a long standing limber gunner and quite browned off, ready to get on my bike and head for Blighty. I don't think we were particularly unhappy but we all had a feeling that at that stage of the war we were merely marking time if not actually wasting that precious substance.

Harry Withers had a splendid interview with our section officer who said that he did not like Harry, to which remark Harry replied that the feeling was mutual. Then my buddy was informed that a week after the departure of Gunner Green 881431, he, Gunner Withers, would be on his bike also. Which piece of information delighted Harry since he had never been an enthusiastic supporter of the military life, feeling that it was no place for a master tailor to operate in.

I have always considered that the authorities were much more wary of Harry than they ever were of me. After all, I could be expected to be a bit bolshie and was probably regarded as eccentric but certainly not of the officer class. Harry on the other hand should probably have known better; as a master man in his professional life he ought to have had a Sam Browne belt, as chief of the military clothing stores possibly.

So when I was informed I would be Blighty bound on 4th January we knew he would be following a week later. Meanwhile I was due away with that stout-hearted gatekeeper Ellison, Flash Ellison who on the third of the month got blotto.

Chapter Twenty

Blighty

Blighty! It might not be Eldorado. It might never be a home fit for heroes to live in. It might have a lot of things wrong with it. But it was still Blighty. And we were heading in its direction.

When Ellison and I got to the school, Lance Burfield put Ellison's mossy (mosquito) net gingerly to one side for the lieutenant quarter master to take a shufti at. I thought it was a bit of a lousy trick on Burfield's part though I had to admit the mossy net was somewhat filthy.

On the fourth we had to take our beds up to the school where, as a start, Flash had to pay out thirty two shillings and sixpence in local ackers for his mossy net and then it was discovered that his bedding was so lousy he would have to debug it before he could take off Blighty-wards. My companion for the journey home was so slow I had to set to and get rid of the bugs for him, otherwise we would have been messing about until the Japanese surrendered, let alone Jerry.

'A bloody fine send-off, Flash, I must say,' I opined. But Flash was impervious to any words of wisdom or censure. In fact he was just impervious.

Back to the gunpark for tiffin and then Harry drove us into Haifa. All our leave taking had already taken place in the canteen. We were the first of the inmates to be on our way. The rest would follow in due course with Harry Withers in the lead.

In Haifa we found it was not all that easy to shake off the dust of Palestine. We were due to board the Cairo Chatanooga Choo-Choo at 3.17 p.m. but the RTO soon found that our papers were not in order. We were minus the all important movement order which the school office had forgotten to supply. We were

a bit concerned about that little matter. After all, neither Ellison
or myself qualified for VIP treatment and thus the train was
not likely to be held while our papers were sent to the RTO.
But the Don R arrived with seven minutes to spare. He was
cussing very vigorously because he had been so messed about
when in fact he should have been resting his weary limbs.

He did not wave us goodbye. Probably his arm ached.

I certainly had mixed feelings about taking off. I had got used
to the place and rather liked being here despite the fact that like
everyone else I was always complaining about 'the poxy place'.
But of course there was no denying that Blighty was Blighty
and that meant home.

We crossed the canal on a newly erected bridge. We no longer
had to cross on foot as in days of yore, but carried on until we
reached Cairo main station. It was always a great fascination for
me to see again the Nile Valley. One moment the landscape was
a brown desert, after all we had crossed the Sinai, and then
suddenly there was the bright green of the Nile Valley cutting
through the landscape like a broad green playing field, edged
by desert to the east and to the west. At the station we were
picked up by ROAB lorries and transported to the base depot
at Heliopolis. I say lorries picked us up, not because Ellison and
I were supplied with one each but because there were large
numbers off the train and all Blighty bound. Base depots during
the war were places to be given a miss if possible and Heliopolis
was one in particular to be avoided. The powers-that-be at that
base depot seemed to have ideas from which they could never
deviate. For example, it took us all day to pass through their
camp admittance procedure. It took near enough the same
amount of time to pass out again when we left. One of the jolly
habits of the army was to have frequent FFIs which I suppose
meant full frontal inspections. We had them at fairly frequent
intervals; fair enough, one had to keep an eye on health. But we
had had one when we left the school and blow us all down if
we didn't have one on arrival at base camp and again when we
left base camp. One of these inspections took place in front of

a crowd of giggling native women and somewhat surprised native children.

Another brilliant stroke was to take down our lines of tents and move them a few feet to one side, fill in the shallow holes in which each tent was set and then dig another line of shallow holes in which to re-erect said tents. They must have been carrying on like that for years! We were to find out later that our Woolwich depot could go one better than that!

It was from Heliopolis that we had sallied out in 1940 into Cairo, when the bootblacks doing business outside the main gate were treated like dirt by the regular army soldiers. Bootblacks would polish and polish and polish and would also do the insteps of boots. I had seen bootblack boxes sent flying and bootblacks kicked as they were told that they were lazy wogs and not fit to be paid.

Ellison and I were somewhat taken aback when we went out of the main gate for the first time on this second visit. For one thing the bootblacks seemed to have grown enormously in size. They appeared to be a kind of male Amazon, tall and with broad shoulders, in strong contrast to the mixed bag of weedy con-scripts with hunched shoulders, white knobbly knees and looks of bewilderment. These fellows were being instructed to place their feet on the stools where the shining boots were given a brief flick with a dirty rag and the boot owners were ordered to pay up at once, which they did, happy no doubt to escape from that Egyptian tyranny. Ellison looked at me and I looked at Ellison. I knew that he would not do what he was told. If our colonel could not get him to open the gunpark gate I was damned certain he wasn't going to oblige a bootblack. He didn't. He just shoved the one who commanded him to put his boot up to one side and shoved on. A man who had paid out thirty-two and six for a lousy mossy net wasn't going to listen to a native demanding money with menaces. As for me, my man told me to put my foot up onto his stool. I said, 'What did you say?' he looked up into my sun tanned face and grinned. I slowly pulled up a trouser leg and pointed at my darkened skin. 'I haven't got knobbly knees nor white ones either.' He grinned again cheerfully as I pulled my trouser leg back into place.

'OK, George,' he said. 'Your boots very good,' which was not true: my boots were never good, let alone very good. It was quite clear that he was really a good democrat and not a bully boy at all and after all it was a good idea for the Egyptians to stand up for themselves, wasn't it?

In the camp I came across many of the old lags from the battery though I saw nothing of Fred Smith or Stan Ward. So we had reunions almost daily.

> The one five three in the firing line,
> The one five two behind them,
> But when they looked for the one five one,
> Buggered if they could find 'em.

Not that they could ever find the 151, they being almost all prisoners of war. I was lucky enough to get put on the Mena house guard. It meant I was shot of the base camp for a while. We were there when the war minister, Sir James Grigg, was staying there. I wrote some verses about him, a person not very popular around our way. There is only one verse extant, the rest having been nicked off my bed in Germany along with many other masterpieces.

> When we have grown old
> And our uniforms sold,
> When we aren't worth even a tanner
> We, the small and the big
> Will do to old Grigg
> What's often been done to big Anna.

The reason for our resentment is no longer knowable. We had probably been denied a wage increase or had been kept in the Middle East too long. It certainly wasn't about the cigarette issue; we had got painfully used to that long ago.

The guard itself wasn't bad; we were away from the hell of

Heliopolis, the food was fair, the trees were shady and the guard duty itself tolerable.

I managed to get into Cairo where I bought myself an over-priced wrist watch which, on the way home, gained twenty-five hours in twenty-four. I also bought a pair of Bata shoes which, when I wore them in Blighty, promptly fell to pieces in the first heavy shower of rain. Ellison and I also had a favourite dish, eggs and chips, the chips being of the sweet potato variety.

The number fifteen tram was the one which we took into and out of Cairo and it was the tram route which passed right by GHQ. The trams were usually two cars attached with a driver and conductor, the latter usually, when not collecting tickets, standing in the centre, ready to blow his horn at the slightest provocation. They were little round short men wearing the inevitable tarbush on their heads. The route had become noto-rious for the gangs of muggers which frequented them. Nothing would happen between Cairo and GHQ because there were always plenty of squaddies on the trams until then. But once that stop was passed the number of soldiers got less and less until there were few about and it was then that the gang would jump aboard. There were some unpleasant accounts circulated about the happenings to lone soldiers on the long run out to the pyramids.

One night when Ellison and I were travelling back to camp a bunch of bandits, or so they looked to me, jumped aboard and sat down like perfectly normal passengers but when Ellison and I were alone with them their obvious leader, a somewhat hefty character, rose to his feet. I said to my old mate Flash, 'Flash, you follow me to the centre of this here tramcar and put your back to the centre post and against my back.' I had noted that the conductor had disappeared. He wanted no trouble, that was clear.

'Now,' said I, 'Slowly roll up your sleeves, as I'm doing and imagine that some fool is trying to make you open that damned gunpark gate and for Christ sake look fierce, not gormless.' We rolled our sleeves up and I glared around giving the ring leader an especial glare and we waited. If there was going to be a dive bombing attack we were gonna have a go.

After a few minutes the leader put his fingers to his lips and gave a whistle which was of course a signal. I started tensing up as the lot of them jumped up. But instead of attacking in true dive bomber fashion they all followed their leader and jumped off. I congratulated Ellison on his clearly observable fierceness.

'Fierce,' he said, 'I was dead bloody scared.'

We had a different kind of experience one night when with a number of others we got back to Gesa. It was one of those times when there were plenty of us around and there had been no tram gangs to bother us. Flash and I were bracing ourselves for the long walk down the dark road which had its perils since there were always plenty of army vehicles dashing up and down it. Though as far as I recall nobody ever seemed to get a lift in a lorry. We had just put the left leg before the right when a turbaned Indian pulled up on a motor bike and asked us if we wanted a lift. A good thought, since we didn't relish going forward with all those folk staggering home after a night out in Cairo.

The Indian, a fine specimen of his breed, smiled proudly under his turban. I always seemed to see Sikhs smiling and still do. 'I am going home to India tomorrow.' We said we were going back to Blighty soon and good luck to all of us.

Our new friend turned to Flash and offered him a lift down the road. He probably preferred my companion because he was clearly lighter in build than me. Or at least that is how I satisfied my ego.

The Sikh smiled genially. He would be quite happy to drop Flash right outside his camp gate, he only had to say which one and presto! In no time at all he would be deposited there. That was the trouble as far as my old mate was concerned. How was he going to be deposited? It was quite clear from the slight slur of speech and the distinctive smell of his breath that our new found friend had been celebrating.

Flash, sensible fellow, declined the honour and turned to go down the road. Our new found friend frowned and then smiled at me, showing his big white teeth in the dark. 'Is there such a thing as an English coward?' he asked politely. At that moment I could see that Gurkha laddie holding up his hand and indicating half a thumb nail. 'English soldier that much better than a Gurkha.' I knew it wasn't true but I supposed there was a reputation at stake.

I said, 'I am, up to a point, a coward. Aren't we all? But there comes a time in the affairs of men ...'

'What did you say?'

'I said, in the name of Commonwealth unity, England and India and all points west and east I will come aboard.' And I climbed onto the back of his bike knowing full well what he intended to do.

And he did.

We roared off into the dark and I had my eyes firmly closed for a start and I was sure his were closed too. When I managed to take a peep there we were roaring down that damned road at full speed, swerving round lorries and on more than one occasion we were leaping off the road and charging over the desert verge to avoid those oncoming lorry monsters. I thought at one stage that the drink had so far taken over, that he had lost his control. Certainly he was singing in a great roaring voice and I wondered if he was singing hallelujahs to his particular deity. I started wondering if I had one after all and was very soon going to meet him face to face. He swerved at one point to miss a bloody great tank and then towards the end I thought perhaps we had taken off and were now on one of those famous Indian *Thousand and One Nights* magic carpets.

We pulled up outside our camp gate and I eased myself off the rear seat of the machine. That motor cycle man smiled at me in the dark and I am sure his eyes were twinkling. 'Did you enjoy that?' he asked politely.

It had been the most hair-raising journey of my life. I was sure my hair had turned white or at least was now tinged with grey. I hoped I should never experience such another journey. But I felt I had to uphold the honour of the English, the RA or something, so I smiled back at him and said, 'Yes, I did, very much, but I found it just a bit slow.' He roared with laughter, and said, 'You'll do.' And setting his bike in motion charged off down the road probably singing the Song of India.

I waited a long time for Flash Ellison who by the time he reached me had got himself sore feet, a common complaint with gunners when they had to do any walking.

On Thursday 11th January Ellison and I were recalled from the Mena house guard. We were about to start for Blighty but not before we had filled in a few more tent holes and had had another FFI.

Reveille on the Saturday was at 4 a.m. for all those heading for a ship. We had breakfast half an hour later and at a quarter to six we moved off in five trucks in the dark to Abbasia station. There were a number of us, including some from the 153. At nine o'clock we pulled out and that train took us off to Port Said, where we boarded the armed merchantman *Chitral* and had tea aboard. On the Sunday tugs took us out of the harbour and left us to ourselves on the open sea.

There was now no fear of enemy action against us. The Italians had long since jacked it in, Mussolini had ended up hanging upside down and the Germans were back in Germany.

So we were to steam on a straight course until we reached the western Med when we would begin zigzagging. Or possibly once we were past Gib, I forget.

Our ship was smaller than the others I had been on and seemed somewhat cosier. The food was good, the bunks were pleasurable and we found that the ATS were mingling with us herberts of the lower deck, freely. Times indeed had changed.

We gunnery folk discovered that we had been volunteered for canteen heavy haulage work. Twice a day we had to carry boxes of goodies up from the holds of the ship, through the mess decks to the canteen. No doddle as the boxes we carried seemed to contain lead ingots. Our reward for being assistants to the canteen traders, the modern Phoenicians, was to be allowed to spend our money first before the mob got there, because the arrival of such mob meant long queues and patient waiting.

When I began the voyage I had with me a sack of oranges, the intention being to regale the folks at home with the fruit which had been very scarce during the war. I also bought, on board, a large box of Rolo chocolate-covered toffees wrapped up in rows of cylindrical paper wrappers. Needless to say neither oranges nor chocolate toffees left the ship. I am afraid I saw the lot off long before we ever reached Gib, let alone England. We pulled into Algiers for supplies and water and to take on board more troops but as they never turned up we sailed without them, which meant plenty of room and plenty of grub. It was particularly handy for those who had begun to put a little romance into their hitherto drab lives. We sailed along by the shore with the mountains of North Africa in full view. Lights were now allowed since the war in the area was over. It was a curious thing to see lighted towns, even though Cairo had only been partly blacked out. On Saturday the twentieth at around one thirty p.m. we came in sight of the Rock. As we approached, it certainly looked formidable and it was easy to see how difficult it would be to capture the place. Seeing it, I wondered what the devil it had been like to be pent up there throughout the war never knowing what was going to happen next. It reminded me of the story of a bloke I had met in a hospital. He had been serving in Aden which had been and still was such a lousy hole that it was a short stay posting and then the usual practice was to fly people back home when the time came. His time came when he started going round the bend. He naturally played on it a bit and considered as a sergeant he had a good case to go back to Blighty. He ended up doing his nut to me because instead of being sent home he was posted to the Middle East. So, I wondered how claustrophobic the Rock had been.

Lights were on all through the night although depth charges were dropped at the entrance to the harbour every twenty minutes. During the afternoon an Italian corvette went by, followed by an Italian submarine. They of course had changed sides some time before. On the Sunday afternoon we, the canteen navvies, were paraded on deck to be informed that like good honest RA men we had volunteered to man the AckAck guns now that we were going north in the Atlantic where Jerry was still possibly mucking about. Charming!

The 153 in the …

But I could possibly have been knocked down with a feather when I saw who the gallant major was, standing so smartly before us, puffing out his cheeks and exhibiting his magnificent moustachios. It was that gallant officer we loved to hate, dear old Fitzy. I cannot say that we were sorry to lose the slave job but the appearance of Fitzy made those of us who knew him mighty suspicious.

Though I must admit I hadn't done too badly out of the canteen. In fact I had got 500 Gold Flake buckshee, 1,200 other cigarettes at a reduced rate, two pounds of pipe tobacco and cigars at threepence and ninepence each. I must have either considered myself in the future role of a factory chimney or had planned to use bribes in Blighty. How times have changed! I would not now buy anything like that at all.

I can see Fitzwilliams, cheeks puffing, his voice Hum Hum Humming and Ah Ah Ahing, standing in front of four hundred hard bitten gunners and declaring that *we* did not want the navy to protect us but that we were only too happy to help the navy out when we were all in peril on the sea. He had therefore agreed, on our behalf, to man the ship's guns, knowing (puffing out cheeks), knowing how happy we would be to help out that gallant band, those descendants of the old seadogs, of sailors who had contributed so much to our great war effort. (Did I hear a few sobs from the ranks?) Therefore we were volunteered but to do things in the correct manner we would have to find out who had been on guns ashore so all those who had been on guns please take one step forward.

No one moved.

Fitzy's cheeks began to huff and puff as if they were on

overtime. He was unable to understand how it was that out of four hundred veteran gunners no one had ever been been on a gun!

With cheeks going in and out and lips making their usual blowing sounds he walked along the ranks eying the artillery wallahs who had never been on a gun. How the devil could they manage that?

He walked up and down until he saw me.

He stopped in front of me and his eyes lit up. 'Ah Ah, Gunner Green, homeward bound, what what!'

Here was someone he had met before. Someone who had been active on guns from the beginning of the war up till, as far as he knew, the time of leaving my unit. Not only that but here was a person who had camouflaged guns, here was a person who had been limber gunner – a nursemaid to a gun. Here was a bod who had been wounded on a bloody gun! Then again here was a man with a lanyard round his shoulder who had been for some years an active member of the Middle East School of AckAck and CD, camouflaging the guns, limber gunning the damned things and not only firing them or helping to do so but who had been actively engaged in taking them to pieces. Then I wondered if he had realised the truth of the matter, that folk in RA uniform were normally very shy people and never pushed themselves forward. That could be classified as volunteering. However he went on to explain that notwithstanding the lack of gunners among the immediate representatives of the Artillery we had got the job. We presumed that he, Fitzy, having done his duty, retired, exhausted, to the officers' mess, for a cut price cigar and duty free alcohol.

We never saw him again.

We retired to the place where duties were sorted out and I next found myself on watch from midnight till 4 a.m.

The manner of the watch was as follows. I toddled along to the gundeck shrouded in my tatty old bum freezer where I found a gun position sited high up on a platform approached by a dangerous looking vertical ladder. That was the only way into the enclosure and the only exit, thus the quick way of leaving the gun was to be blown off the platform by enemy action or possibly a passing tornado.

I climbed up.

Sitting by the covered up Oerlikon was a dejected looking matelot whose face immediately brightened when he saw me climb aboard.

'Thank Christ you've turned up,' he said.

'Oh! Why?'

'Why? Because I'm a bloody stoker and I don't know the first thing about guns.'

I riposted smartly, 'Me iglorant chlinese cooly bloy, me nlever seen one irlikon glun blefore please.'

He looked at me and I looked at him and the gun stayed covered up.

He explained that he was a stoker, that he was on the gun because the navy saved money that way. If he went into the engine room they would have to pay him the full rate for the job and their lordships didn't like that, the war was too expensive already.

We had a bright thought and cheered up. We would wait for the petty officer to arrive on his rounds. He would sort it all out.

The petty officer eventually hove in sight and called up to ask us if everything was all right. The stoker said happily, 'No, everything is not all right.' He went on to say that someone ought to explain to the gun crew how the gun worked before Jerry turned up. But that petty officer, after listening carefully, merely shrugged his shoulders, said he knew absolutely nothing about guns except that they made a nasty noise and 'Goodnight.' Like Fitzy we never saw him again.

From that time until we stood down we sat on our duty spells, beside the gun which we never uncovered and which we had a shrewd suspicion was never uncovered by anyone else either or if they did the cobwebs were phoney. We did speculate as to what would happen if Jerry did appear in the war zone in a last desperate attack on the gunners and the stoker. We wondered what a pilot of an aircraft would think if he came in with guns blazing and observed a gun nicely covered up and the crew smoking duty free tobacco! We also wondered whether we were the only gun nursemaids not nursemaiding or whether everyone else, annoyed with Fitzy, was doing the same thing. We never found time to find out.

My melancholy matelot mate early assured me that my information about our port of call in Blighty was wrong. He pointed out that I had been told we would reach Liverpool on a certain date. 'For a start, them blokes on the bridge don't know where we are going.'

'That,' I said, 'is unbelievable.'

'Well then,' he replied. 'You wait and see. I bet you they'll never make a landfall in England. They'll miss it completely. Probably end up in Norway or p'raps Bolivia.' He went on to say that when we did arrive somewhere near land they would not even get the day of landing right. And to think that, like so many of us non-naval types, I had assumed that the navy at least knew what it was doing in this war!

We could see the lights of the Hebrides as we went by but it was too damned cold to get excited about that. When our watch ended we hurried below.

The voyage had certainly been unduly long but at last we were approaching the land and we were told we would be landing on the twenty-fifth at Gourock in Scotland! The twenty-fifth being a Thursday. We arrived on Saturday to see snow on them thar hills. Snow!

We landed on old Blighty's shore the following Monday.

The reason given for the delay was a shortage of transport ashore. Bit of a nuisance but since all of us had been away for some years a little extra time afloat would do no harm. Anyway, the billet was comfortable and having stood down on Friday we had nothing to do but wait.

Meanwhile the customs people had come aboard to see what the returning heroes had brought back with them. Ye old warriors were not exempt from passing through ye ancient customs. We heard through the grapevine that the customs bods were pretty hot on sorting out the smuggling tendencies of the overweighted Sam Browne belters but were not too much bothered about the lowly paid sans culottes.

We were shepherded onto a mess deck while a customs man appeared and seated himself in front of us.

'Right lads.' (That sounded friendly enough.) 'Has anyone got anything to declare?' First a long silence, broken by an intense faced, bespectacled, lean looking character who stood up and said, 'Yes, I have.'

The customs man again called out, 'Has anyone got anything to declare?'

The same man rose again and said, 'Yes, I have.' Really, it seemed, honesty knew no bounds. For the third time the customs man asked the question, 'Has anyone got anything to declare?' and again the skinny noodle said, 'Yes I have.' There was a pause and then the customs man said, 'For Christ's sake someone tell him.'

The air turned a bit blue and the honest fellow was pulled roughly back into his seat where he was forcibly muted. No doubt about it, the attitude of that customs man was just the job.

I worked with a man after the war who had been called up into the navy. His experience of the customs was very different. He went into the navy most unwillingly as a conscript but was fortunate in that he was able to pursue his trade in the service. In due course, after serving a term in West Africa, he was sent home on board a naval vessel in which nobody had anything to declare. This was somewhat disconcerting as far as Ralphy was concerned because he could not believe that naval personnel were like that, that is having no goodies picked up in foreign parts that should be declared. The customs authority did not believe them either. Those characters swarmed aboard in overalls and gum boots and proceeded to lay out on the deck a large number of long tables.

'What are they for?' asked the naïve Ralphy.

'You wait and see,' was the reply. He did see.

Nobody having declared anything, the customs men vanished from sight and then, in the course of time, began to reappear carrying armfuls of goods. They fished over the side of the vessel and brought up goods, they emerged from mess decks, cabins, heads, galley, holds and even bilges, carrying parcels of all descriptions: large, small, huge, minute, all sorts of shapes and soon all the tables were full to overflowing.

Then it was announced that anyone who wished could step up to the tables and claim his own. That was how it was done with naval personnel, but then they were always popping in and out of ports.

Then we got the latest information. We would not be landing on the Monday after all but on Tuesday. Old Joe's Red Army was rushing headlong onto Berlin but we were having difficulty getting ashore at Gourock.

However Tuesday did arrive and after breakfast at 6.30 a.m. we were ready to go ashore by 9 a.m. but with all our worldly goods dangling around us, under us or over us we had to sweat it out for a further half an hour. Eventually we staggered aboard a tender, a peacetime river steamer, and off we went. Onto the dock through a customs shed, on to a real Blighty train and all around snow! Girls were running around with tea and cakes; boys, as is their wont the world over, were after souvenirs. Though in some places that meant money or food, here it was mostly buttons that the lads were after. I couldn't give 'em any off my bum freezer; they would not have recognised them as buttons at all. Then, we were off, gliding south towards England. Though some of our Scottish comrades took a dim view of that.

I had left in September 1940; I was returning, late January 1945.

The train took us to Edinburgh, then on to Newcastle where we stopped for *chai* and feed bag and then on again until we made a further stop for more mungaree. Then came London. We crawled around that city till 5.30 a.m. At one time I peered out of a partly blacked out window to find that we were passing through West Brompton station, only a chucking stone's distance from Putney. Then came Woolwich and the troubles connected with getting off a troop train. When we had boarded the thing in Glasgow we had been pushed, shoved and crushed into carriages burdened with as much gear as a camel might have found troublesome. I often wondered what the devil it was like for a poor old infantry wallah with the extra problem in train carriages of a bondook.

So we fell out of the train at Woolwich in confused bundles but eventually got ourselves more or less sorted out and so, by 4 p.m. on Wednesday 31st January, I found myself at long last in Putney.

It doesn't matter how long one has been away, home is home whatever the condition of it. I had a kind of swelling feeling inside me as I started down Putney High Street with someone I had picked up with *en route* who also lived in Putney. It turned out that this man's mother lived in Weimar Street off the High Street. It transpired that his mother worked as a domestic for my future wife in a flat in Kenilworth Court by the bridge. He went to live with his wife in the flat above where my parents lived. At the time I hardly knew the bloke, did not know his mother and hadn't yet met my future wife.

Many heads were turned our way as we tottered down the High Street in true RA style. I daresay we were not the first folk in khaki to walk that way but no doubt we were a bit different. For a start we were still lumbered with army junk and our own loot, we had been travelling for some time and no doubt looked as though we were foreigners to soap and water and certainly the pair of us could do with a shave.

Before I reached home a neighbour had told my mother that she had seen two soldiers in the High Street. 'I did feel sorry for them. They looked so loaded down and worn out.' When I knocked at the familiar door I got no answer. They were out. So Mrs Cox in a flat below, took me in and gave me a cup of tea and there I sat until Pappy turned up.

I was shocked at the appearance of my parents. In 1940 when the air raids were beginning my mother would dart from window to window excitedly watching the searchlights as they endeavoured to pick up a bandit. But now they were, both of them, deathly white with fearful eyes and nervous twitches. The doodlebugs and rockets were indeed a tremendous strain. I tried to cheer them up by playing things down but they could only reply, with, 'You just wait and see.' I didn't have very long to wait and see. One came down with an almighty crash while we were having tea. One moment my mother was sitting opposite to me, the next she had vanished.

I looked at Pappy. 'Where the devil has she gone?' He pointed under the table. 'She's under there.' So she was, crouching hidden completely from view and trembling with fear. Forty years and more on we still have people who voice hatred against people they claim to be enemies, still rave against the Soviet Union which lost twenty million dead in the war against Fascism and were our allies, while no doubt they purchase Japanese goods. There are those who claim sound reasons for the stockpiling of atomic weapons and even the use of them. War may be all right on cinema and television screens but elsewhere it is *persona non* bloody *grata*.

I spent three sleepless nights in the air raid shelter under Edmund's barber's shop. I couldn't drop off among the fearful and the snorers of both sexes and it was extremely claustrophobic. I soon concluded that if Jerry had failed to get me in Tobruk after he had publicly stated he meant to get me and my buddies, he was far less likely to sort me out in the vastness of London, so I told Pappy I was going to make a military strategical withdrawal from the air raid shelter. In future I would take my chance in the flat and I told Pappy that I didn't mind in the least as long as I had my tin hat handy.

He said that he understood and that he would join me. I never found out whether he really didn't like the air raid shelter or whether having been without a son for years he wasn't going to let one of 'em be blown up without him if he could help it.

A few nights later the air raid siren went and I got up. Now, as a long term AckAck performer I had got used to moving fast. So, I was fully dressed and with tin hat in hand was reaching for the door handle when I looked round to see what daddy was doing. He was just about to pull his second sock on! 'Pappy,' I suggested, 'You might just be fast enough for bombers crossing the Channel and even that's a bit doubtful, but hell, you ain't got no chance against one of those damned rockets, no sir' (as the Sheriff would have said), 'you sure ain't, pardner.' He readily agreed and started putting on his shirt.

I took my Aunt Peg (born Rebecca) with me and went over to Kilburn to deliver a photograph album to the mother of Taffy Powell, a certain Mrs Evans. She was delighted to see us and happy to know that her son had been able to keep his head down. But I hadn't gone over there merely on an errand of good will. Taffy had boasted that he had got fourteen suits waiting for him when he got back as against my own none and of course we had expressed loudly and long that Taffy was a liar. So I hinted, tactfully, that I hoped Taffy had plenty of clothing and not that her son was a liar but that no one believed him. So she took me to his bedroom, opened a wardrobe door and allowed me to count the suits. Fortunately for Taffy I could count up to fourteen though I did wonder whether his mum had borrowed a few from friends. But then I decided I was being a bit harsh since she had had no idea that I would turn up. So I had to write to the lads to say that Taffy was not a born liar after all and that he had always spoken the truth – at least about his suits.

Having lost my only civvy suit on the back of a lad caught by a bomb in Putney, and having no clothing coupons, I decided the state owed me something and so went off to Wandsworth town hall. At the said town hall I filled in a form and was directed to the Excise and Customs place on Clapham Common. I must admit it gave me quite a feeling as I went by the gun site on the common where I had had my beginnings along the warrior trail. The man behind the counter was sympathetic but doubted whether I, as a serving soldier could get any clothing coupons. After which speech I launched a blistering counter attack to the effect that having been overseas for years and years and now having returned broken in several things such as health and mental condition and having nothing to wear but poxy khaki because my only pre war suit had been blown up, how would he like to spend a good deal of his time in public saluting idiots in Sam Browne belts who had probably never seen the sun set over Brighton beach let alone the British Empire what what?

He said he wouldn't.

'Well then?'

He said he would see what he could do and so I left peaceably.

I had an uncle Ike (born Bert) who knew a tailor in the High Street — a master tailor who could supply coupon-free suits. So I went with Ikey, got measured and handed over twelve quid.

Then came a letter through the post. It contained 145 clothing coupons and enclosed also was the opinion that I would be unable to get any more — ever. 145 would be enough, especially as I wouldn't need any for the suit. But the kindly Customs and Excise hadn't finished with me yet. They must have called an emergency meeting to discuss my problem because hardly had I put the 145 into my pocket when the postman delivered another nineteen. Later, on returning to Woolwich after my disembarkation leave, a number of 'our chaps' were discussing clothing coupons that they had been able to get hold of. Some had managed half a dozen, some ten and one boasted that he had got twenty. I kept silent as long as possible. No need to cause jealousy in the ranks, envy or the desire to upset the economy by creating a rush for clothing coupons. Then again, they all looked so well dressed and elegant in their army clobber.

But of course it wasn't possible for me to stay for ever tight-lipped. For one thing, no one who had once had a stammer can ever stay that way and for another I was the Dodger and had a reputation to uphold.

'Come on Dodger, how many?'

I blushed. 'A few.'

'Come on, how many, blast you.'

'One hundred and forty five.'

'HOW MANY?'

'One hundred and forty five.'

Not being believed, I proved it.

'But that's not all.'

'NOT ALL?'

'No, the Customs and Excise considered I hadn't been dealt with fairly so they sent me more.'

I will not describe the atmosphere in our billet except to say that the surrounding air was blue for a while.

During that six weeks leave I wrote a letter to the CO in Woolwich requesting an extension of leave on the grounds that I wanted to be with my mum a bit longer. I posted it at 8.30 a.m. and at 8.33 a.m. the postman knocked at the door and handed me an official looking letter. Inside was an authorization for a seven day extension of leave plus ration card. Both my parents were goggle eyed at the speed of reply – three whole minutes. I pointed out that I might be only a limber gunner but I did have some influence, particularly with commanding officers.

I bought some clothes. One pair grey flannels, 15s.8d. and five coupons, a grey sports coat, £3.0s.6d. and fifteen coupons and a few odds and ends such as vests and pants. I then decided that my wardrobe was complete and to hell with Taffy Powell.

I then went off to the Windmill theatre to take in the leg show, making sure that on that occasion I was in khaki because the price of admittance was twelve shillings for the circle and ten shillings for the stalls and half price for anyone in uniform. But the event was marred somewhat. I had to queue for a long time. There were too many damned Yanks about.

It was at this time that I took my mother on one or two theatre trips to the West End, my father not being the type of person to carry on like that. He, in fact, was busy, replacing blown out glass in and around Putney. As soon as glass had been replaced, it seemed a rocket went off and blew the glass out again.

We went to the Prince of Wales theatre one Friday in February to see a Sid Fields show and on coming out were in time to hear an almighty bang as a rocket went down at King's Cross.

We didn't hang about.

On another occasion we went to the Palace to see a Cicily Courtnedge, Jack Hulbert thing. My mother was mad about those two as were many other people. I thought the show was lousy but then I was a Windmill addict. There were plenty of empty spaces in the West End where V bombs and rockets had struck and naturally all that bother affected stage performances. It must have been extremely difficult for actors to do their jobs and for comedians to be funny when at any moment they could be blown to smithereens.

Very soon after I had returned home came the incidents of the bread puddings. I had intended to bring that sack of oranges back but had failed to do so though parcels of sweets I had sent home got there intact. When I arrived home my parents had solemnly presented me with an orange, a rare thing in those war time days. What the devil could I do? I could hardly say no to their sacrifice though I had lived in and among oranges for some years. So I ate it. And back to the bread puddings.

Knowing my fondness for bread puddings and knowing I was due home at any time my mother had hoarded dried fruit, saved stale bread and then at the right time had made four large bread puddings baked in a large flat oven toasting tin. Having obliged everyone by eating three of those enormous puddings I took a stroll round to my grandparents' flat where I discovered to my consternation that my grandmother had made *three* bread puddings of the same size and weight as those my mother had made. I knew that the older a person was the better the bread pudding. I have no idea why this is but I have always found it so. Maybe bread pudding making is a highly skilled art which improves with age, that is the age of the maker not the bread pudding. Knowing this I found it hard to resist those new offerings and in any case when someone takes the trouble to please you and when you also know that some sacrifice has been made, what else can be done but to do a bit of obliging? So I sat down, set to and ate two more puddings while my grandfather smoked one of the Woodbines I had brought him and told tales of the past, of Crowther the antiques dealer, of Tom Stevens the wood merchant and of how the other two had grown wealthy while he himself was where he was. When I staggered home I wasn't drunk, I was carrying too much weight.

My leave came to an end in due course. On one of the last days I got my old bike out and rode over the old route to Kingston via Richmond Park which I had so often taken with Will Simmonds. I had been unable to face his parents, even though they were still friendly with mine. If Will's father had not been so domineering, refusing to let his son join the TA with me, he would probably, almost certainly, have been around now. After all, I had lost hardly any of my old buddies.

Chapter Twenty-One

Blighty Base Wallah

On March the seventh, my leave having at last come to an end, I went back to Woolwich, known by its inhabitants as Belsen. Maybe in the light of what happened in the real Belsen and other such frightful places one should not use the name flippantly. On the other hand that was what we called it at a time when the full horror of the German holocaust was unknown to us. So for the sake of accuracy I have left the name on record as an indication of what the ordinary squaddie thought of the place.

We leave returners had to shake down for the night in any corner we could find. I soon discovered that this wasn't a bad idea after all because that night the rockets came bouncing about all over the place, mostly landing in Charlton. Charlton seemed to intrigue the Germans because they were always dropping their damned rockets there. In fact any of our crowd who went there or worked in the area were quite blasé about it. I had to acclimatise myself to the new situation; we had had in comparison, in the west of London, a quiet time of it.

Next day we got sorted out and I found myself in 2 troop, D section, a section for graded men only. We were domiciled in the Royal Military Academy. Our part of it was an old dining room partly burnt out, not because of enemy action but through the result of a blown fuse in the electrical system.

I noted that rockets were bouncing about the Woolwich-Charlton area as if two giants were playing tennis. One rocket went down just behind the Herbert Hospital killing some orderlies, two fell in the arsenal and one went off not far from my ear one Sunday morning. Some of the mob returning from leave said that a rocket had hit Charlton railway station. So, as we went about our various businesses there was always the possibility of a final fourpenny one and although we were all apprehensive, because, I suppose, of the comfort of numbers we were less nervous in Woolwich than elsewhere. I can well remember one character I was on fatigues with. We were standing at a window in the officers' building when this jerk suddenly spat out, 'I wish to Christ one of those bloody rockets would fall on the bloody officers' mess.'

I looked at him askance. 'Aren't you forgetting one thing?'

'What?'

'We're in the officers' building right now.'

'That wouldn't bother me,' he spat out. 'As long as it got them.'

Charming!

But Jerry never got the officers' building. In fact he never did get any of our barracks, which, I supposed in the long run, was a good thing.

I got an early posting. Eight men were wanted at the Army, Navy and Air Force Association place in Kensington. They needed clerks and it wasn't far from Putney. But the next day they only needed four people so I was struck off the list. Possibly a good thing. I have always found it too difficult reading my own writing to be over anxious to inflict it upon others.

The next day I was posted again but as I had got only one battledress I was taken off that one too. The reason for only having one was because the other had been nicked from my kitbag while it had been locked up in the stores. Thieving in the place was rife, something most of us returned from overseas had not experienced before. Because of the increase in thieving I soon found myself on a patrolling picket, the job of which was to prowl around looking for nickers.

Then I got detailed for a mess hall orderly job, which meant that I had every other afternoon free until midnight. The job came about in a curious way. The barracks held about three thousand men so that mungaree time was quite something. For instance, Fridays were fish days so the cooks would have to fry something over three thousand bits of fish.

When I first turned up at Woolwich the dinner-time wait for grub was painful. The mess orderlies would get the dixies from the cookhouse, set them on tables and then proceed to serve out the food. One man on meat or fish, one on vegetables, one on spuds and one on gravy if any.

The dinner queue would normally stretch across the parade ground and the permanent mess sergeant would be hopping around doing his nut and all because of the situation with the potato server-outer. That important vegetable was nearly always of the dehydrated kind and therefore, when re-constituted, cooked and ready to serve out, was somewhat gooey. The problem seemed easily solvable to me. But apparently no one had ever had the wit to do anything about it. The server had only one spoon and was not allowed to touch the potato with his fingers, in consequence of which he stood behind his dixie scooping out spud and trying to flick it onto a plate and it being sticky it wouldn't flop off the spoon easily. In consequence there was much flourishing of the spoon and food flying through the air. The sergeant would be dancing about and effing and blinding, the spud man would be nervous, nonplussed, irritated or walking off in anger or disgust according to the particular man's bent.

Then it was my turn to dish out the offending horrible tasting but usually eaten spuddo. I got myself a second spoon and was able thereby to smartly sweep potato with one spoon from the other and drop it neatly onto a plate. It was a revolutionary idea. No one had thought of it before. But then of course it was but a small step from being on the fastest gun team in the Middle East to being the fastest server-outer of potato in Woolwich – maybe – I thought – in the whole of the army.

The result of this action was to clear the line of men in very short order. In fact the other server outers had to get their fingers out to keep up with the new racing demon of Woolwich. The mess sergeant was so impressed he asked for me to be made a permanent mess orderly and whenever my name appeared on the posting board he would rush round to the postings office to get it scrubbed off.

From the fastest gun to the fastest spoon! My star was in the ascendant.

Thus I was able to get out and home much more often than most. I was often thwarted though, because the powers-that-be had a nasty habit of organising talks for the troops, usually on my afternoon off. One such talk was given by a Ministry of Labour official who had been in the Ministry for thirty-three years and was a long-standing socialist. He lectured on the government's white paper on demobilisation and was convinced that the government was sincere in wanting to build homes and a glorious future for the returning heroes. We, in the main, didn't want to listen, and a good many, forced to do so, failed to see why a long-term self-styled Socialist should bumble on in praise of *Tories*. After all, the Tories were in power before the war, after the war started, during the bloody thing and were still there and a good many of us had long since come to the conclusion that there were a lot of people, probably Tories, who didn't want the war to end, at least not too quickly. So he spoke to a silent audience whose only reaction came when he said that he was off overseas to lecture troops on demobilisation. The sentiment was expressed quite loudly and clearly that the sooner he buggered off overseas the better it would be for us.

Another lecture on another of my afternoons off was delivered by a Colonial official, retired.

By this time, when the lectures were due to take place all kinds of odd bods were swept up into a kind of listening brigade and marched to the lecture hall, where they sat grimly to be lectured at. These folk would include people like myself who had expected to indulge themselves in time off but who found themselves dragooned into listening to things they were not interested in. In an endeavour to force a little enthusiasm into the audiences a number of officers were to be found seated in the front row who no doubt had no wish to be there either.

Now, this elderly, thin, red-faced, colonial bod started off on the wrong foot by explaining proudly how he had been some sort of secretary, adviser or right hand man to a Maharajah of some place in India and this colonial man kept referring to such places as Poona. He made it clear that without this Maharajah, ably supported by himself, the colonial official, India would have long since been lost to that great British Institution, the British Empire – what!

Long before that hard-working true-blue official had finished there were rumblings from the audience and then came catcalls and remarks which could be easily summed up as, 'If you liked the place so much why did you effing well leave it?' and 'If you think it was so marvellous why don't you effing well bugger off back there?' First murmurings, then catcalls, then remarks, then rising noise, then officer intervention, but as time went on they became more and more ineffectual. After all a number in the audience had served in India and the India they had known had not been quite the same as Indian administrators had lived in.

The lecture came to an abrupt halt when the pukka sahib, unable to make himself heard above the din, stalked out followed by advice on the best way to get to India.

It was becoming clearer every day that the Academy was full of mutinous dogs who somehow had to be controlled. But how do you control three thousand men, most of whom had been in all kinds of duffies including those in the Far Eastern war zone? One way of keeping 'the lads' busy was to line them up in rows on one side of the parade ground and then to advance them in serried ranks across the area picking up bits of paper, dead matches and dog ends. Now, as no handy receptacle was ever provided for such rubbish the diligent scavengers simply picked up the offending articles and threw them over their shoulders, so that at the end of each operation the rubbish was left exactly where it had been found on the ground. If those bits of refuse could have been capable of thought it is certain they would have been bewitched, b– and bewildered.

Fred Smith turned up and Smudger and I went out a great deal together. One of the places of entertainment locally was the

Garrison theatre where we would often go for a laugh or two although our first jaunt was to a dance hall because my old buddy was a keen dancer. We sat at the edge of the dance floor all evening, drinking, smoking and arguing, as had always been our wont. Finally, I thought, as Smudger was a good dancer he ought to go get himself a partner to dance with. He agreed it was about time he found a bint and that one over there looked just the job. He got up, crossed over to the girl, she rose, they walked onto the floor, the band struck up God Save the King and that was the end of that.

However, back to the Garrison theatre which must have been the forlorn hope of the theatrical fraternity. The artistes appearing there always seemed to be lacking something: ambition, desire, hope? One thing was plain, none of them could have looked forward with enthusiasm to appearing there. We wondered if it was the theatrical profession's way of creating 'jankers' for the wayward.

Mark you, we had to feel sorry for them as they confronted all those beady eyes watching, alert for the slightest mistake. And there were plenty of those. One very well built not so young girl appeared in a tight gold outfit showing all her contours and started wriggling about as if she had been activated by a tired out, pensioned off wasp. The advice she was given made me blush and I am certainly not about to describe the act with pornographic imagery.

There must have been a talent competition night because there was one act which could never have been entertained by any pro whatsoever. This character came on slowly, shuffling back and forth across the stage holding a cardboard tube. There was laughter at first but when it became apparent that he could do nothing else but shuffle to and fro across the stage holding the cardboard tube, the remarks began. These were followed by uproar then a few things were thrown as a kind of encouragement – to get off.

But the crowning act as far as we were concerned was the trapeze artiste. She was a young heavily built lady who fancied herself in short skirts and who attempted to walk a tightrope stretched across the stage. She should never have taken the job on. Despite several attempts she never made it from one side of the stage to the other; she always fell off. The advice emanating from the audience was enlightening, though there was a great shout of disagreement when some bright spark suggested she should try putting the rope higher – underneath the roof.

Many of the old gang were turning up including one of the original Bundlers, Stan Ward. He was still basing his life on wine, women and song with not too much song. We went around together, the three of us, when he could drag himself away from his vocation. It may have been at this time that we three, with a few others, having imbibed too much booze in his home lair of Tooting, played follow my leader along the tramlines off Tooting Broadway to see who was Charlie, the first to fall off, and damn the trams: they would have to wait.

Stan came round one day after returning from some sort of compassionate leave. He had left his gaiters behind and as he was going on escort duty he would have to borrow mine and if I needed any I could borrow Fred's or tell the CO to go to the devil if there was a muster parade.

I met someone else who had been on an escort duty and he assured me with much vigour that he would do it 'never again, no, not ever again.'

Having collected his prisoner he made an agreement with the latter. If his prisoner promised no funny business like running away, he, the escort would go the long way round to the military prison. So the bargain was struck and off they went. They did go a long way round, they did visit many pubs and they did arrive somewhat behind schedule. The big gates swung open, prisoner and escort stepped inside and a thundering great disembodied voice roared out, 'Prisoner and escort smarten yourselves up and DOUBLE MARCH.'

The prisoner didn't hesitate, he doubled forward pronto but the escort stood a bit bemused. After all he *was* only the escort and as far as he knew he hadn't committed any crime unless someone had watched them taking their time in getting to the glasshouse. The voice roared again and this time indicated that if the escort didn't do what he was told it would be a long time before he saw the other side of the main gate again, so he too doubled and kept on doing so until he was told to stop and by that time he was a broken if not totally demoralised man.

I met several army personnel who had been over the wall and they all had the same point of view – never again.

The Sheriff put in an appearance. It was he who became involved in the dock strike of that year. With others, he was detailed to go down to the docks and blackleg on the striking dockers. Something, I supposed, no self respecting, war time non-regular would ever dream of doing if he could help it. Certainly the Sheriff would not represent the law when it came to strike-breaking, even though he wore the tin star. So he became a baddie.

When he and others got to the gate they asked the dockers at the gate what they, the blacklegs, could do to help. The dockers could not say what the soldiers should do but did say what the dockers would do if they, the dockers, were in khaki.

Sid found himself with others on the top floor of a big warehouse looking out over the dock area and what he saw amazed him. He saw huge dock cranes lying on their sides. How anyone without the right equipment had managed to turn them over was beyond his comprehension but somehow the lads in khaki had done the trick. While he was standing at the top of the warehouse exterior stairs he was handed a box of what appeared to be brand new valves. He simply followed others and tipped the lot overboard; it was easier than carrying them all the way down to the ground. He said it would have been impossible to assess the amount of damage those blacklegs were doing but it was certainly considerable.

Those baddies sure were making a mess of that goddarn town.

The military were quickly withdrawn.

I had one of my weekend passes in my pocket when Smudger joined me, saying he had decided to have a weekend off too though he didn't have a pass like honest Dodger had. A pass was vital when going on leave through London. The Redcaps swarmed at the main line stations though were never seen at the local ones, possibly because they would be exposed to some sort of military mugging. So we devised a plan of campaign. When I got to Waterloo, I loosened my tie, undid my collar, unbuttoned my jacket, took off my side hat and slouched across from the Woolwich line to the main line station and, as expected, when halfway across was told to halt by a bull-like voice. A couple of dehumanized beings in red hats stood before me and wanted to know what I thought I was up to. I saw out of the corner of one eye Fred slipping by unobserved. I decided not to explain in detail to the Redcaps what I was up to, merely mumbled mumbles and showed them my pass on demand.

I was given a lecture on how to dress. I could have told them that where colonels and adjutants had failed Redcaps were unlikely to succeed. After an overlong harangue I was allowed to proceed.

I joined Smudger on the train.

Ralphy, who had been in the navy, always maintained that the naval Jonties were really not human. He swore they were built like tanks, were as wide as they were tall and possessed no human feeling whatsoever. He reckoned that one day at Chatham when he was off on leave he reached the main gate in apple pie order with nothing out of place. At the gate one of those naval creatures above mentioned appeared and growled something or other in a gorilla type jargon. Ralphy didn't hesitate. He said at once, 'How much?'

The Jonty growled, 'How much you got?' Ralphy, who was a tough nut in his own Battersea right, again didn't hesitate. He pulled out his wages and showed them. The Jonty growled, 'Half,' took it and thumbed my old mate forward. So our own Redcaps weren't really all that bad, I suppose.

All sorts of changes were now taking place. Himmler had taken over from Hitler and then Admiral Doenitz superseded the latter villain and all around them in Germany the balloon was going up. The Red Army had linked up with the Americans and the end of the hostilities in Europe was just around the corner. Then came VE day.

Meanwhile another character out of my recent past had turned up – Harry Withers. A week after I had left the school he had been handed over to the medical people, had been found guilty of being unfit and before his feet could touch the ground, found himself in Blighty in hospital and out of the army, medically unfit officially speaking, though he and I agreed it was probably because he was a buyer of the *Daily Worker*. We had no illusions about folk in high places. The Russians might be our allies until the end of the war but there were those in our country who considered the Soviet state evil and that it should be destroyed.

Whatever the real reason it was clear that he was no longer wanted.

But Harry was troubled, not by being demilitarised but with what was going on in his own backyard.

He had always scoffed at those men who complained about their wives carrying on with other men while their husbands were away, while the men themselves frequented brothels. But when he heard that his own wife was carrying on with someone in a muffler and cap he was highly indignant. When I visited him in hospital he was really doing his nut. Here he was with his own wife messing about with a cloth cap and muffler herbert. It was absolutely unforgivable.

'It's the cloth cap and muffler,' he complained. 'If only he wore a collar and tie I wouldn't mind but a cloth cap *and* a muffler!' We went out together several times, often to take a canoe out at Maidenhead. One day we were parked in the middle of the river with Harry ruminating on his misfortune when a gun went off up-river and the next moment I looked up and there, bearing down upon us, was a fleet of sailing yachts, an English fleet in full sail and we a mere cockleshell. Scared stiff, we drove ourselves ashore and toddled into a pub. Me, scruffy as I was, after a day on the river, would have gone where I belonged, into a public bar. But Harry was a master tailor so I followed him into the saloon bar where every drink was a short. Every eye turned on us and most of them switched to me and I knew that with my pint of beer I should have been in the public bar. Ah! What price freedom, what price democracy!

I often saw Harry after his divorce and he still persisted on mulling over the merits if any and demerits of cloth caps and mufflers. I wondered if his carelessness with money had anything to do with his problem. While at the school he had received an income tax demand for ninety pounds back taxes. He had written back to say that he was fighting His Majesty's enemies and he couldn't therefore see why His Majesty couldn't excuse him paying taxes as well. The upshot of the discussions he had as soon as he reached Blighty, still in His Majesty's uniform, was that the income tax powers-that-be would accept back repayment at the rate of a penny a week!

I also went up to Maidenhead sometimes with Fred Smith but those journeys did not have the same leisurely pace as did those with Harry. I remember one outing vividly. Fred decided that we were not on the gentle bosom of old daddy Thames but were in a dugout canoe on one of the great North American rivers the names of which he never knew. That bit of rushing water was not a Thames weir to be avoided but a great set of rapids that we had to negotiate to avoid them advancing redskins. For a man who before the war was supposed to have a weak heart my companion had a very powerful thrusting stroke as I discovered as we drove toward the weir-cum-rapids. I was not keen on the idea so I began paddling in the opposite direction as if the Indians had captured the rapids. We had a long hard struggle, Fred paddling south, me battling north. Fortunately I won that battle and we made it to the safety of the opposite shore with both my half of the canoe and his going in the same direction.

After that incident, whenever he made enthusiastic overtures about returning to the mighty Rockies, the Great Lakes or a powerful river I would point out that I was waiting for my new waterproofed socks and could not venture into the wilderness without them. But he wasn't finished with me yet. At one time he was stationed on the east coast at Clacton. I went down to see him and much against my native wisdom I followed him into the sea. It was not the Med and I came out in very short order a delicate shade of blue and with teeth rattling like knucklebones. Then he got me on to one of those funfair dipper things which swing and twist human innards into knots and create biliousness in human beings. I fell off that thing feeling that while Jerry hadn't got me, the funfair had.

Chapter Twenty-two

VE Day and After

Fred and I visited the Strangers Gallery, but couldn't distinguish between the Tories and Labour members since they all seemed to be wearing black jackets and pin-striped trousers. Outside the chamber it was easy to pick out MPs from the rest by their aforementioned uniform. We hoped to see Jimmy Maxton and his long hair but we didn't. We wondered if our failure to distinguish between them was an omen for the future. Would the brave new free world show there was no real differences between Tory, Labour and Liberal? If so, would this be a good or a bad thing?

So, on the eve of VE day we departed from the house of Commons and went to Madame Tussauds which we found not very interesting. Then to the Forces Centre in Trafalgar Square and picked up two tickets for 'Another Love Story'. We didn't think much of that either. We then mingled with the huge crowds in and around Piccadilly Circus. There was a joyous atmosphere everywhere. The morrow would be VE day to celebrate the end of the war in Europe and so everyone was very happy. On the day itself great crowds invaded the centre of town and great bonfires were lit all over London. Searchlights became London's floodlights and the pubs stayed open until midnight.

There were fireworks on Woolwich Common but none of us in the barracks were enthusiastic about them. We had seen enough fireworks in the RA to last us a lifetime. In any case celebrations were a bit premature for squaddies still being posted abroad and we had to bear in mind that posting overseas could mean the Far East where the Japanese hadn't yet jacked it in. We were also pondering the Minister of Labour's (Bevin) assertion that we needed re-allocation of labour, not demobilisation.

The latter would only take place slowly. Maybe all right for the economy but after years in the army we wanted out – and quick.

On 18th June groups one and two would be demobbed. Thereafter two groups per fortnight. I worked out I would be out by Christmas. By that time I was not only still in the army but was out of the country once again.

Meanwhile, at Woolwich we had a couple of old soldiers who were in group two and who were permanently celebrating VE day and taking verbal potshots at some of us greenhorns of the later groups. They swore they would come and visit us in our gaol as soon as they themselves got out.

Then they found their names stuck up on the posting board. Not only that, they discovered they were posted to the *Far East*!

'Far East,' they raged and no doubt spluttered. 'Far East. Never mind the Far East,' they considered, 'We're being let out in a fortnight. Far East be damned.'

So, round to the posting office they galloped as if they were still in the Horse Artillery, to get their names scrubbed off that 'stupid list'.

They were in for a surprise.

It was explained to them that the postings were not local but had come straight from the War Office and there was nothing that they could do about it locally. There was no doubt about it, they would have to go.

It was a bit sad perhaps, a bit potty perhaps, but they would have to go. But not to worry, it wouldn't be for long.

And so amid many cheers, corny jokes, such as, 'Give the Japs one for me darlings,' amid FFIs, issues of tropical kits and special rations plus their very own personal transport provided by the kindly authorities, they started out to fight the Japs, knowing they were going by sea, would have to arrive, get a posting to the battlefield, defeat the Japanese, and get demobbed – all in a fortnight! Off they went, being given a thunderous send off by more or less the whole of the personnel which certainly numbered thousands.

Arriving at the Rock of Gibraltar they were hailed by some launch or other and told to hop off the boat and go pay a visit to the Rock. They probably told the monkeys there that they, the monkeys, were not the only ones about.

From the Rock they were flown back to Blighty where at our Belsen they marched in to the thundering cheers of their contemporaries. They handed in their kit, if they still had any, and marched straight into civvy street.

The war, at least in Europe, being over, Churchill and the Tories decided to go to the country, probably in the belief that everyone understood they had won the war, with the help of Monty, and they ought to have the mandate to get on with winning the peace. I had no idea what the people in my brother's army, the infantry bit, thought. Were they all like him then I daresay they were Tories to a man. But in the army to which I belonged, we knew that Montgomery, who had tossed Players cigarettes from boxes when touring in his jeep, while we were issued with poxy Victory vees, and Churchill, who indulged himself with big fat cigars, had had a great deal of help from us. Those characters, Tory politicians and senior army wallahs, were no longer *persona grata* apart from Wavell and Rommell.

I was in the Lower Road Putney when the Churchill election cavalcade drove past and turned over Putney Bridge. There was only a thin crowd watching and boos mingled with the cheers. No doubt of course that Churchill had been a good war leader but there were other things to be totted up on the debit side of the Tory party. In Woolwich I seemed to be living a permanent life of argument and arm waving. I was constantly surrounded by a crowd of Labour supporters all telling the world what a lousy lot the Tories were and how marvellous Clem Attlee and his cohorts. At meal times when we orderlies went to the cookhouse I would be surrounded by what I might, in all modesty, describe as my followers.

The mess sergeant got a bit worried about all the schemozzle. He was probably concerned about the dire fate that might be waiting for his spud server outer if that character kept up his political activities. I tried to reassure him by pointing out that when we came to power we wouldn't hurt his feelings by making him man the barricades, he could still be mess sergeant and I would train a replacement for yours truly. We used to wander through the billets advising everyone to vote Labour or get duffed up. We were a strong armed mob quite incapable of even flicking a bit of dust off someone's coat.

But we were bothered by the fact that so many squaddies, being far from home, would not get a vote. So part of our policy was to urge everyone to fill in a proxy voting form and send it off and of course most of them did just that. The only thing was that after the election in which Attlee and company had well and truly defeated Churchill and his mob, one of my cronies happened to be doing a bit of cleaning in the adjutant's office where he discovered a pile of proxy papers in a drawer which had never been sent off! According to my informant they were all Labour votes. Ah well, elections, war, what's the odds.

On one memorable occasion many of us got rounded up and the cattle drive once again took place on one of my days off. So I was not best pleased to find myself down in Grand Depot which turned out to be the corral for the intelligence testing procedure. The idea appeared to be to find out what we were fit for during the rest of our stay in His Majesty's Forces. Since nearly all of us had no ambition to stay a moment longer than was necessary, the interest in the business on hand was nil. No one wanted to do anything during any remaining service.

We were directed into a classroom where, seated at desks, we were handed twelve sheets of questions to answer and told not to cheat. The first page of questions began with a request to answer such questions as two and two, three plus two, three take away two, one and one, one minus one and so on until one arrived at such academic requests as draw a square, a triangle or a circle. I am sure one question was make a dot.

After answering six pages of questions I put my pen down, folded my arms and made it clear I had finished work for the morning, possibly due to brain fatigue. The other six pages I left blank. I told the man next to me that if they wanted the rest filled in they could jolly well do it themselves, whoever themselves were.

He was somewhat surprised but I quietly pointed out that I could no longer exercise my cerebellum, cerebrum and medulla oblongata on such weighty matters as differentiating between a square and a circle, a blot and a smudge and a dot and carry one. He could if he wanted to but my brain was reeling with all the effort.

In the afternoon we had to return for an interview with a psychoanalyst, or was it a psychologist or psychopath? We sat in a hall with a number of doors leading off to rooms into which men, in their turn, disappeared to be interviewed. Everyone seemed to be in a hurry. The average time per interview was five minutes. I said to the bloke sitting next to me, 'You can time me and if I'm out in less than half an hour you can have my spud ration for a week!'

He considered that a lousy idea since according to the lay out of things he would have to wait until I came out. I assured him he should be patient, it was all for the cause, though the cause referred to clearly escaped him.

When my turn came I stepped into a poky little room not fit for a limber gunner, let alone a Sam Browne man, and there was one sitting behind a desk on which stood a pile of books. Having had many discussions with the dog collar fraternity I realised at once that this man would be no trouble. I fingered the books, opened a couple, nodded and put them down again. He said, 'I see you are interested in books.' I knew then that his brain was working, a point in his favour. I said, 'Yes, I read books.' I would have wagered two weeks spud rations that no one else had bothered to even glance at the books.

He suggested that I sat down, relaxed and for the time being forgot I was in the army. I sat down, gazed fondly at my uniform, stared hard at his, looked carefully around and then gazed intently out of the window. What was I looking for, he wanted to know.

'Ways and means of forgetting that I am in the army, but frankly I can't see any.'

He smiled and then said, 'The papers you filled in or did not fill in this morning are the most remarkable I have seen since I have been on this job.'

When he went on to say he had been on that job for nearly five years I nearly gave up. My instinct was to walk out but I remembered in time my vow to stay for half an hour. Besides, I liked spuds, even the dehydrated horrible variety.

He pointed out that the idea was to try and find out what sort of job each of us would be suitable for during the remainder of our stay in the army. I could not help but wonder why a character like him, who had been sitting comfortably in a chair, wearing a Sam Browne belt, for five years, could not sort out a suitable job for a bloke like me. I told him what I thought.

I wanted to know how much influence he had got. That depended. What he wanted to know was what I most desired. He was a bit dim after all. I said I wanted what every non-regular soldier wanted – my ticket. He said he was afraid he couldn't help much in that direction so I had to point out that he didn't seem to have much influence after all. There was I, a building worker, and out there were buildings Jerry had bulldozed needing to be sorted out, spaces to be cleared and new buildings erected and here I was poncing about serving out gluey spud and he, asserting his job was to help, in reality couldn't because he had no power. So we developed a political discussion until on the half hour by my watch I said I thought I ought to go otherwise he might find himself on overtime. We rose to our respective feet and he said it had all been very interesting but it was perfectly clear that he would be unable to fit me into any job category. I told him he shouldn't worry about it since I had a splendid job already.

'And what is that?'

'Serving out mashed potatoes with two spoons instead of one.'

I said goodbye politely and left. My companion was quite eager to know how I could take so long; after all, everyone else had gone home. The long delay had peeved him a bit though I suspected that it wasn't really that. Fact was, he wouldn't get those extra spuds now would he?

After that interview I had a similar experience on my way across Belgium to Germany. The same sort of set up, the same sort of Sam Browne belter and questions, the same contrived air of relaxation. Only this time I didn't get the chance to do any such easy come easy go relaxation exercises. In fact, my feet scarcely touched the floor. I went in, the man behind the desk read out my name, said thank you very much for calling or words to that effect and good day to you, then I was out. The whole operation from start to finish probably taking no more than thirty seconds.

What they would have made of Harry Withers I hate to think. While he sojourned in the land of milk and honey he had to go off and be analysed from time to time, because of his so called nervous condition. It seemed that the powers-that-be, the analysing medical fraternity, were determined to find causes for the condition in Harry's pre army tailoring past. Getting a bit browned off with things in general he decided to give them at least one hefty clue. He invented a very old great great aunt Emily who had been well known as suffering from nervous twitches and who had had a spell in a mental institution. From that day forward everyone seemed quite satisfied and Harry never again had to attend one of those nervous sessions.

Time rolled by. I had my short leaves and my long leaves. I went out with Smudger with Wardy in attendance sometimes; on other occasions it was me and old Harry. But things never stay still and while many of the old bunches I had known appeared, in due course they were dispersed again to all points of the compass. Meantime the business of being the fastest server outer of mashed potatoes in the British army was beginning to pall. Demobbing was dead slow, there was too much bull being forced down the throats of men who were more and more resentful of being in the army. Discipline was getting harder and harder to maintain.

It was time for revolution or a trip abroad. Not too far away – say Germany.

Six months to the day after disembarkation leave I found myself on embarkation leave once again. Arthur Mayes and Fangs King were on the same draft with a few others of the old gang. Taffy Powell had gone off somewhere, Sheriff Sprang had been sent to a POW camp. It was time to hang up my crossed spoons and move on.

It was during that nine day leave that we heard of the dropping of the atom bombs on Japan. Clearly a terrible weapon and one which would change the world we all knew. But at the time of its dropping on Hiroshima and Nagasaki it seemed to a great many of us justifiable in that it would hasten the end of the war with Japan. It might still be possible to justify the action if it had all ended there and then with a determination to have no more bombs. But it was not an end, just a beginning.

In August came the cease-fire in the Far East and VJ day was celebrated on the fifteenth of that month, though few of us were in a mood for celebrations.

It was at this time that many of us who had never bothered to pin on the Africa Star did so. We had never bothered since we had been given to understand that the first folk to wear it were the NAAFI girls of Cairo. And the whole thing seemed pointless if everyone in the Middle East could bung it up. It didn't mean anything. But now we came across lads who had been having their nappies changed while we had been out there, who seemed to think that us old codgers had been skulking in back kitchens some place. So we shoved the ribbon up.

I happened to be home a little later when the usefulness of the Africa Star was made plain. A couple of conscript lads had got in the habit of taking on board a few drinks at the Half Moon pub and then standing outside the flats shouting the odds and explaining how they had won the war for people like my mother and father in the flats. As soon as my ears caught the gist of what was being said I yanked on my bemedalled jacket and made for the front door. My mother, who had been raving on about the lads, tried to repress my enthusiasm, fearing I might get hurt or something. This I thought was a bit of a joke. If I couldn't handle a couple of mindless twits like them my name wasn't Dodger.

I went out of the door and down the stairs fast and arrived ready for action just as one of them bawled out, 'We won the war for you, you silly old cow.'

As I advanced upon this enemy I called to them, 'Did you win the war for me? I just want to know what you think before I flatten the pair of you.'

That ribbon was quite conspicuous and they hurriedly began backing off, protesting it was all only in fun, a bit of humour, no harm intended. They kept up a strategical withdrawal and I carefully explained to them that they may have won some other war but this one they were facing would be won by me. I would mash 'em into small pieces and flush them down the handiest drain hole. I especially advised them not to come down Bigg's Row again and as far as I know they never did.

On my returning to the flat my parents were eager to know what I had said. I told them the truth when I said I had told them to go away.

After leave, back in Woolwich, or more strictly speaking to the RMA, straight to the draft office for a kit check and another FFI, then to be drafted into sections and then, believe it or not, we were allocated tents! The trouble with the bloody tent I found myself in was that the perishing thing leaked!

We all got another weekend leave and we toddled off out of it. I cannot remember why I was on that draft and had been relieved of my spud serving role. Perhaps our mess sergeant had got his just rewards as the chief spirit in the speed up the spuds campaign or maybe they had found someone able to do the job but with less propensity to supplement the serving out with political polemic.

On Monday the twentieth we had to pass through the kit store once again where it took me two hours and ten minutes to get a pair of pants and a hat changed and to draw a rifle. Funny thing about that rifle; the powers-that-be waited until the war had ended before issuing RA personnel with rifles. We had often wondered if there would have been much difference to the outcome if the 151 had been given small arms on Crete when faced with German parachute troops.

After such a tiring day I popped off home for the evening.

We had an inspection by a major at 5 p.m. on the Tuesday and some of us had to stay in to re-blanco our webbing under the eye of Sergeant Spud Murphy, who had never seen the English coast, let alone any action.

On the Wednesday we were inspected by some brigadier or other who wanted to know what demob groups were on the draft. He was told twenty-three and over. Then someone pointed out that he was actually group nineteen and that rather put the cat among the pigeons. That night a number of men were taken off the draft. As it turned out, although I was group twenty-six I was in Germany far longer than expected. It seemed to us that the discharging process got slower and slower until it pretty well bogged down altogether, leaving a mass of men getting more and more browned off, unwilling to co-operate and harder and harder to control.

Chapter Twenty-three

The Warrior Goes
Abroad – Again

I remember as the mob of us marched off, about four hundred men, we cheered, we laughed and we sang and especially did we cheer when we went through the barrack gates. We were happy to get out of Woolwich and as the war was now over the going abroad could be classified as a Grand Tour. We went off in Full Marching Order. Fully togged up as we were it was pretty hard going; after all it was August, the sun was hot, our wind was short and our legs were not those of infantry wallahs. We boarded a train at the station in the usual manner, being rammed into carriages never built for soldiers hidden by masses of weighty equipment.

We puff-puffed through Kent and got to a place just outside Dover which turned out to be a 1939 Hore Belisha barracks. At six o'clock we had tea, at eight o'clock supper, then went to a money exchange where I changed £2 for 350 Belgian francs, leaving myself a bit of old England coin to squander in the local NAAFI. Trucks took us down to the docks at ten thirty, where we boarded a boat and I got myself a comfortable bunk. We had one mug of *chai* on the boat and someone said we were supposed to wear life jackets as we were poodling through a mined area of the hoggin.

We reached Ostend at ten thirty the next morning and marched to a transit camp for a meal and a third blanket issue. Hey Ho! I was reminded that in the Middle East I had had my blankets for around three years before anyone got around to the idea that blankets should be cleaned and fumigated.

The one five three in the firing line,
The one five two behind them,
But when they looked for the one five one
Damned if ...

Then we set off again and with an extra blanket stuck round each one of us there was no mistake about it, we could have been taken for camels. We boarded a German train after I had bought some Belgian pears and we were taken across Belgium to a holding depot in a place called Eingen. We supposed it to be a typical small Belgian town, with cobblestones which rang to the sound of our boots and a tramway on which ran what appeared to be four-car trains pulled by ancient steam engines. I bought some more Belgian pears.

The citizens of Eingen were having a bit of a ball. They had just renamed their main street Rue de Montgomery. Us Middle East wallahs didn't go much on that. One old sweat told us that he had known Monty when he was made a colonel. He said the best way to describe him was to call him a 'Right Bastard'. Someone said he had good points. He would always speak to you and hand out cigarettes. But the old sweat soon put that into perspective. 'He doesn't bloody well smoke or drink, does he?'

Some of us went to a little dump of a cinema, paying ten francs for the privilege, and sat sweating for over two hours while the film rolled on, sub-titled in French and in Flemish. What the spoken language was I don't think we ever found out, the noise was too great. The next night we paid seven francs and went into a much better cinema – the Roxy – but really no Odeon. We saw an ancient cowboy film, 'Pony Express', which seemed to be all about stage coaches.

Meanwhile some of our blokes had been into a local café where, they said, the beer had tasted similar to water. They were all, or rather we were all, somewhat taken aback upon discovering that men and women used the same public urinals and also that the locals thought nothing of passing water in the streets. It was quickly found out that it was possible to get a bash at sexual intercourse for a bar of soap, and also get change!

We all had to pay another visit to the psychologist Sam Browners but as related above, no one was a bit interested in me. I carried on with my policy of keeping my head down.

It was at this barracks that those domiciled on the top floor had to descend eighty-four steps to get anywhere and ascend eighty-four steps to get back again. Thus the nights were full of interest. The lavatories were all on the ground floor so that buckets had to be placed on each landing. It can be left to the imagination the state of the landings each morning and not only the state of but the smell of as well. That particular fatigue, emptying buckets, was not a popular one.

It was a huge barracks, chock full of military personnel from all sorts of units, infantry corps and ourselves. One of the favourite ways to keep the troops occupied was a route march. So one was organised and we in the RA contingent marched out of the main gate, round the corner, and along a road which ran through the wood. The man in charge, probably a staff sergeant (they seemed to pop up all over the continent), stopped us and explained that the last thing he intended to do was to go off on a ten or fifteen mile route march and he didn't expect us to do so either. So as soon as he fell us out we had better go get ourselves into the woods and stay there till the rest of the marchers had gone by and whatever you do, keep out of sight, there could be nosey people about. So we fell out and spent the day lazing around in the woods, making daisy chains, conjuring up the woodland fairies, smoking ourselves to death and, most usual of all, sleeping and resting our tired limbs. In the late afternoon the marchers came raggedly past us, footsore and weary, tired out and worn, sweaty and swearing. They all looked forlorn and dejected.

As soon as it was estimated that the last of the hikers had passed by we fell in and our gallant leader said he thought we ought to march back into that poxy barracks as if a ten to fifteen mile route march was what we normally did before breakfast.

And so we swung through the gates of the barracks all nicely in step and doing the RA ninety steps to the minute. It was perfectly amusing to notice that we were observed by a lot of expert infantry marchers with their jaws dropping. Afterwards assurances were given that we were not used to such piddling walks, we were much more in line with the Roman army and their thirty miles a day and building a temporary camp at the end of each march.

Then came the morning when we crashed down those blasted stairs to form up below in FFMO to be sorted out into batches and then to be despatched to various units in the area. We moved off in trucks en route for our new outfits. Mayes, the only one left of the old brigade, was headed for the 63rd Medium regiment while I was off to the 10th Medium.

We arrived in Ghent in the pouring rain so to cheer myself up I bought some pears to eat while waiting for the train to pull in. But there was not enough room in the train for all of us, so 102 squaddies including myself went off to the Leopold barracks to await the means of getting to wherever we were going. In the evening there was a tolerable ENSA concert, better than most that we had suffered in the Middle East. It was said that the entertainment in Ghent was of a high order as an inducement to keep the soldiery off the streets of the most immoral town in Europe which was, of course, crawling with VD. None of this was of any interest to me. After all, there were plenty of luscious pears about.

Next day we took a train to Germany via Antwerp which had been knocked about by Jerry rockets. I found a contrast between Belgium and Holland. Belgium felt close, hot and shabby. Holland appeared clean, neat, with its flat well tended fields and its Friesian cows and there were plenty of flags and bunting in Holland. When we crossed over into Germany which looked, to me, darkly rugged with hills and trees, a curious and very large notice met the eye, none could miss it. It read:

NO FRATERNISATION.

What a silly idea, everyone thought, and the British soldier and for that matter all other soldiers proved it.

At that time it was quite natural for there to be hatred of the Germans and more particularly of the Nazis. When some of us saw the devastation in the centre of Hanover we laughed. When we saw the appalling wreckage of Hamburg we laughed. It was soon apparent that the Allies had done far more damage to German cities than the Germans had done to ours so we laughed. We had given him a taste of medicine he had handed out. It was a satisfying general laughter over a large scale devastation.

At one point a train going in the opposite direction stopped alongside ours. It was filled with men, women and children in all kinds of odd pieces of military uniform. They were French folk returning home, having been released from the Nazi horror camps. My war, our war, had been to a great extent full of comedy in the long intervals between the nasty bits and even in those, humour was never far away.

But those people were a part of another war, a much grimmer, more frightening war of which we in our army knew very little. As far as we were concerned, Jerry was the enemy to be shot at and knocked over before he shot at us and knocked us over. Although he was a bastard he was still in the same boat as ourselves and probably like us only wanted to get the hell out of it.

We were told we were the masters now and were instructed to push Germans out of our way, knock them where they belonged into the gutter. I never saw anyone do that. I certainly saw plenty of blokes make way for civilians, particularly elderly ones.

As we approached the centre of Hanover we began to notice how the red tiled roofs of buildings were pock marked with shrapnel holes. But this did not prepare us for the sight of the centre of Hanover which had been blasted all to hell. The railway station was a right old junk heap. Steel girders were twisted into shapes as if they had been pieces of wire. Rubble and collapsed buildings everywhere and people walking about as if they were still dazed. We found out later about the terrible fire storms that had been visited upon towns and cities and we wondered how anyone could have survived and remained sane.

No fraternisation was a non-starter. The British in uniform are in the main an amiable lot and not likely to act in the ways that the Nazified Germans had done. They were more likely to share their food with civilians and I doubt if most of them would eat in front of starving children. Then of course there was that other incentive; one could pick up a bint and keep her permanently with bars of chocolate. If one had packets of coffee then one could rise into the world of high finance. I drew no pay while I was in Germany and I doubt whether many others did either. A few cigarettes would pay for all one's needs for a week and of course the great thing was to be sure to return from Blighty leave with coffee.

I found myself in 83 Battery 10th Medium regiment stationed at a village called Wustrow more or less on the Elbe and therefore not too far from the Russians. There was a curfew at 10.30 for civilians and 11 o'clock for us. We were billeted in houses evacuated by the local people. There was still furniture around, that big old fashioned stuff which the Germans seemed to go in for. But as the winter went on that furniture diminished, followed by doors and then floorboards as everyone tried to keep warm. Fuel was scarce and fires in billets were *verboten* but the furniture still went up in smoke along with anything else combustible. It was ever thus with bivouacked armies. On the night of our arrival there was a battery concert in which ten local women and a blind German male accordionist took part. Beer was plentiful, cigarettes were enough if one didn't overdo the black market business, and the village itself had not been damaged during the war. The food was all right, the canteen fair enough, there was table tennis but no cinema. This latter was always missed because my generation had been brought up on the cinema. It had not been unusual before the war for people to go the cinema twice, three times and even four times a week. But mobile cinemas were promised.

A stream ran past the back of the garden where some of us were billeted, from which we drew washing water and the wherewithal to shave. As the winter advanced so the problems of shaving increased until we had to break the ice to get the water, besides sometimes removing disturbed tadpoles. We shaved in cold water because smoking chimneys were detectable during the hours of daylight.

On Tuesday 4th September I took myself into the canteen to listen to a Mozart recital given by a German girl. There were more civilians in the audience than soldiers. Nowt so queer as folk. The Allied soldiers had fought against the perpetrators of evil, the Nazis, and didn't bother about Mozart, while those who had either supported Nazism or who had submitted to it, delighted in the music of Mozart.

Officially we newcomers were being given elementary small arms training while the long time residents of the 10th Medium were being given advanced education in the subject. It was a hard slog for the instructors because no one cared and no one wanted to listen. The war was over and we wanted out and didn't want to be mucking about with useless small arms.

Actually I came to like Germany, though we didn't get much chance to know the ordinary people. It was too soon after the war for that and anyway they were too busy staying alive, while we were too busy trying to keep warm.

The infantry training was supposed to be fitting us to face expected trouble from DPs (Displaced Persons). The main problem, I think, was that the DPs were being forcibly persuaded to go to places to which they had no wish to go, on the grounds that the people they were being sent away from didn't want them. It all became somewhat confusing.

Fortunately for us, the man in charge of training, a certain Lieutenant Evans, was just as browned off as we were. He had just returned from a very stiff tough-tactics training course which had not been very stiff at all, so he in his turn devised a very tough looking training course for us which wasn't very tough at all. In practice it consisted of a bit of arm flapping which hardly interfered with us broken-winded types. One day we were asked whether in our hard training we would like to have either PT or basketball. We were strongly advised to pick the PT as it would prove less strenuous but in our collective wisdom we chose the basketball.

'How long d'you think you should play?'

'Well, we suppose, the usual football time, three quarters of an hour each way.'

The PT instructor thought we ought to settle for ten minutes each way and then see how we were making out. We laughed at the idiot. Tough cookies like us and he talking about ten minutes each way!

We started the game. Hardly anyone stayed the course until half time. Smoking and drinking and possibly the other thing had taken their toll. We were all flopped out at half time, the second half never took place and sporting activities for most of us were gradually abandoned. I suspected it was like trying to turn bears into ballerinas. In fact the battery went on to win the area sports championships but I do not think that the teams competing contained many of us draftees from overseas.

While we were waiting one chilly September day for a truck to take us over to 84 battery for a bit of unwanted sports practice we watched a young woman stagger off down the road. She appeared to be wearing only a coat and shoes and nothing else. Someone pointed out that she was whoring herself to death, being one of those unfortunate German women who sold herself to the troops so that she, and possibly others, might stay alive.

On the way over to the 84th we came up with a truck which had collided with a local cow. There were a number of 84th blokes milling around including one called Martin whom I had come out from Blighty with. He had a slight facial cut because of the accident but no one had been seriously injured apart from the poor old cow. While the truck was smack up against a tree the cow was lying in the roadway with its insides coming out of its backside. Somehow the local farmer got the cow to stagger to its feet. It was urged onto the roadside where, with the aid of a local woman's knife, he cut the poor cow's throat.

On Saturday the 29th we were all volunteered to go watch the area sports from which I had been dropped early on as not good enough for the tug-o-war team. The 10th Medium won quite decisively and a good many of the old regimental personnel cheered. All the time throughout this period we were being trained or attempts were being made to train us for this new-fangled infantry role. It was, as already stated, said to be for the purposes of constraining, restraining, retraining or doing anyway something with the DPs. Though some of us did wonder whether some bods in high places were dreaming of sorting out the Russians, which caused a laugh since it was getting quite cold enough in Germany without thoughts of some modern retreat from Moscow. One exercise entailed marching in sections in various directions, bondooks slung, to eventually surround a German village. Our section set off on a jolly ramble round the outskirts of the village until, arriving at the rear of a row of houses with large gardens, I espied not a pear but an apple tree in a garden, so being in the lead, I wheeled to the left and we all went through the back gate, all except our gallant section leader who kept on going straight ahead down the road; as soon as he realised he was alone he high-tailed it back and joined us in the rear as we went through the garden and back to the front road through a gap between two houses.

Now just in front of that passageway, standing in a large bowl, were many apples with one very large one stuck right in the middle. As we went under the tree everyone plucked an apple and as we passed the bowl so everyone took another one. When I looked back, damn me if the bowl hadn't emptied apart from the very large apple which everyone had politely left alone.

Once out on the main road we turned toward the meeting point with the other sections in the centre of the village and every man jack of every section was chewing an apple! Then a jeep hove in sight bearing the major in charge of the operation and the BSM suggested we should conceal our prizes on the grounds that it was an offence to be caught looting. Not being anxious to find ourselves on fizzers for eating apples, we hid 'em behind our backs as the jeep rushed up to us. The driver was eating an apple, as was the major. They had an advantage over us in that they had a jeep.

In the early part of October we moved from Wustrow to Winsen, still more or less on the Elbe. While we were moving one German woman kept anxiously enquiring whether or not we were taking any furniture with us. We said we were not but she needed a great deal of reassurance. We couldn't see why she was fussing. None of us were interested in humping pieces of heavy German furniture about. We might burn some of it but not hump it about.

We boarded trucks and moved out of Wustrow, leaving it in the hands of the advance party of the new unit taking over. Some of our blokes were not keen on the move, complaining that they were leaving behind bits of nifty frat. I knew about the frat business though I was never part of it myself, having decided that all future adventures into the realm of sex would be for real – for love only.

I had occasion to go across one day where two blokes I knew were billeted, to return to one of them some books I had borrowed. I knocked at the door as any polite military man should do and upon getting an invite to 'Come right in,' found the two squaddies in bed. One in one bed on one side of the room, t'other in a bed on the far side and neither were alone. They had both got in bed with them a tasty piece of frat with whom I assumed they kept themselves warm. I was cordially invited to sit down, have a drink, make myself at home and not to mind them one little bit. I was advised that if I so desired they were sure I could join in. But I was still devoted to the arts, to the study of political economy and I was also in the middle of writing one of my unperformable plays and a lengthy poem about everything possible, which would have needed several bookshelves to contain the volumes if I had ever finished it. In any case four's company, five's none, and so I hastily took my leave of them so busily engaged with the fleshpots of this world.

Winsen we found to be a small village on the Hamburg road, about twenty miles from that blasted heap of rubble, also roughly twenty miles from the military seat of government, Lüneburg. I found myself in fairly comfortable circumstances in a large room of a large house with four other characters who, I discovered, thought the Russians were a crude dirty lot. They themselves soon got into the habit of urinating out of our first floor French windows at night because they could not be bothered to nip downstairs. A certain Lance-Bombardier Welch and I copped one of those spot check jobs that were all the rage around that time. We were taken in a lorry somewhere along the main road and dumped down in the middle of a crossroads in the middle of a village and told we were a patrol station, there to check all civilians to make sure their papers were in order. If they weren't we were told to arrest them. It sounded very positive and simple but the truth was we had no place such as a calaboose in which to detain wrongdoers. Another problem manifested itself at once. All the passes were in German and neither of us had a clue about that language and the identification was a thumb print. We could not see for the life of us how we could compare the thumb print on the pass with the thumb print on the thumb.

We found four persons without passes, advised them in English they were breaking the rules to which they nodded in reply in German, then we sent them about their business.

Some of us got detailed for a seven day guard at a Jerry ammo dump, six of us, I think, with an NCO and a couple of civilians to do the chores including the cooking. We were always very short on rations and on that guard they were particularly poor but one of the Germans was a baker by trade, so we handed over our ration of flour though we had no baking powder. That we had to get from the nearby village. All worth while because that German baker made some damned fine cakes.

The guard duties were pretty easy really. It was a double

guard, two hours on four off at night, but four on and eight off during the day. I teamed up with Verril, a man with a most enquiring mind. So it was that on the first day I found myself assisting him with his first experiment. The guards before us had spent their nights in deep gloom; a power cable to the huts at the entrance to the ammunition dump had been cut somewhere so that oil lamps and candles had had to be used.

But Verril had other ideas.

That which could be broken could be mended and that is what he proposed to do – a bit of mending. So we set out to trace the fault in the main cable which ran from the huts across a field and on into the autumnal distance. After tramping through damp fields for some time we agreed we must have missed the break somehow and so retraced our steps. We found the break eventually, not far from the guard house. We got hold of a rubber mat, put it on the ground for Verril to stand on and then taking a screwdriver he tested the cable to see if it was alive. Flashing sparks indicated that it was alive all right. So we put on our woollen gloves for a bit of protection and between us we carefully joined each bit of wire to its rightful end and with much sparking and flashing we restored power to the buildings and light for ourselves.

One day Verril and I decided to patrol round the whole of the site on the outside of the perimeter. We noted a number of gates giving access to various sunken ammo stores. At one of these we found a gate open and proceeded to close it. There was a German at one of the dumps with a horse and cart and we wondered what the devil he was doing. 'If we were a Jerry guard,' Verril said, 'There is no doubt about it, we would have shot that character stone dead.' No doubt he was right at that. Meanwhile the German, having seen us, jumped onto the seat of his cart, got the horse moving and drove toward us with some vigour, gesticulating violently and indicating that he would like to have the gate opened for him. This we obligingly did and he drove through and away, leaving us to carefully close the gate after him.

During off periods Verril and I would take our rifles and go off hunting deer. There were roebuck and red deer beside rabbits and hares. But although a Scot on that guard managed to shoot a roebuck so that we all had a first-rate supper that night, the local animal population was perfectly safe when Verril and I were around.

At one point we came to a place where there was a wide open piece of ground between woods. I must point out that all the timber in the area was covered in soot and oily matter. There had been a heavy tank battle. So it was no fairyland but rather a place stark and grim with plenty of broken trees.

We stood for a long time waiting for a deer to poke his nose or perhaps one of his antlers out of a wood. We made no movement, imitating the actions of all hunters throughout eons of time, until at last a roebuck emerged from the smaller of the two woods, walked to the centre of the plain, stopped and looked down the plain straight at us. I just didn't have the heart to point my rifle but Verril had his bondook ready and lined the deer up in his sights. The animal continued to stand motionless watching us. I hissed into Verril's ear, 'Go on, *now.*'

The deer turned his head slowly in the direction in which he intended to go and then walked slowly across to the other wood into which he disappeared.

'What was the matter, you idiot?' I demanded, with thoughts of roebuck soup fading rapidly from my mind.

'I just couldn't,' he replied. 'He was just daring me to shoot and he knew damn well what I knew, that I couldn't.'

Once Verril had recovered his lost nerve we devised a new plan. I would enter the wood on the right by the water tower making as much noise as possible and driving the deer out to the waiting Verril and his rifle. So off I went, round to the back of the wood and entered it by the water tower, making as much noise as one man could possibly make. I kept going, shouting and singing and crashing about in the sooty undergrowth, hopefully driving all before me onto the waiting .303 in Verril's hands. I emerged from the wood covered from head to foot in soot to find myself right by the tower from where I had started, having made a perfect U turn inside the bloody place! We decided there and then to end our huntsman role and go back to common soldiering.

I was on that guard twice, the second time with Smudger Smith, the poacher from Uttoxeter. He was the character who managed to hurt his ribs laughing at my unperformable plays. It was he too who gave an example of his peacetime activities which enabled him to apply his natural skills to army life.

As a member of the local football club committee which ran raffles to raise funds, Smudger on one occasion offered his mantel clock as a prize, which was gratefully accepted. Then he and the club chairman organised the event. They filled a jar with peas, dry peas that is. The object of course was to guess the number of peas, winner take all. Having put the peas in the jar Smithy told his mate exactly how many peas were in the jar and in due course his mate won the clock and everyone went happily about the club's affairs until one day, owing to an emergency, the committee was forced to meet in the Smiths' front room. The first thing that the members spotted was Smudger's clock standing where it had always stood, on the front room mantelpiece, the last place it should have been. So, as my new buddy explained, he found himself sprinting as hard as he could go for the safety of the countryside with disgruntled members of the committee in full civilian battle cry behind him. The word *verboten* meant nothing to a man like Smith so that in next to no time on the second guard we had a supply of beautiful German potatoes which went down well with all of us. I didn't know how he had come by them and I never asked.

Although I did know how he got hold of fuel for our billet fire at night. Ours was about the only chimney which ever had any smoke coming out of it. We even had one orderly officer who used to come into our place for a warm. As he pointed out, officers were not allowed fires in their billets and so he hoped we didn't mind when he stepped in.

The day came when our pile of logs was looking very small

and I hastened to point this out to the poacher. He nodded and said he would see to it and not to worry. He quite understood fires were just the job and fuel was just the job too and certainly he would see to it all.

He vanished and I stoked the fire up, confident in the ability of my comrade to keep the home fires burning. I wondered what he would bring back: an armchair, a door, sawn up floorboards? Then came a thumping at the door which when opened revealed an enormous, bulging sack; well hidden behind it was the small sized poacher. The sack was full of logs, forbidden fuel. As soon as we were comfortably ensconced before a blazing fire I asked for an explanation, how had he been able to pluck the forbidden fruit?

'Simple,' he said.

'Simple!' said I.

'Yes, no trouble. I went from civvy door to civvy door and if a woman or elderly person came to it, "By order of the military commandment two logs per household for the British army," and they coughed up and usually gave more. If the door opened and a big hairy ex-Nazi paratrooper appeared I would rub my hands together, breathe on 'em and ask him if he could spare a few logs for shivering *Soldaten* who only wanted to get home out of it and leave every German log for the use of the German people. They always coughed up.'

Meanwhile back on the German ammo guard, Smudger and I used to get into the kitchen as soon as it was our turn on at night. We always volunteered for the worst turn, early hours of the morning, to get the spuds sorted out, washed and put on the stove to bake. As for the night patrol, we never bothered about that. We never knew what our other comrades in arms did on their turn but on ours, the Germans, French, the Russians or anyone else could have helped themselves to any amount of poxy ammo, our only concern was the potatoes.

So each early morning before dawn broke we lined the spuds up in a row, plonked on the margarine, the salt, the pepper and ate our way through a row of potatoes from one end to the other until verging on bursting point and we could lounge back and talk about the days of our youth when we spent many hours, he in Uttoxeter, me in Putney, scrumping other people's fruit.

On the last night of the seven day guard the wind got up, the rain came down and the world outside was dark, windy, wet and just plain horrible. So when I was roused up for my turn I decided it being such a shocking night I would let the poacher sleep on. I put my head down and pushed off outside and into the storm to make my way to the kitchen. I got the potatoes washed and cooking and settled back with some impatience for them to be done, feeling I was a noble character to let my old buddy sleep his way through the violent weather.

I was just lining up and getting the condiments ready when the door burst open, letting in a whole heap of howling wind and German rain and there stood the poacher in his shirt and boots, gripping his bondook, and the abuse he hurled at me made me blush. What the devil did I think I was doing robbing him of his well earned supper? Or was it breakfast? After all he had done for me too. He thought it a poor reward to be robbed by his old mate.

I explained I had only tried to be friendly by allowing him to sleep on. He didn't think it was a friendly act, especially as he noted that I had baked the same amount of potatoes for one as for two. However, he tucked his wet shirt between his legs and after eating his share of the spuds he sank back mollified.

There was already talk of Blighty leave but my expectations were dampened somewhat when I discovered my leave date was 7th December. But I did have the consolation of knowing that I had completed my latest *magnum opus*, a 100-verse eight-line account of my travels so far. It was in the bundle of papers later stolen from off my bed.

Back at the unit we once again found ourselves messing about with infantry training. At one time we were hard at it taking a Bren gun to pieces and putting the bits back together again. This was an aimless activity as neither instructor nor we were at all interested, considering the war to be over and not being of the stuff to use machine guns on refugees and displaced persons.

Then some of us found ourselves on a fatigue trying to repair an old rifle range which had signatures scrawled at the target end going back to the early nineteen hundreds, a pile of Jerry steel helmets and gas masks at the back plus a latrine that may well not have been cleaned out since the late nineteenth century. There were also beds and bedding stored, in a dry room. This we reported to the quartermaster who promptly sent a truck and took them into custody.

Meanwhile our troop was divided into sections with the result that Verril went into one and I into another, so that Verril ended up occupying my bed and I his. The idea was that when men got demobbed the sections would lose men on an equal basis. As usual it did not work out as planned.

Chapter Twenty-Four

Memories of a
German Campaign

I remember vividly the winter months of '45 and '46. It was very cold and certainly there was too much ice and snow with winds tearing across Germany from Poland and the even colder east. I remember one bitterly cold night when Verril and I were standing guard in a vast expanse of snow, stomping up and down trying to keep warm while we were guarding something that was not worth the bother of keeping an eye on. Then our guard commander hove in sight flapping his hands and arms across his body and expressing some really unkind thoughts about the weather. We heartily agreed but pointed out that he had no cause for complaint, all things considered, since he could shelter in the guardroom most of the time. To this he readily agreed, then added that he was a compassionate sort of a cove and that he would make a special journey out to us with something special to warm us up. We stomped on with the wind biting through our balaclavas and the snow creeping into our boots, while we speculated on the possibility of a hot toddy from our generous and kind-hearted guard commander. Indeed he was as good as his word for, sometime around three in the morning, we observed him coming across the snowy waste carrying a bucket which, for all we knew, held a container with something hot. He held it out to us with a shout of triumph. 'Drink up, boys, it's nearly Christmas.' And he presented us with a bucket containing beer! Well, what could Verril and I do? The guard commander did have a kind heart and he had shown consideration, forethought and a desire to carry a bucket of beer through the snow. So we took turns, Verril and I, to up the bucket and drink down. The result was, of course, once the two sentries were alone, they had to stomp up and down a bit harder because we were not only freezing on the outside but on the inside as well. We argued with chattering teeth that we supposed it could have been schnapps, a special local concoction which had filled a hospital with soldiers round the bend after drinking the stuff, a special brew, based, it was asserted, on petrol.

Another guard I fell for was at regimental headquarters. This was the real 'bull' job with one of us standing outside the main door freezing to death but saluting captains and under and giving the full works to majors and above. The powers that were demanded it. We supposed it was something to do with boosting morale which in that cold climate was reasonably low. A few days later I was walking past RHQ with one of our well known wags, when the sentry at the door gave the full treatment salute and my waggish friend immediately returned it with gusto, calling out at the same time, 'Very good, my man.' Whereupon a sepulchral voice behind us said, 'But I didn't think it was very good at all.' Of all the times the colonel could turn up it had to be then. He took such a dim view that my companion and I found ourselves peeling spuds for a week.

It was around this time that I burnt the sole of one boot when I had my feet too near our stove. Smudger was full of compassion when he considered what could happen to anyone who molested army property as I had done. But the worst thing was that with no fires ever lit officially other than in the cookhouse, the burning of the boot had to be classified as a self inflicted wound. Oh my! My! He was certain it was a clear case for a court martial and certainly there was no point in reporting it.

I went to the unit cobbler for a consultation but he, being an original Tenth Medium man who had landed with the unit when all the fighting had streaked off miles ahead, refused to mend 'em. So, after giving him a piece of my dirty mind I departed and spent a long time in and around snow-bound Winsen with a hole in one boot. Of course, after a period of time in which he made me suffer, Smudger solved the problem. He found a

German cobbler who repaired both boots for a few cigarettes and thus was I saved from hell fire and damnation.

Several of us stood a guard duty one day at a local magistrate's court along with Jerry police. The magistrate was a second lieutenant of no particular vintage. One man got three months for not stopping his car when ordered to do so. One boy who had two revolvers and ammunition for same was put on probation for a year and I suppose the only consolation for that day was that we were in the warm. Meantime the food situation remained bad. One day's army feeding might run thus: breakfast, one ladle of sugarless porridge sufficient to cover the bottom of a mess tin, three half-slices of bread with margarine sufficient for two, one tinned sausage and one mug of sugarless tea. Dinner: potatoes, a spoonful of cabbage or beans or both, one small piece of meat plus gravy then possibly a piece of duff. Tea: three half slices of bread, maggy Anne for two and jam for one, a small section of cheese and a mug of sugarless tea. Supper could be soup, cheese or beef sandwich.

The trouble was we were heading into a bitter German winter, most of us had appetites fit for horses and I suppose we would have still been peckish if we had been regaled with five-course lunches starting with roast beef and Yorkshire pudding. The civilians were of course worse off than we were. Germans would stand by swill bins because even with our short rations there were uneatable tough bits.

On 11th November we were all ordered into a large room where we were instructed to remove our hats and bow our heads observing a two minute silence. Nobody bothered to explain why but we assumed it had got something to do with armistice day. Though what that was supposed to mean after a bloody six years of war we never quite fathomed.

On the afternoon of 17th November a sergeant came buzzing around for ten men for some sort of job or other and muggins fell for it. After piling into an armoured truck clutching bondooks we were told we were off to help the Russkies. Apparently there was a camp containing thirty or so DPs who were Russian citizens but who declined to go there. Our job was to help to persuade them that they should toddle off home.

We were led by a handlebars moustache in a Sam Browne belt, a Russian officer and one of their sergeant majors who appeared to be wearing a very warm and comfortable uniform made of wool. He spoke English and German. This contrasted well with our sergeant major who, it was alleged, could neither read nor write. Our leader, whom we named Handlebars, gave us our instructions as we drove up to and into the camp.

'I want you to jump out smartly after we have stopped and look fierce and then I want you to surround the camp.'

When the vehicle came to a halt we jumped out as if we were a load of tramps ordered towards a bathtub and started ambling toward the distant horizon. Handlebars roared out an order to 'double'. So we broke into a staggering trot and the myriads of gaping children broke into peals of happy foreign laughter. We were possibly the funniest thing they had seen in their lives. An Englishman never looks his best in KD shorts and the next thing he is not very good at is ambling away into the distance wearing a uniform which somehow never quite seems to fit him.

There were a number of huts and the area surrounding them was vast. But that did not seem to deter Handlebars because he kept on insisting that we should surround not the huts but the site. So the ten of us trotted off into the blue distance, spreading out into a circle as we went, until we were beyond rising ground, whereupon we halted, gathered into a bunch, sat down and got our cigarettes out. We had arrived at 2.30 p.m. to relieve four men who had been there since 10.30 that morning trying to get the DPs to go back to the Soviet Union.

According to the Russian sergeant major, the people in the huts were Germans who had settled in Russia or Russians who had settled in Germany or they were descendants of the parties that had done the settling. We were sure the Russian knew what he was talking about which was a damned sight more than we did.

We kept an eye on Handlebars and Co, anxious to keep our

own peace, but eventually we drifted back to the huts where all hell was breaking loose. The women did not want to leave and by jingo they were not going to either, but eventually the rank and file found themselves helping to pack the DPs' gear which they seemed to have a lot of, including two sacks of flour and one sack of potatoes. The interior of the huts really hummed. It would seem that no windows had ever been opened and while one family in one room seemed to be pretty clean, another lot appeared to have lived in absolute filth. There were many women but a damned sight more kids running around. One young woman made eyes at one of our blokes (not me) and offered to keep him warm in bed. After a great deal of commotion we got the women (there were no men) out of the huts into lorries and we saw them on their way. Two of our number, one to each lorry, went with the DPs to a Russian camp where there were plenty of Red Army men to assist in unloading. Our blokes said the Russian camp was floodlit and they noticed large pictures of Lenin and Stalin. They were taken to a huge marquee for a meal where they were earnestly prevailed upon to eat everything set before them but they failed to comply, there being too much food for that. They were also sloshed with Russian booze and came away with difficulty and certainly befuddled with drink. As for the rest of us, as there was no transport available so late at night – and it was very late – we had to thumb lifts back to base, Handlebars having left earlier than us.

Verril, a character called Schwartz and I decided to organise ourselves into a company to buy up small items such as German jewellery and then take them home when we went on leave, to flog the loot there. We hoped thereby to make our fortunes but as it turned out the only people who may have made their fortunes were the German black marketeers. All that happened in our case was that we spent our money on one small, semi-precious stone not worth the money we paid for it. We gave the business up after abortive attempts to contact a black marketeer in Hamburg. The place was swarming with Redcaps trying to catch black market operators red handed. We returned to our base and went into the canteen for a consolation drink, only to discover I should have already gone on leave! I had forgotten one started leave on the day before the date on the notice board. So with all speed I slung myself together in half an hour, knowing full well I would never live down such a disgrace as forgetting about leave. I arrived in Lüneburg to discover I had just missed the leave party and would have to wait until the next batch left the following day. So I spent my time between the NAAFI, the YMCA and the Christian Fellowship place, lining up for tea and two wads.

I should mention perhaps that in the big towns a number of such clubs were set up in the least wrecked of the buildings. There were United Services clubs and the Salvation Army for example. At such places we would form long queues, usually winding slowly up stairways, until after long waits we could buy the usual tea and two wads and nothing else. There were usually chairs and tables around, a haze of smoke, much talk and usually a small German band playing away like billy ho.

I got away eventually and the train took us to the Hook of Holland via Minden where we stopped for a hot meal in the middle of the night. Not much of Minden had been left standing as far as we could make out in the darkness. We stopped again in the early hours of the morning for *chai* and sandwiches and so arrived at the Hook where the cold was so great, many of us were to be found walking about almost bent double. And so by boat to Harwich and Liverpool Street.

Talk of tea and sandwiches recalls to mind an incident which I had almost forgotten. Every six months from 1941 onwards and for ten years thereafter I used to go down with malaria. I remember one day we were messing about on some sort of military ploy and I was just getting over a bout of malaria, feeling weak and with a lousy mouth, when we all flopped by the road side pretty well done in – least I was – waiting for the chuck wagon. This duly turned up with our midday meal which turned out to be – of all impossible things – a cold fried fish sandwich! I have never been able to think of anything worse than a cold fried fish sandwich when staggering about with the aftermath of malaria.

On that leave I popped along to see Harry Withers who had been out of the army some months. Before the war he had been a master tailor employing twelve women; now he rented a bench in a workshop in Carnaby Street where he could turn out a coat a day at five pounds a time. So he wasn't doing too badly but being Harry, he spent money as fast as he earned it. He was not too happy with civvy street. His big problem was a shortage of cigarettes. He had been unable to get on friendly terms with a tobacconist and in consequence could only get his cigarettes through his mother. There were shortages everywhere.

Holly and mistletoe were easy to come by but other things were in short supply.

It was estimated, for example, that one in ten families would be eating turkey on Christmas Day. An aunt of mine went to buy herself a pair of indoor slippers only to be told to come back in February when some might be available. Someone in Fulham wrote to my parents advising them that she had chickens for sale at thirty bob a time when the official price of a dressed chicken was around four and six. In one of my mother's cupboards she had set aside a small bottle of barley wine and a bottle of beer obtained from under the counter, for their Christmas festivities. Me, I went to a local off licence to see if I could scrounge anything but drew a grave shake of the head and a 'sorry, we are out of stock'. This, despite the fact the counter was stacked with bottles of beer. I went after the manager but I might just as well have argued with a discoloured brick wall – it did me no good.

Toys were at a premium. There were many wooden toys displayed in shops, many made by service people, which were not of the best construction but brought good prices. The controlled price of whisky was around £2 8s. 6d. a bottle but no one got any under £4 a touch. All in all, things had been fairer during the war. Better get back to the army where we did at least have a fairer distribution of whatever was going. Or did we? I nipped off down to Stratford to see the Sheriff, who was having a whale of a time among Italian prisoners. We had some booze, went to the pictures, and I went home again. Twenty first December and the end of my leave and so I started back for Germany and the environment I felt at home in. I had to make sure of getting back on time because anyone overstaying leave by only one day was liable to find himself over the wall and far away. The glasshouse was not considered very funny. One bloke I met had prided himself on being a tough nut but admitted that by the time he had been sorted out in a military prison he was capable of grovelling and licking anyone's boots. Everything was done at the double, even shaving. This man said that one of his jobs had been to take nails out of a bucket of water and polish them after which they were returned to the bucket for future polishing.

I had no intention of over-staying my leave. No, Sir!

Poacher Smith was due to return on Christmas Eve. He told me that under no circumstance would he spoil his leave by returning on such a stupid date to poxy eyed Germany. He would have Christmas at home with his wife and kids and the army could go to the devil. I did point out to him that it was much more likely that he and not the army would trot along to meet Lucifer. I did also say that, after all, the longer he was away the less leave someone else got. But poachers have their own way of thinking. He just laughed and went off on his leave.

On Christmas Day in the morning questions began to be asked of his old mate, me, as to the probable whereabouts of Smudger.

I said I did not know.

On Boxing Day the questions were still being asked but more frequently. The next day speculation grew as to how many days Smudger would get over the wall and I was pressed harder – 'Where was that scrounging git?'

I still did not know.

Then he came back and as soon as he stepped over the front doorstep, so to speak, he found himself under open arrest. Now it had been known for delinquents such as Gunner Smith of Uttoxeter to get as much as thirty days over the wall but it did not seem to worry the villain one jot. But something was worrying me and I told him so.

'What's up?' he enquired, 'You've no need to worry, it's my nut they're after, not yours.'

'My concern,' I pointed out, 'is not your punishment but mine.'

'Yours? How the bloody hell can you suffer?'

I looked at him as if he were some poor dumb creature with no idea of the ways of the world. 'You're not the only Smith fish in this military swamp. I've got another buddy, a Fred Smudger Smith and the army seems always to want to bracket Smith and Green together. I am sure there is an army fixation about it. We went on guards together, fatigues together, duties together, leaves together, until we were known as Smith and Green. We went boozing together, swimming together and we could even exchange thoughts without speaking. And have you noticed anything about us?'

'No, what?' A strange remark coming from a dedicated poacher.

'We get shoved together, you and me, same guards, same fatigues, we're in the same billet and the universal question is, who is the biggest scrounger, Smith or Green?'

'What are you babbling about?'

It was true I was sounding a bit hysterical, perhaps I was babbling but there was an uneasy idea in my head and I said I had had a terrible thought. 'So with all this Smith-Green business it is a dead ringer that when they announce who your escort will be, it will be me?'

'So?'

'So when you start telling the tale as you will, to the old man, how am I going to keep a straight face?'

'Don't worry,' he said, 'It won't happen.' But of course it did.

There it was on the notice board as plain as a pike staff for the whole outfit to note. 'Gunner Smith prisoner, Gunner Green Escort.'

The evening before the great trial Smudger went carefully over the story he was going to tell the old man once he was in front of him. I couldn't believe that even a Smith could get away with the yarn he was going to tell. There again, as I pointed out, how the devil was I going to prevent myself from laughing right out? But all he would say was that I ought to be able to keep my ugly mug under control. I was not just unhappy on that terrible morning, I was greatly disturbed and had difficulty in eating my breakfast. I only finished it because that Smith fellah said he could easily finish it for me if I liked. The sergeant major fell us both in outside the great man's office. The sergeant major wasn't a bad bloke, in fact he was quite a genial soul. He never liked falling out with anyone and was not happy with his present job and that soon showed.

He brought the prisoner and escort to attention and then, as was the rule, knocked the prisoner's hat off. But he carried out the operation a bit nervously in so far as in knocking off the hat he hit the prisoner on the forehead, which was against the rules. Smudger said, 'Oy, whatcha think you're trying to do – brain me?'

The sergeant major said he was sorry, and meant it, while Smudger muttered dire threats. 'Prisoner and escort RIGHT TURN.' He then should have said 'Quick March,' which would have brought the prisoner and escort nicely into the judge's court but he did not utter those vital words. Instead he said, 'Prisoner and escort DOUBLE MARCH.' This meant that he had made a second mistake with the escort in front when he should have been in the rear to prevent the prisoner escaping and now the order DOUBLE MARCH! Now the escort, understanding the duty of a soldier was always to obey the last order, immediately galloped into the tiny office with the prisoner belting after him so that the two of them went crashing against the end wall, apparently endeavouring to get through it. The sergeant major with lightning speed realised his mistake and shouted, 'PRISONER AND ESCORT ABOUT TURN.' Those two worthies, so anxious to please, speeded up into a military gallop as soon as they had turned and the escort led by the prisoner immediately disappeared out of the office and continued on down a long passage until the by then fairly flustered master of ceremonies bawled out, 'PRISONER AND ESCORT ABOUT TURN.' Prisoner and escort, still anxious to please, about turned and speeding up a bit into a real horse artillery gallop went once more belting into the office to carry out another attack on the wall. This time the SM got something right because he cried, 'HALT.' Which we did while the colonel concealed his mouth behind his hand – he had to remain neutral.

But our dear old organiser was not finished yet. He had yet another surprise up his sleeve. He should have said, 'Prisoner and escort, right turn.' This would have brought us face to face with the awesomeness of military law. But he didn't. Instead he said, 'Prisoner and escort LEFT TURN,' which brought us face to face with the blank wall with our backs to the presiding judge. Then the sergeant major did the unbelievable. He said, 'Prisoner and escort left turn quick march.' This last order must have come about through reflex action; after all it was a very common parade order. So away out of the office once again went the prisoner and his escort, this time at the artillery pace of ninety to the minute. Our kindly colonel came to his office door and said, 'Sarg'n major, just let the lads come in and see me.' It sounded as if he was already on the prisoner's side. So we re-entered the office nonchalantly as if we were taking a stroll in some park or other. He invited me, the escort, to stand at ease, while he did his very best to look sternly at the red-faced prisoner (red-faced because he liked a drink and had certainly had more than his share during his leave).

Once the charge had been read and the seriousness of the crime explained, the colonel asked the prisoner if he had anything to say for himself. Of course that damned poacher had got plenty to say and while he was saying it I had great difficulty preventing myself being choked to death by my huge silent guffaws.

He had gone home, had the prisoner, full of great happiness at the prospect of once again being united with his beloved wife and especially with his beloved children who were dearer to him than his own life. Then just before he was due back he was more or less forced at the point of civilian bayonets to go to the local pub with some of his old and very dear friends from the football club (I assumed he had made it up with them) and he had drunk too much of that treacherous thing, beer. He had staggered off home, not knowing what he was doing, and when he woke up in the gutter next morning he found that his wife had gone back to her mother and taken the children along. He was sad, bitter and contrite. What could he do? He did the only thing a man could do, he went to his mother-in-law's house and pleaded with his wife to come back and he would join the Band of Hope and would never drink anything again, not even water. His dear, dear wife had forgiven him but by that time he had overstayed his leave and as he ended his pitiful tale I caught out of the corner of an eye the tears beginning to ooze out of the prisoner's eyes and damn me if the bloody old man didn't pull out his handkerchief and blow his nose!

The judge slowly shook his head and noted for all to hear that it was a sad tale. He hoped that Gunner Smith had learned his lesson and Gunner Smith admitted that he had and he now knew that drink was the curse of mankind and probably of the whole world and he would never drink again. While the colonel was again blowing his nose I just managed to prevent myself having what may be known in medical circles as strangled tonsils. Whether the colonel was really impressed or whether he enjoyed a good tale, I know not. All I do know is that the prisoner was awarded one day's Royal Warrant which in effect meant the stoppage of one day's pay.

When we got away from the court a crowd full of curiosity gathered round because no one had escaped dire punishment for such a crime as my friend had committed. Smudger kept mum, ordering me to do so. He suggested we run a book on how many days in the glass-house he had been awarded or how many years jankers. I refused to stoop so low, remembering the peas in the pot, and of course the whole affair was inexplicable. We had no more dealings with higher authority but we were not yet finished with the BSM. Came the day when we decided it wasn't worth the bother going on their silly muster parades, after all we were never likely to desert since in a fairly short time we would be civilians again. So we got in the habit of pleasing ourselves whether or not we would allow ourselves to be mustered. Then one morning we swung round a corner in Lüneburg and came face to face with the sergeant major who, no doubt, had not forgotten the episode of the trial.

'Ha Ha!' he cried in a dramatic and joyful fashion. 'You are supposed to be, the pair of you, on the muster parade and seeing that you are here, that spells trouble for both of you.'

I looked at my companion with astonishment. 'Did you hear what the sarg'nt major said?'

'Yeah, I did.'

'And?'

Smudger tried to look solemn. 'I would like to ask the sarg'nt major. Who always takes the muster parade?'

Our friendly sergeant major opened his mouth and then shut it again, gave us both a good glare and without more ado walked off in a different direction to ours. Those muster parades had become a sort of fetish with the 10th Medium hierarchy. Everyone had to be on them, even the cooks who were supposed to be excused everything apart from cooking and breathing. But somehow the parades never seemed to reach a very high muster as time went by and men were sent off to Blighty to be demobbed and other characters appeared to replace them, so that the folk in charge became more and more confused until one day . . .

The sergeant major appeared before the congregation, opened his important portfolio and began checking off names. Some were there, some were not, some were sick, some had gone home. On that particular morning he came to an old familiar name, a bombardier of long standing in the regiment. After repeating the name a number of times he said, as he licked the end of his pencil, 'Ah yes, demobbed.'

A voice from the ranks said, 'No he ain't.'

'He doesn't answer, he must have gone.'

'No he ain't.'

Our father figure lowered his portfolio and looked thoughtfully at the owner of the voice. 'Why do you say that?'

'Because he's still 'ere.'

'I haven't seen him about,' said the sergeant major, as if not seeing him was proof enough to establish his absence.

Somebody else butted in with, 'Well you wouldn't, would you, but the blokes in his billet do.' Did we note a touch of envy, a note of malice in the voice?

'What d'you mean, they see him when I don't?'

'Well they takes their breakfast into them from his farm.'

The first voice came again, 'It's general knowledge he's shacked up with a farmer's daughter. He's moved in there and expects to inherit the place.'

Did we note agitation on the face of our chief? Had some suspicion or other dawned on him. 'Just a minute, what farm are you talking about?' Both the voices told him as one voice.

He stood rooted for a long moment, an expression of disbelief dawning on his rugged, careworn face. Then rage got the better of him as he flung his list to the ground and roared out for the whole of the area to hear, 'But that's *my* Fräulein and *my* farm.' With that he jumped on his portfolio and roared off into the distance, leaving us to dismiss ourselves from the muster parade. I cannot recall the sequel, if any. I know the sergeant major was still around and the breakfasts still turned up at the billet when I hit the trail for Blighty.

It was a damned bitter winter with snow and ice and sharp winds driving in from the east. As mentioned already, fuel was short and fires were banned in billets, something the poacher and I were wont to ignore, in the belief that he and I between us had done something towards winning the war and how could we victors be constantly cold? However, there was one place where fuel was vital – the cookhouse. That had to be fuelled by soft German coal and my buddy and I decided that, as victors in the war, we were entitled to at least a small share in the local coal tonnage dropped in the cookhouse yard. So, one night, before the rise of the moon, we went off to the cookhouse with our poacher type bags and slipped through a back way into the yard and silently, with great skill, we began filling our sacks with the forbidden fruit. A light went on in the adjutant's office so we made a proper British army strategical withdrawal and melted into darker shadows to await the extinguishing of the offending light. As we waited came the sound of quiet movement and then a shadow slipped from one dark corner to another. This daredevil did not seem to heed the light from the adjutant's office so we concluded it was someone utterly reckless or a bit thick. The light went out and the moon, as if in support of the light, came on and Smudger dug me in the ribs to which I hissed 'Don't do that again, you fool, it hurts.'

He ignored me as he usually did on our forays and said, 'Dodger, d'you see who that is?'

I peered as hard as I could and having seen, nodded, 'It's *him*.'

'That's him all right, the bloody old rogue, the robbing effing wheelbarrow, it's the BSM.'

Indeed it was our dear old sergeant major helping himself at the coal exchequer.

'Come on,' said my companion, 'Let's go and say good evening.'

We crept up on each side of our dear friend and began filling our sacks. The BSM straightened himself up, holding his partly filled sack, and he gave no sign of shame, showed not a spark of guilt. He said, 'What do you think you pair of scrounging gits are doing?'

The poacher was quick, 'Putting the coal back that other scrounging scallywags have pinched. What are you doing nicking it?'

We filled our sacks and went our several ways and that clinched the business of the muster parades absolutely. We did not go mustering any more; it really was a waste of our valuable time.

Someone in the higher echelons of power must have had a right old brainstorm because twenty of us found ourselves sharing two open-backed lorries heading for Hamburg to collect bricks. We never found out why bricks were needed but then of course we never had very enquiring minds in the depth of that German winter.

Arriving at the frozen wreckage of Hamburg where, it was estimated, thirty thousand dead were still missing, we soon discovered that there were plenty of bricks lying around for anyone who desperately needed them. Of course the desperate need did not apply to any of us. Someone did stumble across a loose brick and threw it into the back of one of the lorries. No other loose brick was ever found. They were all, soundly, solidly, frozen onto and into the ground. Even ammunition boots wouldn't shift 'em. Soon the work of flapping arms about and jumping up and down on the spot to keep warm became tiring so we drifted off in groups to the local NAAFI, Church Army or other such clubs to stand in the long queue to buy a cup of *chai* and a couple of wads to be consumed to the sound of music from small German ensembles.

At four of the clock, when our military working day ended, we climbed wearily onto the lorries and returned with our one brick to Winsen for a hot meal, which we thought we had richly deserved. We did opine that picks and shovels would have been of more use than army boots in the collection of bricks but then it was possible that we would either not have had the strength to use such deadly weapons or we might have left ourselves open to serious injury.

One good thing did emerge. One very good thing indeed. We were never again asked to go collect bricks, not even a wheelbarrow full.

Coal was not easy to get hold of and so it was decided to augment the supply to the cookhouse with firewood. Our unit had been allocated a small section of forest, a rectangle in the middle of other sections, wherein the true native foresters cut down and dressed trees, stacking them into neat piles with all the lengths cut to a precise size.

We landed in the middle of this German neatness and me-
thodical working with axes and double handed saws. You can
of course imagine what the ordinary man in khaki thought of
those long double handed log saws. They were far too exhausting
for our bodies in the state of frostbite into which they had fallen.
But the axes were different. Everyone knew how to handle one
of them, even those who had never held one before. Soon the
forest rang with the sound of axes bashing away at the poor old
trees, suffering under the onslaught. Of course everyone had
seen, in films, Canadian lumberjacks at work and so everyone
knew that as the tree was about to fall one cried out in a
stentorian voice, 'Timber!'

What no one seemed to understand was that one called out
'Timber!' *before* the tree *began to fall*, not after or when it had
more or less reached the ground. Thus we all diced with death.
At one time Smudger and I were happily swinging at a tree
with my partner missing more times than he hit with his axe,
when a tree came crashing down with a heavy branch just
missing my hoppo's ear. A feeble voice then called, 'Timber!'
Smithy yelled out, 'I'll split your bonce right open if you do that
again.' Considering the times that my enraged companion had
missed the tree nearest to him with his axe I considered that
'feeble voice' was in no danger whatsoever. The trees kept
coming down but in no particular order so that in a short space
of time the area was criss-crossed with fallen trees. One character
with an abundance of muscle delighted in axing down trees with
no concern whatsoever how or where they fell and as for calling
out 'Timber!' we decided that he was either dumb or couldn't
spell. In the end, with trees falling everywhere, Mrs Smith's son
began to lose his cool.

'Let's show the bastards what's what, shall us?' and he began
a savage attack on his tree with such vigour and as it turned
out, for a change, with some skill so that the tree began to topple
toward the man who we thought was either dumb or couldn't
spell. However, I lost my nerve and called out 'Timber!', allowing
the offending party to take his brake off and run like the clappers.

But novelty wears thin after a time; in our case in very quick time. Before tiffin some of the lads had built a fire, and gradually each man downed his weapon and made for the warmth of the fire, until we were all round it. It was less energetic warming by the fire than keeping warm with an axe. The sandwiches came out and someone brewed up. That was the conclusion of all woodwork. The scene around us was one of complete devastation. I wondered what the local woodsmen must have thought of us as they passed our site going to their own well ordered places of work. It seemed as if a whirlwind had passed. Trees were strewn everywhere, there were untidy piles of them, trees lying alongside each other as if attempting a comforting embrace, trees jumbled across one another as if exhausted after riot. By the middle of the afternoon we were in no mood to care. Then someone, someone supposed to be in charge, suggested we might collect up the axes and the saws. This of course turned out to be something of a problem in so much as there were no tools in sight. They were buried beneath the fallen timber. We therefore had to exert ourselves, shifting trees about to find the missing tools. Having somewhat hopefully collected them all up and tossed them aboard our transport we wearily followed them and went back to Winsen. Nobody had ever considered putting any of the timber on the truck. After all, back at the village who would be doing the sawing up? Thus it was that my poacher friend and I still had the only warm billet in the village.

I suppose in that episode we had excelled ourselves. In the jaunt to Hamburg we had, at least, returned with one brick while on the woodcutting exhibitions we had not only not brought back any timber but had most certainly left some tools behind. We no doubt comforted ourselves with the thought that the tools would fall into more capable hands than our own.

The unit mounted a night guard in the village of Winsen which meant in effect that we were the curfew patrol. A couple of us would go round the place during the hours of curfew which began each evening at 9 p.m. Our orders were quite explicit.

During the curfew any civilian or for that matter anyone else was to be challenged and if the person or persons did not stop then we were to open fire. We were also told that if we fired without permission we could be court martialled.

We have no doubt all seen films and read stories of German guards and for that matter any other foreign type guards who shoot at the slightest opportunity and think nothing of it. No doubt they would be imbued with a sense of patriotic duty. Anything that moved in fact should be shot at. But this general rule in regard to sentries did not apply to us. When Verril and I were patrolling the perimeter of the ammo dump we politely opened the gate for the German civvy with his horse and cart, who was clearly helping himself to something he wasn't supposed to have in a place where he should not have been. One night I was standing in a doorway with Verril, acting as the curfew patrol, banging our arms about trying to keep warm while pointing out to each other what a stupid thing this guard business was, when we heard the sound of approaching footsteps.

'Someone's coming,' my companion hissed in true conspiratorial style. 'He's breaking the curfew.'

A young German hove in sight whistling away merrily to himself and anyone else who cared to listen.

'Halt, who goes there?'

Neither of us thought to cock our rifles. Understandable. After all we were artillery wallahs and not used to that sort of thing. Fact was, our rifles were still slung over our shoulders. It was too cold to muck about.

The young man politely said, 'Good evening.' We naturally said, 'Good evening' in reply and then Verril said in broken English so that benighted foreign type could savvy.

'You is breaking zee curfew, ya?'

The young man explained that he had been visiting his girl friend and explained the situation in very good English, which prompted the thought, why do foreigners so often speak English while often the English, particularly Geordies, find it difficult to express themselves in their own language? Then there was another thing, what the devil was a German male doing, talking about his German girl friend? It was a bit disconcerting as it had long been considered the German Fräuleins had become purchasable property of the Allied armies.

The young German was told to shove off and we warned him to beware of the patrol, who might shoot him if he was caught breaking the curfew. He bade us a cheerful goodnight and walked off. My partner looked after him quite thoughtfully and then looked just as thoughtfully at me. 'We've warned him to beware of the patrol, haven't we?'

'Of course,' I said, 'best to warn 'em case they meet the patrol.'

'But,' he answered, 'aren't we the patrol?' and of course we were but the kind of military patrol that would have found it difficult to shoot a passing rodent.

I was standing outside the guardhouse one very early morning wishing it was warmer and hoping time would get a move on when a bedraggled figure presented itself before me. I was taken aback at the sight of the creature, wet and decidedly chilly looking.

'Goodness gracious me,' I said, or words to that effect. 'Where did you spring from?'

He spoke extremely good English though he was clearly one of those plaguey foreigners who kept popping up everywhere.

'I haf just swam the Elbe,' he answered with a bit of teeth chattering.

'Funny time to go for a swim,' I rejoined quickly, 'The dawn hasn't broken yet so it's very early on a winter's morn. I don't think I would care to take my pleasures in that way.'

'You do not understand, I think.'

'I understand that it is a very queer way to spend a very early winter's morning, swimming the Elbe.'

'I have swam the Elbe to escape from zee Russians.'

I didn't say so but I did wonder whether the Russians would be bothered about a case like him.

'Now I vish to be taken to your intelligence officer, I haf

information for heem.' I called the guard commander. A character insinuating that we had an intelligence officer or intelligent ones was in need of more help than I could give him. We took the bloke inside and gave him a cup of tea and the drinker kept asking for the intelligence officer and even gave us his name, something neither I nor the guard commander nor anyone else on the guard could do. Then in the course of a number of exchanges in which our visitor became extremely agitated if not angry, he revealed that he knew the names of *all* our officers. Was he in fact a foreign type Sam Browne Belter down on his luck?

We continued our discussions for a long time and became so absorbed in what we were doing that no one thought of going outside to do a bit of guarding; the lord alone knew how many curfew breakers, enemy agents, Elbe swimmers, Russians with snow on their boots or Japanese wearing big round spectacles were sneaking past our post. Our man from the Elbe kept demanding to see someone of importance, which really annoyed us since we all considered ourselves important. Then someone, more observant than the rest of us, pointed out that we were due to stand down from the night guard in a few minutes. So, what were we going to do with this persistent perisher demanding to see the impossible, an intelligence or intelligent officer. A solution was found. First, our guard commander pointed out that if we kept him, someone, probably himself, would be lumbered with looking after the silly idiot until he was taken away, probably to some loony bin or other. That, as far as he was concerned, was not on. He would take no prisoners after working hours. So someone said, 'Chuck the silly sod out and as he obviously likes a swim, tell him to go back and bother the Russkies.' So we took him to the door, opened it, pushed him out into the cold and closed the door behind him. He banged on the door several times but as by this time he must have been drying off and in no danger of catching pneumonia, we ignored his knocking. When we cautiously opened the door there was no sign of him. Whether he ever made contact with the impossible, whether he jiggered off into some other area or whether he decided he would be better off re-crossing the Elbe and pestering them there Russians, we never discovered.

By 1946 things were really slipping. Morale was on the slide. No one wanted to bother any more and the only real topic of conversation was how long it would be before we got out of that perishing khaki. Fraternisation had been the order of the day ever since the non-frat notice had appeared and I suppose in consequence VD was on the increase. The black market was booming. I drew no wages during the nine months I was in Germany. What to do with all those blasted inflationary Marks? Then an idea circulated. Why not *send it with flowers?* One could spend up to five quid sending flowers to mum or wifey. There wasn't much else we could do with our loot anyway. So I sent off the money along with ten thousand million others serving in Deutschland with the obvious result that there were not enough flowers in the world to satisfy the demand. That idea quickly fell flat and I only ever paid for one bunch of flowers. The next idea was to send off to Blighty a fiver and get sent home five pounds worth of records and this I did. I had the set of Tchaikovsky symphonies for years. But that idea too was soon clobbered and so I never sent off any more fivers. So with not much of an outlet available I gave up my interest in the black market dealing; there really was no future in it for amateurs like me.

Females at that time never bothered me and booze was not easily obtainable and I was certainly not in the market for the petrol type schnapps, so I spent a great deal of my time writing verse and un-performable plays. The latter I wrote, chiefly, to make the poacher laugh and indeed at one time he hurt his ribs laughing, which for an unpublished author was praise indeed. But even this business came to an end. I used to have my papers, poems, plays and stories kept together in a large brown paper parcel. I was wont to leave it lying around the principle that no one could possibly be interested. But I was wrong.

Someone was interested. It was either a would be author who

could not write himself or a plain black marketeer who imagined he had got hold of a brown paper parcel full of goodies. I never saw my *magnum opuses* again and neither did I ever come across anything published that could have had anything to do with me. Maybe some disgusted character tossed the lot into the Elbe where only unhappy swimmers might bump up against it. So, we went on with our somewhat aimless activities such as firing a Bren gun at a tin hat and getting a hole in the rim after a long burst of fire.

We in the 28 group were waiting for the time when we could push off, collect our tickets and go home. In due course the call came and I knew I would be away in a few days. The poacher, in a slightly higher group, would follow later. Hey ho, the wind and the rain, we'll be off to Blighty again.

I am now about to record an action in this German campaign which even after nearly fifty years, might cause some concern, some embarrassment, some chance of retribution. I don't know. So the principal actors in the following scene are not named, though I doubt if either of them would care a tinker's cuss what anybody said or did.

One day He had to go the adjutant's office to do a bit of cleaning. He thought that part of his duties was to investigate all the drawers and cupboards in the place. In consequence He discovered a number of army pay books – unused. He helped himself to a round dozen – he liked even numbers – then proceeded to lay them in front of Charlie. Charlie hastily pointed out that he was not only not an official army paymaster but even if he were, that particular one would not have the where-withal to pay out so much money.

But He was not to be denied.

'You'll be going back to Blighty soon, won't you?'

'Y-e-e-s.' Charlie said, looking decidedly suspicious.

'By the time you are demobbed I will be on my way, won't I?'

'Y-e-e-s.'

'As you know, when anyone goes to a transit camp he is entitled to draw one day's pay.'

'Y-e-e-s.'

'With a number of partly-used pay books anyone could draw quite a bit of pay, especially if anyone went the long way home, say through Germany, Holland, France, Malta, Gibraltar, Canada, the Bahamas . . .'

'You are completely nuts, that's my opinion.'

'I'm not asking for your opinion, only signatures, plenty of scrawled signatures in pay books and I will see to it that they are well worn.'

Later that year, when both He and Charlie were out of the army, Charlie went north to see him, his old companion in arms. One warm and sunny afternoon the pair of them were lazily stretched out watching the local cricket team at work. It was then revealed to Charlie that the scheme had worked wonderfully well and as He spoke about it He smacked his lips with great relish.

Charlie himself went home as honest as he could be.

Our draft home consisted of a large number of other ranks led by a staff sergeant of no mean ability. There was quite a crowd of us, probably the usual four hundred or so. At any rate there was quite a daffy and all hard bitten, going home and the rest can go to the devil types.

Before leaving our respective units we received our travelling rations including our weekly supply of free issue cigarettes and then we got together and moved off Blighty-wards. Arriving at a large barracks with an enormous parade ground we dumped our kit and led by our new found leader we headed for the headquarters building and in particular the quartermaster's stores. In doing so we had to cross a corner of that enormous parade ground on which a powerful looking, mustachioed RSM, with regular army written all over him and his cane tucked underneath his arm, was happily drilling his latest batch of eighteen-year-old conscripts.

Led by our intrepid leader we slouched across our corner of a foreign field with hats on or off according to fancy, collars undone, boots unpolished, hands in pockets, with many mouths drooping with our free allowance of fags. We could not have looked much like an all-conquering army.

The RSM must have thought so too, because he roared like the proverbial bull, 'WHAT DO YOU THINK YOU ARE DOING ON MY PARADE GROUND?'

We collectively took no notice and mooched on. Came the bull voice, 'HALT!' We slouched on, understanding that our man in charge was the staff sergeant and he was either stone deaf or bolshie, because he shuffled on, puffing at his somewhat bedraggled cigarette.

The voice screamed, 'YOU LOT, HALT!' And the RSM marched towards us with one of those light infantry treads as if his trousers were on fire at the rear. He seemed to smash himself in front of us, demanding who was in charge. Our leader paused awhile, we supposed to admire the RSM's smart rig. Then our staff leered in a most unmilitary manner and said, 'I suppose I am.'

'Then you are a slovenly creature leading a bunch of slovenly people not fit to be called soldiers and I've a good mind to put you under open arrest, in fact a mind to put *all* of you under arrest.'

Our staff drew heavily on his cigarette and blew the smoke into the irate man's face.

'Have you been able to notice,' he said in a conversational tone, 'That we are *not* a bunch of conscripts?'

'All I have noticed is the way that all of you are dressed and the way in which you are crossing *my* parade ground.'

'And now', said the staff sergeant, 'I give you notice that if you don't bugger off I'll flatten you with this,' and he brandished his fist under the somewhat startled RSM's nose. 'And I daresay the lads here might just tread all over you. So be a good chap and go back and play with your conscripts and leave the man's world to men.' He moved on, with us shuffling along around him.

What could that regular infantry man do but return to his creche and his nursing, leaving us to go on our benighted way.

This we did until it brought us to the very door of the quartermaster's store. The door was closed so the staff gave it a good hearty kick and a heavy thumping with his fist. When time went by and we got no response we all joined in until the door opened and someone with a couple of stripes stood there. It was easy to see that he was used to dealing with greenhorns from Blighty because he framed his lips to say 'no'. It was a negative response, one not to be tolerated and he was told to run along and fetch the proper man in charge and he had better hurry up. He soon returned with his superior who informed us that we had had our tobacco ration. Everyone had an issue before leaving their units and it was no use asking him for any. He obviously had some idea of what we wanted because we hadn't so far asked for any supplies.

Our staff sergeant raised his eyebrows and turning to us said, 'I don't recall getting a leaving present. What about you lot, did you get any?'

There was a chorus of 'No No's' and 'Of course not's.'

So you see, 'explained the staff, 'Nobody at all has had any. We have all been deprived. Must have been a general oversight. So will you be good enough to rectify the situation and give us our weekly smokes?'

'Oh dear, I don't think I can do that.'

'In that case I am afraid we will have to come in and issue them ourselves.'

'Oh dear! You can't do that, that's against KRRS.'

Our leader took a couple of steps forward and beckoned us to follow, which we did, quite happily. The war was over and the bull was still around along with the red tape and petty dictators and all we wanted to do was to get home out of it – but smoking. 'All right,' the QM said, 'I'll see what I can do.'

The staff sergeant shook his head sadly. 'You'll have to do better than that. Tell you what, we'll be democratic and give you five minutes and then, after that, we'll come in and do the rationing ourselves.

We got the issue in under five minutes which, as someone pointed out, was just the job. We were asked to hang about for a bit because the colonel of the outfit or whoever was in charge would like a word with us. He was warned to tell the bloke concerned to hurry up since our legs were tired and we couldn't hang about too long. The important Sam Browner arrived pretty quickly and began talking to us like a right old Dutch uncle. He had, he explained, the heavy responsibility of a lot of young conscripts and therefore had to avoid things which might be called irregular. It would be very much harder for him if the old soldiers did not set an example and would we not help out? During the speech which I have given roughly correctly, the lads became more and more restless, a few raspberries were blown, some cussing took place but we stood to the end when, I suppose, we gave the speech a collective nod and shuffled off, most of us contentedly smoking.

It was no use lecturing us. During the war we had accepted discipline as a necessary means of fighting the enemy. But now the war was over it was different, and all over the army similar views were held.

We were housed on the top floor of a huge barrack building forming one side of a large quadrangle and it became clear on the first night of our stay in that hotel that lights were switched off at what we considered to be an incredibly early hour – 10 p.m. Most of us had not experienced barrack life, having spent our time under canvas, on gunsites and isolated posts. So that the idea that grown men should have to have their lights put out was anathema to all of us. In fact it just wasn't on. We watched on that first night as the lights in the other buildings went out. Then some infantry corporal appeared at the door of our large dormitory and actually, without warning or by your leave, *switched our lights off!*

Someone immediately switched them on again.

The corporal returned, passed some remark and switched them

off again. As he went out an ammo boot crashed against the door jamb narrowly missing the miscreant and the lights were switched on again. But the officious corporal did not re-appear. Instead we had the privilege of a visit from none other than the orderly officer who might well have done himself proud at Sandhurst but now had to prove himself at the door of our billet.

He addressed us in a friendly enough manner. 'The lights must be switched off,' he explained. 'We must maintain discipline because of the youngsters we are training.' He didn't look too old himself and someone told him to go push off and go visit the nursery where, no doubt, his nanny was waiting. He said he would have to report us and we said he could do what he liked as long as he left us lot alone. He left and we made our own decision as to when our lights would go out. Thus, we were not left long in the barracks and we soon found ourselves on our way down to the coast. Once there we had to pass through customs control and change our ill-gotten or hard-earned money, according to how you viewed it.

There was a reasonable rule that one man could change up to 400 marks into sterling and that would be the absolute limit. Only a dumb cluck could expect a situation where thousands of men were allowed to change unlimited quantities of marks into sterling. But I had such a one right in front of me.

It was a long slow queue and the squaddie in front of me was protesting indignantly at the limit to the amount of marks he was allowed to change.

'I'm not having that,' he said.

'You're not?' I said in reply.

'No, I'm not. I got my marks legit and I want 'em changed. Didn't I help to win the war – didn't I? I bet them officers get 'em changed all right, I bet they do.'

Someone did point out that as it was a universal rule it applied to everybody.

'Not on your Nelly,' he insisted, 'I earned my marks legit when working that there farm in Germany and they just gotta change 'em and that's final.'

It was now his turn and so he plonked a great pile of marks down in front of the pay clerk.

The latter looked up in utter astonishment. 'How much have you got there?'

'Forty fousand marks and I want 'em changed. You can count 'em if you like but I can tell you they are all there.' Which might not be said of himself.

The pay clerk choked and said, 'I CAN T CHANGE FORTY THOUSAND MARKS!

'Course you can, they are legit all right.'

The pay clerk at heart was one of us and, trying to be helpful, suggested that the irate customer should keep his voice down as there were two Redcaps over there backed up by a full blown captain.

'I'm not keeping my voice down and I want my forty fousand marks changed, NOW.'

The pay clerk tried to be reasonable.

'If you keep yourself quiet and to keep the queue moving and the Redcaps away I'll risk my neck and change eight hundred marks.'

'Eight hundred poxy marks! It's forty fousand or nuffink.'

The law so far had had cloth ears but now the applicant for millionairism was really raising his voice and the keepers of the military peace strolled over to the cause of the flap going on at the counter.

The pay clerk saw Nemesis approaching. 'Listen, this your last chance, cock; behind those Redcaps coming up is a Redcap officer and behind that Redcap officer is a dirty big jail, so take eight hundred and go.'

'I want what's rightfully mine – forty –'

He never finished his sentence. The Redcaps went alongside, to use a nautical expression, fully aware of the situation. They said not a word but picked up the offender by his elbows and carried him away. His feet were definitely not touching the ground and his voice could still be heard, though gradually getting fainter and fainter, 'I want my forth fousand marks, they're legit, I tell you.'

Whether he got a short sentence or is still in jail I never found out.

On the boat across the Channel I remember one thing vividly, a large notice which read: ALL JEEPS MUST BE DECLARED. As we passed through customs one character, well loaded with gear, broke away from the rest of us; he had something to declare. He plonked a camera on the table in front of the customs official saying that as it was an expensive German camera, he thought he had better declare it. The official picked it up, looked it over and then handing it back, smiled and said there was no value in it since it didn't even have a lens in it. So the owner said he was hoping to get a lens in Blighty. The customs bloke shook his head, 'I doubt it,' and they parted company. On the train I asked the camera man what it had all been about as I said I thought everyone knew there was no chance of a lens for a German camera at home. He grinned and said he knew all about that but what about knowing about this. He then proceeded to open his pack to reveal the truth of the matter – it was packed tight with brand new cameras!

There was another character on a train though I may have met him earlier while going on leave. He had landed soon after D-day and had been in the advance on Europe.

As they were strolling through some small town or other he and his mates observed a man standing at a factory door and he beckoned to them to come over. The civvy took them inside the building which turned out to contain roll upon roll of silk. What the devil it was doing there remained a mystery. Why hadn't the Germans cleared off with the goodies themselves? They never found out but were invited to help themselves. Naturally they took advantage of the opportunity and staggered off down the road with silk rolls. So they indulged themselves with silk sheets which they threw away when they got dirty, merely tearing themselves off other strips when needed. Some story, we all thought, as we sat in that train carriage. A damned good yarn no doubt.

'Don't believe me?'

'Not really.'

He shrugged, produced his water bottle, uncorked it and proceeded to pull out yards of silk, 'For the missus.' It was staggering the amount of silk that could be pulled out of an army water bottle. As he pointed out with a grin, 'Customs people never look into army water bottles.'

Chapter Twenty-five

A Warrior Stands Down

Once arrived at the demob centre in Woking we got brooms shoved into our mitts and were advised to sweep the billet floors.

We were quickly passed through the chucking out procedure on the following day. We were offered ready made suits, brown, navy blue stripes or sports coats and flannels. There was no trilby hat or any kind of headgear to fit my cranium but though I never wore a hat in civvy street and avoided them when possible in the army, I insisted on one being sent to me when they had my size in stock. When it eventually arrived I gave myself a great deal of pleasure in kicking it all round my parents' flat. Silly boy!

We looked a strange lot in our none-too-well fitting demob suits and we could hardly recognise each other. The following day, wearing our new suits, we were asked politely if we would mind sweeping the billet floors. Dear me, how times had changed! It felt strange to be able to walk out of that demob centre knowing, as your own master, you could please yourself and do more or less what you liked without being accountable to anyone. But could you?

And so to the point where I must rest my pen, the point where so many of the characters I served with slipped into history. Most of them appreciated the futility of war and hated it. They also knew who paid for it.

I lost sight of most of them pretty quickly. I had the impression that now it was all over they wanted to forget all about it. Harry Withers I continued to see until I asked him if he could lend me a hundred pounds so that I could put down key money for a flat when I was about to get married. He himself could never save money and must have choked on a scrounged cigarette when I phoned him. I certainly thought I heard gurgling sounds.

I never heard from him again.

Smudger the poacher lived in Uttoxeter and I spent a week with him and his wife in their somewhat dilapidated rented house where door panels had wide splits in their unpainted panels. At least the bedroom I was in had such a door. I just assumed that mine host was being his natural self and keeping an eye on someone he would consider to be a fellow poacher.

That was the last we heard of him.

My old buddy Fred Smudger Smith found civvy street irksome. He rejoined the army and went to Korea in charge of a tank. I never heard from him any more.

My mother started to write a letter to Montgomery thanking him for winning the war. I asked what she thought I had been doing all those years.

She never sent the letter.